P9-DMQ-150

RICHARD TUCKER

JAMES A. DRAKE

RICHARD TUCKER

A BIOGRAPHY

Foreword by Luciano Pavarotti
Afterword by George Jellinek
Discography by Patricia Ann Kiser

E. P. DUTTON, INC.   NEW YORK

Frontispiece: Richard Tucker as Canio in Leoncavallo's *I pagliacci.* (Henry Grossman)

Page vi: Top, as Des Grieux in Puccini's *Manon Lescaut;* bottom left, as Alvaro in Verdi's *La forza del destino;* bottom right, as Riccardo in Verdi's *Un ballo in maschera.* (Metropolitan Opera Archives)

Page x: Top, as Mario Cavaradossi in Puccini's *Tosca* (Louis Melancon/Metropolitan Opera Archives); bottom left, as Eléazar in Halévy's *La Juive* (Metropolitan Opera Archives); bottom right, as Turiddu in Mascagni's *Cavalleria rusticana* (Sedge LeBlang/Metropolitan Opera Archives).

Copyright © 1984 by James A. Drake

All rights reserved. Printed in the U.S.A.

No part of this publication may be reproduced or transmitted in any form or by any means, electronic or mechanical, including photocopy, recording or any information storage and retrieval system now known or to be invented, without permission in writing from the publisher, except by a reviewer who wishes to quote brief passages in connection with a review written for inclusion in a magazine, newspaper or broadcast.

Published in the United States by E. P. Dutton, Inc.,
2 Park Avenue, New York, N.Y. 10016

Library of Congress Cataloging in Publication Data

Drake, James A.
   Richard Tucker.

   Discography: p.
   1. Tucker, Richard, 1913–1975. 2. Singers—United
States—Biography. I. Title.
ML420.T88D8 1983   782.1'092'4 [B]   83-16615

ISBN: 0-525-24194-9

DESIGNED BY EARL TIDWELL

Published simultaneously in Canada by Fitzhenry & Whiteside Limited, Toronto

10 9 8 7 6 5 4 3 2

COBE

To Fathers Everywhere, from Grateful Children

Foreword

No one who was at the Teatro alla Scala in Milan on the night of May 20, 1969, will ever forget the ovation the Italian audience gave Richard Tucker. I know I will never forget it, because I was there. Along with hundreds and hundreds of others who came to hear Richard in *Luisa Miller* that night, I too shouted "Bravissimo!" the moment Richard finished singing "Quando le sere al placido."

I was also singing at La Scala that season, and I can attest that the reception which greeted Richard Tucker went well beyond anything I had ever seen. The audience didn't merely applaud, they *erupted*—there is no better word for it. The people screamed. They stamped their feet. They tore up their programs and showered him with confetti.

Someone might ask, in retrospect, what made this scene so unusual. After all, many great Italian tenors had been given thunderous receptions at La Scala. But what made this night so unusual, and therefore so memorable, was that the tenor who earned this incredible ovation was not an Italian but an American—a Jewish-American who had first sung as a cantor. What made this all the more unusual was that Richard Tucker was making his La

Scala debut that night—at age fifty-five, nearly twenty-five years into his career, in a Verdi opera that had not been heard at La Scala since well before he was born.

I was not at all surprised at the perfection of Richard's singing in *Luisa Miller*. When I was studying voice, he was one of my idols. I heard many of his recordings, and I learned a great deal from them.

For me, Richard Tucker was, and always will be, an "Italian" tenor. Like Jussi Bjoerling, he proved that one does not have to be Italian-born in order to win the critics and public in the Italian repertoire—which explains the reception Richard was given at his La Scala debut.

But let us not forget that Richard Tucker was more than one of the greatest "Italian" tenors of our time. His sense of style was so adaptable, and the timbre of his voice so pure, that he became a great interpreter of French opera, a highly acclaimed oratorio singer, and a widely respected bel canto tenor. Personally, I always found it hard to choose which repertoire—Italian, French, oratorio, bel canto—I preferred hearing Richard in. But he did each of them so inspiringly that I never really *had* to choose.

What made Richard Tucker such a phenomenon?

First and foremost were his voice and technique. His voice was not only beautiful—shimmering, silvery, and very powerful—but also incredibly enduring. For thirty years his voice remained youthful and vibrant, and his technique as close to perfect as one can get. Considering the length of his career and the diverse repertoire he sang, I dare say that not ten tenors could have kept their voices so fresh for so long.

Yet his voice alone does not entirely explain his great success. We have to look also at Richard Tucker the man for a complete explanation. I came to know Richard during my first seasons with the Metropolitan Opera Company. I was not well known in the United States at the time, though Richard, of course, was one of the giants—the real "stars"—at the Metropolitan. I found him to be a superb colleague—always encouraging, always ready to share the wealth of performing knowledge he had amassed during his long career.

As a man, Richard was an intriguing combination of qualities. He was not only a great artist, but was also a very caring, very sweet, man who took people into his heart just as they took him into theirs. Any artist who gives himself to the public—and who gives his best every time he steps onto a stage—will never be disappointed by the public. Richard Tucker gave himself to his public, and his public not only admired him but loved him for it.

I cannot find the words to express the loss I felt on the day of his death. But since that sad day in January 1975, I have had the pleasure of honoring his memory by singing (and once serving as Master of Ceremonies) at the annual Richard Tucker Gala Memorial Concerts at Carnegie Hall.

I was also honored to be chosen by Zubin Mehta and the Tucker family to sing in Israel at the dedication of the Richard Tucker Memorial in Tel Aviv. There especially I felt his presence in his ancestral homeland, and I saw how much he meant to the Israeli people.

One of my fondest memories of Richard's singing came near the end of his long career, in a matinee performance of *La Bohème* broadcast "live" from the Metropolitan. Because Rodolfo is very dear to me, I listened to the broadcast and was utterly astounded at the style, lyrical approach, and sheer beauty of voice Richard brought to the role. By the time the broadcast ended, I was so moved that I telephoned him in his dressing room.

"This afternoon you've shown us again," I said, "that you are the master of us all."

In death, as in life, Richard Tucker is still a master, still a model and inspiration. May the memory of the man and the artist endure as long as opera itself.

LUCIANO PAVAROTTI

New York, New York

Prelude

Richard and Sara Tucker often made the drive together: down Seventh Avenue, from their midtown Manhattan apartment, to West 57th Street; a right turn on 57th to Tenth Avenue; up Tenth until it becomes Amsterdam Avenue, where the immensity of the Lincoln Center for the Performing Arts comes into view. One more turn, and then they would arrive at the stage door of the Metropolitan Opera House.

At precisely six-fifteen on the night of a performance, Richard Tucker would stride into the Metropolitan, climb the flight of stairs to the backstage area, and walk briskly down the long corridor to his dressing room. His gait would be rapid, his posture arrow-straight, and his expression intense. Those he passed along the way—from the guard and receptionist at the stage door, to the many technicians backstage—greeted him warmly but always formally. They did not expect him to return their greetings except with a nod. He was preoccupied, they knew, and did not want to use his voice until he went onstage.

In his dressing room—a comfortable, buff-colored room with a piano and a couch among its utilitarian furnishings—he rested quietly in a crimson robe, reviewing parts of the vocal score of

the evening's opera while seated in a large swivel chair in front
of the bright lights of the makeup mirror. At seven o'clock sharp,
Victor Callegari, the Metropolitan's chief makeup artist, would
begin to transform Richard Tucker into Radames, or Manrico,
or Canio, or any of the other characters his repertoire encom-
passed.

At half past seven, still in his robe, Tucker would break his
silence and begin to sing—softly at first, then gradually louder,
traversing the scales from the middle of his range to the bottom,
then to the top. "I don't go in for long warm-ups," he often said.
"A 'pro' is always ready." His son Barry once timed his father's
warm-up routine: it lasted one minute and forty-five seconds.

Hairstylist Nina Lawson and wardrobe master John Casa-
massa would then dress Tucker in costume and wig, completing
the transformation. At seven forty-five, in costume and ready to
go onstage, he would telephone the other dressing rooms to wish
his fellow cast members good luck. To his Italian colleagues, he
would offer an "In bocca al lupo"—their equivalent of "Break a
leg!" To an American co-star, he might say, in a husky whisper,
"Are you with me, Kid? We're gonna give this audience a performance they won't forget!" Ten minutes later, he would be in
the wings, ready to go onstage.

Sara would be waiting for him in the wings the moment he
made his exit, whether at the end of an act or even in the middle
of a scene. As they had for most of their thirty-nine years of
married life, the Tuckers would then walk arm-in-arm to his
dressing room. It was a ritual they had begun at the old Metropolitan Opera House, and one they brought to the new house at
Lincoln Center; a simple ritual that conveyed a unity, closeness,
and rock-like security rare in any marriage, much less a theatrical
one.

The Tuckers would then make their way quietly to Richard's dressing room amid the frenetic activity backstage. On the
nights when he performed his heavier roles—in *Il trovatore, La
forza del destino Turandot, Pagliacci*—Tucker would maintain his
concentration between acts and his dressing room would be silent. Yet on other nights, when lighter music—*Bohème, Traviata*—allowed him to relax a bit, Tucker might gather a group
of the stagehands and watch television with them in the green
room.

But on this day—Friday, January 10, 1975—there would be no performance at the Met. Sara Tucker made the drive to Lincoln Center not with her husband, but with her sons and their families. They spoke hardly a word as Lionel Daniels, the Tuckers' longtime driver, threaded their Cadillac sedan through the midmorning Manhattan traffic.

The bustle of the streets escaped Sara's notice. She sat in numb silence, awaiting the sight of the Metropolitan Opera House.

That morning, rather than have Lionel circle behind the Opera House directly to the stage door, Sara asked him to pass by the front of the complex. The expansive square was filled with people. They formed long queues in front of the five entrances of the theater's glass-paneled facade.

More than three thousand fans, colleagues, and friends had come to honor Richard Tucker. But for the first time in Metropolitan Opera history, an audience had come to the opera house not to applaud, but to mourn the death of a great singer. Two days before, while on tour with Robert Merrill in Kalamazoo, Michigan, Richard Tucker had died suddenly of a heart attack.

He had died a mere two weeks before the Metropolitan was to have feted him for his thirty consecutive seasons there as a *primo tenore*—the astral category in which Enrico Caruso, Giovanni Martinelli, and Beniamino Gigli had shone.

Caruso, Martinelli, Gigli—their names had been mentioned often during Richard Tucker's three decades of singing. The morning after his debut as Enzo Grimaldo in Ponchielli's *La Gioconda,* in January 1945, a New York critic said that not since Gigli's had a tenor voice so inherently beautiful been heard at the Metropolitan. Thirty years later, Tucker had come within three seasons of equaling Martinelli's milestone—thirty-three years as a first-rank tenor at the Metropolitan. Tucker sang most of the Italian roles that Martinelli and Gigli had inherited after the death of Caruso. And for nearly twenty of his thirty years at the Met, Tucker had been openly compared to Caruso himself.

"The American Caruso," the press labeled Tucker—quite to his satisfaction. Sir Rudolf Bing had helped initiate the comparison many years earlier. "Caruso, Caruso—that's all you hear!" Bing had told the news media. "I have an idea we're going to be proud someday to be able to tell people we have heard Tucker!"

The hundreds of thousands of people who heard him in person—in the United States, Latin America, Australia, Europe, the Orient, and Israel—and the millions more who heard him on radio, television, and recordings would scarcely forget Tucker's legacy: thirty-three roles in thirty years, nearly nine hundred operatic performances in the world's greatest opera houses, and almost as many concert and regional-company appearances on three continents. Those who crowded into the Metropolitan Opera House on the bleak morning of January 10, 1975, came to pay silent tribute to this legacy, and to confirm the sense of personal loss they felt. They came to honor a man who, in the fullest sense of the word, had indeed lived—a man whose boundless energy made it all but impossible to accept the reality of his death.

Richard Tucker had neither looked, acted, nor in any way seemed daunted by his sixty-one years—not physically, mentally, and certainly not vocally. Only a handful of his legendary predecessors—Gigli, Martinelli, Schipa, Lauri-Volpi—had passed their sixtieth birthdays while still actively performing in major opera companies. Of these, only Gigli, arguably, had possessed the same degree of tonal purity and technical perfection that Tucker boasted at the same age.

But, unlike Gigli, whose health became uncertain in his early sixties, Tucker seemed not merely impervious to age but somehow invincible to those who knew him. Conductor James Levine, himself the age of Tucker's sons, spoke of his "endless energy," both as an artist and as a man. Sherrill Milnes, half Tucker's age, was always astounded by his vigor. "He gave all of us the impression that he could have gone on forever," Milnes remarked.

But a few of his colleagues—and even his wife, Sara—had occasionally seen ominous signs. To them, it seemed as if Richard Tucker were in a race of his own making, a race that ruled out slowing down even slightly, let alone retiring—a word that seemed increasingly absurd to him as the years went on. He ignored signs of fatigue, and disregarded any pleas that he alter his pace. "I have enough energy," he maintained, "for two men, let alone one."

This limitless energy, usually expressed in pragmatic terms—building and then maintaining his illustrious career—ultimately arose from Tucker's intense feeling of personal destiny. Throughout his life, he believed he had a special mission—a calling almost religious in nature, perhaps a personalized extension of his identity as a Jew, one of the Chosen People. He believed that God had given him a wondrous gift—the gift of song, the gift of the biblical David—and had chosen him for an extraordinary life.

From tens of thousands of young Jewish boys on the Lower East Side of Manhattan, Tucker had been chosen by a respected cantor for serious study because of the purity of his youthful alto voice. When that alto voice matured into a compelling lyric tenor, Tucker was then selected for the cantorate. And while at the height of his cantorial career, he was at last chosen for a Metropolitan Opera debut. To be sure, hard work, self-confidence, and a measure of luck were important ingredients in his success; yet, inwardly, Tucker considered his "special mission" preordained— an unprecedented challenge that he uniquely had been offered. It gave meaning not only to his life, but to his music. "Richard Tucker was a man totally dedicated to the full and generous use of a voice and a marvelous talent that the Lord had given him," said Terence Cardinal Cooke in the Metropolitan's ecumenical funeral service. "Richard was always ready to share that tremendous talent because he had a generosity founded on faith."

In a definite way, this sense of mission, of personal destiny, also intensified Tucker's zest for living. He loved to defy odds, to challenge limits—to live, as it were, "on the edge." Near his sixtieth birthday he told an interviewer, "Everything I did in life was always big." He meant it. He feared nothing at any point in his life—and his unshakable self-confidence was as infectious as it was genuine. When asked whether he had ever doubted that he could become a major opera star, he unhesitatingly gave a one-word answer: "No."

After the funeral, and the ritual week of *shivah* that followed, Barry Tucker, the eldest son, took responsibility for removing his father's belongings from the opera house. It was early morning when Barry went to the Metropolitan. The immense auditorium was dark, and its stage almost barren. The corridor to the dressing rooms was empty. Only the hollow echo of his own footsteps broke the stillness. As Barry walked, memories flooded back to him. His father had walked the same corridor after every act of every performance. Barry packed his father's belongings—several robes, a prayer shawl, a pocket-size book of rabbinical wisdom, family snapshots, publicity photographs, record albums—and thought of the crowds inside the dressing room after those performances. Celebrities, politicians, colleagues, old friends, longtime fans—all the people who came to congratulate Richard Tucker, to celebrate with him, or just to seek an autograph.

As he left the dressing room, Barry noticed familiar faces among the crew members who were readying the stage for an afternoon rehearsal. Barry and his brothers had literally grown up backstage and knew many of the crew on a first-name basis. As he walked he nodded to them, as they did to him—but no one knew quite what to say.

One of the men at last broke the awkward silence. "A lot of us have been around a good while, and we've seen singers come and go," he said. "We're just part of the crew, so we don't often get to know them. But we *knew* Richard Tucker. When we were around him, we felt he was one of us. That's how he made people feel."

"When we lost your father, Barry, we lost more than a great singer. We lost a *man*."

1

Q: Are you nostalgic about your boyhood in Brooklyn?

A: Nostalgic isn't the right word for it. If people ask me, "Would you like to bring back the old days?" I don't even let them finish the sentence—I say, "Definitely!"

For a life that ended so suddenly, so unexpectedly, Richard Tucker's began simply enough in a tenement in the Williamsburg section of Brooklyn, New York. He was born there in 1913, the sixth and last child of Israel and Fannie Ticker—immigrant Jewish parents who, like hundreds of thousands of others, had crossed the Atlantic in steerage, leaving behind the oppression and intolerance of Eastern Europe, choosing instead the boundless optimism of life in America. They and the other threadbare European Jews who crowded the decks of the ferryboats that steamed past Liberty Island were soon shunted from the Ellis Island processing center to the swollen streets, decaying tenements, and tinderbox sweatshops of the Lower East Side of Manhattan.

The Tickers made their way into the maelstrom of lower Manhattan with no money, no place to live, and four children to feed. A farmhand and for a time a peddler in Sucharan, a *shtetl* in the Carpathian Mountains near the Russian border of northern Rumania, Israel Ticker entered the New World with no appreciable trade. Only the generosity of a Rumanian synagogue, whose congregation he joined, and a nearby settlement house on the Lower East Side, helped him sustain his family until he earned his first American dollars—selling chocolate squares at a candy stand. Following the accepted Melting Pot practice, Israel soon anglicized his biblical name to "Sam," though he resisted the Americanized "Tucker" that his children would eventually adopt.

Those who remembered Fannie Ticker in later life, when she was chronically overweight and wracked by diabetes and hypertension, could still recognize the refinement of her facial features. She had passed these on to her surviving daughters—Minnie, Rae, and Norma, all Rumanian-born—and to the daughter she and her young husband had lost: a doll-like girl, Chaiah, who died in a fire in the Sucharan ghetto when only four years old. The tragic death of little Chaiah, perhaps even more than the oppression of Jews by the Rumanian government, made Sam Ticker decide to emigrate. For more than a year, he had stood by helplessly as his wife sank deeper into depression over the loss of her child. A self-contained and undemonstrative man, he could not comfort her. Ultimately, he decided to pack their meager belongings and begin anew in America.

Not long after they settled in lower Manhattan, Fannie became pregnant. The pregnancy eased her depression and, not unexpectedly, led her to hope for another girl. Sam very likely hoped for another boy. Louie, their only son, was then seven years old and was growing up amid nothing but women. Sam moved his family to the tenements of Brooklyn's Williamsburg section shortly before he became a father for the sixth and last time. There, on August 28, 1913, he stood by the bedside as Fannie presented him with a doe-eyed baby boy. A week later, at the infant's *bris,* the proud father named the child Rubin.

Still partly dependent on the charity of the synagogue, and with yet another mouth to feed, Sam intensified his attempts to find steady work in Manhattan's garment district. He found no work among the dressmakers along Broadway in the upper Thirties. He tried the milliners' sweatshops along Sixth Avenue and still found nothing. But adjacent to the milliners, in the Jewish-dominated fur market between Sixth and Eighth avenues near 30th Street, he found his niche.

Apart from the high-priced apparel that emerged from its factories, the fur industry was no more glamorous than any other in the garment district. Its manufacturing end was a pyramid of skilled craftsmen and semiskilled laborers, with the "cutters," the "dressers," and the "operators" near the apex, and the "finishers" and "nailers" somewhat below them. Having no expertise as a craftsman, Sam Ticker entered the fur market from its side door: the lucrative "piece business," in which the cutter's waste materials were bought in bulk and transformed into intricately sewn "plates." These plates were then used in lieu of actual pelts in the manufacture of cheaply made, high-profit hats, glove linings, jackets, and even full-length coats. Sam became one of dozens of middlemen in the fur market—men who bought the cutters' wastes and sold them in volume to other immigrants, most often Greeks, who tediously sewed them into the rectangular plates.

Sam Ticker was an Orthodox Jew in a fundamental Old World sense of the term. He remained devout and observant despite the sunrise-to-sunset workdays he endured to be able to feed and clothe his family. His religious devotion gave his younger son lifelong memories of the importance of rituals in everyday life. Each morning, young Rubin watched his father don a prayer shawl and *tefillin* and thank God for creating the new day and for renewing his strength through the night's sleep. At dinner each night—however meager the meal and no matter how late it was served—Sam recited the Hebrew blessing, giving thanks to "the King of the Universe, Who dost bring bread out of the ground."

But apart from the religious example he set, Sam Ticker was a remote father—partly because of his temperament, and partly because of his demanding work schedule in the fur market. For Rubin, especially, it was his mother rather than his father who shaped his basic personality. Fannie Ticker, in contrast to her self-contained husband, was warm, outgoing, and affectionate. As Sam's steadily increasing income enabled him to move his family to a better section of Manhattan and, then, back to Brooklyn into a more spacious apartment in the Borough Park section, Fannie readily immersed herself in the activities of the synagogue congregations her husband joined. In each of them, she was known for her warmth, wit, and especially her willingness to work.

A reasonably literate woman, she fulfilled her responsibilities for her children's religious upbringing by reciting the biblical verses she had learned from her own mother, and reading them snippets of Yiddish and Hebrew wisdom from New York City's then-prosperous Jewish newspapers. Though Sam was dutiful, it was Fannie who reinforced her children's identities as Jews, underscoring the meaning of the Book of Jonah: "I am a Hebrew, and I fear the Lord, the God of Heaven, Who hath made the sea and the dry land."

To foster in her children a sense of communal responsibility as Jews, Fannie Ticker used what she had learned of the Talmud. A gem she frequently quoted to her younger son—her "Ruby," as she called him—was the parable of men in a boat at sea. Far from the shore, the parable went, one man began to bore a small hole in the bottom of the boat. When the others admonished him to stop, the man responded, "But I am boring the hole under my own seat." Only when his comrades pointed out that he would cause all of them to drown did the self-centered man stop what he was doing. "So it is with Israel," the Talmud declares. "Its wealth or its woe is in the hands of every individual Israelite."

Sam Ticker was innately musical. In his home each Friday night, the Sabbath Eve, he sang traditional Hebrew melodies in his light baritone voice—a pleasant-sounding *"Shabbos* voice," as its kind was called in lower Manhattan. He encouraged his children to join the singing. They looked forward to these *Shabbos* evenings and, many years later, remembered them warmly. For it was on these evenings—and rarely any others—that the Ticker children saw a different side of their father. The *Shabbos* music transformed him from a quiet, detached, authority figure into a smiling, loving father.

When Minnie, his eldest daughter, joined in the singing, Sam recognized the emerging purity of a fine soprano voice. Years later, Richard Tucker would remember it as a "beautiful lyric soprano," and wondered what it might have become had Minnie seriously studied singing.

About his son Rubin's boy-alto voice, Sam had no doubts at all. It had all the ingredients—a plummy tone, perfectly even vibrato, steady pitch, and a columnlike evenness throughout its range—to enable the boy to stand apart from other child singers. Confident in young Ruby's promise, and hopeful that his voice might ripen into a cantor's, Sam was determined to place his son's vocal development in competent hands.

"I was at the ripe old age of six," Richard Tucker would later recall, "when my father first took me by the ear to Cantor Weisser." Samuel Weisser, born Joshua Samuel Pilderwasser of Bessarabian lineage, was cantor of the Tifereth Israel synagogue on Allen Street on the Lower East Side. "Just like the biblical story of Jacob serving seven years," Tucker was fond of saying, "I sang as a boy alto in his choir for seven years." Weisser was a highly respected cantor despite the fact that the timbre, or tone quality, of his sizable tenor voice was not especially beautiful. Whatever the merits of his voice, however, his excellence as a teacher was unquestioned. He was demanding and selective, especially where youthful voices were concerned. Despite the testimonials of well-meaning relatives who assured him that their little boys had great voices, Weisser's keen ear usually told him otherwise and led him to refuse most of the children who were brought to sing for him. The few genuinely promising voices—of which young Ruby Tucker's was one—he placed in the Tifereth Israel choir, where he could refine their technique and monitor their development.

Under Samuel Weisser's tutelage, Ruby developed slowly but steadily. He spent nearly four years in the choir before he was given his first solo to sing at Tifereth Israel. Though there is no eyewitness account of this event, his delivery was probably marked by the same characteristics that his boyhood acquaintances remembered: he sang easily, he did not stray from pitch, and, most of all, he seemed completely free of the nervousness that sometimes marred other boys' solos. As his development continued, Weisser often took him along to weddings and other services, where he had Ruby chant the responses to the cantor's prayers.

In 1973, in a long interview for the William E. Wiener Oral History Project of the American Jewish Committee, Tucker lapsed into unabashed nostalgia as he described this period in his boyhood. "We appreciated everything we had, even if it was just a piece of bread with a little jam or jelly on top." He spoke of "running home from school to play a half-hour of ball in the street, running to the Talmud Torah to learn about our Jewish faith, running home to have supper with my folks, doing my homework, and then running to a choir rehearsal at the Allen Street synagogue." The one word that pervaded this remembrance was *running*. Even as a boy, he was always on the move, invariably trying to crowd in more than the day would allow.

How much of this nostalgic recollection is accurate and

credible depends on the weight one is willing to assign the many activities Tucker mentions. One inference seems certain: his schooling, most of which he received at P.S. 124 and 164 in Manhattan, held relatively little interest for him. One may surmise, consequently, that when he spoke of "running home from school to play a half-hour of ball in the street," he would rather have spent the day in the street if he could have gotten away with it. As a boy, Tucker was an excellent athlete, and shone particularly at stickball. As he grew into his teens, he frequently saw real baseball at Brooklyn's Dexter Park or Ebbets Field, where such colorful players as Jake Fournier and Floyd "Babe" Herman helped the Brooklyn Dodgers maintain their reputation for zaniness on and off the field. Years later, when Robert Herman, the Babe's son, became assistant general manager to Rudolf Bing at the Metropolitan, Tucker accorded him an extra measure of respect he felt was due the son of a baseball hero.

There is a certain independence that pervades Tucker's reminiscences of his boyhood. The implication that he may have had more freedom than parental supervision is inescapable, and to a fair degree true. He was the baby of the family, the favorite child of a mother whose disposition always inclined more toward affection than toward discipline. He was also the only child still living at home. All of his sisters had married rather young. Minnie had married Danny Nacman, an American of Russian-Polish descent. Rae, the middle girl and the most outgoing of the three, had married Abe Parness and had begun a family of her own. Norma, the youngest, married especially well by her parents' standards: her husband, Philip Schaffer, was a textile retailer whose Madison Avenue business address underscored his success.

Louie, eight years Ruby's senior, also had left home early. An extroverted, back-slapping good-timer when life was treating him well, he was regularly victimized by his volatile temper and poor judgment. Louie's adult life, despite the constant support of his wife, Celia, would prove to be a long series of bad breaks, many of them stemming from a lack of ambition that regularly put a distance between himself and Ruby. Even as a youngster, Ruby brimmed with energy and self-confidence. But Louie, in the words of a family friend, was a case of "not much push, too much play, and too little *mazel*."

The picture that emerges of Richard Tucker as an adolescent

is that of a high-energy, enormously competitive youth who, in a sense, was already leading two lives. Three afternoons a week (in addition to the *Shabbos*) he spent studying under Cantor Weisser, perfecting his technique and learning the basic cantorial literature. As a student, he was eager, dedicated, and rather unassuming; he deferred to Weisser in everything, and accorded him the respect he would have shown a great rabbi.

But outside the synagogue, in the raucous streets of Brooklyn's Boro Park, a different Rubin Tucker emerged: a street-wise, physically imposing boy who, in the words of a friend, could "raise hell with the best." His disposition was consistently sunny and, unlike his brother, Louie, he was generally even-tempered. Yet his easy-going demeanor disguised a temper that became mercurial on the few occasions when it reached a boiling point. Most of the time, he avoided fights, choosing instead to limit his aggression to athletics. But if a fight was picked by someone else, his strength and endurance, fueled by a volcanic temper, almost always proved too much for an opponent. As a result, though he was never a troublemaker, he was at ease on the streets and feared no one.

The young Tucker was also a gambler, to whom playing cards and a pair of dice were possessions as essential as a fielder's mitt, a rosin bag, and a well-seasoned Louisville Slugger. A deck of cards was as natural to him as to the Duke of Mantua. "I can still see him sitting on the sun porch, playing poker by the hour with his friends," Claire Nacman Witkowsky, his niece, would remember. "Win or lose, he loved every minute of it. Ruby liked to challenge the odds."

It was his prowess at sports and his taste for gambling, more than his voice, that distinguished Tucker in and around Boro Park. Few of his adolescent friends, even in retrospect, thought him destined for a great career—even as a *hazzan,* a cantor, let alone an opera singer. His voice was lyric and sweet, but hardly distinctive; it was still in its chrysalid stage, and it would remain so until he was in his middle twenties. The members of his "gang"—Manny Schwartz, Teddy Sloan, Phil Silverstein, Harry Singer, Sid Ziering, Sam Sherman, Bill Landesman, and Bernie and Sam Steinhaver, among them—thought of him more as an athlete than as a singer.

Rather curiously, as a youth Tucker lacked the compulsion

to perform that usually marks singers in their formative years. He shied away from amateur nights and other forums for the self-impressed, choosing instead to sing mainly in the synagogue. Nor did he listen intently to the music available to him on radio or phonograph recordings—religious, operatic, or popular. The only recordings he seems to have listened to with more than a passing interest were a few pre–World War I Victor "Red Seals" by Enrico Caruso, which the Metro Music Company in lower Manhattan played over loudspeakers to passersby in the spring and summer months. He made no serious study of the recordings of Yossele Rosenblatt, Mordecai Hershman, Gerson Sirota, Zavel Kvartin, or other renowned cantors. And while he may have danced with a date to the rhythms of the latest hits by the Paul Whiteman Band, Rudy Vallee's Connecticut Yankees, or the Coon-Sanders Nighthawks, he had no deep interest in popular music.

Both as a youth and as an adult, music was the source of Tucker's personal fulfillment and the measure of his accomplishments, but never a source of relaxation and amusement. Gambling and sports—usually in that order—were his ideas of unrestrained fun. As a young man, he engaged in them vigorously and regularly, and often managed to combine the two: it was more fun to bet on the outcome of a race or a basketball game than merely to compete in one. Self-assurance was the strongest pillar in Tucker's personality, and he was always willing to bet on himself—even when he had little reason to think he might win. Whatever the outcome, recalled his boyhood friend Manny Schwartz, "Ruby had enough *chutzpah* for any three people."

Sid Ziering was one of the Boro Park gang's "sharpies," and thus an obvious target for Tucker's competitive edge. Loath as Ruby was to admit it, Ziering usually bettered him at poker and pool—both of which Ruby practiced ardently, often with an eye to "cleaning out" Sid Ziering.

Once, after a particularly sizable Ziering victory at the card table, he and Tucker got into an after-school argument over who was the best pool player. Deciding to settle the issue once and for all, they headed for one of the pool halls then plentiful in Brooklyn. Once inside, they were reminded by the proprietor that the game would cost ten cents, no matter who won.

"Got some money on you, Tucker?" Ziering goaded.

"Sure I do! *You* got money, Ziering?" Tucker shot back. "If you think you can whip me, let's see you put some of your poker money on it!"

"You're on!" Ziering answered, pulling a fifty-cent piece from his pocket.

Twenty minutes later, Ziering pocketed the last in a string of difficult shots—some of them made from angles that mystified his hapless victim. When the call came to pay up, Tucker confessed that he didn't have fifty cents to his name.

"Aw, hell, just pay the dime for the game, then," said the victorious Ziering.

"I don't have a dime, either," Tucker said with a shrug.

The victor paid for the vanquished.

Tucker, Ziering, and the rest of their Boro Park friends earned the pocket money that supported their wagering from a number of after-school sources. They served as errand boys for local proprietors, clerked occasionally in small stores, and in the summers sold confections at Dexter Park. But one of the many summer jobs Tucker took on had a lasting effect on him. He worked for a time as a "runner" on Wall Street, carrying bids and paperwork to and from stockbrokers. The electricity of the New York Stock Exchange and the win-or-lose challenge of the market itself lured him in a way that shooting craps and playing poker had also gripped him. He viewed the stock market as the game table of the rich, and he hoped one day to learn it and manipulate it to his advantage.

Not unexpectedly, Tucker did his gambling without the knowledge—and certainly without the approval—of his adoring mother and Orthodox father. Several times Sam came close to catching Ruby gambling—but he never came quite close enough. "We were in the basement shooting craps one day when Ruby's father suddenly came down the stairs," Manny Schwartz recalled laughingly. "Ruby sure had to think fast!"

Sam had thought he heard the rattle of dice as he descended the stairs. Fortunately for his son, a large boiler blocked Sam's view.

"Dice? Down here?" Ruby said innocently. "Naw, we're fixing my bicycle. What you heard was the *chain* rattling!"

If Fannie Ticker heard from time to time that her young son had a passion for crap-shooting and cardplaying, no doubt she dismissed it. If she asked him, he probably acknowledged the charge, but made no mention of playing for money. She would have pressed the issue no further because, to her, Ruby was the perfect son—just as she, in his eyes, was the perfect mother. Their relationship was so mutually protective that Ruby often interceded for her when he (or perhaps she) thought Sam should provide more. As her health slowly declined from her worsening diabetes, she needed increasing bedrest. She suffered especially during the hot summer months—so much so that Ruby would regularly urge his father to take her to the Catskills for a week so that she might be spared the oppressive heat of the city.

In the summer of 1932, mainly at Ruby's insistence, Sam arranged a week's stay for her at Loch Sheldrake, a Catskill resort. Sam could not free himself from the fur market for the week, and sent Ruby in his place. Minnie, who was staying with her children at a small summer cottage nearby, met her mother and young brother at the West End Hotel. There, Fannie seemed to recover much of her strength after a few days' rest.

Midweek, relaxed and in far better health, Fannie went with Ruby, Minnie, and her children to the hotel's casino, where Ruby attracted his share of the teen-age girls whose parents were vacationing at the hotel. He danced with them and enjoyed showing off his command of the latest dance steps for the benefit of his mother. As the dancing went on, the bandleader eventually called for a Russian *sher*—a folk dance meant especially for the elders, many of whom, like Fannie Ticker, were Jewish immigrants from Eastern Europe.

The crowd applauded in delight, and immediately began to group into the four-couple, scissorlike formations the *sher* called for. Ruby proudly escorted his mother to the dance floor, and the *sher* began. Partners changed, then changed again, reuniting mother and son—and at that exact moment, Ruby's mother collapsed into his arms.

The music stopped. Other dancers offered their help as Ruby lifted his mother and carried her into a small room near the casino's entrance. Minnie knelt at Ruby's side as he cradled his mother's face in his hands.

Fannie opened her eyes, gazed at Ruby, and then closed them. *"Yets gei ich,"* she whispered in Yiddish—"I am going now." Those were her last words.

Ruby clutched her lifeless body to his, and looked helplessly at Minnie. He sobbed so wrenchingly that he could hardly catch his breath.

The death of his mother marked the loss of the most important person in Ruby's young life. It also marked the end of his family home. Sam Ticker would marry four times in all, three times outliving his wives. He married for the second time a year after Fannie's death, when Ruby was twenty. The new Mrs. Ticker insisted they move from Brooklyn, where most of Ruby's friends lived, to the Bronx, then later to Brighton Beach. Sam acceded to her wishes—at first without the enthusiasm of his son. It was not long, however, until Ruby grew fond of his second new home in Brighton Beach.

What finally won him over was Brighton's twofold promise of swimming and shapely young girls to attract and conquer. At twenty, Ruby had no difficulty attracting girls—and, if one can infer from the rather measured testimony of some of his Borough Park friends, he did more than his share of conquering. Youthful snapshots show him to have been handsome and muscular—a confident, responsive, good-looking boy who had developed a sense of bodily pride that he displayed eagerly at Brighton Beach in the summertime. A sun-worshipper even as a youth, he tanned easily and deeply, and relished the advantage his looks gave him in pursuing girls.

Any "steady" girl tended not to remain in his life very long, especially if she demanded exclusivity. If she was content to let him "play the field," Ruby would continue seeing her. On dates, he might take her to a baseball game, to a movie, to a Sunday dance, or, more often than not, for a long ride in the rumble seat of Manny Schwartz's Whippet roadster. On balmy summer nights, if their dates seemed in a cooperative frame of mind, the two boys would take their pleasures along a secluded stretch of beach or in the shrouded privacy of a tree-lined country lane.

At least one such intimate sojourn, however, was brought to an abrupt end when the Whippet failed to cooperate. "We had met these two girls a week or so earlier," Manny Schwartz recalled, "and to our surprise they seemed as eager to find a quiet spot as we were. I was driving, and from what I could see in the side mirror, Ruby was doing very well in the rumble seat. Just about then, the ignition coil gave out and the car coasted to a stop. We had to get out and push—and Ruby cursed that Whippet every foot of the way."

Tucker's two-world existence continued throughout 1932 and 1933. Dutifully, he kept up his studies with Cantor Weisser, who now taught him how to undergird his maturing lyric-tenor voice with the muscles of his thickening torso. Away from the synagogue, Ruby concentrated his attention on girls, gambling, and sports—each of which he pursued vigorously. He was happy living in two different worlds, yet he had no clear vision of a future—no ultimate goal on which he could focus his considerable energy and self-confidence. But in the winter of 1934, all of this would begin to change with a telephone call to a girl he had yet to meet.

2

Q: Who would you say has been the most influential and most important person in your life?

A: Sara, my wife. She's been by my side all the way, and she has inspired me to achieve the goals I set when I proposed to her.

It was well past sundown when Ruby made his call. The winter weather seemed unreasonably cold and made him grateful for the momentary shelter of the wooden telephone booth. It was warmer in there than it had been on Delancey Street, where the trolley from Brooklyn had discharged him hours earlier. But then, at least, the sun had been out.

He fumbled for a five-cent piece and wedged the cold receiver between his shoulder and neck while he dialed her number. Her uncle, Abe Posner, had written her name—Sara Perelmuth—on a small scrap of paper. That was weeks ago, and the frayed piece of paper showed it.

At the other end of the line, a woman's voice greeted him in Yiddish. Her voice was too commanding, too mature for a girl of twenty. He concluded, rightly, that he was speaking with her mother. He apologized for the intrusion and said he hoped he wasn't disturbing the family's *Shabbos*. When Anna Perelmuth assured him he wasn't intruding, he asked to speak with her daughter.

As he stood in the booth waiting to hear her voice, a knowing smile crossed his lips and his coal-black eyes shone with confidence. He was sure that Abe Posner had given him a good build-up with her—and *he* would take it from there. Bolstered by his summer conquests at Brighton Beach, he was certain that this newest object of interest, like the ones before her, would find his looks and charm irresistible.

"Hello, Sara, this is Rubin Tucker," he said when he heard her voice. He lingered musically when he spoke her name, letting his voice rise a bit in pitch, as if to show her that merely saying hello to her gave him great pleasure.

"Rubin who?" she said indifferently.

"Rubin *Tucker,*" he reiterated. He awaited a show of exuberance.

"I'm awfully sorry," she said kindly, "but I think you must be calling for somebody else. This is Sara Perelmuth you're talking to."

"Look, I *know* you're Sara Perelmuth," he said. "This is *Rubin Tucker.*" He continued to speak his name so confidently that Sara began to wonder whether she was having a lapse of memory.

"I'm sorry, but I don't know who you are," she said after a moment's pause. "Is there something I can do for you?"

What the hell kind of a matchmaker is Abe Posner? he asked himself, quickly trying to change his strategy.

"Maybe I could help you," she added, "if you tell me what you want."

"I thought your Uncle Abe would have told you that a long time ago," he said. "Didn't he mention me to you? He sure told me a lot about you. He even told me to go ahead and call you, and ask you to go out with me."

Suddenly, things began to make sense to Sara. Abe Posner had a special interest in her and, like the rest of her family, wanted her to meet someone who would be right for her—someone handsome, good-hearted, and especially someone who would be a good provider. At least in Abe's estimation, Sara supposed, the unseen party at the other end of the line must have met those requirements. *But who is he?* she wondered, growing more curious about him as their awkward conversation continued.

"Can I come to your house and see you?" Ruby asked, opting to get right to the point.

"When?" she asked warily.

"Right now. I'm in a phone booth a few blocks away from

your house. I can be there in just a couple of minutes. And anyway, it's very cold out here and I'm sure it's nice and warm in your house."

Sara knew her parents would hardly approve of this, especially on the Sabbath Eve.

"Look, tonight is out of the question," she said, matching his firmness. "This is *Shabbos* and my family is here together, and they're certainly not expecting to meet you. And besides, I'm supposed to meet a girl friend of mine in just a few minutes. You'll have to make it some other time."

"But—but I'm all alone," he said pleadingly. "I don't know anyone here, I'm from Brooklyn, I'm far away from home . . . and it's *so* cold out here!"

"If you're from Brooklyn and you're all alone," she said, "what are you doing here?"

"I'm studying to be a *hazzan,*" he said proudly. "I have to sing a service near here tomorrow, so I came in tonight. Otherwise, I'd have to walk from Brooklyn because I don't ride on the Sabbath."

She accepted his explanation without comment.

"So, you see, I'm all alone," he reiterated. "I don't know anybody here and I'd just like to come to your house and meet you. And it's *awfully* cold out here!"

Who is this boy? Doesn't he understand what "no" means? Once more Sara told him that he couldn't come—and once more he pleaded with her.

Finally, she gave in.

"All right, all right—you can come," she said in desperation. "But you're going to have to promise me that you'll only stay for a minute. My family isn't going to think this is right."

"On my word," he said, "I promise!"

Sara had hardly hung up the receiver when Ruby knocked at the door. When she opened it, he strode into the room, his hat in his hand, and flashed a victorious smile at her. As formalities were exchanged face to face, they studied each other and were pleased with what they saw. Each found the other attractive—her silky brown hair, well-proportioned figure, and womanly countenance pleased him, and his handsomeness, accented by his large jet-black eyes, fascinated her. Only his clothing made her feel that some finishing touch might be missing—he was wearing an ill-fitting tweed suit, a faded wool muffler, and a functional but drab-looking overcoat. Yet his undistinguished and mismatched dress did little to undermine the refinement of his features.

"My name is Rubin," he told Sara as he took her hand, "but everybody calls me Ruby."

She took him into the dining room and introduced him around the table. Her three brothers were there—Sender, the youngest; Mac, the middle son; and the eldest, Jan, whose wife, Alice, was also at the table—and one by one Ruby shook their hands. Ruby could hardly conceal his delight when Jan returned his handshake; he knew Jan's reputation as a singer, and admired him greatly.

Though the Metropolitan Opera, his ultimate goal, still lay some seven years in his future, Jan Peerce was already a formidable figure in the New York musical world. Success had come neither immediately nor easily to him; there had been constant obstacles along the way. When he eloped with Alice Kalmanowitz in 1929, he had only a semblance of a career. His talent and persistence enabled him to build enough of a following in the Catskills to sustain his wife and children through his lean years—most of them spent trying to break into Broadway or, preferably, into opera. Casting directors frequently judged his voice too large for Broadway—and, just as often, opera savants thought his voice too lyric for opera, probably better suited to Broadway.

Through a fellow musician, drummer-turned-booker Abe Pizik, Jan had gotten an important break by being featured at an Astor Hotel black-tie affair honoring vaudevillians Weber and Fields on the occasion of their fiftieth anniversary in show business. Everyone who was anyone on Broadway attended the affair. Late in the evening, when the orchestra had exhausted its material, Peerce, then billed as Pinky Pearl (a derivative of his real name, Jacob Pincus Perelmuth), made his way to the stage and sang Irving Berlin's popular ballad "Say It Isn't So."

The applause was hardly more than polite.

When he sang, next, "Yours Is My Heart Alone," the critical Broadway crowd applauded louder and longer. No doubt many were taken by the *chutzpah* this unknown amateur showed in playing to such a group. The third time he stepped to the front of the stage, singing the popular Italian folk song "O sole mio,"

Joe Weber and Lew Fields joined in the show-stopping ovation that greeted Peerce. Samuel Rothafel—Broadway's "Roxy," the man who masterminded Radio City—was at the Astor that night. He believed in Jan, and went on to make him a star.

The Jan Peerce to whom Sara introduced Ruby Tucker that evening in the winter of 1934 was well on his way. Ruby was still beaming when Sara led him back into the hallway. For a moment, she wasn't sure where his real interest lay—in her, or in her brother Jan.

Mrs. Perelmuth, perhaps wanting to scrutinize her daughter's uninvited guest a bit better, left the dining room with Ruby. Sara went to the phone to call her girl friend and tell her that she would be late. As she was dialing, she noticed, out of the corner of her eye, that Ruby was slowly taking off his coat. Mouthing her words silently so her mother wouldn't notice, she said to him, "Remember your promise!" With the look of a boy who had just been caught with his hand in the cookie jar, Ruby thrust his arms back into the coat.

Knowing that Sara felt it was time for him to leave, Ruby then began a spirited conversation with her mother; he told her about his family, and about his studies for the cantorate. Anna Perelmuth was the motive force in her household, and Ruby clearly sensed it.

When is he going to leave? Sara mused to herself, well aware of his strategy. As the situation grew more awkward, Ruby merely kept on talking.

"Maybe you and I can go for a short walk," he finally said to Sara. She looked at her mother, who did not seem to disapprove. As Sara viewed it, in any case, agreeing to go for a walk with Ruby would extricate her from a situation that showed no signs of concluding otherwise. Soon they were walking down Madison Street, the freezing wind penetrating their coats and stinging their faces. "It was one of those winter nights that wouldn't let you get warm," Sara would remember, "and I wished I had put on a heavier coat. As for Ruby—well, Ruby didn't seem to notice the weather, at least not for a while. He was too busy talking!"

That was the first thing she learned about him: he was a talker. He didn't exactly hold forth—and he certainly didn't seem a know-it-all. He just liked to talk. As they walked, he told her much about himself—not egotistically, not really self-servingly, but in an ebullient way that bespoke complete security, absolute self-confidence. He told her proudly of his studies under Cantor Weisser, and of the weddings, *bar mitzvahs,* and other services at which he assisted. More and more, he said, he was officiating instead of merely assisting another cantor. Ultimately, he hoped to secure an annual position at an Orthodox synagogue; if so, he could quit his job as a silk-lining salesman in the fur market and concentrate instead on the cantorate.

After a while, the bitter weather led him to interrupt his monologue.

"How about a movie?" he asked. "It will be warm in the theater."

Sara thought he was joking. Cantors were not supposed to be seen in movie theaters or any other entertainment places on the Sabbath. When she voiced her concern, he dismissed it.

"Oh, well, nobody around here knows me," he said indifferently. "Anyhow, the way I figure it, we're just going to the theater to get warm. You see?"

She didn't exactly, but they endured another two or three blocks until they encountered a marquee announcing *The Barretts of Wimpole Street.* They took their seats as the last of the credits rolled by. "We thawed out, all right," Sara recalled, "but we might as well not have gone. He kept right on talking, with me shushing him now and then, until there was no point trying to watch the movie."

Halfway through it, Sara tactfully suggested that they leave. Soon, their conversation was shifted to a nearby ice-cream parlor. The new locale was his choice rather than hers; he was hungry and, as usual, wanted to indulge his sweet tooth. This time, Sara didn't bother to verbalize her concern for his image. True, ice-cream parlors were no more fitting places for a cantor to be seen on *Shabbos* than were the movies. But, she told herself, if the one didn't matter to him, the other mustn't either.

Their date—or what there was of it—ended over a pineapple-chocolate soda, followed by a long walk back to Madison Street. It had all been pleasant enough, but, as was clear to both of them when they parted company that cold winter night, neither one had sparked anything extraordinary in the other: that singular rush of excitement, the obliviousness to time and circumstances, simply wasn't there. They said good-bye that night without having any reason to suspect that much would ever develop between them. Ruby did not call again—nor would Sara have wanted him to.

But something did eventually develop—and it was purely a matter of chance. It happened at Brighton Beach several months later, in the summer of 1934. "My best friend," Sara recalled, "was a girl named Sarah Zuckerman, who lived in our building on Madison Street. She was the one I was supposed to meet the night Ruby first called, when my uncle had given him my phone number. One Sunday, she and I went to Coney Island, and it was such a gorgeous summer day that we decided to walk to Brighton Beach. We spent the day there and then took the train back to Manhattan.

"I went up to the turnstiles on the passenger platform and was standing there waiting when a train pulled up. The first person to get off was a very handsome, deeply tanned young man— he was so good-looking, in fact, that my eyes couldn't help following him. I looked and then looked away, but I noticed that he was looking at me, too. It was Ruby, though I didn't recognize him at first."

Tucker's memory of that moment mirrored hers exactly— including how the summer sun seemed to enhance her attractiveness. "The train opened up and Sara was standing right in front of the door. I looked at her and said, 'How are you?' and she didn't recognize me. So I dashed out of the train and the doors closed." He had found her attractive before, he remembered, but in the summer sunshine "all of a sudden she became beautiful."

Impulsively, he asked her to meet him the next weekend at Brighton. She agreed, with one stipulation—that he find a date for her friend Sarah. Sarah Zuckerman was an outgoing, bubbly, very attractive girl, and Tucker claimed he would have no trouble talking one of his friends into a blind date. All was set, and the two girls agreed to meet at the Perelmuths' the next Wednesday night, where Ruby would call them and finalize their weekend plans.

"Every time the phone rang that Wednesday," Sara recalled, "we would spring from our chairs trying to get to the phone. Sarah Zuckerman was just as excited as I was, and from seven o'clock on we were sure every call was going to be his."

Eight o'clock came and went. Then nine o'clock. Nine-thirty. Ten, then ten-thirty. Finally, Sarah Zuckerman had to go home. By then, the two girls had exhausted every possible reason why he hadn't called. They were left with only one: Ruby Tucker had stood Sara up.

"After that night," Sara said, "I detested him. I couldn't even stand to hear his name mentioned. It wasn't just that he had stood me up. That I could live with. Worse than that, he had embarrassed me to my best friend. Now *she* knew that he stood me up."

She had all but forgotten him when Abe Posner, her matchmaking uncle, happened to see Tucker at a *bar mitzvah* at which he sang. When asked whether he had ever called Sara, Tucker acknowledged that he had, but neglected to add that he had also stood her up. Abe Posner innocently encouraged him to call her again, which he did, only to have Sara almost hang up on him. He kept her on the line, and then he talked, pleaded, soothed, and cajoled her until she not only accepted his apology but agreed to go to a New Year's Eve dance with him.

"This time, I promise I'll be there," he assured her. It was his last chance with her, and he knew it.

"I honestly didn't know whether he would show up or not," Sara recalled. "But he surprised me, and gave me a wonderful New Year's Eve. He treated me like a queen that night."

That memorable evening at the St. George Hotel in downtown Brooklyn, Ruby gave Sara a first glimpse of the exalted place he would accord her throughout their married life. His Boro Park friends, many of whom were at the St. George ringing in the New Year, considered him special, and he knew it; he considered Sara special, and he made sure *they* knew it. The corsage he gave her was more lavish than the ones most of the other girls wore. He complimented her repeatedly, and praised her appearance to his friends.

It was clear to everyone who saw them that New Year's Eve that indeed Ruby Tucker had designs on Sara Perelmuth. But Sara Perelmuth was not at all sure how she felt about Ruby Tucker.

At times, his behavior puzzled her—as an event that night at the St. George only served to underscore, much to Sara's embarrassment. "A girl at our table kept shooting daggers at me all evening. At first, I tried to look away, but I couldn't keep that up very long because she just kept glaring at me. After a while, I grew really uncomfortable. I was able to avoid her until all the girls at the table decided to go to the powder room."

Sara was hardly inside the doorway when her antagonist confronted her. "So!" the girl said mockingly. "Rubin Tucker stood *me* up to go out with *you!*"

Sara was dumbfounded. After a few moments of stunned silence, she mumbled that at least the girl was lucky to have gotten another date for the dance.

"That's my brother!" the girl said, rolling her eyes to confirm her desperation. "Thanks to *your* date, he's all I could get with one day's notice!"

Sara was in a mild state of shock when she returned to the table.

"You're terrible!" she lectured Ruby under her breath. "One day's notice! You're worse than terrible, you're horrible!"

"Aw, forget her," he said with a wave of his hand. "We're here together, so let's enjoy ourselves. Don't worry about her. She'll get over it."

None too gently, Sara reminded him that he had done nearly the same thing to her. He ducked the issue long enough to get her onto the dance floor, where he could charm his way back into her graces.

"That was then, and this is now," he reassured her in an apologetic voice. "From here on, Sara, you won't be able to get rid of me."

As with every subsequent promise he made her, this one he kept. "We saw each other quite often," Sara remembered, "and we thoroughly enjoyed ourselves. He was a perfect 'date'—always so attentive, so much a gentleman in the way he treated me—and yet he was so spontaneous that being with him was really exciting."

Early in their courtship, he arranged to sing for her. *Arranged* is quite the right word, considering the lengths to which he went in planning it. He took her to a Rumanian restaurant on Second Avenue—a café rich in atmosphere, accentuated by the competent playing of two strolling violinists. Ruby patronized the café as often as his salesman's wages permitted, and he knew the headwaiter and some of the other help. With their cooperation, and with a dollar or two paid to the violinists, Ruby serenaded

Sara in the presence of other diners, singing the verse and refrain of the popular ballad "One Night of Love."

When she kissed him good-bye at the end of that special evening, she burst into the cramped kitchen of the Perelmuth apartment and said to her mother, "Ruby *sang* for me tonight, Mama! Why, he sings just like Jan!"

"What?" Mrs. Perelmuth said in disbelief. "You don't know what you're talking about. Rubin Tucker is just a boy. He *can't* sing like Jan. Do us both a favor and go to bed. Maybe tomorrow you'll get this out of your head."

Mrs. Perelmuth's reaction was blunt, protective, and entirely logical—as were most of her judgments, whether of people or events. Though these qualities had come to her naturally, they had grown stronger when circumstances had forced her to become the breadwinner for her family. Her husband, Levi, once a presser in the garment district of the Lower East Side, became a victim of the unrelenting harshness of the sweatshop—the twelve-hour workdays, the unsanitary conditions, and especially the constant pressure from management to produce more goods in less time. After years of coping with this strain, he developed a serious ulcer and nearly died before an operation repaired most of the damage.

Anna Perelmuth's emergence as the dominant figure in her family began with Levi's hospitalization and long recuperation. "She didn't have any choice," Sara said in looking back on her family's situation. "Papa was sick, there was no money coming in, so she *had* to take charge of things." For some time, Anna had augmented Levi's meager wages by taking in boarders—some of them newly arrived immigrants who needed a place to sleep for a week or two, others young working people who needed long-term lodging. With at least three boarders to feed, plus her husband and four children, she was accustomed to cooking large quantities of kosher food.

With Levi out of work, she began serving kosher meals in their five-room apartment. "Most of the people who ate at our table were workers," Sender Peerce, the youngest of her three boys, recalled. "Usually, they were Orthodox Jews, which meant they were looking for kosher food that was *really* kosher. Word got around the neighborhoods that you could eat at the Perelmuths' on Madison Street, and for two bits you could get a four-

or five-course dinner that was guaranteed kosher. So, one person told another, that person told two more, and before long we had what amounted to a small restaurant in our apartment."

As Levi's strength slowly returned, he took odd jobs to bring in extra money. During the day—often with Jan and the younger boys, Sender and Mac, helping him—he sold dry goods on consignment in the open-air markets of Orchard and Water streets. At night, he worked the cloakroom concession at a banquet hall on Ludlow Street; he worked until the last of the customers called for their coats and hats, which was often at one or two in the morning. When the owners of the hall opted for a larger one uptown and offered to sell the facility to any employees who might be interested, Levi and one of the waiters, Gershon Smith, put up their joint savings for the down payment, borrowing the rest from East Side lenders. They renamed their enterprise the Grand Mansion. Anna ran the kitchen, and Levi and Gershon Smith gathered the bookings for the weddings, receptions, lodge meetings, and *bar mitzvahs* they catered.

As its clientele grew with its reputation, the Grand Mansion became a family enterprise. Sender and Mac worked on and off at the Grand Mansion while they were in school; when he grew older, Sender took over the booking end of the business. Jan provided the musical entertainment until he began playing the better resorts in the Catskills. Mac often played the drums in the five-piece band Jan put together for his Grand Mansion engagements.

Though Levi and Anna Perelmuth endowed each of their children with parts of their own personalities as parents, all four mirrored more of their mother than their father. To varying degrees, all of them inherited her fast pace, black-and-white views of right and wrong, and intuitive ability to size up a person. Even her eldest, Jan—from whom she expected the most, and who resisted her hard-line discipline just as strongly as she imposed it—had to acknowledge that he had inherited much from her in temperament. "My mother was a wonderful woman with love in her heart," Peerce has written, "but she had a temper and a powerful way of telling you off; in other words, she was very much like me when something irks me." Perhaps this admitted similarity, and the contest of wills it occasioned during Peerce's adolescence, accounted for his less than flattering portrait of his mother in his memoirs.

Ide Levine saw the Perelmuth family from the more neutral vantage point of a neighborhood friend, and provided a more balanced overview of Sara's parents in middle age. "They were both rare people, different as they were from each other," she recalled. "Mr. Perelmuth was a quiet and kindly man, a man whom you could readily confide in, a man who was wise in the biblical sense of the term. He set a wonderful example of religiousness by the way he lived—and yet I never knew him to be judgmental of anyone else. He accepted someone's failings, especially if he saw that the person was trying to improve himself.

"Mrs. Perelmuth was less accepting, particularly if a person shirked an important responsibility or did something dishonest. She had very high standards, especially where work was concerned—she worked harder than anyone I have ever known, and she expected everyone around her to work just as hard. She was extremely organized, and could carry on a half-dozen projects at once, always seeing the straightest line to the best results in each one. Now, if you happened to be standing in the midst of that straight line, she might move you out of her way in mid-sentence, and maybe without much finesse. Yet if you knew her, you grasped how special she was and you were never offended." Other friends and family members remembered the Perelmuths the same way—Mr. Perelmuth with reverence, and Mrs. Perelmuth with awe.

Perhaps predictably—and aside from her secondhand assessment of his singing—Mrs. Perelmuth was a catalyst in Sara's engagement to Ruby Tucker. Though the two dated steadily, their feelings for each other had not yet ripened into the kind of love that demands a lasting commitment. Only when Sara's mother confronted her about her relationship with Ruby did Sara realize how deep her feelings went.

One Sabbath Eve, Sara and Ruby went out on a date; they intended to take in a movie and, if time permitted, to stop for dessert at an ice-cream parlor. As was often the case, Sara's brothers and Jan's wife, Alice, were at the table with her father and mother when Ruby came calling. To Sara's surprise, no one had left the table hours later when Ruby brought her home.

"The moment we walked through the door," she recalled, "Ruby and I could tell that we had been the topic of conversation. It was nothing explicit, mind you, and nobody was saying anything about us when we walked in. But the way they all reacted gave them away. Ruby and I looked at each other and knew what had been going on."

Ruby grew uneasy and politely declined Mrs. Perelmuth's offer of tea and cake. He bade Sara a hasty good-night and whispered that he would be waiting for her at noon the next day outside the Falstaff Press on Fifth Avenue, where she did clerical work. He sensed that she would be in for a motherly grilling and he knew that her family's estimation of him was sure to be discussed. He could hardly wait to find out how the Perelmuths viewed him.

As soon as he left, Mrs. Perelmuth asked Sara to join her at the table. Characteristically, she went directly to the point. "What's it going to be with you two?" she asked Sara. "You're seeing each other very often, and you don't go out with many other boys. That tells me you're serious about Ruby. You *are* serious about him, aren't you?"

"Mama, I don't really know," Sara replied honestly.

Her mother pursued a different line of questioning, comparing Ruby to other young men Sara had dated and asking her how different her feelings were in each case. Mrs. Perelmuth made particular mention of a young doctor whom she had encouraged Sara to date. He was one of her motherly attempts at matchmaking, but, as had been the rule for some time, Sara's affection for Ruby Tucker had precluded anything coming of it. Ultimately, this new line of questioning on Mrs. Perelmuth's part yielded predictable results: Sara underscored Ruby's charm and appeal, and made clear that she had more feeling for him than for anyone else she had ever dated.

Jan, who had listened patiently, now spoke up.

"Appeal is very nice, very important, and so is charm," he said, "but also you've got to have food on the table. Ruby Tucker is a nice guy and I'm sure he means well. But you've got to ask yourself whether he's going to be able to provide for you."

Sara replied that she believed in Ruby, and believed that he would earn enough to meet their needs, whether as a fur-market salesman or, in time, as a full-time cantor.

"It's good that you believe in him," Jan said in a protective older-brother tone. "But if you look at where he is and where he says he wants to be, belief alone isn't going to make it happen. He says he wants to be a cantor, but I tell you, Sara, he's got a very long way to go. What are you going to do in the meantime? Your parents can't be taking care of you after you're married, you know."

Much as Sara respected Jan, she felt he was underestimating Ruby—and was forgetting his own past as well.

"You didn't have so much either," she reminded him, "but you and Alice worked together—and look at you now. You believed in yourself, and Alice believed in you. That's how I feel about Ruby. I really believe someday he'll make it as a cantor. He's got wonderful ideas for the future."

"But, Sara, ideas alone won't put food on a table," Jan said a bit impatiently. "I'd like to be able to say that Ruby is going to make it, that he's going to do everything you and he think he can do. But it's not that simple. Making it as a cantor is very hard, Sara, and I'm not sure Ruby can do it."

Sara had no effective reply. Jan, after all, knew singing and knew more than she about the pitfalls of a career, even a cantorial one. Yet she wouldn't yield her confidence in what Ruby could do. The discussion ended without any resolution, although everyone in the Perelmuth family, including Jan, made clear that they liked Ruby a great deal. "They were all fond of him," Sara would say later, "but the problem was he was poor."

The Peerces left for their West End Avenue apartment shortly before midnight. Sara was in bed not long afterward, but couldn't sleep at all; at seven the next morning, when she began readying herself for work, she was still mulling over what she would say to Ruby when she saw him. To relate the dinner-table conversation, she would have to bring up marriage—an awkward topic for a girl to have to bring up to her boyfriend, especially when he had never directly broached the subject himself.

When her half-day's work at the Falstaff Press ended at noon, Ruby was waiting for her just as he had said. As they made their way down Fifth Avenue, he quizzed her eagerly on what had happened after he left. She had debated how she would tell him, but finally she put it bluntly—she was, after all, her mother's daughter. She said her parents wanted to know whether the two of them were planning to marry.

Ruby sensed her awkwardness and took her hand in his.

"Look, Sara, I'm very fond of you," he told her softly. "I promise that if you stick with me, I'll really make it. And I don't want you to worry about having to go to your family for anything. As long as we're together, you and I can make it on our own."

Then he told her something that momentarily took her aback. He confided that he intended to become an opera star. Not merely an opera singer, but an opera *star*. "You mark my words, Sara," he told her firmly, "someday I'm going to make it big in opera."

"Ruby, have you ever *seen* an opera?" she asked incredulously.

He shook his head no.

"Well, if you're going to be an opera star, don't you think we ought to start going to some operas?"

He told her he had been planning to take her to the Hippodrome, where the low-budget San Carlo Opera Company put on the more popular Italian operas.

Sara said nothing for a moment, and merely kept on walking. Her silence made him uneasy.

"You're really serious about this, aren't you?" Sara asked him. "When you say you're going to make it big, I have to believe you because I know you won't give up."

"It may take me years," he said to her, "but this I can promise you: like a rosebush, I'll bloom and bud every year and I'll make you proud of me."

This was all the promise Sara needed. She returned it with a vow to stand by him—no matter what hardships the future might bring, no matter where it might take them.

3

*Q: You and Mrs. Tucker seem to have one
of those rare "model marriages" that we only
read about. What was it like when you were
starting out?*

*A: We both love and respect each other, which
is why we've made it this long. How did we
start? Comically, when I look back on it. We
lived with Sara's parents—which was hell for
me, much as I loved them. Then, we squan-
dered our money on a Bermuda honeymoon,
and that got ruined, too. A hell of a start!*

On February 11, 1936, in the presence of three hundred guests at
the Grand Mansion, Sara Perelmuth became Mrs. Rubin Tucker.
The wedding took place just over nine months after their engagement was announced. As weddings go, theirs was unusual
in at least two respects: Sara received her engagement ring not
from Ruby but from her mother, and Ruby—normally the essence of punctuality—nearly missed the ceremony.

Shortly after Sara accepted his proposal, Ruby made the engagement official by presenting her with a simple but elegant ring.
She thought him oddly apologetic for the ring's minute stone.
Though she treasured the ring as if there were no other like it in
the world, he felt compelled to assure her that one day he would
give her "a diamond so big you'll have to wear sunglasses when
you put it on."

Sara's mother would have preferred a shorter wait. When Sara
showed her the ring, Mrs. Perelmuth said aloud, "My daughter
isn't going to wear that!"

"But, Mama," Sara said in Ruby's defense, "it's all he can
afford, and *I'm* happy with it."

"You shouldn't be!" Mrs. Perelmuth said bluntly. "People

will think you're marrying someone in the poorhouse! It may be all *he* can afford, but it's not all *I* can!"

With that, she took her own diamond ring from her finger—a much more ornate ring with a sizable stone, which Mr. Perelmuth had given her after the Grand Mansion began earning money. She handed the ring to Sara. "From now on, you'll wear *this!*"

Sara knew better than to argue with her mother when her mind was made up. But rather than offend Ruby, she alternated the rings for several days, wearing Ruby's when she was with him, and her mother's when she was at home. Eventually, her ruse caught up with her, and Ruby demanded an explanation. Sara could find no graceful one, so she told him what her mother had said.

"Needless to say, he was crushed," Sara remembered. "He said I would wear his ring or none at all—and he was determined to have it out with my mother over this."

That Sabbath Eve, as Sara's mother prepared the meal, Ruby quietly went into the kitchen and, trying to conceal his anger with a respectful tone of voice, he asked her why she had forbidden Sara to wear his ring.

"She's my only girl, Ruby, and I want to give her something special," Mrs. Perelmuth said unapologetically. "I couldn't think of anything more special than my own diamond ring, so I gave it to her and asked her to wear it."

"But she's *my* fiancée," he protested. "She's supposed to wear *my* ring, not yours!"

"Don't be mad at me, Ruby," she answered. "As long as I'm alive, let her wear my ring. Let me enjoy seeing it on her finger, won't you?"

There was nothing more to say, and he knew it. Ruby swallowed his pride and deferred to Anna Perelmuth. "How do you say no to your future mother-in-law?" he would say of the incident years later. "She was such a marvelous woman—a wonderful mother to Sara, and a really great mother-in-law to me. Anyway, she was so strong-headed that there was no point arguing with her."

Tucker would always regret that his own mother did not see him stand with his bride beneath the *huppah,* the wedding canopy, and receive the marital blessings of the Jewish faith. In keeping with Orthodox tradition, he fasted on his wedding day and honored his mother's memory by visiting her grave. The blustery February weather, worsened by an early-morning snowfall, made the journey to her Long Island gravesite difficult. His sister Rae and her husband, Abe Parness, drove him to the cemetery in what they thought was more than enough time to visit the grave and return to the Lower East Side for the ceremony.

On the way out of the cemetery, however, Parness's sedan suddenly skidded off the road and teetered on the edge of a deep ditch. After an hour of railing at the snow and ice, and climbing in and out of the ditch while his brother-in-law rhythmically worked the clutch, Ruby arrived at the Perelmuths' Madison Street home hungry, exhausted—and late. But he revived quickly among the three hundred guests who crowded into the Grand Mansion's main banquet room. After the ceremony, with Sara never more than an arm's length away from him, he partied with his Boro Park friends—Manny Schwartz, Sid Ziering, Teddy Sloan, Harry Singer, and the rest—all of whom were members of the wedding party.

The honeymoon had been planned far in advance—at Sara's insistence. "In those days," she recalled, "the classy thing to do was to take a honeymoon cruise to Bermuda. I had never done anything like that in my life, and I wanted it so badly that I practically made it a condition of our wedding. I told Ruby that we would have the wedding when he and I had saved enough to sail to Bermuda."

Though his income was hardly enough to pay rent on an apartment and sustain his cantorial studies, Ruby didn't balk at Sara's high-priced request, but used some of the money from their wedding gifts to pay for the honeymoon cruise. He was as adventurous and social-minded as she, and anything that Sara wanted he took as a challenge to provide. Well before the wedding, he booked passage on the *Monarch,* one of several liners that sailed weekly from Manhattan to Bermuda.

The *Monarch* was to set sail on February 15, a Saturday. Owing to the lucrative weekend bookings at the Grand Mansion, Sara and Ruby were married on a Tuesday. "Business was business with my parents," Sara recalled, "and they couldn't change a booking even for my wedding. They gave us a Tuesday, which

was fine because Jewish people consider it a lucky day." Lucky
or not, it left the newlyweds with three days and four nights to
fill until their honeymoon cruise began.

They decided to spend the intervening days at the Park Central Hotel in midtown Manhattan. Sara remembers that their first
night as husband and wife was not quite what either expected.

"It was very late when we left the Grand Mansion for the
Park Central. Naturally, my brothers made a big deal out of what
was going to happen at the hotel. Even as we were pulling away
from the curb, they were embarrassing the hell out of me—you
know, 'Take it easy on her, Ruby, she's just a kid,' or 'Get plenty
of sleep tonight, the two of you.'

"When we finally got into the hotel—we had just a small
room, nothing fancy—we hung out the DO NOT DISTURB sign and
bolted the door. We had waited too long for this moment, so we
dispensed with formalities. Ruby was the one with the experience,
so I followed his lead. He told me it would be very romantic for
us to begin by taking a shower together. He had no more than
suggested it than we were out of our clothes and under the water.

"We stayed in the shower a good long time, totally unaware
of anything but each other. But, stupidly, we had forgotten to
put the shower curtain *inside* the tub. When we went to get out,
the bathroom looked like a pond. There must have been at least
three inches of water on the floor!

"I started to panic because all I could imagine was the water
leaking through the ceiling of the room below, then the manager
banging on our door, plumbers coming into the room, charges
for damages—the whole thing became a nightmare, but at the same
time it was funny beyond words. It got funnier when we decided
to mop up the water, and found that there were only two towels
to work with. We spent till three o'clock in the morning wring-
ing out wet towels. We were so exhausted afterward that we
just fell into bed—the lovemaking had to wait till the next morning."

Between Wednesday and Friday, the newlyweds took in as
many movies, vaudeville revues, and Broadway shows as their
budget would allow. On Saturday morning, many of their friends
boarded the *Monarch* and gave them a bon voyage party. One of
Ruby's friends, Harry Singer, had just taken the two-and-a-half-
day cruise with his new bride. He offered some advice for Sara,

whose queasiness on the water worried Ruby. "He told Ruby to order me a tray of appetizers—finger sandwiches, that sort of thing—as soon as the boat got under way. He advised both of us to snack on the finger sandwiches, even between meals, so that we would always have something in our stomachs. That way, we wouldn't get seasick."

But Ruby's compulsive noshing led him to devour the first tray of sandwiches before the boat left the dock. *"Eat,* Sara, you're gonna get sick otherwise," he lectured her as the finger sandwiches quickly disappeared. She ate sparingly, only to have him lecture her again as the *Monarch* made its way out of the harbor.

Their first night on board had been planned almost to the minute. They would dress in their best evening apparel, she in a specially made gown and he in a black silk tuxedo. They would have a formal dinner at their own candlelit table for two. After dinner, they would make their way to the dance floor, and afterward stroll along the moonlit deck.

To Ruby's chagrin, the script had to be rewritten shortly after they sat down at their table in the dining room. "When we ordered dinner," Sara remembered, "Ruby didn't say much of anything, and seemed uninterested in the menu—he just ordered for the sake of ordering. I didn't think much of it because I was having such a good time. As the waiters passed by our table carrying trays of food, he got greener and greener. All of a sudden, he shot out of his chair and headed for the nearest bathroom. He dodged in, out, and around the line of waiters like some football player on his way to a touchdown. I ended up having a candlelit dinner by myself."

Trying to make the best of the situation, Sara accepted a few invitations to dance. When Ruby failed to return, she got worried and went to look for him. She found him hunched up in a chair on one of the upper decks, swathed in blankets like a sick child. "He was so worn out from being seasick," she remembered, "that he was afraid to talk, afraid to move, for fear he would get sick again."

She was asleep when he finally crawled into bed. He tossed, turned, and periodically moaned until the morning sun rose above the gray horizon. As soon as it was light enough to find his way back to the deck, he rewrapped himself in the now-moist blankets and, looking like a monk on his way to the Judgment, he slowly climbed the iron stairs and slumped into the deck chair.

"Except during the night when he was asleep next to me," Sara said, "he stayed in that chair and refused to move." For the next two days, he ate no solid food at all. He was even afraid to drink water for fear he couldn't keep it down.

He stirred only when the Bermuda shoreline came into view—and with it the prospect of the comforts of the Elbow Beach Hotel, where he had made reservations. "As soon as the *Monarch* docked," Sara remembered, "Ruby ran down the gangplank, dropped to his knees, and kissed the ground." Once they were inside the hotel, his appetite returned. "As soon as we checked in, he ordered a huge tray of food. When that wasn't enough, he ordered more. He ate so much that first day that he actually made himself sick again!"

On the return trip, temperate eating put his stomach at ease, and Ruby began to enjoy himself in the ways he had imagined—until, halfway back to Manhattan, a series of violent thunderstorms reawakened his queasiness and sent him back to the deck chair. The worst was yet to come. "Just as we got through most of the storms," Sara recalled, "the captain announced that he had just received an SOS from a liner that had lost control of its rudder. He said that the *Monarch* might be needed to help rescue passengers. So he turned the boat around and we sailed right back into the storms."

The rudderless ship was repaired at sea and the *Monarch*'s help was not needed. Ruby seemed to recover again and for a time the ocean grew calm enough for the newlyweds to contemplate an evening of dinner and dancing. Though he was pale and drawn from seasickness, Ruby was too proud to admit his exhaustion to his ever-eager bride. He reached for his tuxedo and said with a wink, "I'm gonna give you an evening you'll never forget. I feel like dancing all night."

Amid this display of bravado, his collar button slipped from his fingers and rolled beneath the bed. He bent down to retrieve the button—and fell flat on his face. "There went his act," Sara said. "He was so weak he just lay there and moaned. He couldn't get up until I helped him. He mumbled that he was never going on a boat as long as he lived. He was even mad at the tuxedo—he said he was never going to wear anything but plain black suits for the rest of his life, just so he wouldn't have to chase collar buttons."

Once back in Manhattan, the "welcome home" party the

Perelmuths gave Sara and Ruby at the Grand Mansion helped make up for their thwarted honeymoon plans. This was a private party for family, friends, and the employees and suppliers of the Grand Mansion, many of whom had known Sara since she was a young girl. Perhaps predictably, it was an affair that all but exceeded their wedding reception.

One of the party's most memorable moments took place when the musicians who had been booked for the affair struck up the love song "Because." Jan Peerce took his once-familiar place at the center of the Grand Mansion's small stage, amid the cheers of clients and workers who had known him years before the coast-to-coast "Chevrolet Hour" and the Radio City Music Hall had made him a star. His flawless technique and superb musicianship transformed the familiar wedding song into great music, and his admiring audience applauded a polished, mature artist. Sara and Ruby vigorously joined in the applause. Jan had sung to them, and they were both touched by his gesture.

In the din afterward, before the festivities resumed, a few well-meaning guests called for Ruby to sing. At first he declined; the moment was Jan's, not his. One or two guests kept after him. With some encouragement from Sara, he mounted the stage and sang a chorus of "One Night of Love."

The guests applauded politely, almost sympathetically.

At some of the tables, there were quiet expressions of wonder about Sara's new husband. A nice fellow, yes. A cantor? Well, perhaps—with a lot more study. A tenor like Jan Peerce? Hardly. The contrast was too obvious—leading some of the guests to question whether Rubin Tucker really knew his own limitations.

At that moment especially, Tucker himself might have granted their concerns, but with one important difference. Amateur that he was—especially when compared to a professional like Peerce, who was nine years his senior—Tucker harbored no doubt that with the proper guidance, time, and hard work he would *become* a great singer.

Self-assurance, then and later the Tucker trademark, was not in itself a bankable commodity in the depths of the Depression. When he married Sara, Tucker was earning $25 a week as a salesman in the fur market. As a wedding present, his boss awarded him a $5-a-week bonus. He worked for the Reliable Silk Company, then located at 328 Seventh Avenue in the heart of the fur market.

Owned and managed by the Rosenblatt family, who were Russian-Jewish immigrants, Reliable Silk was one of many small-firm "jobbers" that supplied bolts of material to the furriers in Manhattan from the silk mills in Paterson, New Jersey. Not unexpectedly, Tucker got his entree to Reliable Silk through his father, who had dealt several times with the patriarch of the Rosenblatt family.

Ben Herschaft, a respected furrier who would spend more than fifty years in the Manhattan market, made Tucker's acquaintance in 1935, shortly after the Rosenblatts had hired him. "Ruby's job was to go door to door, from one factory or showroom to another, displaying his silk samples," Herschaft recalled. "He was very young—maybe ten years younger than I, just in his early twenties. I had seen him around before he called on me in my showroom, but I didn't know that he was Sam Ticker's son until he told me. I also knew his father very well. I liked the way Ruby presented himself when he called. He was confident, always very 'up,' an all-around nice guy who you sensed had something special about him. I gave him some business, and I got to know him."

This was the beginning of one of the longest and closest friendships of both men's lives, one based initially on a business relationship but soon deepened by Herschaft's interest in the cantorate. "I had heard most of the great cantors who had appeared in New York," Herschaft said. "When Ruby told me, after I got to know him, that he was a *hazzan,* a cantor, it made him all the more special to me."

Several times, when they were alone in his showroom, Herschaft persuaded Tucker to sing for him. "At the noon hour, when my people would be at lunch, Ruby would often drop in and we would spend the hour together, eating a sandwich and just talking. After a while, I might remind him of a *z'miroh,* a *Shabbos* song, or maybe a folk tune from the Purim holiday, or a Passover seder melody. I'd say to him, 'Come on, Ruby, open up the voice!' He would draw himself to his full height, that barrel chest of his bulging out of his suit coat, his head cocked slightly upward, his eyes fixed in the distance—and then he'd let loose that voice! I used to sit there in awe, thinking to myself, 'Here's a young man who one day is going to be sitting on top of the music world!' "

As yet, the musical world of Rubin Tucker was limited to

*bar mitzvah*s and weddings, each of which netted him an average of $10—enough, when added together at the end of an especially good month, to cover his lessons. After his engagement to Sara, the Perelmuths occasionally booked him for wedding parties at the Grand Mansion. Though the Grand Mansion had an "official" cantor—Jerusalem-born Joseph Mirsky, a well-schooled *hazzan* then in his early thirties—Tucker eagerly took any engagements that Mirsky had to decline.

With Mirsky's help, Tucker was engaged to chant the High Holydays services for an Orthodox congregation in the Washington Heights section of Manhattan, at the Beth Midrash Hagodol synagogue. It was his first major engagement in the pulpit, and the beauty of his voice as heard during the Rosh Hashanah and Yom Kippur services quickly earned him a promising reputation. Then, in the winter of 1935, the first prospect of a major break came his way. He was given an audition—and with it the prospect of an annual appointment, assuring him a steady income—at the Rumanian Synagogue near the intersection of Rivington and Forsyth streets in lower Manhattan.

Ben Herschaft attended the service. "It was a tough tryout because it took place on the Sabbath during Hanukkah. I came in from the Bronx and, though I got there early, the synagogue was already jammed. Besides the regular congregation, there were connoisseurs from all over New York who had come to hear this young *hazzan* that people were beginning to talk about.

"Ruby sang wonderfully that day. I don't mean just the way his voice sounded, which was great. More than that, it was the heart he put into the music. He was 'on' and he knew it. I was sure he had the contract in the palm of his hand."

As the congregation filed out, Herschaft listened intently to the comments they made. "You'd hear a lot of them saying, 'This young fellow is terrific!' Others were saying, 'He's good, he's still young, and he'll develop into something.' But the older connoisseurs were shaking their heads as if to say, 'What's all the fuss about? He's nothing special. He's just a kid, and he's got a lot to learn.' " The board of directors of the Rumanian Synagogue inclined to the latter opinion and did not award Tucker a contract.

Levi Perelmuth had a formidable grasp of liturgical music, and sought to help Tucker identify what those connoisseurs found lacking. At Mr. Perelmuth's suggestion, Joseph Mirsky, the Grand Mansion's cantor, took Tucker as a pupil. Though there was no

need to improve his technique, thanks to the thorough ground-
ing he had received from Cantor Weisser, Ruby soon learned important stylistic nuances from Mirsky—perhaps a certain inflec-
tion in one line, an unwritten but telling bit of ornamental phrasing
in another, all of which could be learned only by concentrated
study.

"Ruby and Joe Mirsky became inseparable," Sara recalled.
"Ruby would go to his home after Joe had chanted the Sabbath
service, and the two of them would pore over the cantorial texts
for hours." Mirsky, reflecting on this apprenticeship in a 1983 interview, judged that Tucker's innate musicianship and keen re-
tentiveness best explained his rapid progress. "Ruby had an astonishing ear and a faultless memory," Mirsky has said. "He was
so easy to work with because I only had to demonstrate something once and he would be able to repeat it perfectly. He retained everything so thoroughly that once a piece of music was
in his mind, it was there for life."

Between the spring and autumn of 1936, Tucker's progress
under Mirsky was so rapid, and the results so clearly apparent,
that he got his first annual contract: the board of directors of the
Temple Emanuel congregation in Passaic, New Jersey, offered him
$1,200 a year to chant their services. At last, the young *hazzan*
had his own pulpit.

In keeping with the Orthodox family tradition of *kest,* in which
a bride's parents offer living space in their own home as part of
a dowry, Levi and Anna Perelmuth gave Sara and Ruby a room
in their already crowded Madison Street apartment. Mrs. Perelmuth approached the matter more from a pragmatic than a traditional vantage point. She pointed out to them that it would make
sense for them to live on the Lower East Side because they both
had jobs there. After a hard day's work, she reminded them, they
wouldn't have to worry about meals; they would have all the food
they could possibly want. This meant that Ruby would eat well
and keep in good health—which, she underscored, would keep
him from missing a day's work at Reliable Silk or, worse, missing out on a singing engagement.

Tucker sensed a more implicit point in Mrs. Perelmuth's
reasoning: she was highly protective of Sara, and clearly didn't
want her to leave home.

Respecting the idea of living in *kest* (whatever the underly-

ing motives of his mother-in-law) and still unsure of their immediate economic future, Tucker gathered his belongings, said
good-bye to his father and stepmother, and moved in with the
Perelmuths. His belongings were more meager than Mrs. Perelmuth had imagined. "When a son left home to marry," Sara recalled, "it was traditional in Jewish families to give him the best
of clothes, the best of belongings, so that he would go out into
the world feeling good about himself. Ruby arrived at our Madison Street home carrying an old, scuffed, weatherbeaten suitcase. There wasn't much of anything in it."

Sara's mother blanched as she unpacked Ruby's undercloth-
ing, all of it in desperate need of darning. "*Gott,* such a poor
boy!" she exclaimed as she poked her thumb through one of the
holes in his briefs. "This is what happens when a boy doesn't have
a mother," she told Sara. "Until now, he hasn't had anyone to
look after him, not even to darn his underwear. Well, from now
on, he has you—and he has me." If Tucker needed or was seeking a mother substitute, he found her in Anna Perelmuth. "The
first thing Mama did," Sara remembered, "was to put his tat-
tered underclothes back in that old suitcase, lock it shut, and throw
it in the trash. She marched out the front door, walked over to
Rutgers Street, and bought him a full supply of underwear at a
haberdashery."

What initially drew Mrs. Perelmuth close to Ruby was his
self-assurance, iron determination, and enormous capacity for hard
work—qualities of her own, those by which she apportioned not
only her respect but her support of anyone around her. Her son-
in-law got the full measure of both—and, at the same time,
brought a measure of difference to the Perelmuth household by
his unshakable ebullience and his affectionate ways.

Though they were loving parents, Mr. and Mrs. Perelmuth
were not overly demonstrative, especially by Tucker's standards.
Soon they found themselves the recipients of his displays of affection. "Even my father used to kiss Ruby when he would greet
him," Sara said. "Ruby's own father, who I doubt ever put his
hand on Ruby's shoulder before, got more than a little jealous
about that. He finally started kissing Ruby, too."

The affection Ruby continually showed Sara pleased and yet
puzzled her family. "He was always holding my hand, putting
his arm around me, or hugging me, even if I was doing some-

thing trivial like washing dishes," she remembered. Quite often, as might be expected, he had something more in mind with his young wife than simple affection.

In the end, his romantic appetites undermined his living with his in-laws. As the months went on, what initially seemed an ideal arrangement degenerated into a barely tolerable one—especially when Ruby wanted any intimacy with Sara. "Two of my brothers, Mac and Sender, were living at home at the time," she noted. "Particularly around them, I was very nervous. I even felt strange lying in bed with Ruby. After all, it was my family home." When no amount of cajoling could make her relax, Ruby limited his lovemaking overtures to the relatively few moments when they had the Perelmuths' apartment to themselves. Even then, Sara was tense. "I hate to think what I put him through every time he touched me," she said. "My ears got so good I could hear footsteps before anybody's feet ever touched the stairs!"

Eight months of living with a skittish bride in her parents' home exhausted Ruby's generous supply of tolerance. After yet another tryst ended prematurely, he told Sara forcefully, "We're getting out of here, and out of the whole damned East Side. We're going to have our own place, or I swear I'll go nuts!"

A family friend volunteered to help them find an apartment to rent, and soon located a spacious three-room unit in a comparatively new six-story building at 60 Thayer Street, in the Fort Tryon Park section of upper Manhattan. Sara and Ruby took an immediate liking to it and gave the landlord a deposit. Amid their happiness at the prospect of having their privacy at last, they underestimated Mrs. Perelmuth's reaction. "Mama was very unhappy about it and said she would never be able to see us," Sara recalled. "Because she hardly spoke English, she didn't venture much outside the Lower East Side. When she did, she would mark the subway or trolley stops by their billboard advertisements—which was fine as long as nobody changed the ads. When I told her where Ruby and I were going to live—it was near 200th Street, which was the last subway stop in those days—she reacted as if we were moving to Canada."

Tucker, knowing the length of Mrs. Perelmuth's apron strings, found the distance rather to his liking. Grateful as he was to Sara's parents for their generosity, he tended to date his marital happiness from his and Sara's Thayer Street years.

"We paid fifty-six dollars a month for our first apartment,"
Tucker recalled in an interview he gave in 1966, as his thirtieth
wedding anniversary approached. "Between the thirty dollars a
week I was making at Reliable Silk, the twenty-six a week Sara
was getting as a sort of 'girl Friday,' and the twelve hundred dollars a year they were paying me as a cantor in Passaic, we were
living pretty well." As often as possible, he and Sara went out—
often to the Hippodrome, to see the San Carlo Opera Company's low-budget productions. There the future *primo tenore* saw
his first performances of many of the operas in which he would
be acclaimed—*Cavalleria rusticana* and *Pagliacci, La traviata, Il trovatore,* and *La Bohème*—most of them cast with minor singers and
set among two-dimensional backdrops in lieu of expensive scenery.

The largely Italian audiences tended to be more tolerant of
the scenery than of the singers. More than once the Tuckers heard
shouts of *"Porco!"* ("Pig!") resound through the theater, directed
at a hapless tenor whose high C failed him in the third act of *Trovatore,* or a baritone who could not negotiate the A-flat at the
conclusion of the Prologue to *Pagliacci.* Tucker usually directed
his own comments only to Sara, but often he wasn't impressed
either.

Verdi's *Aida* was the first opera Richard Tucker heard at the
Metropolitan Opera House. With mid-Depression ticket prices still
out of his and Sara's reach at $4 to $7, he waited for the so-called
Spring Season—four weeks of performances in May, a month after
the end of the regular season—when ticket prices were reduced
to the $1 to $3 range. In the role of Radames, he heard the English tenor Arthur Carron—a protégé of the English soprano
Florence Easton, and later a modestly received addition to the
German Heldentenor ranks. Whatever the merits of Carron's
eventual Wagnerian performances, his Radames failed to impress
Tucker. He told Sara he felt sure he could sing it better.

Those who want to find the source of the young Tucker's
inspiration among the great tenors of the 1930s need not consider
the fledgling Carron—or, for that matter, Giovanni Martinelli,
Giacomo Lauri-Volpi, Tito Schipa, Aureliano Pertile, or many of
the other legendary names of the generation of tenors who inherited Caruso's mantle. Tucker hesitated to discuss most of them
in interviews because he never heard them in the theater in their

primes. What he knew of Pertile and Lauri-Volpi (whom he came to know much later) he derived mainly from their recordings; of the two, he especially admired Lauri-Volpi, whose range and flair were legendary. As for Schipa's voice, though Tucker admired the technique behind it, he found it too lyric for his personal taste—and Martinelli's he always judged steely, forced, and uncompelling.

Of all the great tenors of the past, Beniamino Gigli was Tucker's major inspiration, without any question. He admired Gigli not only vocally but also, in the Italian repertoire, interpretatively and stylistically. Tucker considered himself fortunate not only to have heard Gigli in person but to have met him. In 1957, when Gigli toured North America for the last time, Richard took Sara to Toronto to hear Gigli, who was then sixty-seven years old and still in exceptional voice. When Tucker called on Gigli in his dressing room after the concert, he was taken aback when Gigli not only recognized him but praised his singing, especially in the Puccini repertoire.

The degree to which memories of Gigli remained with Tucker became evident on the day of his death in Kalamazoo. When an inventory of his personal belongings was made, a Catholic funeral-prayer card for Beniamino Gigli was found in his wallet. In 1969, more than a decade after Gigli's death, the Gigli family had welcomed Richard and Sara to their palatial estate in Rome. The tenor's widow had given Tucker the prayer card, along with one of Gigli's medals. Since then, Tucker had sent money anonymously to St. Patrick's Cathedral to have a Mass said annually in memory of the great tenor.

The newlyweds were apart for the first time for ten days in July 1937. Mr. and Mrs. Perelmuth rented a room at the Gibber Hotel at Kiamesha Lake, in the Catskills, and invited Sara and Ruby to join them. To his chagrin, Ruby could not free himself from his work at Reliable Silk. Rather than ask Sara not to go without him (and mindful, no doubt, of Mrs. Perelmuth's lingering dislike of having her daughter very far away from her), he reluctantly told Sara to go alone. Though they had been married a year and a half, Ruby found it difficult to cope with her absence, short-term as it was. Rarely one to put his feelings in writing, he wrote Sara three letters during her stay at Kiamesha Lake.

He wrote the first of these letters on July 20, 1937, while he awaited a client at the Friedlander Brothers factory on West 28th Street:

> My dearest Kitten,
>
> At the present moment I am at a customer and with nothing to do, so I thought of writing to you. How are you feeling since I last saw you? Are the folks well? I hope this week passes quickly so you will be able to come home, and I will be able to enjoy the life of a good husband with a beautiful housewife.
>
> Since I left you Sunday, nothing exciting has happened, for when I came home that evening, I went to the park for a stroll. I climbed to the top of the hill where we both once walked, overlooking Riverside Drive, and sat down wondering what you were doing and of course at the same time wishing you were here beside me, for I was a bit jealous looking at the other couples walking about. . . .

Three days later, on July 23, he had talked with her by phone and was not only lonely, but envious of the fun she was having.

> If I did not want you to enjoy a good and earned rest, I would order you home this very day for to be truthful about it, I really am lost without you. It seems that wherever I want to go or do, you are missing from my side and that leaves me feeling very blue. . . .

Late in the evening on July 27, he telephoned to tell her of an unexpected break he had gotten. The "Jewish Daily Forward Hour," sponsored by the widely read newspaper and aired weekly over station WEVD in Manhattan, had offered him his first solo appearance on the program.

> As I told you over the phone, I am going to sing over the "Jewish Forward Hour" this Sunday morning. Last night, after I spoke with you, I had a little lesson with Joe Mirsky, and then went to the Apollo Theater. I got out at midnight and seeing it was late, I spent the night at your Mama's and Pop's house. Darling, I know by your letters and our phone conversation that you are enjoying yourself, but it is *so* lonesome without you. When I finish my work in the evenings, I roam around, no place to go, and maybe I finish up at the movies. This endurance is none too good for me, but I suppose you feel it, too.

As soon as Sara received the letter, she showed it eagerly to her mother. Though Ruby did not know it as yet, Mrs. Perelmuth had gotten him the solo on the "Jewish Daily Forward Hour." Jan Peerce's phenomenal success on radio had made her aware how important the medium was to a budding career. She had regularly urged Jan to intercede for Ruby with the management at WEVD, but no invitation came forth. Taking matters into her own hands, she marched into the lower Manhattan office of a powerful housing-project administrator who had connections with the radio program. When his secretary informed her that she would need an appointment, Mrs. Perelmuth informed the secretary that she would sit outside the man's office until he would see her.

When the man finally emerged, not knowing that she was awaiting him, Mrs. Perelmuth immediately sat him down and began promoting her son-in-law. When she informed him, in Yiddish, that she was the mother of Jan Peerce and a respected businesswoman, he paid closer attention to what she said. In short order, she extracted a promise that Ruby would appear on the "Jewish Daily Forward Hour."

"My Ruby won't disappoint you," she told the man confidently.

Tucker himself made good her promise. Because of the success of his first appearance, he sang frequently on the program and built a steady following among Jewish listeners in and around New York City.

Tucker's letters to his young bride, apart from the good news about the "Jewish Daily Forward Hour," were different in that all were signed, "Your loving husband, Richard." Following the example of his brother-in-law, who had progressed from Pinky Perelmuth to John Pierce and ultimately Jan Peerce, Tucker had anglicized his first name. He did so with a definite eye toward more secular singing. Though his cantorial career would have prospered under his given name, the mixed images it might cause elsewhere—as in the Midwest, where "Rubin" had definite hillbilly overtones—led him to choose an Americanized first name.

Once he and Sara agreed on a choice—"We went through Ralph Tucker, Robert Tucker, Raymond Tucker, anything that began with an R," she remembered laughingly—they opted for the Peerces' strategy of never reverting to the original name. Yet when the Tuckers tried to adhere to "Richard," they could manage it only outside their home. To Sara and to his family and friends, Tucker remained "Ruby." But to the music world he became Richard Tucker.

Not long after she returned from Kiamesha Lake, Sara learned that she was pregnant. Overjoyed as she and Richard were at the prospect of becoming parents, motherhood came with a price tag for Sara. She could no longer work, which meant that Richard would have to make up the loss in their income. As it was, money problems had continued to plague them despite their better-than-average joint earnings. "We spent every dollar, that was the trouble," he reflected years later. "We never saved any money."

A great part of their money problem, though Tucker was not about to acknowledge it in an interview, was his penchant for gambling. "The five-dollar-a-week bonus which Mr. Rosenblatt, Richard's boss, gave him when we got married should have made a noticeable difference in our finances," Sara remembered. "But I was having trouble accounting for that five dollars whenever I added up what we had. One day I was cleaning out his suit pockets and I found what looked like a coupon book. When I looked closer, it was a loan payment book—the kind they give you at a bank. Without ever telling me, he had borrowed money and was paying it back, five dollars a week."

What Sara did not realize, until she confronted him, was that Richard had borrowed the money to cover a gambling debt.

"When he came home that night, I laid the payment book on the table. I was *very* hurt, and I told him so. Once he admitted what he had done, I budgeted even tighter so the loan could be paid off quickly. From then on, whether he won or lost—and no matter how much it was—I always knew what he was spending."

Gambling, defying the odds, was still an integral part of Richard Tucker's makeup. Over the years, as his career reached Olympian proportions, it never surprised those close to him that he was always willing to take a chance, whether it involved his artistic reputation in a new role or part of his fortune at a roulette table. Both metaphorically and literally, gambling was part of his nature. To Sara's credit, she understood this and was able to help him contain his impulses within reasonable bounds.

When their son Barry (named for Berel Posner, Sara's maternal grandfather) was born in March 1938, the Tuckers' finances began to worry them. Proud father that he was, Richard wanted the best for his firstborn, and looked forward to the prospect of having more children. Fatherhood forced him to take stock of his financial situation—and, by extension, the progress of his cantorial career.

His income in the fur market, he knew, was essentially fixed. Unless he asked to be put on a commission basis, which he was reluctant to do because of the uncertainty involved, there was no way he could be paid a higher salary at Reliable Silk. With some of the furriers, his second career as a cantor sometimes worked against him. "They figured he was making money as a cantor," his friend Ben Herschaft affirmed, "so they didn't think he was hungry enough to care about this or that deal. He was so good-natured that he didn't give them any reason to think otherwise."

Tucker knew that the cantorate was the only avenue to long-term security open to him. But in Passaic, at Temple Emanuel, he was only a part-time *hazzan* and it was netting him far less money than he had expected. His contract called for him to sing only two services a month, one every other Sabbath, for which he was paid $100 a month. But there were added expenses that he could not avoid. On Friday nights he had to stay overnight in Passaic; though he stayed cheaply at the Lincoln Hotel near the temple, his lodging still cost money—as did his train tickets and the meals he ate during his stay. When he took Sara along, as he often did, it cost him even more.

Money aside, Passaic was but a stepping-stone to a larger, more permanent annual appointment, and Tucker had always viewed it as such. Hence, when Saul Salzburg, one of his clients in the fur market, told him that the cantor at Temple Adath Israel in the Bronx had resigned, Tucker quickly made his interest known to Henry A. Schorr, the temple's rabbi.

A magnificent structure on the Grand Concourse at 169th Street in the Bronx, Temple Adath Israel was the oldest congregation in the Bronx and served a sizable Jewish population. The congregation was Conservative rather than Orthodox, even to the extent that the cantor sang to organ accompaniment rather than a cappella. The temple's musical director was Zavel Zilberts, a prolific arranger of Yiddish folk songs and the composer of art songs based on Yiddish poetry. Formerly a cantor, Zilberts was educated at the Warsaw Conservatory and had been choral direc-

tor of the Moscow Central Synagogue. By the mid-1930s, well
after he arrived in America, Zilberts had come to be considered
one of the finest musicians and choral leaders in New York City.
The annual Zavel Zilberts Concerts at Town Hall always merited
New York Times reviews, even though their programs featured
predominantly Jewish music and attracted mainly Jewish audiences.

Saul Salzburg was president of the Adath Israel board when
Rabbi Schorr, as a formal audition, invited Tucker to sing a service for the congregation. Dr. Danny Jacobson, who succeeded
Salzburg as board president, recalled the negotiations that surrounded Tucker's coming to Temple Adath Israel. "His reputation was already growing, so the audition was basically a formality," Dr. Jacobson remembered. "We wanted him if he wanted
to join us, so we made him an offer. We would pay him twenty-
five hundred dollars a year to be our *hazzan,* and we also promised we'd give him a respectable annual raise."

With a week to say yes or no to the offer, Tucker sought
advice from Sara's and his families. The Perelmuths were encouraging, even if—as Levi Perelmuth very diplomatically said
to him—it would have pleased him more if Richard served an
Orthodox congregation. Sam Ticker was considerably less diplomatic. "You are selling yourself for money!" he told his son
angrily, vowing that he would never cross the threshold at Temple Adath Israel because of its non-Orthodox orientation. "He
eventually came to grips with it, although he never enjoyed coming to Adath Israel to hear me," Tucker said, looking back on
the conflict it caused. "When I left the cantorate for opera, he didn't
mind—in fact, he was very proud of me. You see, to him opera
was something else, so anything I did there, except for singing
on the Sabbath, was all right with him. But if I was going to be
a cantor, if I was going to sing to the Lord, I was going to do it
only in an Orthodox way or he wasn't going to come and hear
me."

Jan Peerce, whose sense of contracts and negotiations Tucker
respected, looked at the Temple Adath Israel offer far more ob-
jectively. At a Sabbath Eve supper at the Perelmuths', Richard
and Sara asked his advice.

"How much have they offered you?" Jan asked.

"Twenty-five hundred a year," Richard answered.

At this time, Jan was earning nearly that sum every two

weeks; the lucrative "Chevrolet Hour" alone brought him $750 for each program. Prosperous as he was, Peerce had never lost sight of his earlier struggles, and never took any of his success for granted. In Tucker's eyes, this gave his opinions added weight.

"What do you think I should do?" Tucker asked directly.

"Maybe you ought to think about this very hard," Jan answered, his look conveying a reservation, a concern, that Tucker could not pinpoint.

"Is there something wrong with the terms?" he asked. "Do you think they're not paying me enough?"

Jan paused, and let out a deep breath. "Do you *really* think you're ready for something this big?"

Though some of the implications of the question momentarily escaped Tucker, they stung Sara. She thought them too reminiscent of Jan's earliest attitude toward Ruby's ability—an attitude which, she felt, should have changed now that Tucker was modestly successful.

"Sure, I'm ready," Tucker said, shrugging it off. "I've done all right in Passaic, I know what I'm doing, I can handle it fine."

"This is a hell of a lot bigger than Passaic," Jan said. "This is a big responsibility."

Tucker thought the point self-evident, but Jan kept underscoring it.

"Well, what can I tell you?" Jan concluded. "If you think you're ready, then I guess you're ready."

Tucker signed the contract and returned it to Rabbi Schorr. Yet he went to Temple Adath Israel not fully believing that he had gone with Jan's support and confidence. Whether Peerce actually questioned his ability or his readiness to hold such an important annual position—or whether he was deliberately challenging Tucker by pretending to doubt his abilities—can only be guessed. He had not heard Tucker regularly enough to have a clear impression of his progress as a *hazzan*.

Whatever his motives or concerns, Peerce was at least consistent: he reacted in virtually the same fashion, making the same points and raising the same questions, when Tucker came to him five years later with an offer for the cantorship of the prestigious Brooklyn Jewish Center. Then, as he had before, Tucker came to the same conclusion. "He felt that Peerce was discouraging him," said Dr. Jacobson, recalling Tucker's comments at the time. "He couldn't understand why—and it hurt him."

4

Q: *What made you decide to head straight for the Metropolitan, rather than making your debut in a smaller house, or perhaps in Europe?*

A: *Everything I did in life was big. I have always had a very strong will. To me, it was a case of being either a king or a bum. I was heading for king.*

"A singer has to be blessed with two honest people," Richard Tucker reflected at the zenith of his long career. "One is your vocal teacher, and the other is your coach." Though Tucker had a number of excellent coaches during his career—Angelo Canarutto, Emil Cooper, Frank St. Leger, and Wilfred Pelletier in his early years, and later Joseph Garnett, who prepared him in most of his roles—he had but one voice teacher, Paul Althouse, to whom he credited the perfection of his operatic technique.

Zavel Zilberts, whose judgment Tucker respected, gave him in large measure the encouragement he felt was lacking from Jan Peerce. Once Tucker shared with Zilberts his desire to sing opera, Zilberts recommended a realistic pathway to his goal: study voice with a well-known teacher, refine the technique and extend the range of the voice under proper guidance, and then study *Lieder,* oratorio, and Mozart before studying grand opera per se.

It was Peerce, nevertheless, who introduced Tucker to Althouse, with whom he was acquainted through mutual friends. This was actually Peerce's second attempt at helping Tucker find an operatic teacher, on the advice of Zavel Zilberts. The first interview, which Peerce had arranged with Giuseppe Boghetti, one of his own teachers, had ended with Boghetti saying within earshot of Tucker, "The boy hasn't got enough to work with." Everyone fared better the second time, in the autumn of 1940: when Tucker was introduced to his prospective teacher at a party next door to Althouse's studio and apartment on West 72nd Street, Paul Althouse immediately took a liking to him. An audition was arranged later in the week, and soon Tucker was one of Althouse's pupils.

Paul Althouse was a tall, silver-haired, square-shouldered man with the ample girth of a Heldentenor, a man whose round face, expressive eyes, and easy smile conveyed a fatherly countenance. He was in his early fifties when Tucker began studying with him, and had only recently concluded a performing career that had spanned twenty-seven years. Strictly speaking, Althouse had had two careers. The first lasted some twelve years, beginning with his debut at the Metropolitan in 1913, where he was the Met's first Dmitri in *Boris Godunov;* the second commenced in 1934, when he reemerged at the Met as a Wagnerian tenor after nine years of study in Europe.

When Althouse eventually distinguished himself as Siegmund in Wagner's *Die Walküre* and, shortly afterward, became the first American tenor to sing Tristan at the Metropolitan, critic Max de Schauensee was not surprised that he had at last found his niche. Recalling Althouse's Pennsylvania German upbringing, De Schauensee wrote that "his voice, tastes, and temperament were always strongly Teutonic." One of Althouse's best-known pupils, Eleanor Steber, disagreed with part of De Schauensee's conclusion. "Paul's temperament was almost more Latin than Teutonic," Miss Steber maintained. "He was a very warm, very affectionate man. To me, Paul was not only a great teacher but a great friend."

As a promising young tenor, Althouse had left his native Reading, Pennsylvania, for New York City, where he became a pupil of Percy Rector Stevens. In Stevens's studio he met another gifted young American, the baritone Reinald Werrenrath, whom Stevens was to launch on one of the most successful concert and recording careers of the World War I years. Werrenrath was to become Stevens's contribution to the concert platform, and Paul Althouse became his contribution to the operatic stage.

In an era when virtually all American-born singers—legend-

ary artists such as Lillian Nordica and David Bispham before the
turn of the century, or, afterward, Louise Homer and Geraldine
Farrar—had had to prove themselves in Europe before they were
accorded Metropolitan Opera debuts, Althouse became a "first"
in the annals of American opera. Though the New York press
would eventually accord the distinction to Rosa Ponselle, it was
Paul Althouse who became the first native-born, native-trained
singer to debut at the Metropolitan Opera with no prior European experience. Whatever the merits of his voice and artistry—
and critics generally agreed that the quality of each was admira-
ble, even formidable at times—Althouse had the misfortune of
singing in two different repertoires at the Metropolitan when each
was dominated by a super-tenor: Enrico Caruso in the Italian
repertoire and, later, Lauritz Melchior in the Heldentenor roles.

The vocal techniques and principles that Althouse passed on
to Richard Tucker were essentially those that Percy Rector Stevens had taught. A teacher steeped in the bel canto tradition, Stevens had deplored the strained singing and general decline in vocal quality that the newer *verismo* operas of Puccini, Leoncavallo,
and Mascagni had wrought. "He had nothing against new music," Althouse once said of him, "but he felt that these operas,
like Wagner's, could be sung properly, without 'forcing' the voice
and without making gods of volume and range." Stevens was especially adamant on the subject of volume in singing. "You hear
it said that this or that person has a big voice and can sing with
great power," Reinald Werrenrath remembered him saying. "A
brass band can make a lot of noise. It is knowing how to use the
voice with the least possible effort, coupled with the right kind
of diction, that will make the greatest effect."

This was precisely the approach Paul Althouse used with the
young Tucker, whose voice was initially rather small, but whose
effortless technique and superb diction laid the proper foundation
for the expansion of the voice as the years went on. Tucker was
never obsessed with the size of his voice—which was fortunate,
considering that the thunderous Mario del Monaco was one of
his contemporaries—and, for that matter, he often made a joke
of it. As public-relations gimmicks backstage, his young sons often
sported hand-lettered signs that read: SOME TENORS CAN SING LOUDER
THAN TUCKER, BUT NONE CAN SING BETTER.

When Althouse first greeted his cantor pupil, he asked him

why he wanted to sing opera instead of liturgical music. Tucker told him of his youth in lower Manhattan and Brooklyn, and the mesmerizing effect that Caruso's recordings had had on him.

"Now, tell me, Mr. Tucker," Althouse asked, his brow furrowed in concern, "is that how you want to sing—like Caruso?"

Tucker replied that he didn't know whether he had the same potential in his voice.

"So much the better, then," Althouse said. "If you want to sound like Caruso, I would tell you to put on your coat and hat and close my door behind you!"

Tucker asked him to explain.

"I knew Enrico Caruso very, very well, and I heard him in most of his great roles," Althouse went on. "He was one of a kind, and every other tenor who has tried to sound like him has ended up a failure. No disrespect to the man, but he didn't really have a perfect technique. He sang his own way and he did things that no one else could do quite the same way. The last thing I want you to do is to try to sound like him. For that matter, I don't want you to sound like Gigli, Lauri-Volpi, Pertile, Paul Althouse, or anybody else. I just want you to be Richard Tucker—that's all, and that's enough."

Althouse went on to give Tucker three cardinal rules and made him promise he would abide by them throughout whatever career he would have. First, he admonished him to let his voice expand slowly, naturally, with age and experience. "I don't want you to study one role without first clearing it with me," Althouse said. "The worst mistake a young man like you can make is to take on roles that are too much for the voice at this stage of its development." Echoing one of Stevens's bon mots, he told Tucker to regard time and age as friends, not enemies. "There's no shortcut to developing the voice," Althouse said. "In singing, the short way is the long way."

Next, he warned Tucker not to overtax the voice before singing an engagement—whether that engagement was a *Shabbos* service, an oratorio performance, or a grand opera. Favoring the analogies and similes of his mentor Stevens, Althouse made his point by asking Richard if he drove a car. Richard said no, but mentioned that he had learned to drive his friend's Whippet roadster.

"Well, now, if you wanted to take that roadster out for a

spin," Althouse said, settling into a simile, "you wouldn't spend a half-hour riding it around in your yard just to see if it would run, would you?"

Richard shook his head no.

"It's the same thing with singing," Althouse continued. "If you've got your technique right, all you have to do is limber up your voice with a few vocalises. These singers who claim they have to do all these fancy exercises two, three hours a day are just kidding themselves. It's not necessary, if you know what you're doing in the first place."

How literally his pupil took this advice is borne out by the recollections of Richard Tucker's family, colleagues, coaches, and friends. With very few exceptions, Tucker never sang unless he was required to sing. Before a performance, he might be found perusing the score in the wings instead of vocalizing at any length in his dressing room. "I remember in the last series of *Lucia*s he sang at the Met," James Levine recalled, "I noticed him sitting at the stage manager's desk reading the score. I said to him, 'Richard, you've been singing *Lucia* practically all your life!' He said to me, 'But sometimes I forget the little words, Jim, so I have to look them up!' "

Particularly in his early career, Tucker would demonstrate an ability to redirect his concentration completely before, during, and after a performance that astounded everyone who knew him. He was always able to "shift gears" from one part of his life to another, as Sam Mintz, one of his friends, once put it. When Tucker was the cantor of the Brooklyn Jewish Center, Mintz was writing radio scripts for Orson Welles's "Mercury Theater" and other network programs. Mintz and his wife, Selma, lived across the hall from the Tuckers, and though Sam was not musically inclined, the couples became close friends.

"One Saturday evening, Richard asked me if I would mind driving him to the St. George Hotel in downtown Brooklyn," Mintz recalled. "I wasn't doing anything at the moment, so I said okay. On the way there, I asked him what was going on at the St. George. He said there was a Zionist rally that night, and that Rabbi Abba Hillel Silver (who eventually championed the cause of Jewish statehood to the United Nations) was going to be speaking. The St. George, in those days, had the largest auditorium in New York, and that night it was literally overflowing with people. As we entered, Rabbi Silver was mesmerizing the crowd. He and a group of prominent Jewish leaders were in the center of the auditorium, speaking from a platform way above the heads of the audience.

"As Rabbi Silver concluded his speech, Richard marched down the center aisle toward the platform. He walked up the wooden steps and quietly introduced himself to one of the men on the dais. It was obvious that this man was expecting him, and he passed a note to Rabbi Silver, who finished his address to thundering applause. The next thing I knew, Richard was being introduced. He began to sing 'El Mole Rachamim,' the Hebrew 'Prayer for the Dead.' A hush came over the whole auditorium. People sat there with their heads bowed and you could hear many of them sobbing as he chanted the prayer.

"When he finished singing, hundreds and hundreds of people sitting in those simple wooden chairs were crying into their handkerchiefs, holding on to one another—for me, it was one of the most moving experiences of my life. But there was more to it than just the singing. I had watched this perfectly ordinary, likable neighbor of mine—a nice guy who I'd have a beer with on a hot summer night—enter an auditorium unnoticed and within minutes exert a kind of power over hundreds of people that no politician, no great orator, could possibly rival.

"When he walked down the stairs of the platform, he headed right for where I was standing, way in the back of the auditorium. I was so overcome that I could hardly talk. He sort of winked at me and said, 'Okay, time to go home.' When we got outside, he said to me, 'Well, how was I?' I was still too choked up to say much of anything.

"As I looked at him, I could see how unimpressed he was with the power he had over the people in that auditorium. His mind was now on something else entirely. He snapped his fingers as if he'd just remembered to do something, and said, 'I've got to get to a telephone.' With that, he went to a pay phone in the lobby and rang up Sara, who was at home making supper and taking care of the boys. Soon he was asking her what kind of cake, from which downtown bakery, would go best with that night's supper."

Paul Althouse also instilled in Tucker a clear distinction between his home life and his life as a performer. At the very beginning of his career, Tucker heard Althouse say repeatedly, "Your home

is where you live with your family, and the opera house is where
you sing. When the curtain rings down and you've taken off your
makeup, go home and enjoy your life." Althouse also admonished him not to involve himself in too much socializing, and
certainly not in opera-house politics. "All of a sudden, you're going
to be important, and everybody will know your name," Althouse told him. "But don't let it go to your head. One day, it's
all going to pass and all you'll have are the memories. Meantime,
don't lose sight of your home life, because that's where your permanence is. Your wife and children are your greatest assets."

This, too, stayed with Richard Tucker—even to the extent
that he rarely sang a note of music in his home, except to intone
the prayers for meals on the Sabbath or other religious occasions.
Though the Tucker home on Long Island sported a paneled music room, there is no clear agreement whether he ever practiced
in it. Certainly, he studied there—whether opera scores (which
he could sight-read rather well), cantorial texts, or, only slightly
less important, stock-market reports and the sports pages of *The
New York Times*. But he studied silently—on that much there is
agreement from his family.

By the time he moved his family to Long Island, however,
Tucker was already in his fourth season at the Metropolitan and
was therefore an established artist. But even before his debut, he
did not often practice at home. "When you have small children
and you live in an apartment," Sara observed, "it's not exactly
ideal for practicing singing." Instead, Richard did most of his vocalizing and rehearsing either in the soundproof studios of radio
station WEVD, where his accompanist and coach, Joseph Garnett, worked as a musician, or else he did his vocalizing in empty
classrooms at the Brooklyn Jewish Center.

In an era when conservatory training for young opera singers was more the rule than the exception, Tucker came to Paul
Althouse with a liability: he had no knowledge of music notation
and had never studied an instrument. In time, however, he became an adequate sight reader. "Although Richard could sight-
read the treble line in a piano-vocal score," recalled Alex Alexay,
his longtime accompanist, "he couldn't really sight-*sing* a difficult line unless it was played for him first. He was an instinctive
rather than a trained musician, but his concentration, memory,
and especially his consistency were really phenomenal."

Once a coach or accompanist played a passage on the piano for Tucker, he could almost always repeat it unerringly. "Even in the most difficult cantorial music," said Alan Chester, choral conductor of the Brooklyn Jewish Center and the Park Synagogue in Chicago, "Richard could hear a line and then sing it without a mistake. His ear made up for anything he lacked in musical training."

Late in his career, Tucker's near-photographic memory for music almost precluded any in-depth study. Yet he insisted on playing out a ritual that his sons remember. "He'd go into his study, pull out a score, put on a recording of the opera, open the score to Act I, stretch out in his leather lounge chair, and review the score while he listened to the record," Barry Tucker remembered. After a while, this would begin to bore him. "Many times, David, Henry, or I would walk past the study and hear Dad snoring away. He'd wake up when the record-changer automatically shut off. When I'd catch him sleeping, I'd wait till he woke up and deliberately ask him how this 'study session' had gone. He'd be yawning and stretching and his eyes wouldn't be focused yet, but he'd say to me, 'Fine, great . . . just wonderful!' "

As a teen-ager, Henry Tucker eventually grew puzzled about why his father never sang at home. "One day, it just struck me that I had never heard him sing except in the opera house or maybe on television or radio," Henry said. "I remember telling Mother that I felt I was missing something. She said to me, 'Why don't you go into the study and ask your father to sing for you?' That was the obvious thing to do, so I did."

Henry never forgot the puzzled look on his father's face when he put the request to him. "I don't think he ever gave a thought to singing around the house—I mean, he never even sang in the shower!—so he seemed a little perplexed when I said I'd like him to sing for me."

There ensued the momentarily awkward matter of what his son wanted to hear.

"Oh, anything," Henry replied. "Just a little bit from one of your operas. Maybe *Tosca,* or *Rigoletto,* anything's fine with me."

One chorus of "Parmi veder le lagrime" later, Henry Tucker went back to his homework, and Richard Tucker, alias the Duke of Mantua, went back to the Dow Jones averages in the *Wall Street Journal.*

Exactly how Paul Althouse taught Richard Tucker to sing—or, more accurately, how he transformed Tucker's mature cantorial voice into a lyric tenor of operatic proportions—is largely a matter of conjecture. Tucker was not a person to whom eloquence came easily, even where his method of singing was concerned. When Janet Bookspan asked him in her oral-history interview how he would describe his technique, he replied, "Very simple. It's a method that is used only with certain vocal exercises to achieve the 'ping' and also the flexibility and agility in the voice."

Elsewhere in the long interview, he referred to the technique he had learned from Althouse as "bel canto, very important, which is dead today." Beyond these remarks, he was mute on the subject of his singing technique. In this, Tucker was by no means alone. Relatively few great singers have been able to articulate the intricacies of their vocal techniques. In 1919, Enrico Caruso gave musicologist Harriette Brower what was to have been the premiere interview for *Vocal Mastery,* her volume on the methodology of singing. But not once in the fifteen-hundred-word interview did Caruso utter anything about his technique. Beniamino Gigli, Tucker's idol, had a vocal endowment nearly as rich as Caruso's, but fared no better than his predecessor in discussions of method and technique.

We have Tucker's own word that when he began with Paul Althouse he had neither the range nor the evenness of tone that he had when he finished his studies. To Robert Merrill and a few other colleagues, he acknowledged that before Althouse had taught him how to extend his range without impairing the beauty of his tone, his top note had been a B-flat, and not always a reliable one. His cantorial singing had not suffered because of it, since Jewish liturgical music generally makes its greatest demands in the agility rather than the compass or extension of the voice. Nevertheless, the free exercise of musical creativity and interpretation on the part of the cantor may extend the music well above the staff—as with the legendary Yossele Rosenblatt, who dominated the cantorate in the era when Caruso reigned supreme in opera, and who frequently used his keenly developed, flutelike falsetto voice to extend his range and achieve a coloratura effect in his improvising. Tucker, however, eschewed the use of falsetto and instead limited his liturgical singing to an agreeable, full-bodied tenor range.

Tucker's reference to "certain vocal exercises" that Paul Althouse taught him in order to "achieve the 'ping' " were probably those that Althouse had learned from Percy Rector Stevens—groups of three or four successive tones, each a full step higher than the last, on which the vowels were sung by means of the nonsense syllables *zah, zay, zee, zoh,* and *zoo.* The quality of the *z* sound, Stevens believed, put the tone in a plane slightly above the soft palate of the throat and the middle of the nose; there the tone would resonate fully and give the voice a bright-sounding "ping," like the ring of a delicate piece of china or a finely cast bell.

Following Stevens's example, Althouse laid heavy stress on vowel sounds in his teaching. "The first six months I spent with him," Tucker recalled, "I only sang vowels. Imagine not singing a word for six months! You have to have patience and believe in your teacher to be able to do that." Only after those six months of exercises, when all the vowels resonated as they should and the voice was properly equalized, did Althouse finally put a vocal score in the hands of his hard-working pupil. He gave Tucker art songs to study first—Giordani's "Caro mio ben," then Schubert *Lieder,* and especially Mozart vocal masterpieces, in both Italian and German. As Tucker rapidly progressed, Althouse had him prepare Mozart arias, on the order of "Un'aura amorosa" from *Così fan tutte.*

Understandably—and naïvely—Tucker had wanted to begin studying Italian operas immediately. He wanted Verdi and Puccini, but Althouse gave him Mozart instead. "A tenor with a pretty good technique to begin with," Althouse had told him, "can bull and bluff his way through the big Italian operas—for a while. But fairly soon, what he didn't learn in the first place—that is, the real *discipline* of singing—will catch up with him." Mozart, Althouse reiterated, was the best source of discipline and refinement. In later years, Tucker would repeat one of Althouse's metaphors to overeager young tenors who chose weighty Verdi arias for their auditions. "You've got your diet all wrong," Tucker would say emphatically. "You've got to learn Mozart before you try Verdi. Put the milk before the meat."

In time, the Mozart songs and arias nourished Tucker to the point that his teacher indeed thought him ready for Verdi. In mid-August 1941—when, with the birth of his son David, Tucker be-

came a father for the second time—Althouse gave him a leather-
bound edition of Verdi's *La traviata,* the first opera he was to call
his own. Coincidentally, the opera became Jan Peerce's first as
well. On November 29, 1941, Peerce's years of dedicated study
and hard work culminated in his Metropolitan debut, as Alfredo
in *La traviata.* The next day, *New York Times* critic Olin Downes
praised not only "the appealing quality of his voice and his manner of using it" but also "a genuine histrionic talent which enabled him to impart a touch of ardor and reality" to his portrayal
of the young Germont.

The annals of the Metropolitan Opera note that Richard Tucker
sang his first *Traviata* on December 15, 1945, in the performance
in which Robert Merrill made his debut as the elder Germont. As
Tucker was quick to point out, however, this was not the first
time he essayed the role of the younger Germont. Rather, his first
Traviata—his first performance anywhere as an opera singer—took
place at the Al Jolson Theatre in the autumn of 1941, under the
banner of the Alfredo Salmaggi Opera Company. Salmaggi, who
was quartered mainly in Brooklyn, was to opera in New York
what the Brooklyn Dodgers were to baseball—unpredictable,
rowdy, low-budget, and immensely popular. Tucker was but one
of many eventual notables who first stepped onstage amid the
painted canvas backdrops and antiquated footlights of a Salmaggi
production. Another debutante, soprano Herva Nelli (who would
later sing Aida to Tucker's Radames under the baton of Toscanini), exemplified Salmaggi's casting practices. The young, inexperienced soprano merely answered Salmaggi's ad in the *Brooklyn
Eagle* for a *Cavalleria rusticana* cast.
    Tucker sang two performances of *Traviata* for Salmaggi—
the first in Manhattan, at the Jolson Theatre, and the other at the
Brooklyn Academy of Music a week or so later. Except for the
recollections of his family and friends, little is known of his debut; there were no reviews of it, and, on Tucker's part, the more
successful he became, the more he tended to dismiss his two Salmaggi performances with a nostalgic laugh. "Half of the audience at the Jolson that night was Jewish," he once told an interviewer. "My Boro Park friends were there, and, of course, half
Temple Adath Israel was there, too. My costume didn't fit worth
a damn—it was an old swallowtail outfit which made me look

like a mortician." Those of his friends who, like Dr. Danny Jacobson, remembered the performance agreed with Tucker's funereal comparison. "He was so stiff he looked like he had rigor mortis," Dr. Jacobson recalled. "I don't think he moved three feet during any of the acts!"

Rehearsals were as minimal and perfunctory as the scenery. Overall, Salmaggi expected little more from his performers than good singing. In turn-of-the-century European fashion, the cast members advanced to the footlights, faced the audience, sang their solo arias, bowed and waved to acknowledge their applause, and then returned to whatever semblance of realism the plot allowed. If the audience was particularly demonstrative—as it was during Tucker's second performance, at the Brooklyn Academy, when he repeated "De' miei bollenti spiriti"—the singers were free to launch into an encore. Whatever the merits or demerits of Salmaggi performances in general—and the consensus is that they varied considerably over the years—for Tucker they were a necessary first step. Until then, his singing had been done in the pulpit of a synagogue, at weddings or *bar mitzvahs*, or in front of a microphone at the WEVD radio studio. He had never been in costume, had never portrayed a character, had never faced an audience through the haze of stage lighting—and, most of all, had never paced himself in an actual opera performance. The Salmaggi *Traviata*s afforded him his first genuine theatrical experience.

Undoubtedly, the success of Peerce's Metropolitan Opera debut was a factor in Tucker's decision to attempt to advance his own career out of its embryonic stage as rapidly as possible. Though the refinement of Peerce's artistry was furlongs ahead of Tucker's at the time, the fact that Peerce had succeeded there made the Metropolitan seem more attainable to Tucker. Against the advice of Paul Althouse—the first and last time he would oppose his mentor's judgment—Tucker decided to take a long-odds gamble on his future.

At Althouse's suggestion, Angelo Canarutto, a respected coach, had taken Tucker under his wing and had prepared him in *La traviata*. Before he heard him sing, Canarutto, as had many others, had been inclined to regard Tucker as a would-be Jan Peerce—a cantor who, probably because he had an opera singer for a brother-in-law, wanted to become one himself, but who probably lacked the phenomenal vocal resources that Peerce boasted. Viewing Tucker this way, Canarutto was quite unprepared for the quality of voice and refinement of technique that he heard when Richard first sang for him.

What especially amazed Canarutto was Tucker's Italianate singing style and clear command of the lyric line—the sources of which Canarutto himself, an Italian, could not find in questioning Tucker about his background. They were just innately there. Thirty years later, when the Metropolitan was preparing to honor Tucker on his silver anniversary with the company, *Opera News'* Frank Merkling found this similarly puzzling. "A Jewish American by birth, Tucker has made his reputation almost exclusively in the French and Italian repertoires," Merkling wrote. "This is all the more surprising in the light of his training. His teacher, Paul Althouse, specialized in Germanic roles; his coach, Joseph Garnett, is a Pole." Inadvertently, Merkling excluded Angelo Canarutto from this list. Although Canarutto's association with Tucker was unfortunately brief—he was killed in an automobile accident in 1944—his influence on Tucker, especially on the refinement of his natural Italian "line," was deep and lasting.

After they began working together, Canarutto began to extol Tucker's merits to conductor Wilfred Pelletier, who had a studio in the same building. Canarutto kept praising Tucker's singing until Pelletier grew curious enough to want to hear him.

A French-Canadian by birth, and a piano prodigy as a youth, Wilfred Pelletier accompanied or else coached many of the legendary singers of the Golden Age of Caruso. His first prominence came in Montreal, where he accompanied the genial baritone Emilio de Gogorza in his Canadian concerts; a decade later, as a young coach in the French repertoire at the Metropolitan, he helped prepare Caruso in *Samson et Dalila* and subsequently in *La Juive.* When he became a conductor at the Metropolitan during the 1928/29 season, he launched a long if not universally acclaimed second career. As basso Alexander Kipnis said of him, echoing the sentiments of singers more than critics, "Pelletier was a good conductor who gave singers a lot of freedom, who was very good at preparing ensembles, but who was not always imaginative in his interpretations—certainly not in the league of a

Fritz Reiner or Bruno Walter. [But] at least he did not claim to have discovered the 'true' Massenet or Bizet."

Pelletier had never abandoned his first love—coaching young singers—and had taken charge of the Metropolitan's "Auditions of the Air," inaugurated in the spring of 1937. Sponsored by the Sherwin-Williams paint company, the "Auditions" afforded young native-trained singers the opportunity to compete for a Metropolitan Opera debut. A string of promising baritones dominated the first years of the "Auditions" competition, beginning with Thomas L. Thomas, who debuted as Silvio in *Pagliacci*.

In the spring of 1938, another baritone was named "Auditions" co-winner—Leonard Warren. Born of Russian-Jewish immigrant parents in lower Manhattan, Warren, like Tucker, had made his living in the garment industry. Warren's powerful, rich, dusky baritone was already so refined that Pelletier, as he listened to him rehearse through the loudspeaker in the control room of NBC's Studio 8H, thought the technicians were playing a joke on him. "I thought they had put this boy up to mouthing the words to a phonograph record, just to fool me," Pelletier remembered. "Finally, I went down to the stage area to hear this voice for myself. As I listened, I knew that he would win the 'Auditions'—no other beginner could possibly have sung better than that."

When he heard the young Richard Tucker, Pelletier had the very same feeling. "When he heard me, he thought I would be a cinch to win," Tucker recalled many years later. "He told me he didn't think there was anyone who could touch me in the 'Auditions.' "

Paul Althouse saw it differently.

"Suppose Pelletier is right and you win," Althouse told him. "You'll get a contract with the Metropolitan and then what? You don't even know *Traviata* well enough—you've got the notes in your head, but the music isn't part of you yet. You don't have a repertoire at all. You're like a grocery store about to announce a grand opening without any groceries on the shelves."

"I went back to Pelletier," Tucker remembered, "and I told him what Paul had said. I was worried, so I said to him, 'Maestro, I don't think I should try out because I don't have anything to offer the Metropolitan.' But he kept telling me I was going to win, that I couldn't possibly lose. So, I told Paul I was going through with it anyway."

On Sunday evening, December 20, 1942, confident as always, Tucker stood with Virginia Card, a coloratura from the Los Angeles area, and faced the studio audience in an early round of the "Auditions" held at Rockefeller Center. Milton Cross was at the microphone, his eyes scanning his introductory notes as he awaited the engineer's signal to begin the broadcast at six-thirty sharp.

At six-forty, after Virginia Card had fared better than expected in the taxing roulades and runs of "Una voce poco fa" from *Il barbiere di Siviglia,* Tucker rose from his chair, bowed politely to the studio audience to acknowledge its applause, strode to the center of the stage, and proceeded to gamble everything he had learned from Paul Althouse and Angelo Canarutto.

His confidence at a peak, he dispatched the "De' miei bollenti spiriti" from *La traviata,* and followed it with a rousing performance of "La donna è mobile" from *Rigoletto.* He sang tastefully, precisely, and effortlessly—and stood by helplessly as the panel of judges advanced Virginia Card in the competition for the 1942 "Auditions of the Air."

For the first time in his professional life, Richard Tucker had gambled and lost.

5

Q: You had a goal, but there was a long haul before you finally made your Metropolitan debut. Did you ever get discouraged?

A: No. I had confidence going for me at all times.

Not long after the "Auditions of the Air" setback, the impulse to gamble struck Richard Tucker again. Rather than opera, the stakes this time involved his livelihood, the coat-lining business—although his operatic ambitions had much to do with the gamble he took. With a wife and two children to support, and with Paul Althouse and a growing list of accompanists, *répétiteurs,* and coaches to pay, Tucker was regularly finding himself in need of extra money. Still working in the fur market and dividing his remaining time between Sara and the children, his congregation at Temple Adath Israel, and his singing lessons and coaching, he was forced to limit his most reliable sources of outside income—weddings and *bar mitzvahs*.

Confident, nevertheless, that he was within reach of the Metropolitan, Tucker wanted to earn the most money he could in the meantime. Simple arithmetic convinced him that if the end-of-the-year earnings of Reliable Silk, a relatively small jobber, were large enough to support four salesmen, he could make far more money if he were doing what they did—namely, acting as a conduit between the silk mills and the furriers. Challenged by the prospect of becoming his own boss, Tucker decided to go into business himself.

On paper, at least, it seemed an easy business to start. He wouldn't need much of an office—a place with enough square footage to house a small supply of stock, and room for a desk and a filing cabinet. It wouldn't be necessary to keep many of the huge bolts of silk on hand because almost any large order could be shipped directly from the mills in New Jersey. Customers, he felt sure, would be no problem. With the help of his father, and with his own contacts in the fur market, he would have more than enough of a clientele to yield a respectable profit. Best of all, he would have complete control over his own schedule at last.

Simple as all of it seemed, he quickly found himself in need of far more money than he had originally thought. To establish credit with the mills, he needed several thousand dollars in security deposits for borrowed stock—the sixty- or ninety-yard rolls of material that he would eventually sell, but that might sit in his storeroom-office for several months. When he totaled what he needed to capitalize his business—the office, some used office equipment, the security deposits, and a modest amount of cash to tide him over until he could collect on his first sales—he found it came to a staggering $10,000.

With written promises of accounts in hand, he went to several Manhattan banks. Without collateral, he was told, a loan of such a large amount would be out of the question. After his last turndown by the banks, Tucker put aside his pride and went to Philip Schaffer, his brother-in-law, who had amassed considerable assets as a textile retailer.

Schaffer, too, said no to him.

Sara, who saw his desperation growing by the day, suggested the obvious: together, they would go to Jan for the money. Jan not only had a large income, but had invested well; though $10,000 was a lot of money in 1942, he could afford to lend it more easily than anyone else the Tuckers knew. "Richard didn't want any part of it—on principle," Sara said. "He didn't want to be beholden to anybody. But even one of his own family had said no to him, so Jan was our last hope."

When they approached Peerce, he asked for time to think over the loan, but soon said yes. Tucker was grateful and assured him that the money would be repaid promptly. A few days later, when he and Sara met Jan at his attorney's office, Richard signed the requisite papers. Jan's attorney then said that Sara, too, would have to sign the note; should Richard default for any reason, she would be liable for the unpaid balance. Sara willingly signed—but Richard boiled inside as he watched her. To hold Sara accountable for money that he had promised Jan he would repay—whatever the legal considerations behind having her cosign—was a clear indication, as Tucker viewed it, that Peerce somehow doubted his word.

Fortunately, the new business began to prosper almost immediately. Tucker did well—so well, in fact, that he was able to repay the note long before it was due.

Amid the uncertainties of starting a small business and the disappointment of the "Auditions of the Air" setback, the Brooklyn Jewish Center gave Tucker the real balm he needed: in the summer of 1943, the board of directors of the large, prestigious congregation approached him with an offer to be their cantor. It was to be the plum assignment of his cantorial career—and, after the "Auditions" debacle, his hedge against any other unforeseen detours along the road to the Metropolitan.

Julius Kushner was vice president of the Center's board when Tucker was approached. "We were a prestigious congregation in search of an equally prestigious cantor," Kushner explained. "There were many excellent cantors in the New York area, but by then Richard had developed the largest and most enthusiastic following of all of them. He had made an excellent name for himself with Zavel Zilberts at Temple Adath Israel, and on the 'Jewish Daily Forward Hour' as well. He was our first, last, and only choice—if only he were interested in joining us. We invited him to a dinner meeting, and the president of the board asked him very directly whether he wanted to be our cantor. When he said yes, we didn't even discuss money until later—we just celebrated!"

Dutifully, Tucker approached the directors of Temple Adath Israel and gave them an opportunity to match the Jewish Center's offer of $3,200 a year. "Naturally, we didn't want to see him go," recalled Dr. Danny Jacobson, "but there was no way we could pay him what the Brooklyn congregation offered him." Sara had secretly hoped that Adath Israel would do anything to keep him. "It was very difficult for me to think of leaving," she said, "because of the irreplaceable friends we had made at Adath Is-

rael. Most of the board members were young and successful, and
we all had so much in common. We became so close that even
when they took their winter vacations in Florida, they would insist
that Richard and I and the boys go along with them."

Tucker signed his contract with the Brooklyn Jewish Center
on his thirtieth birthday, in August 1943. The following Sabbath
Eve, Rabbi Israel H. Levinthal, the Center's founding spiritual
leader, formally introduced him to the congregation and welcomed him to the pulpit. "His voice spoke to the Lord with beauty
and compassion," said *The Synagogue Center,* the newsletter of the
United Synagogue Movement, after he had sung his first service,
"a strong tenor, partly lyric and partly dramatic, with powerful,
full, ringing tones in the higher register."

The Brooklyn Jewish Center, which Tucker now served as
hazzan, was a pioneering concept of Mordecai M. Kaplan, a distinguished professor at the Jewish Theological Seminary and a
seminal figure in the development of Conservative Judaism in
America. In the Jewish Center concept, Kaplan sought, as historian Moshe Davis expressed it, "an integration of religion, education, and recreation based on the traditional threefold function
of the synagogue as a place of worship, study, and fellowship."
The Brooklyn Jewish Center, completed in 1921, therefore housed
not only a fully accredited day school and an afternoon Hebrew
school, but also an expansive library and a swimming pool,
gymnasium, and health club.

For all of Kaplan's influence in its design, it was Israel Herbert Levinthal, its founding rabbi, who truly shaped the Brooklyn Jewish Center. The mortar on the outside walls was not yet
dry when Levinthal began conducting services in the basement of
the complex. Under his stewardship, the congregation quickly
expanded to twenty-five hundred prominent Jewish families in the
New York area. Public figures and world leaders regularly addressed the congregation at Rabbi Levinthal's invitation. A friend
as well as confidant of many leaders, both Jewish and Gentile, he
was respected not only for his "erudition in many fields," as the
New York *Herald Tribune* once characterized his Renaissance education, but also for his warmth, humility, and wise counsel.

Levinthal was a toddler when his parents left Poland for
America in 1891. He worked his way through a bachelor's degree at Columbia University, and went on to obtain four other

degrees in law, philosophy, and Hebrew literature after he became a rabbi in 1910. Despite this formidable education, he never
abandoned the simple, homiletic style of preaching he had polished as a seminarian. "This Rabbi," a Boston newspaper once
observed, "has the sermonic gift." In particular, declared the *Herald
Tribune* in reviewing a book of his sermons, he had the "facility
of making an ancient parable or an ancient Hebrew word illu-
mine a modern theme." His delivery, Julius Kushner remembered, was "low in volume, never excited nor impassioned, though
his sermons were full in content to such an unusual degree that
they affected everyone. Those who were less knowledgeable left
the synagogue feeling enlightened, while the more knowledgeable understood his homilies in a different way."

One of the most important—and certainly most prescient—
addresses of Rabbi Levinthal's career, "The Book versus the
Sword," illustrates his mastery of homily. Albert Einstein was
the guest of the Jewish Center when, in December 1934, the board
of trustees inaugurated the American Library of Nazi-banned
Books, in response to Hitler's book-burning rages.

"When God gave the Torah on Sinai—at that very moment—there came down from the heavens *Sefer Vesayof*—'a book
and a sword'—bound one against the other, as if wrestling in
combat," Levinthal began. "And a heavenly voice was heard to
cry: 'Choose one or the other! If you choose the book, life will
be yours; if you choose the sword, death must be yours!' This
simple legend tells us in clearest fashion the struggle of Civilization. It was the Book versus the Sword; it was Mind versus Brute
Force. The Nazis chose *Sayof*, the Sword; and their boast is a
Hitler! We chose *Sefer*, the Book, and our boast is an Einstein!
They prefer fire, destruction, symbols of Death! We take our stand
on the side of thought, feelings, ideals—symbols of Life!"

Levinthal spoke these words in the depths of the Depression,
a full five years before Hitler would engulf Europe in war, and
more than a decade before Allied troops would see firsthand the
horrors of Auschwitz, Dachau, Buchenwald, and the other death
camps in the bowels of Nazi Germany.

As Tucker signed his contract with the Jewish Center in 1943,
North Africa became the first battleground on which American
soldiers engaged in combat with Nazi troops. As the nightmares

Hitler wreaked upon the conquered Rumanians, Poles, and Russians were shown graphically in each week's newsreels—and as
fears of a reputed "final solution" for the Jews of Europe haunted
the American Jewish community—Tucker had wanted to enlist
and fight in Europe. When the draft was inaugurated in 1942,
however, he had taken a deferment at the request of Temple Adath
Israel's Rabbi Schorr, whose widening civic responsibilities frequently took him away from the pulpit. As Jewish tradition dic-
tates, when Schorr was visiting hospitals, participating in inter-
faith councils for the war effort, or was otherwise unavailable,
Tucker as cantor had to officiate at Sabbath services and see to
the needs of the congregation in Schorr's place.

But as the war deepened and casualties mounted, Tucker felt
less and less comfortable with his deferment—a predictable consequence not only of his patriotism and firm Jewish identity but
also of his physical energy and his penchant for proving himself.
At thirty years old, despite his thinning hair and thickening
waistline, he felt and looked the part of a tackle awaiting the next
play. What better place to test himself than on the front lines?

When Tucker left Temple Adath Israel to join the Brooklyn
Jewish Center, he did not leave the paradox of his continued deferment behind him. As more Nazi horrors continued to unfold
in 1943 and 1944, Tucker turned more and more to Rabbi Levinthal for guidance and solace. Levinthal reminded him repeatedly that the spiritual messages of his cantorial art were vital to
the maintenance of hope among Jewish-American families, and
to the reaffirmation of the Jewish religious commitment to the
long and gradual perfection of mankind. This counsel momentarily eased Tucker's frustration, as did his singing for fund-raising causes—although he lacked the prominence as yet to draw
substantial attention to the causes he represented. But nothing he
did during the war was ever enough, in his view. Tucker was left
with a gnawing feeling that he had a debt to repay to his country.

Apart from his personal uneasiness over his deferment, Tucker
was affected by the war in a way he could not have foreseen. As
the war progressed, silk became the preferred fabric for the par-
achutes of the Allied airborne troops—and Tucker watched his
small company's profits dwindle as supplies all but vanished. The
ledgers showed an increasingly dismal bottom line, until Sara urged

him to sell the business and take his losses. "What else was there to do when things were getting worse by the day?" she said, remembering the frustration Richard felt. "He finally sold out, but it was a setback—and it affected him more than he let on."

In the autumn of 1943, Tucker was greeted at the Brooklyn Jewish Center by a handsome, gray-haired man whose face seemed familiar to him. When it became clear to the distinguished-looking gentleman that Tucker did not recognize him, he smiled and extended his hand. "I'm Edward Johnson," he said, and, directing Tucker's attention to another well-groomed man who stood nearby, "I'd like you to meet my associate, Frank St. Leger."

Puzzled at meeting the general manager of the Metropolitan Opera Association in the vestibule of the Brooklyn Jewish Center, Tucker knew that this was hardly a casual visit. Johnson affirmed this when he said that he and St. Leger had come to hear him sing a service. When Tucker wondered aloud why a Sabbath Eve service would interest the most important man in American opera, Johnson told him that he had more than a passing acquaintance with cantorial music. "When I was starting out as a young lyric tenor, after coming to this country from Ontario," Johnson explained, "I was told I could earn extra money in some of the small synagogues that had no regular cantor. So I learned the Passover service phonetically, and eventually other services as well—and I sang them several times, especially in a synagogue in New Jersey."

After the service, Johnson told Tucker that he had heard much about him from Wilfred Pelletier, Angelo Canarutto, and others after the "Auditions of the Air." The very mention of the "Auditions" prompted a spontaneous reaction. Tucker quickly declared that the "Auditions" had been a grave mistake, that he had gotten what he deserved, that he did not have enough to offer the Metropolitan, and had been foolish not to listen to his teacher.

"My boy," said Johnson, halting this unexpected stream of self-criticism, "if you can satisfy the critical ears of two thousand people in this prestigious temple, you can satisfy any audience at the Metropolitan Opera House!"

As Frank St. Leger nodded his agreement, Johnson came directly to the point: he wanted Tucker to go through a formal audition. But, remembering the "Auditions," Richard said that he would have to speak with his teacher before giving Johnson a definite answer.

Paul Althouse told him to go through with the audition. Johnson's presence at the Jewish Center, Althouse noted with pleasure, indicated a serious interest in Richard; certainly, there would be nothing to lose by auditioning. In all likelihood, the audition was little more than a formality; Johnson, himself one of the tenor luminaries of the Metropolitan in the 1920s, had already heard Tucker and could verify the high praises Pelletier and others had accorded him. The real test, Althouse explained, would come when contracts and repertoire had to be discussed. "If they offer you a small contract full of minor roles," Althouse warned, "they will not be giving you a pattern that will let you grow as an artist. If that is what happens, I am going to insist that you say no—for your own good."

When Tucker dutifully reported the three arias St. Leger had given him to prepare for the audition—"Che gelida manina" from *La Bohème,* "Di rigori armato" from *Der Rosenkavalier,* and "Cielo e mar" from *La Gioconda*—Althouse had no specific reaction to their significance. "I don't know whether they're just testing what you can do," he said, "or whether they might be thinking of *Bohème* or maybe *Gioconda* for you. We'll have to wait and see."

Surely the three arias would be a test—that much was clear. Rodolfo's well-known narrative from the first act of Puccini's most popular work, *La Bohème,* would test Tucker's mastery of *legato,* the ability to blend phrases in a fluid, seamless way; it would also test his top notes, as the narrative reaches its climax on a customarily prolonged high C. The *Rosenkavalier* aria—popularly known as the "Italian Tenor's Aria" because it is sung by the stereotyped Latin whom Richard Strauss added tongue-in-cheek to the levée scene in the opera's opening act—would involve four minutes of intense lyricism in an often torturous range. And Ponchielli's expansive "Cielo e mar," an apostrophe to sky and sea, would test how Tucker's legato singing would fare in weightier music. Both the aria and the character who sings it, Enzo Grimaldo, had long been associated with Caruso—a clear indication of the power of voice expected, if not necessarily required, to sing the music.

Angelo Canarutto coached Tucker and accompanied him at the piano during the audition. Johnson sat in the middle of the cavernous Old Met, while St. Leger listened from various boxes in the upper strata of the house to get an impression of how well Tucker's voice carried. If there were any surprises for Johnson, they probably centered on the perfection of Tucker's Italian and his complete lack of nervousness during the audition.

Afterward, Johnson asked Tucker to come to his office. Complimenting him on his performance, he offered him a limited contract, essentially requiring him to serve as a "cover" in a range of operas that included *Gianni Schicchi, Ballo in maschera, Rigoletto,* and *Cavalleria rusticana.* The only role he would sing with any assured frequency was the Italian Tenor in *Der Rosenkavalier,* in which he would make his debut.

Since its revival in January 1935, when Lotte Lehmann brought her formidable Marschallin to the Metropolitan, *Rosenkavalier* had increasingly endeared itself to the operagoing public. In 1943/44, the season in which Tucker was to debut in it, Strauss's masterpiece would be elevated to even loftier heights by the conducting of George Szell, to whom the composer had been an early mentor. Though Lehmann was absent, owing partly to the war (her singular Marschallin having been temporarily assigned to the lesser-gifted Irene Jessner), Tucker was to sing the Italian Tenor in casts that included veteran artists Emanuel List and Jarmila Novotna, and a coterie of promising newer arrivals—among them Risë Stevens, Eleanor Steber (who was also studying with Paul Althouse), and Nadine Conner.

When Tucker brought the news to his teacher, he found Althouse singularly unimpressed by the offer. Althouse dismissed the role of the Italian Tenor with a wave of his hand. "You walk on, you sing for four minutes, you walk off, and nobody hears another note from you," he said disdainfully. In recent years, he reminded Richard, the role had done nothing to advance anyone's career. True, Raoul Jobin and Kurt Baum had sung it in their first seasons—Baum, in fact, in his debut—but neither man had built his reputation upon it. Two others who had sung the Italian Tenor in their debuts—John Carter and Elwood Gary, both "Auditions of the Air" winners—also had not been well served by the part. The same fate might await Richard Tucker.

As for the rest of the contract and its gaggle of "cover" roles, Althouse was contemptuous. Though times and circumstances were undeniably different, perhaps his memory of several of the roles that Giulio Gatti-Casazza, Johnson's predecessor, had assigned Althouse himself—roles that were difficult but never as plummy as the ones that went to the more popular Giovanni Martinelli—made Althouse wary of the fare now being offered Tucker.

"This is *not* how you build a career," he told Richard emphatically.

Tucker had asked Johnson for a few days to think over the terms of the contract. After he spoke with Althouse, he and Sara went to Jan Peerce, seeking additional insights. Peerce, though by all accounts pleased for him, felt he had little advice to offer. "You've gotten this far doing what you thought you should do," Peerce told him, "so what can I tell you? If you think you're ready for the Metropolitan, and I guess you do, then it's your decision to make."

When the time came to give Johnson a final decision, Tucker took stock of the situation, calculated the odds, and decided to gamble.

"Talk about *chutzpah,*" he would say from the safe vantage point of twenty-five years, "I gave the word a new meaning. I looked Eddie Johnson, Frank St. Leger, and the others right square in the eye and I told them I wasn't going to do *Rosenkavalier* and I wasn't going to be anybody's cover. I said that when I would come to the Metropolitan, I was going to come through the front door, not through the back."

The *chutzpah* aside, as gambles went, this was actually a reasonably safe bet on Tucker's part. The war had taken a sizable toll of the Metropolitan ranks, especially in the lyric-tenor repertoire—so much so that for the first time in memory the Metropolitan Opera was without a tenor king in the Italian repertoire.

In past decades, including the World War I years, the departure of a star tenor had always been followed by the crowning of a prince-in-waiting—Enrico Caruso immediately after the retirement of the dashing Jean de Reszke, Beniamino Gigli after the death of Caruso, and Tito Schipa after Gigli left the Metropolitan over a salary dispute in 1932. When Schipa left the Metropolitan in 1935, to return only for a single season in 1940, another brilliant career was already in the making. From the moment he first walked onstage in 1938 as Rodolfo in *La Bohème* and set the Grand Tier aflame with a magically spun "Che gelida manina," Jussi

Bjoerling rekindled vivid memories of the young Caruso among older operagoers. But Bjoerling had hardly begun to settle into his regal status when the war took him back across the Atlantic. The tenor ranks suffered accordingly.

So did the soprano ranks suffer from the departures of the dramatic soprano Maria Caniglia to Italy, the promising new-comer Zinka Milanov to the Balkans, and, most of all, from the return to her native Norway of Kirsten Flagstad, the most cele-brated Wagnerian soprano since the turn of the century. Yet, as Irving Kolodin has written of this period in his book *The Metro-politan Opera,* "The expectable influences of the war were evident . . . [but] not all of them were adverse." It was the wartime "curtailment of operatic activity abroad," Kolodin points out, that "made available Bruno Walter as the first in the series of such conductors as [Sir Thomas] Beecham, [George] Szell, [Fritz] Busch, [Fritz] Stiedry, [Fritz] Reiner, and [Jonel] Perlea, who con-tributed so much to the Metropolitan in this decade [the 1940s]."

But, all things considered, as of 1944 Edward Johnson could do little to help his company but hope that the European war would end reasonably soon. Fortunately, the dramatic-tenor ranks were secure: Lauritz Melchior was still there to sing Wagner, and Martinelli to sing Verdi—especially *Otello,* which Johnson had revived for him in 1937. In the *lirico-spinto* repertoire—the gray area between the purely lyric and clearly dramatic, requiring voices with lyric flexibility but approaching dramatic power—a group of well-seasoned veterans including Charles Kullman, Armand Tokatyan, René Maison, and the versatile Frederick Jagel kept the Met foundation secure, although no one among them had ever achieved first-rank stature with the public or with the critics. Johnson was able to strengthen their ranks by securing the talents of such promising young tenors as Kurt Baum, Emery Darcy, and Raoul Jobin.

Still, with Bjoerling in Europe for the duration of the war, the usually rich lyric repertoire remained impoverished. The sit-uation was not helped by the retirement of Richard Crooks—for ten years one of the finest lyric tenors the Met had ever known, and an artist whose style epitomized elegance in singing. Then in his mid-forties, his operatic debut (in Germany, ironically) more than fifteen years behind him, Crooks had brought his career to a graceful ending near the time Bjoerling made his exodus.

With faint promise found amid such "Auditions of the Air" victors as Morton Bowe and Elwood Gary (who, to be fair, was drafted before his Metropolitan career could be launched), Johnson opted for popular-music solutions in lieu of any other alternatives. From radio he recruited James Melton, whose career began in the early 1930s, when he replaced another pop tenor, Franklyn Baur, in a radio-and-recording group called the Revelers. Melton's main contributions to the lyric repertoire at the Metropolitan—Tamino in *The Magic Flute,* Pinkerton in *Madama Butterfly* (which was banned after Pearl Harbor), Alfredo in *La traviata,* and Ottavio in *Don Giovanni*—led most critics to conclude that he often needed a microphone to be heard without forcing his voice. Two others in this parenthetical period of Johnson's reign—Nino Martini, a radio tenor who had achieved no great distinction when he first sang at the Met in the mid-1930s, and the French Canadian tenor Jacques Gerard—had small voices and, with the exception of Martini's Almaviva in *Il barbiere di Siviglia,* made small contributions to the repertoire.

The limitations of Melton, Martini, Gerard, and the others only underscored the attributes of Jan Peerce, who vocally came the closest, perhaps, to filling the void left by Bjoerling's departure. But Peerce was only one lyric tenor, and Edward Johnson clearly needed more like him. Why not his brother-in-law? If Tucker's artistry was not yet as mature as Peerce's, owing mainly to the differences in their ages and experience, his voice seemed to Johnson every bit as promising.

Taking into account the times and circumstances, Tucker's gamble for a better contract found him with the odds in his favor—though only as long as the European war dragged on. But the Metropolitan was not his only gamble: his operatic intentions were now undermining the security of his position in the cantorate. As Tucker himself pointed out years later, "Rabbi Levinthal, the board of directors, and the congregation at the Brooklyn Jewish Center felt that if the Met took me I would almost have to leave the pulpit. I knew that a lot of them didn't like the idea. I was supposed to be a cantor, not an opera singer, as far as they were concerned. What if Johnson wouldn't have given me a second chance when I said no to *Rosenkavalier?* Would the Jewish Center take me back? I had no way of knowing. I might have lost everything I had worked for."

Richard agonized over this repeatedly to Sara. Ultimately, he decided that the odds for a Metropolitan contract were in his favor, and he settled into what he hoped would not be a long wait. Meantime, he signed with an agency—the National Concert Artists Corporation, which, with Sol Hurok, also represented Peerce—and began augmenting his income through a series of radio appearances. His first radio exposure outside the WEVD "Jewish Daily Forward Hour" was as a guest on the "Squibb Hour," where he sang the Serenade from *The Student Prince* and an English version of "Le Rêve" from Massenet's *Manon,* with Lynn Murray and his orchestra providing the accompaniment.

Some sources credit Tucker's "Squibb Hour" appearances with his subsequent engagement, by *Chicago Tribune* magnate Colonel Robert R. McCormick, for the popular "Chicago Theatre of the Air" program—Tucker's first professional break, and first taste of national prominence. Broadcast weekly over the *Tribune*-owned station WGN, the "Theatre of the Air" presented capsulized grand operas and operettas in English translation. Soon, Richard and Sara were boarding the Twentieth Century Limited in Manhattan, arriving in Chicago in time to attend rehearsals in the Medina Temple, where the broadcasts originated.

A high-budget production known for its smooth pace, meticulous timing, and extensive promotion, the "Theatre of the Air" brought Richard Tucker's voice and name to much of the country for the first time. Critics reacted favorably to his easiness in front of the microphone—which he shared with Miriam Stewart, Selma Kaye, or, most often, Marion Claire, whom McCormick had singlehandedly made a star. Claire's husband, Henry Weber, conducted the studio orchestra for the broadcasts.

Tucker's singing on the program earned him continual plaudits. Not even the sometimes awkward and maudlin translations of Verdi, Puccini, and Mascagni librettos—including an English version of Rodolfo's narrative from *La Bohème* that grated on the ears with such unsingable lines as "Alas, my dear, I am a poet without income!"—gave Tucker any measure of difficulty. The greatest advantage the "Theatre of the Air" afforded him was an opportunity to expand his understanding of such familiar heroes as Mario Cavaradossi, Rodolfo, and Turiddu, all of whom he would eventually re-create on the stage of the Metropolitan. In the meantime, the "Theatre" led to lucrative guest spots on other network shows—including the "Westinghouse Hour," on which he replaced the Metropolitan's John Charles Thomas five times in a single season.

Finally, Marks Levine, director of the National Concert Artists Corporation, notified his client late in the spring of 1944 that Edward Johnson wanted another audition. This time Tucker would be asked to sing only "Cielo e mar" from *La Gioconda*. Johnson assured Levine in so many words that if the audition was good, Tucker would debut in *Gioconda* and would also have the opportunity to sing other major roles during the 1944/45 season. At the audition, as in the previous one, Angelo Canarutto accompanied him at the piano. Johnson, St. Leger, and Emil Cooper, a recently arrived Russian conductor, were in the audience.

Thirty years later, Tucker recalled the scene:

"It happened at the end of the season, after the tour. The Old Met was dark—there was nothing but a bare bulb lighting the part of the stage where they had wheeled the piano. They asked me to sing 'Cielo e mar.' I finished and I heard a voice say, 'Thank you very much.' Then Edward Johnson came up onstage and asked me to come to his office. Maestro Cooper must have gone to the office already, because I don't remember him going with us. Eddie Johnson said to me, 'Richard Tucker, you're going to be a very big star one day.' Then he said to Maestro Cooper, 'Will you take the responsibility?' What he meant was, would the Maestro take the responsibility for making sure that I was prepared. Emil Cooper said yes, he would.

"They handed me a contract, which I gave to my agent to look over. Then Frank St. Leger sat me down and said, 'Richard, these are your orders. You're going to study two operas for us every year, starting right now with *Gioconda* and *Lucia*. And you're going to sit on your fanny until we tell you that you're ready to perform them. You're not going to let yourself be used up.'

"My contract called for me to make my debut in *Gioconda* on January 25, 1945. Then there was a tragedy. Angelo Canarutto, who was going to help prepare me under Maestro Cooper's direction, died in an accident that summer. So I worked directly with the Maestro. I remember that when we were leaving the Met after the audition, the Maestro smiled at me and said, 'You're a green potato right now, Richard, but by mid-December you'll know every note of *La Gioconda* like you know your ten fingers.' And it was true. I don't think I ever studied harder than I did in the six months I spent preparing *Gioconda* with Emil Cooper. I got so that I actually dreamed the music in my sleep."

As anticipated, his Metropolitan contract marked the end of his tenure as cantor of the Brooklyn Jewish Center. The decision to leave, however, was not Tucker's own. Perhaps because of his almost filial relationship with Rabbi Levinthal, or because of a momentary insecurity about his future at the Metropolitan, Tucker did everything he could to stay on as the Center's *hazzan*. Though Rabbi Levinthal was reluctant to replace him, most of the board members felt that he could not, and should not, live in both worlds. When it fell to Rabbi Levinthal to decide the matter of Tucker's future, he told the board that he would solicit the opinions of five distinguished rabbis throughout the country, and would abide by their majority recommendation. When their opinions were received, the tally was three against, and two in favor of, Tucker's staying on as *hazzan*. Dutifully, Richard tendered his resignation.

Leaving the Jewish Center not only took Tucker away from Rabbi Levinthal, his spiritual mentor as an adult, but also left a void in his musical life. While at the Center, Tucker had enjoyed a deeply satisfying association with Sholom Secunda, the prestigious composer of religious and secular Jewish music. A Juilliard graduate and a student of composer Ernest Bloch, Secunda served as music director of the Brooklyn Jewish Center. Many of his religious compositions were written specifically for Tucker, who, under the direction of Alan Chester, first performed some of the earlier ones at the Center.

Self-assured and every bit as aware of his worth as was his favorite interpreter Tucker, Secunda was not always generous in his opinions of the works of other liturgical composers. "Why do you bother with such trivia, such *drek,* when you could be singing *my* music?" he would chide Tucker whenever a non-Secunda work might appear on one of his cantorial programs. Fortunately, their association continued throughout Tucker's operatic career, and their relationship enriched both lives.

La Gioconda, the only enduring opera of the nine written by Amilcare Ponchielli, had been given at the Metropolitan Opera House during its premiere season; Christine Nilsson, the comely soprano who had opened the new theater as Marguerite in *Faust,* was heard in the title role. Though its spectacular sets and fiery drama showed the new Metropolitan stage to its highest advantage, *Gioconda* was performed only four times and then relegated to obscurity. It was revived in 1904 with a cast that should have guaranteed its popularity—Enrico Caruso, Lillian Nordica, Louise Homer, and Pol Plançon—though it stayed in the repertoire a scant two seasons and was heard all of eight times. The opera fared better, at least with the critics, when it was revived under Toscanini in November 1909, again with Caruso as Enzo. But only with its next revival, in the 1924/25 season, did *La Gioconda* take hold with the public. With Rosa Ponselle singing the title role in casts that sported, in its first season, the awesome voices of Titta Ruffo, Margarete Matzenauer, José Mardones, and Beniamino Gigli, and with Tullio Serafin at the podium, *Gioconda* endured eleven seasons and eventually went out of the repertoire shortly after Ponselle left the Metropolitan in 1937. It reappeared, however briefly, in the 1939/40 season, when Edward Johnson found in Zinka Milanov a soprano who could wear the mantle of Rosa Ponselle. Unfortunately, Giovanni Martinelli, then near the end of his Metropolitan career, was no longer in command of the lyric beauty of voice that the role of Enzo demands. Five seasons later, Johnson was certain that in the young Richard Tucker he had found an ideal Enzo.

The story of *La Gioconda,* drawn from a play by Victor Hugo and adapted for Ponchielli's use by Arrigo Boito, was set in the seventeenth century, in the time of the Inquisition. The drama was as convoluted as Verdi's *Il trovatore,* and Lillian Nordica, one of the greatest of all Giocondas, admitted that she had never been able to explain the plot to anyone. Its complexities aside, the characters on whom the action hinges, though admittedly stereotypical, are nevertheless vivid.

Frank St. Leger announced the cast for *Gioconda* early in the autumn of 1944. The Rumanian soprano Stella Roman, whose extensive European career had shown amply in her 1941 Metropolitan debut as Aida, would sing La Gioconda to Richard's Enzo Grimaldo. The veteran American baritone Richard Bonelli would sing the role of Barnaba. Bruna Castagna, considered by many critics to be the finest Carmen of her day, would lend her molten contralto to the role of Laura. Nicola Moscona would portray Alvise. Margaret Harshaw, who had progressed from the "Auditions of the Air" to major roles during the war years, would sing the part of the blind mother, La Cieca, and John Gurney and Osie Hawkins would be heard in smaller supporting roles.

For Emil Cooper, this would be his first *Gioconda* at the Metropolitan. It was but the first of what proved to be many performances of the Ponchielli masterwork under his baton.

Early Thursday evening, January 25, 1945, Richard Bonelli stood in front of the lighted mirror in his dressing room. He was nervous and would remain so until he was onstage, immersed in the character of Barnaba. Only then would he be able to release the tension that invariably mounted as he awaited the opening measures of the overture.

Yet, preoccupied as he was, Bonelli suddenly thought of what the young and inexperienced Richard Tucker must be going through. Tucker was about to lay his future on the line in a role worrisome enough for any veteran, let alone a complete novice. Imagining Tucker enduring the tortures of the damned, Bonelli tried to reach the backstage area a bit early, in case his moral support was needed.

The Richard Tucker he encountered here was not the one he had let himself imagine. Richard was standing in the wings, trying to catch a glimpse of Sara, his hands calmly planted at the back of his sash, and his eyebrows arched in an expression of eagerness. "Now and then he would stand on his tiptoes, probably recognizing a friendly face in the audience," Bonelli recalled in a 1948 interview. "A few minutes later, he was glad-handing some of the backstage crew, then he came around to each of us and wished us good luck. Imagine him wishing *us* luck!"

Nearly forty years later, Stella Roman confirmed Bonelli's recollections. "I had been impressed by Richard from our first rehearsal, when the high quality of his Italian diction and, of course, his excellent voice made him seem much more experienced than he was," she said. "The night of the actual performance, he did not really seem nervous."

When Bonelli mentioned Tucker's calm to Emil Cooper, the maestro sought out Tucker backstage.

"Are you nervous, Richard?" he asked. "Of course you are nervous—we are all nervous until the curtain is up."

"Why, Maestro, I feel just great!" Tucker exclaimed. "I can't wait to get out there!"

"*Be* nervous, Richard," Cooper said emphatically. "A nervous singer gives a better performance!"

Once he was onstage, his performance was, for a debut, exceptionally smooth. He missed none of his cues, though his movements were occasionally awkward. What his acting lacked, the quality of his voice—the primary focus of the critics' attention in any debut performance—more than counterbalanced. Vocally, Tucker could scarcely have bettered his portrayal of Enzo—especially in the romantic fervor he brought to "Cielo e mar" as he stood in the bow of a ship, musically likening the rhythmic restlessness of the ocean waves to his dreamy longings for the woman he loved. "With the stage to himself in the climax of the second act," said the New York *Herald Tribune,* "he seized the moment and won an ovation normally reserved for a Martinelli or a Melchior." Added the New York *Post,* "His lyric voice is of a lovely quality and fullness that was particularly noticeable in the two high B flats in the 'Cielo e mar' aria." The *Sun* concurred that throughout the performance he had sung "mellifluously and well," and that "his highest tone was pure and steady."

Summarizing the critics' judgments in his encyclopedic *The Metropolitan Opera,* Irving Kolodin would later write, "When Tucker finally decided to give his major effort to opera . . . the Metropolitan acquired its most beautiful tenor voice since Gigli's."

Comparisons to Gigli abounded in a number of critics' columns—the sign of an auspicious beginning. But amid the laurels, the words of Paul Althouse stayed with him: "I don't want you to sound like Gigli, Lauri-Volpi, Pertile, Paul Althouse, or anybody else. I just want you to be Richard Tucker—that's all, and that's enough."

Althouse's advice compelled Tucker to take his first success in stride. Now that he had entered the Metropolitan—and through the front door, just as he had said—he had but one remaining goal. Rather than revive memories of Beniamino Gigli, he would perfect his art so that no one would ever forget Richard Tucker.

With Risë Stevens in a televised vignette of Bizet's Carmen, *on Ed Sullivan's* "The Toast of the Town." *As Don José, Tucker made a menacing entrance, thrusting a dagger into one of the props. Camera angles and platforms helped minimize the height difference between Tucker and the much-taller Stevens. (Jerry Saltsberg & Associates)*

By the time Tucker (in costume for Giordano's <u>Andrea Chénier</u>) signed his contract for the 1955/56 Metropolitan Opera season, Rudolf Bing (right) was well accustomed to his negotiating strategies. (Mrs. Richard Tucker)

Tucker (far right) at a testimonial dinner in Brooklyn, singing with (left to right) Robert Merrill, Danny Kaye, and Presidential aspirant Thomas E. Dewey—all of them Brooklyn-born. Dewey had studied voice and once considered a concert career. (Mac A. Shain)

At the Teatro alla Scala, Milan,
recording *Aida* with Maria Callas and
Fedora Barbieri (right), 1955.
(Electrical Musical Industries)

In costume as Ferrando in Mozart's
Così fan tutte, with director Alfred
Lunt. *(Sedge LeBlang/Metropolitan
Opera Archives)*

(ABOVE)

Tucker, as Alfredo, and Leonard Warren as the elder Germont, in the Metropolitan production of Verdi's La traviata, staged by Tyrone Guthrie. (Mrs. Richard Tucker)

(ABOVE CENTER)

With Tullio Serafin, in the cavernous Verona amphitheater, 1947. Under Serafin in Verona, Sara Tucker said, "Richard left his baby shoes behind." (Musical America)

(ABOVE LEFT)

As Dmitri in Mussorgsky's Boris Godunov, backstage with Sara and Paul Althouse, November 1946. Althouse had worn the same costume when he was the Met's first Dmitri at the premiere of Boris in 1913. (Mrs. Richard Tucker)

(LEFT)

Enzo was still a Tucker trademark in 1960/61, when Eileen Farrell (far left) sang Gioconda in her first season at the Metropolitan. (Eugene Cook/Metropolitan Opera Archives)

When Concord Hotel owner Arthur Winarick told Sholom Secunda that he intended to hire "the greatest cantor in the world" to sing the services for Passover and the High Holydays, Secunda promptly recommended Tucker. (The Concord Hotel)

(RIGHT) With Sara backstage at the Metropolitan, in costume and ready for his debut as Enzo in Ponchielli's La Gioconda, January 25, 1945. (Mrs. Richard Tucker)

(OPPOSITE) An ebullient Edward Johnson (right) praises Tucker after the curtain rang down on his debut performance. Left to right are stage director Desire Defrere, conductor Emil Cooper, Tucker, Paul Althouse, and Jan Peerce. (Mrs. Richard Tucker)

(RIGHT) By the time Tucker was named cantor of the Brooklyn Jewish Center in 1943, Sholom Secunda (left) was already a noted composer and arranger of Jewish religious and secular music. Many of Secunda's cantorial works were written expressly for Tucker. (Harcourt-Harris, Inc.)

(BELOW) Tucker's sons were backstage "regulars" at the Metropolitan Opera House, especially in the 1950s. Left to right are Barry, Sara, Henry, and David, with Tucker in costume for Giordano's _Andrea Chénier_. (Sedge LeBlang/Metropolitan Opera Archives)

(ABOVE) Tucker, with his sons David, Barry, and Henry, rehearsing for a 1952 television appearance. Although Tucker's publicists described this as "a nightly event in the Tucker household," the opposite was true—Tucker rarely sang at home. (Elizabeth Winston)

(LEFT) Dr. Israel H. Levinthal, first rabbi of the Brooklyn Jewish Center and a widely respected leader of Conservative Judaism, profoundly influenced Tucker's religious beliefs. (Courtesy of the Levinthal Family)

The bride and groom on their wedding day, in lower Manhattan, February 11, 1936. (S. Chomsky/Courtesy of Mrs. Richard Tucker)

Tucker's first cantorial portrait, taken in 1933. He was still studying under Samuel Weisser and as yet without a pulpit. (Mrs. Richard Tucker)

The "Boro Park Gang," Indian Point, New York, August 1930. Clockwise from the top are Sam Sherman, Sam Steinhaver, Bill Landesman, Manny Schwartz, Teddy Sloan, and Tucker. Contrary to what the photograph suggests, Tucker did not play an instrument— Manny Schwartz merely lent him the banjo-ukulele for the snapshot. (Emanuel Schwartz)

Proud patriarch Israel (Sam) Ticker (center) with his family in 1926. Seated (left to right) are Daniel Nacman, holding his infant daughter, Ruth; Claire Nacman; Claire Parness; Abe Parness, holding his infant son, Larry; Daniel Parness. Standing (left to right) are Minnie (Mrs. Daniel Nacman); Celia (Mrs. Louis) Tucker; Louis Tucker; Fannie Ticker; Rubin, then thirteen; Norma (Mrs. Abe Parness); and Rae Tucker. (Mrs. Richard Tucker)

Ruby and his mother, taken outside the Ticker home in Brooklyn's Boro Park section, 1928. Tucker carried this photograph with him wherever he went. (Mrs. Richard Tucker)

Preparing Don José in <u>Carmen</u> with Sir Tyrone Guthrie, 1951. (Sedge LeBlang/Metropolitan Opera Archives)

With Anna Moffo between "takes" of a <u>Traviata</u> recording session at the Rome Opera House, 1960. (Courtesy of Anna Moffo Sarnoff)

As the Duke of Mantua in Verdi's
Rigoletto, with Ettore Bastianini in
the title role, in a production of the
Lyric Opera of Chicago, 1962.
(Nancy Sorensen/Lyric Opera of
Chicago)

A roster of early 1960s Met stars. First row, left to right: George London, Lili Chookasian, Cesare Bardelli, Renata Tebaldi, Richard Tucker, Regina Resnik, Eileen Farrell, Fernando Corena; second row, left to right: Roberta Peters, John Alexander, Joy Clements, Giorgio Tozzi, Gabriella Tucci, Rosalind Elias, Jess Thomas; third row, left to right: Barry Morell, Calvin Marsh, Ezio Flagello, Frank Guarrera, Lucine Amara, John Macurdy, Irene Dalis, Anselmo Colzani, Anna Moffo, Mario Sereni. (Yale Joel, Life *magazine © Time Inc.)*

(RIGHT) As Dick Johnson in Puccini's <u>La fanciulla del West</u> Tucker inherited yet another Caruso role—and, courtesy of his daughter, Gloria Caruso Murray, Tucker also inherited the leather jacket the great tenor wore at the Metropolitan premiere in 1910. (Courtesy of Alix B. Williamson)

(BELOW) Leontyne Price, as Minnie, pleads that Johnson (Tucker) be spared in <u>La fanciulla del West</u>. Anselmo Colzani (center) is Sheriff Jack Rance. (Louis Melancon/Metropolitan Opera Archives)

6

Q: You and Maria Callas made your debuts in Italy together, at the Arena in Verona. How did the audiences react to both of you?

A: The word in Verona was, "Why have they brought us an American tenor and a Greek soprano? Haven't we got enough Italians to sing opera?" But after that first Gioconda, *they took to me in Verona.*

"The first years of a career," Luciano Pavarotti has said, "are spent in combat—fighting hard to make it, to earn the acclaim of the critics, to put food on the table for the family." Richard Tucker's years of combat began not long after his debut, when a number of internationally acclaimed tenors began arranging their arrival or else return to the Metropolitan after the cessation of hostilities on the battlefields of Europe.

Jussi Bjoerling's return was the most anticipated, and the most auspicious. Between the autumn of 1945 and the spring of 1946 he reestablished his preeminence in the lyric repertoire with near-perfect performances of *Rigoletto, Tosca, Ballo in maschera,* and *Bohème.* If his initial Duke in *Rigoletto* left a few critics suspecting that the luster of his voice had been dimmed slightly, his Cavaradossi in *Tosca* permanently corrected the impression; if anything, Bjoerling was singing even better than before.

Two other lyric tenors also on their way to star stature—Ferruccio Tagliavini and Giuseppe di Stefano—would soon join the lyric ranks in much-publicized debuts a season apart. When the Metropolitan's publicity wing heralded their arrival—or, for that matter, the arrival of any other prominent European tenor—

Sara grew apprehensive about Richard's future. Though he refused to concede that her worries had any basis—"I'm gonna be around long after people forget how to spell their names"—she had good reason to be concerned. Unlike the newcomers, Tucker had arrived at the Metropolitan with virtually no repertoire. Impressive as his debut had been—his "grand opening," to use Althouse's simile—his shelves were as yet unstocked, and it fell to Emil Cooper and Paul Althouse to help him fill them.

Though tempting offers of larger roles occasionally made him balk, he always followed their advice—a few times with the benefit of a second opinion. When Edward Johnson offered the role of Alvaro in *La forza del destino* early in Tucker's career, Althouse advised him to decline it. "It's too early in the day," Tucker remembered Althouse saying. "Unless you want your career to have an early sunset, you'll say no to *Forza* until you're more mature."

Confident, nevertheless, that he would do well as Alvaro, Tucker paid an informal visit to conductor Bruno Walter and asked his advice. After Walter heard him sing the demanding "O tu che in seno agl'angeli" from *Forza*'s third act, he told Tucker quite directly that he agreed with Althouse. "Singing that aria well, which you do, is one thing," Walter said. "But to sustain that level of singing throughout *Forza* is quite another. You're a young man, and your voice has yet to unfold completely. When you're ready for it, *Forza* will still be there."

Instead of *La forza del destino,* Althouse and Cooper insisted that Tucker concentrate on the lyric repertoire during his first three seasons. During his second season, 1945/46, Tucker had a reprise of his success as Enzo when the war's end enabled Johnson to assemble a "dream cast" for *La Gioconda*. Zinka Milanov's Gioconda called to mind the splendor of earlier triumphs by Rosa Ponselle or Emmy Destinn. Tucker, for one, never forgot the ravishing beauty of the prolonged high B-flat, sung in the purest pianissimo, that Milanov sustained during the exit of Gioconda and La Cieca in Act I. Leonard Warren, whose artistic promise was beginning to match his vocal prowess, sang Barnaba as brilliantly as any of the critics could recall hearing. Ezio Pinza, then in his twentieth season at the Metropolitan but still in command of his legendary voice and acting, brought new life to the role of Alvise.

Within this star-studded cast, Tucker more than held his own. "His singing, especially in 'Cielo e mar,' " said Risë Stevens, a very young Laura in those now-famous *Gioconda* performances, "was as extraordinary and beautiful as anyone had ever heard—even in *that* ensemble."

Baltimore was the first city of the Metropolitan tour earmarked for this newly cast *Gioconda*. On opening night in the Lyric Theatre on April 1, 1946, Rosa Ponselle was in the audience. She recalled Tucker's Enzo in a 1977 interview. "Even at that time," she said, "it was clear that Richard had all the makings of a fine career. His voice was lyric, but you could hear the spinto potential in 'Cielo e mar,' in the 'Assassini' in the first act—there was no mistaking it. His technique was as near perfect as you can get. The more I heard him over the years, the more convinced I became that he didn't know how to sing badly! But, most of all, he knew what it meant to be an ensemble singer and not just a 'star.' "

Ponselle had regularly taken exception to the liberties that her Enzo, Beniamino Gigli, had allowed himself in their *Gioconda*s in the mid-1920s. "Great as Gigli was, he tended to sing his best when he had the music all to himself," she recalled. "Even then, in arias with high notes like 'Cielo e mar,' he would hang on to those B-flats until the woodwinds and the brasses almost turned blue. Richard was different. He had good high notes, but he didn't use them to call attention to himself."

La traviata formally entered Tucker's repertoire at the Met when he replaced Jan Peerce, who was ill, in a December 1945 performance that marked the much-talked-about debut of Robert Merrill. At twenty-seven, the Brooklyn-born baritone had progressed from "Major Bowes' Amateur Hour" to musical comedies in the Yiddish theaters of lower Manhattan, the resort hotels of the Catskills, Radio City Music Hall—and finally to the Metropolitan Opera.

Despite their common roots in Brooklyn (even including the New Utrecht High School, which both attended about five years apart), Merrill and Tucker had never met until they were paired at the last minute for Merrill's debut. "I had heard about Ruby Tucker in and around Brooklyn," Merrill remembered, "but he was older than I, and we were going in different directions at the time. He was singing at *bar mitzvah*s and weddings as a young cantor, and I was singing anything and everything, anyplace that would hire me. So it wasn't until I made my Met debut in *Traviata* that we came to know each other." Aside from the title role in the *Traviata* performance, portrayed by the Italian-born Licia Albanese, both *The New York Times* and the *Brooklyn Eagle* proudly pointed out that the two other principals all but made it "a Brooklyn cast."

At the final curtain, as Merrill prepared to take another of his dozen curtain calls, he asked Tucker excitedly, "What the hell, Ruby, was I *that* good?"

"Take another bow," Tucker answered with a slap on the back. "They can't *all* be from Brooklyn!"

In *The New York Times,* amid the acclaim showered on Merrill, critic Noel Straus also served bouquets to Tucker for his "fervor and poetry, manly impersonation, fine sense of restraint, and unfailing taste" as the young Germont.

Not only in *Traviata* but in *Lucia, Rigoletto, Madama Butterfly,* and *La Bohème* Tucker sang some of his first performances outside New York in Philadelphia, Cleveland, Chicago, and other cities. Only a few of these performances were sung with the Metropolitan company, however. Most featured Tucker in productions of respected regional companies, such as the Chicago Opera, or even with touring companies like the San Carlo. Paul Althouse had encouraged Tucker to make himself available to smaller companies when he was not singing at the Metropolitan, so that he could venture new roles outside the New York limelight. Tucker took this advice—and, in the process, unintentionally obscured this phase of his early career. In 1970, Frank Merkling wrote in *Opera News* that Tucker had "prepared all but two of his thirty roles for the Metropolitan." That was correct, insofar as Tucker had indeed prepared his roles for the Met eventually, even if some of his first performances of them were sung under the aegis of smaller companies. But Tucker did not, as his press representatives and even the Met's administration occasionally claimed, "sing his first performances of all but two of his roles at the Metropolitan."

In Chicago, in the autumn of 1946, the presence of many in the audience who had followed Tucker's appearances on the Chicago "Theatre of the Air" perhaps occasioned the applause that led to the Chicago *Tribune*'s comment that whenever Tucker made

an entrance, he "walked right into an ovation." His Edgardo in
Lucia led the critic Claudia Cassidy to wonder whether a finer
Tomb Scene had been heard since the days of Gigli. In *Rigoletto*,
which Chicago and Milwaukee heard late in 1946, the critics'
verdict was quite the same as it would be in New York in February 1947, when, in the words of Irving Kolodin, Tucker "made
his first venture in *Rigoletto* a memorably powerful one." Said the
Milwaukee *Journal* of his Duke of Mantua, "If 'La donna è mobile' ever rang out more brilliantly in this audience's memory, it
must have been on a phonograph record of Enrico Caruso." In
Chicago, his B. F. Pinkerton in *Madama Butterfly* earned him
similar plaudits, although he was compared with the young Giovanni Martinelli rather than Caruso.

    Though Tucker coached most of these roles with Emil
Cooper, he prepared one of his early successes largely under Paul
Althouse—Dmitri in *Boris Godunov*, the role in which Althouse
himself had shone in 1913. When Tucker sang Dmitri to Ezio
Pinza's Italianate Boris on November 21, 1946, he nostalgically
donned Althouse's original costume.

    If Tucker was usually beyond reproach vocally in the early
years of his career, the critics often took him to task for his
semaphoric acting—especially the New York critics. Reviewing
a November 1947 *La Bohème*, in which Licia Albanese sang Mimi
to Tucker's Rodolfo in a benefit for the Hebrew National Or-
phans' Home, the *Herald Tribune* wryly observed that he "played
the part of the Bohemian with all the recklessness of a bank president."

    Claudia Pinza, daughter of the legendary basso and a lyric
soprano during the early years of Tucker's career, remembered
one of the stiff characterizations that had occasioned this kind of
criticism. "Richard, my father, and I sang *Faust* together, and when
we were rehearsing the love scenes, everyone noticed what a distance Richard was putting between him and me. At first, I didn't
give it much thought, as I imagined that he was saving his acting
for the performance. But when we were actually onstage, the same
thing happened. He kept so far away from me in the Garden Scene
that someone who didn't know the story would have thought he
was my attorney, and that we were discussing some business
contract."

    After the performance, Ezio Pinza—a man well experienced

in the art of lovemaking, both onstage and off—pleaded with Tucker to act the part of a young man in love. "Hold her close to you! Kiss her! *Make love!*" Pinza exclaimed.

"Aw, hell, I'm a married man and the father of three kids," Tucker retorted. "Sara is sitting right there in the audience, and I'll feel like an idiot."

Now and then, Edward Johnson took matters into his own hands and, as he was in the habit of doing with other beginners, gave Tucker dressing-room lessons on form and movement. Unfortunately, the stage deportment Johnson tried to pass on had been learned during his glory days in Milan, Chicago, and New York in an era that placed a lesser premium on realistic acting. Eventually, he sent Tucker to drama coach Ann Nichols, but with only marginal results. Experienced colleagues like Bidú Sayão were sometimes helpful. During the last act of *La Bohème,* she whispered stage directions to Tucker between phrases of Mimi's music, gently urging him to move closer to her, hold her hand, and embrace her at the appropriate moments.

Quite the opposite, however, was Jarmila Novotna, the aristocratic Czech soprano who alternated with Albanese and Sayão as Violetta in *La traviata*. Novotna expressly forbade Tucker to act the part of a lover in the final scene of the opera.

"Richard, never, *never* do that!" she chided him in eccentric Garbo-like tones when he tried to embrace her in the death scene. "You *must* understand," she carried on, "that when *I* die, I die a-*lone!*"

"Don't worry, Toots," Tucker muttered under his breath, "you'll die alone—I guarantee it."

"That may have been the only Metropolitan *Traviata,*" Sara recalled, "where Alfredo stood twenty feet from the dying Violetta!"

Only later, when Rudolf Bing would bring to the Metropolitan such formidable directors as Alfred Lunt, Margaret Webster, Tyrone Guthrie, and Garson Kanin, did Tucker's acting begin to approach the quality of his singing. Of these early years under Edward Johnson, Tucker once said tersely, "I spent more time taking acting lessons than any other singer, bar none—and yet the critics always pounced on me for my acting. Well, thank God they never attacked my voice."

Tucker's chrysalid years as a performer were from 1945 through 1947. In the main, they were happy years in Sara's and his personal lives—especially when their third child was born in January 1946. Though she and Richard had been away from the Lower East Side for nearly a decade, Sara wanted to have her baby at the Beth Israel Hospital, partly because she wanted to be near her parents. Though Barry and David had been born at Beth Israel, by 1946 the hospital no longer permitted outside obstetricians to oversee deliveries there. For a time, therefore, Sara resigned herself to giving birth in a Brooklyn hospital. But through her brother Mac Peerce a "deal" was made with an East Side Democratic ward boss: if Richard would sing for nothing at a political fund raiser, Sara could give birth at Beth Israel with her Brooklyn obstetrician in attendance.

On January 20, at an East Side club, Richard sang the Yiddish lullaby "Rozhinkes mit Mandlin" free of charge for the ward boss and his cronies. Ten days later, on January 30, Henry Tucker was born at the Beth Israel Hospital.

Sadly, Anna Perelmuth did not live to see her grandson. In the spring of 1945, she died after a prolonged illness. The decline of her health was the result of a freak accident at the Grand Mansion. A gas leak in one of the kitchen ovens caused an explosion that damaged her heart and lungs; she never recovered her stamina, and spent her last years tethered to a bedside oxygen tank. Bedridden and debilitated, though young in spirit, she died in April 1945 at the age of sixty-six.

The post-funeral *shivah* rite of the Jewish faith marked one of the last moments of unity in the Perelmuth family; during the seven days of the *shivah* ritual, Sara and Richard openly mourned her mother's passing, and shared their grief with Mac, Sender, Jan, and their families. The last years of their mother's life had been marked by mounting tension within her family—tension between Jan and Sender, and most especially between Jan and Richard. The one was mended and passed quickly; the other, unfortunately, only grew worse. Eventually, the ill feelings between Jan and Richard assumed the proportions of an irreconcilable feud, engulfing family and friends and, on occasion, a few of their professional colleagues. The antipathy between them was well known, not only in the opera world but in many quarters of the Jewish community—which, quite rightly, remained equally proud of both men's accomplishments.

Robert Merrill was one of few colleagues who fostered close relationships with both men. Several times, he found himself in the middle of awkward situations—including an airline agent's well-meant attempt to seat the three men side by side on a New York–bound flight (which Peerce tactfully declined, saving Tucker the trouble of doing the same), and a handful of occasions where fans confused their identities, addressing Peerce as Tucker or vice versa (which normally prompted an icily delivered correction). For the most part, however, the difficulties between them rarely spilled into the open. "We all heard that there was some uneasiness between them," said soprano Stella Roman, Tucker's first Gioconda and a frequent partner of Peerce as well. "But they were such great artists and fine colleagues that their personal differences never entered into their work." Unlike the celebrated artistic feuds that affected entire segments of the opera company— Gigli *vs.* Lauri-Volpi, Ponselle *vs.* Jeritza, Del Monaco *vs.* Corelli, Callas *vs.* Tebaldi—this one had little or no effect on the day-to-day affairs of the Metropolitan, either onstage or backstage.

Within the comparatively small world of the Metropolitan Opera, the two men became masters of mutual avoidance. On tour with the Met in the late 1940s, during the long train trips to the South and West, they ate in the dining car at different times, played cards in the club cars with different groups, and in effect took turns socializing with their colleagues—all the while avoiding each other without calling undue attention to it. The same applied to the few family functions that brought them together— a *bar mitzvah,* a wedding, or perhaps a milestone occasion like Levi Perelmuth's eightieth birthday, which the Peerce and Tucker families celebrated in regal fashion. Unforgettable as the event was, the fact remained that this kindly, ever-tolerant patriarch spent his last years dividing his affection among grandchildren who grew up barely knowing one another. Until his death in 1962, at age eighty-nine, he made his home with the Tuckers in Great Neck, but spent one day each week at the Peerces' home in New Rochelle when they were not traveling.

On separate occasions, Robert Merrill asked both men why they had allowed so much to come between them. Neither man could point to a single event, a solitary issue, that had actually caused the rift. Each had his own pet view and readily shared it with almost anyone who asked. Peerce, in the main, seems to have viewed Tucker as an intolerable narcissist whose intelligence and social demeanor were distinctly below Peerce's own; Peerce labeled Tucker an ingrate who neither acknowledged nor repaid what Peerce claimed to have done for him early in his career. Tucker, in turn, saw Peerce as a spiteful, jealous man who hid petty hatred under the cloak of religion. "I don't go showing my dirty laundry in public," Tucker said on the record in his oral-history interview for the American Jewish Committee. "But when people ask the question, 'How is it you two brothers-in-law don't get along?' I say it's simple. There's one word—jealousy. This man can't take it when anybody surpasses him."

Each spared the other two kinds of criticism—as family men and, interestingly, as tenors. Peerce, in his memoirs, wrote of Tucker as "a great tenor who had a great career"; Tucker, in his Jewish oral-history interview, said freely of Peerce, "To me, he was always a great artist." Ironically, it was their peculiar destiny to compete for the critics' acclaim in the same opera company, on the same stage, in some of the very same roles, and for almost the same length of time—Tucker for thirty seasons, and Peerce for twenty-seven.

Even on recordings, there were comparisons. When RCA Victor and Columbia Records marketed competing discs of the "Kol Nidre" as recorded by both men, one reviewer wrote, "Both versions are well sung, but at the risk of promoting a domestic crisis, I must confess a preference for the rich, well-phrased tones of Richard Tucker."

The reviewer need not have worried. The domestic crisis had begun long ago. Regrettably, it never ended.

In the spring of 1947, at the invitation of tenor Giovanni Zenatello, then director of opera productions at the Arena in Verona, Tucker enthusiastically agreed to sing *La Gioconda* in Italy. This was to be his first appearance abroad (and the only one, as it happened, for more than a decade), a foreign debut calculated chiefly to broaden his experience in competent hands.

"After Richard and I took off for Verona," Sara said of their first sojourn abroad, "the TWA staff at Idlewild deserved at least a week's vacation." Though Tucker was not yet well known

enough to warrant a siege of reporters and newsreel photographers, the Trans World staff had smilingly endured all of the
Tuckers, most of the Perelmuths, and dozens of Richard's and
Sara's friends. Levi Perelmuth and Sam Ticker presided over the
brothers, sisters, nieces, nephews, and in-laws who joined the
parade down the runway to the awaiting DC-3. Barry and David—
nine and five, respectively—were too excited to pay much attention to little Henry, who was wheeled to the boarding area in a
stroller. His nursemaid, Gusti Olivier, a Viennese matron then in
her late forties, would help look after all three boys while their
father and mother were in Italy.

When the last snapshots had been taken, Richard and Sara
made their way up the stairway to the plane. As they reached the
top step, just before they entered the cabin, they paused and took
a long look at their children. It would be seven weeks before they
would see them again; they had never been away from them so
long. Understandably worried about them, Sara was suddenly
gripped by a feeling of helplessness and she began to cry.

"When I cried," she remembered, "I started everybody else
crying. Richard did his best to calm me down, but I knew that
leaving the boys was getting to him, too. Finally, he broke the
tension and left everybody on a happy note. He put his finger
inside his cheek, Lawrence Welk–fashion, and made a popping
sound—like the sound of a cork from a champagne bottle. The
older boys started to laugh, and pretty soon everybody was
laughing because *they* were laughing. We gave the crowd a big
wave, and at last we were on our way."

Rome was their first stop in Italy. They stayed there several
days, both to get accustomed to the time change and to drink in
as much of Rome's musical and cultural life as a stay so brief would
allow. When they landed, they checked into the Hotel Flora, where
a messenger soon delivered a packet and a telegram. The packet
contained enough *lire* to allow them to enjoy themselves in Rome.
The telegram was a formal welcome from Zenatello, the *padrone*
of opera in Verona.

Even in an era dominated by Enrico Caruso, Giovanni Zenatello had enjoyed a monumental career as a dramatic tenor. Born
in Verona in 1876, he had been instrumental in launching the famous open-air performances in his native city in 1913. By then,
his singing career had already reached international proportions;

fourteen years earlier, he had made his debut in Naples, as Canio in *Pagliacci*. He had followed Caruso at La Scala and Covent Garden, and had competed with him in New York, where Zenatello sang the heavier tenor roles with Oscar Hammerstein's Manhattan Opera Company. When he left the opera stage in 1930, capping a career that included a great success as Otello, which he sang more than three hundred times, Zenatello and his wife, mezzo-soprano Maria Gay (a controversial Carmen of the 1900s), devoted their lives primarily to teaching. One of their discoveries—Lily Pons—had become an international star largely as a result of their influence. As of 1947, Zenatello was about to figure prominently in the making of another star—the young Maria Callas, who was scheduled to make her Italian debut in the same *Gioconda* in which Richard would make his.

It is not surprising, given the legendary proportions of the life and career of Maria Callas, that the accepted accounts of the near-mythical beginnings of her great career have not always been scrutinized by those who have written about her. This was especially true of her debut in Verona, which had been consistently depicted as having earned Callas instant and universal acclaim, until Giovanni Battista Meneghini, her husband and mentor, emphatically declared otherwise in his recently published memoirs. Of the three young artists whom Zenatello engaged for the 1947 Verona season—Maria Callas, Richard Tucker, and Renata Tebaldi—Tucker and Tebaldi received the greatest acclaim, and Callas almost none at all.

One of the most striking features of the Callas career is that, for a soprano who would eventually be proclaimed one of the most important in opera history, she was anything but an "overnight success." By the time she made her Italian debut as Gioconda in Verona, her career was already in its ninth season.

Maria Callas (or Kallas, as then spelled) had made her debut in 1938 in Athens, as Santuzza in *Cavalleria,* having studied primarily with Maria Trivella and, for a time, with coloratura Elvira de Hidalgo, a contemporary of the Zenatellos. Success in Europe initially eluded her, and she tried to build a career in the United States. Her first bit of fortune was to find, in Eddie Bagarozy, a man with the enthusiasm and the bankroll to invest in her career. A lawyer, the son of a New York agent, and brother

of music critic Robert Bagar, Bagarozy and his wife, the former
Louise Caselotti, had been introduced to Callas by another former singer, Louise Taylor.

Taylor, then retired, had made her operatic debut in the 1910s
and had enjoyed nominal success in Central and South America,
chiefly with the Adolfo Bracale touring company. Much later, she
opened a voice studio on East Ninth Street in Manhattan, and the
young Callas took several lessons there before she began coaching with Bagarozy's wife, Louise Caselotti.

Near the time Tucker had made his Metropolitan debut,
Louise Taylor had persuaded tenor Giovanni Martinelli and, subsequently, Edward Johnson to audition Callas. As has been recorded by most of her biographers, and as Callas herself acknowledged, Martinelli judged her technique imperfect and thus
had little encouragement to offer her. But the audition with Edward Johnson, according to Callas, went very favorably and netted her an offer to sing two roles at the Metropolitan—Leonora in
Fidelio, and the title role in *Madama Butterfly.* Callas supposedly
refused Johnson's offer of a Metropolitan debut because she considered *Butterfly* beneath her talents.

In point of fact—as Tucker heard later through his European representative, John Gualiani, and as has been verified recently by Steven Linakis in his biography of Callas—Edward
Johnson also found fault with Callas's technique, and said so to
Louise Taylor. John Gualiani, soon to be a close friend of Tucker's, knew Taylor, and was introduced to Callas at Taylor's studio in 1946. He was present (at Taylor's request) during Callas's
informal audition with Johnson. Gualiani was an eyewitness to
Johnson's reaction, and heard him say to Louise Taylor, "If you're
her teacher, help her get her upper and lower registers in balance.
If you can work out her problems, come back and I'll give her
another try." When Callas met Linakis at a nearby drugstore after
the audition, she was still seething at "that bastard" Johnson, and
told Linakis that she had even offered to sing for nothing just to
appear on the stage of the Metropolitan.

Probably through no fault of Callas's, the story of how she
came to sing *Gioconda* in Verona is also fraught with inaccuracies.
What is certain is, first, that in 1946, when opera was again heard
in Verona after a five-year hiatus because of the war, Zenatello
assumed the post of impresario and included in his plans for the

1947 season a production of *La Gioconda*. Largely because of his limited budget, he fixed his sights on two young American artists—Tucker, the Metropolitan's newest Enzo, and Pennsylvania-born Herva Nelli, to whom he offered the title role. (Several accounts indicate that Zenatello offered the role first to Zinka Milanov, which Milanov has flatly denied.) From a mercenary standpoint, Zenatello assumed that Nelli and Tucker could be gotten cheaply. He was correct as regards Nelli, whose tenure with the Philadelphia La Scala Opera was in its early stages and who was therefore not in a solid position to demand as much as Tucker could. Zenatello soon discovered that Tucker had forgotten none of his salesman's tactics when he retired his sample cases. Whereas Nelli reportedly agreed to travel tourist-class to Verona and sing six performances of *Gioconda* for $1,500, Tucker traveled first-class and got $2,500 for his Verona performances.

When Eddie Bagarozy learned of the Verona *Gioconda*, he begged Zenatello to audition Maria Callas. Though Zenatello did hear her—and was more favorably impressed than Johnson or Martinelli had been—he explained to the eager Bagarozy that a contract had already gone to Herva Nelli. Bagarozy interceded for Callas by reportedly offering Nelli $2,000 to void her contract. Whatever Bagarozy's tactics, Herva Nelli declined Zenatello's offer, and Maria Callas assumed the role of Gioconda.

The schedule Giovanni Zenatello had drawn up for the Tuckers called for them to stay five days in Rome and then travel by train to Verona. The packet of *lire* that awaited them when they checked into the Hotel Flora had been intended to cover their lodging and sightseeing, as well as first-class travel on the railway line between Rome and Verona. When the hotel presented Richard with the bill for their stay, however, he found himself short of funds and had to wire Zenatello for more money. "The *lire* we were spending was measured in units of a thousand," Sara recalled, "so the prices of what we bought didn't mean anything to us." Only when the hotel bill was presented to them did they become aware of the cost in U.S. dollars of some of their recurring expenses. "We found out, for instance, that a tiny glass of orange juice cost the equivalent of five dollars," Sara said. "Richard had at least three of those little glasses every time he sat down to breakfast."

Zenatello, whose own budget was limited, hastily wired train fare to the Tuckers. Even these extra *lire* were not enough. "We had to dip into the train fare to pay off the rest of the hotel bill," Sara remembered. "When we counted what was left, the cheapest train tickets were all we could afford. We ended up riding in what looked like a battered subway car—no seats, just overhead straps to hang on to. Richard stood all the way to Verona, and I sat on top of a pile of suitcases."

The Verona the Tuckers saw when they arrived from Rome was hardly the city they had imagined. The Nazis had sullied its splendor, leaving a trail of bombed-out buildings and mounds of rubble as they retreated from the Allies in the spring of 1945. As a final touch, they had blown up all ten of Verona's bridges—not merely utilitarian bridges, but even the Ponte Pietra, which Caesar had crossed during the Gallic Wars in 55 B.C. The Nazis had dynamited the ten bridges on April 25, 1945; only two weeks later, the war in Europe ended. Two years hence, Verona was trying to rebuild itself.

Giovanni Zenatello saw to it that Richard and Sara were as comfortable as postwar Verona would allow. They stayed in a structurally sound but worn-looking hotel, the Accademia, where they met Renata Tebaldi and her mother, who accompanied her to most of her engagements. At the Accademia, the Tuckers also renewed their acquaintance with Maria Callas, whom they had met briefly the year before in Chicago, where she had found herself stranded when a new opera company went bankrupt. When Tucker was reintroduced to Callas, he soon anglicized her first name to "Mary"—his way of attempting to create an informal easiness with a new colleague.

At the time, Callas's complicated affair with her mentor Meneghini dominated the conversations of the lunch-and-dinner group that quickly grew up amid the Tuckers' casual, extroverted ways. "The Maria Callas we came to know in Verona," Sara Tucker remembered, "looked and acted almost nothing like the Callas that the whole world eventually knew as a celebrity. In those days, she was grossly overweight, she moved awkwardly on the stage, and offstage she hadn't the vaguest idea how to use makeup. She used all the wrong colors and hues, disfiguring the same features that would later make her famous. She was poor, restless, and confused about her career—and yet all this time Meneghini stood in the wings adoring her, showering her with lavish gifts, and filling her cramped hotel room with elaborate sprays of flowers."

After lunch one afternoon, Maria showed Sara the floral arrangement Meneghini had just sent her. "I don't think I love him," Maria told her, "but he wants me to stay here. He wants me to marry him."

"And you?" Sara asked.

"I want to go back to the States and sing there. I don't like it here, and I think I can do much better for myself in America."

Thirty-five years after that conversation took place, Sara reflected on the young Callas's impulsive ways. "When she asked me what I would do if I were in her place, I gave her the only answer that made sense to me. I said, 'Don't go back to the States—not yet, at least.' After all, there was Meneghini, somebody who had the money she needed but didn't have; somebody who believed in her and who wanted her to become a great star. I told her I thought she ought to let him take care of her. I'm sure most people told her the same thing—it made perfect sense, and ultimately that was what she did."

Richard found Maria Callas a puzzling mixture of contrary qualities—partly cunning and wily, and partly girlish and naïve. One moment, she could be timid and nearly helpless, and, in the next, uncompromisingly demanding. As regards her singing, Tucker thought her technique amateurish at times, yet he recognized the intense dramatic drive she was capable of infusing into an aria like "Suicidio!" in *Gioconda*. For the most part, however, he was too taken with the exquisite lyric voice and flawless technique of Renata Tebaldi—whom Zenatello had engaged to portray Marguerite in *Faust*—to concentrate much of his attention on Callas's singing. Though Callas's range was far more expansive than Tebaldi's, it was the only advantage Callas could claim over her, Tucker felt. For Tebaldi, unlike Callas, had a seamless voice whose beauty of tone was matched by a technique so refined that it seemed effortless to the listener.

Tebaldi had been chosen by Toscanini to reopen the Teatro alla Scala in Milan after the war and was well on her way, Tucker believed, to international stardom. He and Sara were able to draw her out of her basic shyness, and soon had her join an enviable luncheon group—Richard Tucker, Maria Callas, Renata Tebaldi, conductor Tullio Serafin, and Giovanni Zenatello, all at the same table, all contending as best they could with the oppressive heat and shortages of food that plagued postwar Verona.

With food at a premium, whatever there was had to be shared communally. One day, the evening meal for this illustrious group might consist of little more than three or four ounces of meat apiece, served with a small dish of string beans; the next day, it might be steamed vegetables and fruit, or whatever else the cooks could lay their hands on. Fortunately for Tucker, two of his favorite fruits—watermelon and peaches—were in somewhat steady supply. After an especially hot rehearsal, he might have the local police captain take him by car to a roadside market to buy the largest melon he could find. At the hotel, he would carve it for the group, as if it were a prized cut of meat. "I remember the many afternoons in the hotel when he would have the waiters bring out a whole platter of peaches," recalled another guest at the table, aspiring conductor Giovanni Camajani, whom the Tuckers befriended in Verona and who helped them as an interpreter. "We'd sit around the lobby asking anybody in sight to join us—including Tebaldi, who remained somewhat shy."

Camajani also remembered Tucker's ever-active sweet tooth, which he satisfied daily at a *dolceria* next to the Accademia Hotel. "He couldn't pass that *dolceria* without having a brioche or a large malted milk. He might have one at four o'clock in the afternoon, and then sit down to dinner at six. Even in war-torn Verona, the man found simple ways to live it up."

Between rehearsal sessions, the Tuckers saw as much as they could of Verona and its surrounding countryside. War-torn or not, the city had its riches—the Gothic Arche degli Scaligeri, where Can Grande I (literally, the "Great Khan") was entombed; the unscathed Hotel Due Torri with its period furniture and vast art collection; and the church of San Zeno Maggiore, with its mammoth bronze doors and their biblical scenes.

As was always Tucker's custom in any city in which he sang, he sought out the local synagogue and paid his respects to the rabbi. When he learned from the rabbi that the chant of a *hazzan* had not been heard in the once-magnificent Verona synagogue since the early years of the war, he asked him if he might sing the Sabbath service. In the space of one week, the fragmented congregation went from having no cantor at all to hearing a voice

possibly unrivaled by any European cantor of his time. In gratitude for this gesture, the rabbi asked Tucker what memento he
might give him as a modest repayment for his singing. Seeing a
set of eighteenth-century translations of rabbinical texts lying in
a heap of rubble, Tucker asked if he might have them. The rabbi
gathered them, dusted them off, and gratefully inscribed them.

The Arena, for which Verona is best known, lies in the heart
of the city, on the banks of the Adige River. None of the other
surviving Roman amphitheaters can match the one in Verona,
either in size or in splendor. Despite its awesome size—250,000
feet square, with a seating capacity of 30,000—the acoustics in the
Arena are nothing short of perfect. Zenatello and Serafin often
marveled at how thoroughly a handclap from the stage would resound through the rows and tiers of seats.

When, as is the custom, each member of the audience lights
a small candle at dusk, in anticipation of the conductor's downbeat, the Arena takes on the glow of the evening sky, each candle
resembling the twinkle of a star. To view this scene within the
Arena is stirring; to view it from the stage, the vantage point of
the performer, is overwhelming. Sara Tucker remembered the
spectacle as she looked into the vastness of the audience while
waiting backstage with Richard. "I was mesmerized," she said.
"I was so moved I made Richard come and look. Fortunately, it
didn't unnerve him—nothing ever did. It only made him want to
please this vast audience all the more."

Because of Tullio Serafin, the rehearsals and, ultimately, the
performances went flawlessly. Then approaching seventy but still
in full command of his resources, Serafin was Italian opera's un-
challenged *primo maestro*. Those who knew him at various stages
of his long and productive life—he died in Milan in the winter of
1968, a few months short of ninety years old—considered him
the peer of Toscanini in the medium of opera, and unfailingly
warmed to his affectionate but disciplined ways. "Serafin was what
I would call the 'total conductor,' " said Rosa Ponselle, whom he
prepared in most of her great roles, including Gioconda, Giulia
in *La vestale,* Norma, and Donna Anna in *Don Giovanni.* "He
didn't merely coach the principals and let others prepare the rest
of the cast. He viewed each opera, each performance, as a unity
between the orchestra and the singers, a unity flowing from his
own concepts of dramatic and musical effectiveness." Such a ges-

talt approach, Ponselle observed, "left no room for assistants to work out details. He prepared everyone, down to the smallest roles."

No one escaped his attention or, according to Ponselle, his great reserve of patience. "His personality was, at least for me, a key ingredient in what made his method work. Though he could be a stern taskmaster, his direction was done *con amore*. No threats, no temper tantrums, just constant encouragement."

As Tucker soon learned, Serafin's unerring sense of dynamics, when wedded to his expert knowledge of the singing voice, enabled him to give every principal a measure of interpretative freedom where a score might call for it. The result was an ensemble, an overall orchestral and vocal unity, that was almost unparalleled.

Until their first rehearsals, Serafin had never heard Tucker sing and had taken Zenatello's word for the quality of his Enzo. After two rehearsals, the maestro had full confidence in Tucker's basic musicianship, though he began to doubt whether his voice would be ample enough for the Arena. During the rehearsals, Tucker had sung only in *mezza voce,* or "half-voice," and had transposed any high notes an octave downward to preserve his voice for the performances. Eventually, Serafin wondered aloud to Giovanni Camajani whether Tucker would be up to the chasmlike demands of the amphitheater. Accordingly, Camajani pleaded with Tucker to sing out in the next rehearsal. Tucker held his reserve until "Cielo e mar," in which he gave everything he had—including a ringing climactic note at the end of the aria. At that moment, Serafin's worries ceased.

As it was, everyone worried about Maria Callas—including Callas herself. To be sure, few worried about her voice; though it was not undergirded by a polished technique, it nevertheless was reliable and thoroughly exciting in many of the rehearsals. Nor was her acting a concern—that was her strong point, even in the early stages of her career. Rather, what worried Callas and everyone around her was her movement on the cavernous Verona stage. During an early rehearsal, she had slipped and had pulled several ligaments; she hobbled through the rest of the rehearsals and wasn't entirely certain whether she could endure the pain through her first performance.

Once she was onstage, she was secure and in good voice.

Her torn ligaments had improved markedly by the day of the opening performance, and by the end of the first act some of her own concern about her stamina had abated. Nevertheless, Tucker, like a protective brother, watched over her during their scenes together, adjusting his movements to hers whenever he thought she might be having difficulties.

His vigilance and care cost him nothing with the Italian critics. With no exceptions, they singled him out for the highest accolades of the entire cast. Whereas the *Corriere del mattino* judged Callas "a fiery Gioconda, especially in 'Suicidio!' " and one "whom the greatest of all teachers, Experience, may shape into a gem one day," the critic Carlo Bellotti considered Tucker a completely polished Enzo. "A truly beautiful voice—clear, robust, penetrating, and expressive," Bellotti wrote, "a voice of natural perfection which permitted the most pleasing continuity and shading."

In the rival newspaper, *Il gazzettino,* the critic Renato Ravazzin assayed Callas's Gioconda as "dramatically compelling but all too obviously flawed by an unfinished technique." By contrast, Ravazzin devoted a laudatory paragraph to the evening's American Enzo:

> Tucker can truly sing; he handles his middle register intelligently, with feeling, and a penetrating range which emerges with ease and fluidity. His timbre is one of general warmth [and] he ascends the column of sound with admirable facility. His voice, which came from his heart, had a fresh as well as clear Italian accent.

To have been granted the last compliment in Verona by a native critic surprised even Tucker—who, for all the purity of his Italian, was never fluent in the language. Early in the *Gioconda* rehearsals, when Serafin had paid him a similar compliment on the perfection of his Italian, the maestro naturally inquired where it had been learned.

"In Brooklyn," Tucker said with a smile.

Elsewhere in his *Gazzettino* review, Ravazzin (who must have been watching through opera glasses) made brief mention of Tucker's surprised expression when, after "Cielo e mar," thousands in the Arena began shouting *"Bis!"*—the traditional Italian cry for an encore. "I didn't know what the audience was yelling at me," Tucker later confided to a friend. "For a second or two, I thought they were calling me a *beast.*"

Six performances of *La Gioconda* sung to an estimated 150,000 people, each night yielding cries for encores of "Cielo e mar," marked Richard Tucker's Italian debut. Twenty-five years would pass before he would return to Verona, as Radames in *Aida,* at the zenith of his career. In 1947, two years after his Metropolitan debut, Verona proved to be the catalyst he needed. Under Tullio Serafin's baton, Tucker breathed the rarified musical atmosphere of Italy and, as Sara would say later, "he left his baby shoes behind him." He returned to his native country a different artist, and in short order this became clear to everyone at the Metropolitan.

7

Q: *How would you characterize your relationship with Rudolf Bing?*

A: *Cordial, wonderful, never a harsh word between us. I sang in all his best productions, I had eight opening nights under him, and he put me with the greatest directors and finest maestros the Met ever had. Let's say I did well by him, and he did well by me.*

Rudolf Bing became general manager of the Metropolitan Opera Association on June 1, 1950. Thin and pale, he seemed the personification of his own private opinion of the Metropolitan under Edward Johnson's stewardship. The description fit only Bing's physique. The mind that animated his skeletal fame was penetrating, imaginative, and precise. Its humorous turns partly offset his usually austere demeanor, though he remained in stark contrast to the affable, always accessible Johnson.

The contrast of personalities in the two men was mirrored in their differences as executives. Put simply, Johnson was a democrat and Bing an autocrat. Formerly a first-rank tenor, Johnson prided himself on his grasp of the singer's psyche. He felt he understood his artists and knew firsthand the psychological frailties to which they were susceptible. His operating principle was that great artists give their best when they are made to feel the most secure. On this basis, he did everything within reason to provide a comfortable, nonthreatening environment for his singers and he interacted with them in an almost fatherly manner.

Rudolf Bing had no familial inclination toward any of his

artists. "I did not socialize with them, and I did not want to know them in any personal way," he said in retirement. His interest in them was purely artistic and he considered them only insofar as they did what they had agreed to do in their contracts. He was not disposed to soothing nerves before, during, or after a performance. He let singers know that he assumed they were professionals, and that as professionals they were to give their best onstage. He said he would not be long-suffering if they undermined their professionalism, onstage or off. "I can assure you," he told reporters at his first press conference, "that I will attempt to run this house—unmoved by promises or threats—on the principle of quality alone."

It was Johnson, surprisingly, who had made the initial overtures that eventually lured Bing to the Metropolitan from England, where he had managed the Glyndebourne Opera in Sussex. Conductor Fritz Stiedry, with whom Bing had worked at the Charlottenburg Opera in Berlin in the 1930s, had introduced the two men in the spring of 1949. In January, the board of directors had reluctantly accepted Johnson's resignation and had asked him to work informally with them in identifying the best-qualified successor. Some two months later, when the board voted Bing a three-year contract, they urged Johnson to agree to have his forty-eight-year-old successor on hand as a "paid observer" during the 1949/50 season. The idea was the board's rather than Bing's. The rationale behind it was one of hope for a smooth transfer of power, a year in which the incoming manager could learn directly from the day-to-day involvements of the outgoing one. It soon became clear, however, that the arrangement was both unwieldy and unwise. Bing clearly wanted to enact his own plans, with his own administrative team, rather than copy Johnson's. To reiterate Irving Kolodin's epitaph for this ill-conceived transition period, "The bulldozer could make its own way, unescorted by the jeep."

Few of Bing's first dealings with artists showed the psychology of his management style better than his contract negotiations with the Met's tenors. Among the excellent artists he stood to inherit from Johnson's roster were, in the order of their tenure, Lauritz Melchior, Jussi Bjoerling, Richard Tucker, and Giuseppe di Stefano. Melchior, by universal acclaim, was the greatest (some say the only) Heldentenor of the twentieth century.

Coupled with his awesome Wagnerian voice, his twenty-four-year tenure with the Metropolitan gave him unassailable seniority. Bjoerling, in the estimation of the critics, possessed one of the most beautiful voices and most perfect techniques ever heard in opera; his use of his shimmering, silvery sound was consistently on a high artistic plane, and it earned him a critical following equivalent to that of the great lyric tenors of the past. Di Stefano, even by Bjoerling's reckoning, "could be the greatest of us all." He was young, handsome, and blessed with a voice as lyrically sparkling as Gigli's, and he had an incandescence onstage that few could match. His heritage gave him an edge over not only Bjoerling but Tucker as well: he was a native-born Italian. Where Bjoerling, a Swede, and Tucker, an American Jew, could gain the acceptance of the large Italian opera audience only through letter-perfect singing, Di Stefano inevitably held them in the palm of his hand the moment he walked onstage.

Leaving aside vocal comparisons, had Bing's criteria for awarding tenor contracts been public opinion, tenure at the Metropolitan, years of service in Europe, or even indispensability to a particular repertoire, Lauritz Melchior would have been the first to be given a contract. Bjoerling and Di Stefano would probably have been next, and Tucker—a non-Italian with a limited repertoire and only one European engagement in his dossier—might well have been the last. As it was, however, Tucker became the first tenor Rudolf Bing engaged. Bjoerling and Di Stefano were extended offers shortly afterward—and Melchior's contract under Johnson was allowed to lapse.

Bing's official reason for making Tucker his top priority was, as he said in his first autobiography, out of "fear [that] someone in Europe would hear this remarkably beautiful voice and steal this man away." The same rationale, of course, could have been applied to any of the others. It was accurate as applied to Tucker, though it was only part of the explanation. The rest could be found in the differences among the four men as professionals—differences evident onstage, offstage, and backstage, which Bing noted and used in his decision-making.

Bing immediately took a skeptical view of Lauritz Melchior's priorities as an artist. Brilliant as he could be onstage, and indispensable as he was to the Wagnerian repertoire (by 1949, he had sung Tristan more than two hundred times), Melchior had exacted privileges that no other principal singer was granted—but which Johnson, acutely aware of his value, had quietly but grudgingly allowed. Chief among these was being allowed to be absent, free of any penalty, from key rehearsals. Melchior was absent frequently—to the detriment of his own performance (which could be musically erroneous if nevertheless heroic) and the performances of the rest of the cast as well. In the 1940/41 season, he had made news by deserting the stage in the final act of Wagner's *Parsifal,* during the parts of the score in which he was not required to sing. Whether he was tired and wanted to save his voice (his public explanation), or whether he was simply bored (the observation of a number of cast members), he was roundly criticized for this inartistic, self-serving behavior. Lacking a forceful reprimand from Johnson, however, the uncontrite Melchior had merely shrugged off the criticism and had continued to take more than his share of such liberties.

By the late 1940s, the sheer force of his larger-than-life personality had made Melchior a multimedia star. He was under contract to appear in films for Metro-Goldwyn-Mayer, and at RCA Victor he was churning out more popular music than opera on his recordings. (A saccharine version of the Serenade from Romberg's *Student Prince,* paired with a patriotic number titled "My Country," to which the "Melody in F" had been grafted, were among his RCA Red Seal issues of the day, each sung in a variant of English.) Late in 1949, the advertising firm of Campbell and Ewald signed him for two-minute radio jingles for Chevrolet automobiles. With radio conductor Gustave Haenschen leading a studio orchestra in a parody of Wagner, Melchior could be heard in commercials throughout the country, belting out the words, "See the *Yoo*-Ess-Ay in a *Chev*-ro-let!"

None of this smacked of a serious artist to Rudolf Bing. He came to regard Melchior as an example of the kind of unprofessionalism and wrongly ordered priorities that he would not tolerate. When Melchior made it known through his manager, James A. Davidson, that he expected premiere treatment from the new general manager, Bing did not respond. When word was leaked that Leonard Warren and Richard Tucker, each a native and a relative newcomer, had been signed before him, Melchior told the press that he considered such behavior toward an artist of his prominence discourteous and inexcusable. The closer Melchior and his manager came to an ultimatum, the more pronounced Bing's silence became. Finally, no contract was offered at all.

Jussi Bjoerling and Giuseppe di Stefano presented different problems to Bing. Di Stefano, twelve years younger than his Swedish counterpart, was out to make headlines and made no secret of his longing for celebrity. A "natural voice," he had arrived at the Metropolitan from Italy (with a wartime detour in Switzerland, where he also performed) on the sheer force of his unstudied talent. Di Stefano considered himself ready and able to sing both lyric and lirico-spinto roles, and seemed unconcerned about his vocal longevity. Bing judged his unfocused energies temperable, and hoped he could tightly rein Di Stefano's petulant tendencies.

Compared with Di Stefano, Jussi Bjoerling, like his art, was deeper and more complex. His personality was alternately pleasant and abrasive, accommodating and inexcusably selfish, moderately inviting and totally forbidding. Conductor Erich Leinsdorf, who respected his impeccable musicianship, outlined in his memoirs the kind of erratic behavior Bjoerling heaped upon those around him in his moments of blackness. The incident Leinsdorf relates took place at the RCA recording studios and involved the making of a *Madama Butterfly* in which tenor Cesare Valletti sang the role of Pinkerton:

> During a playback of the great love duet that concludes Act One, the producer, singers, and I sat in the control room listening intently. Suddenly there appeared next to me a very drunk Jussi, highly indignant at what he heard; he bent down and began to sing into my right ear how the tenor part *should* be sung. . . . The comments he made while Butterfly sang and Pinkerton rested were not for public print or hearing. . . . I began to perspire in perplexed embarrassment, trying in vain to silence Jussi, but he kept getting angrier. . . . He made sure that we all knew what a mistake had been made in casting.

For the greater part of his career, Bjoerling was a chronic alcoholic. Offstage, he could not control his drinking, and, as Bing charitably put it in *A Knight at the Opera,* his second book of memoirs, "he abused his health and altogether led an undisciplined life." Yet his artistry seems never to have suffered. Once onstage—when and if he got there—he sang, Bing wrote, "as beautiful [*sic*] as ever." Because of his voice and the high artistic level at which he sang (and, perhaps, with a ray of hope for his recovery), Bjoerling was reengaged early in 1950. Bing offered him the tenor lead in a new production of Verdi's *Don Carlo,* which would open the 1950/51 season.

Jussi Bjoerling's erratic ways were both puzzling and foreign to Tucker. By Rudolf Bing's reckoning, Tucker, in contrast not only to Bjoerling but to the others, was a professional in the fullest sense of the term. Where Melchior shunned rehearsals and Bjoerling frequently missed them, Tucker arrived punctually and thoroughly prepared. Where Di Stefano often forgot his cues and directions from one rehearsal to the next, Tucker rarely had to be told anything twice, no matter how complicated. Where Bjoerling ignored all but the most rudimentary stage directions, Tucker followed directions to the letter and helped promote a sense of ensemble. Musically, where Di Stefano was prone to alter note values to display his high notes, Tucker adhered to the score as the conductor wanted it interpreted. Yet, like Bjoerling at his best, Tucker never let his metronomic accuracy undermine the emotional intensity of the music. In his performances, as Robert Lawrence once wrote, Tucker remained "a New Yorker more fervently Italian by temperament than the most outspoken Neapolitan."

Bing had heard Tucker in *La Bohème, Tosca, Ballo in maschera,* and *Rigoletto* by the time he engaged him. Tucker had sung his first Metropolitan *Bohème* late in November 1947, only a few months after his triumphant return from Verona. The results of Serafin's influence were obvious. In only a few seasons, he perfected the role to such a degree that Noel Straus, the *New York Times* critic, was compelled to write, "Not since Caruso have we heard a tenor who delivered Rodolfo's music with more fervor or greater accuracy." In February 1950, opposite Stella Roman in the title role, he sang a *Tosca* that netted further comparisons with Caruso.

"I heard his Duke in *Rigoletto* several times, and in each one there were signs of growth," Bing recalled of Tucker's performances in the 1949/50 season. "I could see him transforming the stage director's or the conductor's directions into improvements in his performing. This kind of steady self-improvement, the desire to do better each time he performed, gave me the assurance that he would do well for the Metropolitan." Not only the beauty of his voice but, Bing added, the disciplined way he took care of it had impressed him early on. "He was very concerned about every role he was offered, because he had been told not to do spinto roles prematurely. This is what separated him from Di Stefano, for instance. Di Stefano believed that his lyric voice was really a spinto already. Tucker was just the opposite—he knew the spinto quality was there but he did not want to hurry it along. This is one of the reasons why I used to describe him as 'a tenor with brains.' Most of them, of course, had none."

Thea Dispeker was introduced to Rudolf Bing not long after he arrived in New York. Their roots were different—his lay in Vienna, and hers in Munich—yet both had been part of the musical life in Berlin in the mid-1930s, although they had never met. At that time, Bing was an administrative associate with the Charlottenburg Opera, which he would later direct, and she was a music educator in a branch of the Interior Ministry. With a series of books already to her credit, the personable and erudite Miss Dispeker directed and hosted a number of popular radio programs, many of them featuring compositions and performances by gifted children. When she and her parents left Berlin for New York during the Nazi turmoil in 1938, her reputation followed her. Lecture-bureau magnate W. Colston Leigh soon engaged her to create a concert bureau, aimed at securing network radio appearances for such celebrity artists as Lawrence Tibbett, Jeanette MacDonald, and Lauritz Melchior. Her efforts on Melchior's behalf led to an invitation to work for James A. Davidson, who represented Melchior, Kirsten Flagstad, and Helen Traubel.

When Davidson eventually merged his interests with the William Morris Agency—a short-lived venture that concluded when Morris found that the dollar return on one Bing Crosby was worth at least ten Lauritz Melchiors—Thea went to work for Morris and, with his encouragement, became an independent representative when the Davidson-Morris association ended. John Brownlee, a protégé of the legendary soprano Nellie Melba in her last days at Covent Garden and a Metropolitan baritone since 1937, was one of the established artists who immediately signed her as a personal representative. Her chief interest lay, however, in emerging artists like soprano Polyna Stoska, whose performances in Smetana's *Bartered Bride* and Wagner's *Fliegende Holländer* had attracted much attention at the New York City Opera.

Tucker and Thea Dispeker met through conductor Thomas Scherman, for whom she also worked, and who had engaged Tucker as a guest soloist on "Opera Cavalcade," a WEAF radio program aired in New York. Scherman also engaged Tucker for his well-received Little Orchestra Society performances in Town Hall, where Tucker sang "Sound an alarm" from Handel's *Judas Maccabaeus* and the "Risposta" from the Pergolesi cantata *Contrasti crudeli*. At the time, Tucker's career was still managed by the National Concert Artists Corporation, with whom he was satisfied but growing a bit restless. "My main achievement for Richard when I became his personal manager," Miss Dispeker recalled, "was to persuade him to leave National Concert Artists and audition for Arthur Judson at Columbia Artists Management, where I was convinced he would do much better."

Judson, one of classical music's most powerful impresarios, was not especially impressed by Tucker's dossier. "I went not once but at least ten times on Richard's behalf," Miss Dispeker remembered, "and each time Mr. Judson would say to me, 'Well, he may be at the Met, but he doesn't have a name yet.' I knew that Arthur Judson was never easily won. But I also knew that once he made a commitment, an artist's career virtually skyrocketed."

Though Thea Dispeker was not aware of it while she was doing her best to persuade Arthur Judson to take Tucker into the Columbia fold, Sol Hurok, Judson's great rival, had been following Tucker's progress at the Metropolitan and contemplated making an overture to manage him. Hurok shared his thoughts with Jan Peerce, who was then one of the top-drawing artists in the Hurok stable (though Hurok represented only his opera career) and a close friend of Hurok. Peerce, according to one member of the Hurok organization, reacted angrily. "If you take Tucker, I'll leave," Peerce reportedly said. "I don't want to, but I will." Hurok, seeing the depth of Peerce's feelings, assured him that he had no intention of immersing his organization in "family politics"—and thus did not pursue an offer to Tucker. Meanwhile, Peerce brought to Hurok a teen-age coloratura who would soon become one of his brightest stars—Roberta Peters.

After a dozen visits to Arthur Judson, each time pleading Tucker's cause, Thea Dispeker finally wore down Judson's resistance. He agreed to audition Tucker at Steinway Hall, and asked that he sing three arias from the familiar tenor repertoire. When, at last, Judson heard Tucker toss off "Che gelida manina," "La donna è mobile," and his trademark aria, "Cielo e mar," he all but apologized for not believing the advance press Thea Dispeker had given him. Judson signed Tucker as a client and grew to like him greatly. "He saw Richard as modest, uncomplicated, and very eager to make a career for himself," Miss Dispeker recalled. "Richard had about him a rare blend of gentleness and ambitiousness, and Mr. Judson could not help but warm to him." Tucker basked in Judson's attentions and wondered why he had never received the same treatment from National Concert Artists' Marks Levine. "At National, Jan Peerce was the star tenor," Miss Dispeker explained, "and he was also the favorite of Marks Levine. [National handled Peerce's concert career.] There, they used to call Richard the 'little tenor.' But at Columbia Artists, under Arthur Judson, National's 'little tenor' became Columbia's biggest."

"Columbia" soon figured prominently elsewhere in Tucker's career. Early in 1947, he signed a contract with Columbia Records and made his first complete opera recording—*La Bohème*, recorded with an all-Metropolitan cast featuring Bidú Sayão as Mimi, Francesco Valentino as Marcello, and Mimi Benzell as Musetta, with Giuseppe Antonicelli conducting. *Bohème* was one of the first of a series of "official cast recordings" of Metropolitan Opera performances—a series conceived by Goddard Lieberson and brought to fruition by Columbia president Edward Wallerstein, who sold Edward Johnson on the concept. The resulting contract called for Columbia to record and issue four operas a year, and guarantee the Metropolitan a minimum of $20,000 in royalties each year.

Goddard Lieberson wanted Tucker not merely for the *Bohème* recording but as an exclusive Columbia artist. An aggressive young executive who would later become president of Columbia Records, Lieberson had an eye (and ear) for emerging stars and saw a diverse market for Tucker's artistry—complete operas, oratorio selections, cantorial pieces, perhaps even a few popular ballads. Through his attorney, Al Gins, Tucker negotiated what he described as "a six-figure recording contract"—an agreement

by which Columbia was to pay him $10,000 dollars a year for
ten years, with royalties payable after the company recouped its
annual investment. Sara, for one, was not entirely in favor of these
terms, but Richard was insistent that he get his "six figures"—
even if they were spread over a ten-year period.

In 1947, the state of affairs in the recording industry made
the terms of the agreement seem favorable to both parties. During the war years, restrictions on the importation of shellac—the
basic material of the 78-rpm record—had crippled the industry.
Labor problems brought into focus by the American Federation
of Musicians—problems that led AFM president James Caesar
Petrillo to impose a virtual ban on instrumental recordings between 1942 and 1944—all but put an end to the already ailing industry. But by 1946, the gloom of the past had disappeared; as
Roland Gelatt, editor in chief of *High Fidelity* magazine wrote,
"almost anything with grooves sold well in 1946." The ledgers
of the three major companies—Victor, Columbia, and Decca—
underscored the literal truth of Gelatt's assertion. Between 1945
and 1946, record sales had more than doubled—from 130 million
discs in 1945 to 275 million in 1946. In 1947, the year-end total
would be a staggering 400 million.

As had long been the case in the industry, the largest sales
of recordings were of popular rather than classical music. A major technical development at Columbia, however, carried with it
the promise of redressing the balance between popular and classical record sales. Since 1944, engineers Peter Goldmark and William Bachman had been secretly working with a team of engineers on the refinement of a long-playing disc record, and early
in the project, codeveloper Bachman had coded the experimental
disc "LP." When Columbia introduced the new disc with great
fanfare in June 1948, Bachman's tentative label became the official one. In a press release, the company described its new Columbia LP as "a revolutionary unbreakable microgroove phonograph record which plays 45 minutes on one 12-inch double-faced
record with full fidelity and absence of distortion hitherto unknown in this field." The release went on to point out that the
new combination of "extraordinary fidelity and uninterrupted
listening" made the LP "especially suitable to the recording and
reproduction of major instrumental and vocal musical works."

Since 1946, most classical-music sessions at the Columbia

studios had been recorded with an eye to issuing them in the standard 78-rpm form, and ultimately in the soon-to-be-perfected long-playing form as well. The Tucker-Sayão *Bohème* recording, initially issued in the 78 format, eventually became one of the best-selling titles in the Columbia LP catalogue. Early in his tenure with Columbia, Tucker enhanced not only the company's sales ledgers but also its reputation with the critics by contributing other full operas (among them a *Madama Butterfly* with Eleanor Steber and a *Fledermaus* with Lily Pons), recital albums of tenor arias, and two best-selling albums of cantorial selections and Yiddish songs.

The cantorial selections, issued in both 78 and LP form as *Richard Tucker Sings Cantorial Jewels,* affected an entire generation of singers—primarily young cantors, but in one notable instance an emerging popular singer as well. In 1953, in an old frame duplex in a working-class neighborhood in Memphis, Tennessee, a struggling young Orthodox rabbi, Alfred Fruchter, often played 78s from his cantorial collection for the teen-age son of the downstairs tenants in the duplex. Though the boy understood not a word of the Hebrew prayers on the recordings, he was especially drawn to the voices of two cantors—Moshe Kussevitsky and Richard Tucker.

The teen-age boy was Elvis Presley.

Years later, when the Tuckers took in a Presley appearance in Las Vegas, Sara wanted to go backstage and meet Elvis. "The lines will be so long, and there are so many bodyguards around him that we'll never get near his dressing room," Richard told her.

"But you're in the business too," Sara said, "so maybe that will get us in."

"Don't kid yourself," Richard said with a laugh. "Elvis Presley wouldn't know me from Adam."

Late in 1948, Arthur Judson helped make possible one of the plum engagements of Richard Tucker's early career. Under the auspices of the National Broadcasting Company and RCA Victor Records, arrangements were completed for a concert performance of Verdi's *Aida,* under the baton of the legendary Arturo Toscanini. The *Aida* performance was to be the fifth in a series of operas in concert form featuring the maestro and the NBC

Symphony Orchestra, which had been asembled for him at great expense by David Sarnoff, president of the Radio Corporation of America. Beethoven's *Fidelio* in the winter of 1944 initiated the historic series. By 1954 the list would encompass concert versions of Puccini's *La Bohème* and five of Verdi's masterworks, *La traviata, Otello, Aida, Falstaff,* and *Un ballo in maschera.*

The *Aida* performance—to be broadcast two acts at a time, a week apart in late March and early April 1949—would be special in two respects. For the conductor, it evoked memories of a hot summer evening in Rio de Janeiro in June 1886, when he laid aside his cello, mounted the podium, and quelled a hostile audience at his totally unplanned debut as a conductor. The opera was *Aida* and Toscanini was nineteen years old at the time.

For audiences throughout America, the concertized *Aida* would be special in another way: it was the first in the series of performances to be telecast. For the first time on coast-to-coast network television, a major opera would be both seen and heard. In late November 1948, Easterners had been treated to a telecast of *Otello* with Ramón Vinay, Licia Albanese, and Leonard Warren; although aired from the Metropolitan Opera House, the telecast had been marred by irregular lighting and was only a limited success technically. The Toscanini–NBC Symphony *Aida,* on the other hand, would be telecast from Studio 8H at Rockefeller Center, where the lighting and acoustics could be expertly controlled. The performance would be broadcast simultaneously over NBC radio, guaranteeing the maximum audience for the event.

Toscanini had already begun to assemble the principals of the *Aida* cast—basso Norman Scott as Ramfis, baritone Giuseppe Valdengo as Amonasro, mezzo-soprano Eva Gustavson as Amneris, and soprano Herva Nelli in the title role—when he agreed, at Arthur Judson's prodding, to audition Tucker for the role of Radames. It was a singular opportunity, but one Tucker approached with a hint of trepidation. He knew only too well that he had nothing to recommend him but his success in Verona.

When Tucker entered Studio 8H for the audition, Toscanini merely nodded to him. For moral support, Tucker had brought along Sara and Al Gins, his attorney, who had helped at various points in securing the audition. For once, Sara observed, Richard actually seemed a bit nervous. Toscanini, seated at a rehearsal piano, all but dispensed with any introductions.

"Now you sing, Tucker," the maestro said in broken English as he struck up the chords to the aria "Celeste Aida."

Tucker merely stood there.

"You *sing,* Tucker!" Toscanini said firmly, striking the middle F loudly to signal both the moment and the tone on which Tucker should have begun vocalizing. Again there was silence.

"I don't really know 'Celeste Aida,' " Tucker admitted.

"No? So why are you in this place?" Toscanini asked, confounded. "You say you want to sing Radames, but you do not sing. Now you say, 'Maestro, I don't know the aria.' Tucker, why you bother me? No, Tucker—why *I* bother with *you?*"

Tucker explained that he would not feel he could do justice to *any* of *Aida* unless Toscanini himself were to coach him in the role. In so doing, he inadvertently suggested to the maestro just what he wanted in a Radames—a beginner who had no preconceived ideas of the "correct" approach to Verdi's masterpiece. Tucker could be molded, and Toscanini clearly sensed it. When Tucker at last sang "Cielo e mar" for the maestro, Toscanini nodded his approval to Bruno Zirato, the Philharmonic administrator who served as a liaison between the maestro and the management. In Italian, Toscanini told Zirato that the search for Radames had just ended.

Toscanini then informed Tucker that the initial preparatory sessions for *Aida* would begin almost immediately.

"But, Maestro," Tucker pleaded, "I can't rehearse right now—why, I've got to go on tour, and I won't be around for another four or five weeks."

"Per Dio!" Toscanini exclaimed to Zirato. "I get another tenor!"

Not about to let this once-in-a-lifetime opportunity disappear, Tucker promised the maestro that he would learn the score at first with Joseph Garnett, his coach, and would be totally prepared for the major rehearsals. "If you don't think I'm ready on that first day," Tucker said, "you won't have to say a word, Maestro—I'll go away on my own!"

In a rare concession, especially to a young artist, Toscanini gave him the role. "You learn the music," the Maestro said in parting, "and then I teach you the Radames of Giuseppe Verdi."

At his first rehearsal, Tucker soon grasped how literally Toscanini had meant this comment. It became clear when Richard sang "Celeste Aida" the first time. He had no more than launched into the aria, having sung a stentorian recitative, when the maestro silenced the orchestra.

" 'Ce-les-te Ah-*ee*-dah/for-ma di-*vee*-nah!' " Toscanini sang in his hoarse, unfocused voice. "Is beautiful woman you sing about here, Tucker. 'Aida! You are goddess! Your body is beautiful, divine!' You, Tucker, are singing this like you are telling about your brother. Now, sing like a lover!"

Richard began the aria again—and managed to get to the next couplet before the maestro rapped his baton.

"What I tell you, Tucker? Aida is a woman, not a building. Put feeling in this. Better you put your *pants* into this! Now sing again."

This time Richard finished the aria, concluding it on a ringing high note.

"Bad, very bad," Toscanini exclaimed, shaking his head.

Tucker was sure he had sung it well and could not understand why the maestro judged otherwise.

"Repeat last line, Tucker—sing for me, 'ergerti un trono vicino al sol.' Then I tell you mistakes."

Dutifully, Tucker sang it again, ending the line on a ringing B-flat, just as the score dictated.

"You do not sing Giuseppe Verdi, Tucker. You sing Caruso 'Celeste Aida,' or Gigli 'Celeste Aida,' or Pertile 'Celeste Aida,' but you do not sing *Verdi* 'Celeste Aida!' "

"But I'm singing it from the score, Maestro," Tucker maintained.

"No, Tucker, this is *big* mistake in score," Toscanini said excitedly. "This is not how Verdi write this line. Verdi was genius, Tucker—Verdi does not make big mistakes. I show you."

He called Tucker's attention to the composer's markings for the final line of "Celeste Aida," which in the printed score was marked *"pp morendo"* on the concluding note.

"Tucker, you know what *pianissimo* means?"

Tucker answered yes—feeling, no doubt, as if he had been transported back to an elementary music class at New Utrecht High School.

"And, Tucker, you know what *morendo* means?"

"It means 'dying,' " he said like a schoolboy. "Like the tone is supposed to die away when Radames sings it."

"But, Tucker, is *impossibile!*" Toscanini replied firmly. "What tenor sings such a high note *morendo?* This is not what Verdi want!"

With that, the maestro reached into his breast pocket and retrieved a photocopy of a letter Verdi had written apparently in 1875, four years after *Aida*'s world premiere in Cairo. In the letter, Verdi illustrated an important change in the conclusion of "Celeste Aida"—an accommodation made for tenor Giuseppe Capponi, Verdi's first choice for the role of Radames.

The letter, which Toscanini had found in the *Carteggi verdiani,* a compilation of the composer's correspondence published by Alessandro Luzio in 1935, indicated that Verdi had received reports not only from Capponi but from tenor Ernesto Nicolini indicating that the B-flat in "Celeste Aida" could not be sung as marked. The letter read as follows:

> I understand that it is hard to leave the B-flat in the way it has been written, but for this inconvenience, I myself have taken steps to remedy it, adding for Capponi these three notes. [Here Verdi penned the musical notation to which Toscanini alluded.] I repeat that in this case you should ask Ricordi [the publisher] for this alteration, because I have no authority—or, to express myself better, I cannot assume this power.

The correction in the score, Toscanini pointed out, would enable the final phrase of "Celeste Aida" to be repeated an octave lower. There, in the middle of the tenor range, Verdi's *pianissimo-morendo* dynamics could be followed. "I do not know why Ricordi did not change the printed score," the maestro said in conclusion.

As was heard coast to coast on the evening of March 26, 1949—and as can still be heard on the RCA recording of that famous broadcast—Tucker proved himself capable of unerring technique and musicianship under the most demanding of circumstances. Though a few critics found an element of passion occasionally lacking in his Radames ("Tucker's voice is steady, clear, and powerful," judged B. H. Haggin, "but lacks warmth, luster, and ease of flow"), there was little disagreement about the rocklike security of his technique and the basic beauty of his tone.

Early in the telecast, when Radames's concluding tribute to the absent Aida—"Ergerti un trono vicino al sol/I'll build you a throne near the sun"—was sung so differently by the youthful but confident Richard Tucker, no doubt some of the cognoscenti wondered whether, in his eagerness, he had made a mistake. Tucker did not worry what anyone might have thought. His defense rested securely in the maestro's breast pocket.

Before Arthur Judson and Columbia Artists had begun to represent Tucker, Rudolf Bing approached him about the renewal of his Metropolitan Opera contract. Rather than wait until arrangements with Judson were finalized, Tucker chose to negotiate his own terms with Bing. Thea Dispeker accompanied him and remembered how, during the cab ride to Bing's temporary office at Broadway and 39th, Tucker rubbed his hands excitedly.

"Just watch me work this guy!" he told Thea. "You haven't seen me in action. It'll be a piece of cake. You and I are gonna walk into his office with me making four-fifty a week, and we're walking out making *seven*-fifty—and I mean seven-fifty for every performance!"

Thea reminded him that Bing was known for his shrewdness and was very difficult to read.

"That's what they said about Eddie Johnson," he chuckled. "He was paying everybody else a hundred and twenty-five a week, but I got *two-fifty* a week out of him!"

Amazed at his ability to effect a 100-percent increase, Thea asked him how he had done it.

"I was a salesman, remember?" he said with a wink. "With Johnson, I used every trick in the book. When he wouldn't budge, I finally pulled out pictures of Barry and David to show him!"

Again Thea urged him not to underestimate Bing. From Melchior's manager, James A. Davidson, she knew that Bing could be cold, calculating, and absolutely rigid.

"Listen, I don't give a damn whether he's as cold as ice or as hard as a brick," Tucker said with a shrug. "I'll wear him down, and I know how to do it. You see, *I* know what I'm worth."

He described his plan of attack for Thea. He would begin by telling Bing exactly what figure he wanted. "I'm layin' it right on the table—no talk of eight or eight-fifty and working backward, no beating around the bush." He would cite his reviews and his success in Verona to establish a basis for requesting a per-performance rather than a per-week contract. He would then describe his responsibilities as a husband and father, pointing up the fact that he now had another child, Henry, to feed, clothe, and one day send through college. ("Hell, that's gotta be worth an extra hundred bucks right there!") If Bing still would not bend, he would offer to take him to lunch, where the atmosphere would be more congenial. There he would further soften Bing's resistance, but in more subtle ways.

Precisely at eleven o'clock, Bing invited Thea and Richard into his office. Dispensing with formalities, he immediately took his place behind his desk.

"We all know why we are here," Bing said with a trace of a smile, "so let us proceed to agree on a reasonable fee, Mr. Tucker."

Richard leaned forward in his chair and riveted his large black eyes on his adversary. "I couldn't agree with you more, Mr. Bing," he said with a nod. "On the way over here, I said to Thea, 'Mr. Bing doesn't seem like the kind of guy who wants to dicker. He's gonna want me to be straight with him.' Isn't that what I said, Thea?"

She nodded her agreement, enjoying this opening volley between Old Vienna and lower Manhattan.

"Well, Mr. Bing, I'm not gonna disappoint you," Tucker went on, leaning forward another inch or two. "I'll be very happy with seven hundred and fifty dollars per performance—which is really, I think, very reasonable for an artist of my caliber."

At first, Bing thought he had heard him wrong. "Do you mean seven hundred and fifty dollars per week?" he asked.

"Not per week, per performance," Tucker quickly clarified.

"That's absurd! You are making four hundred and fifty dollars a week, even if you do not sing during a particular week. What can be wrong with that?"

"Only one thing," Tucker said with a knowing smile. "You can make me sing three, maybe four times that week—and I still only get four-fifty."

Bing glanced at Thea Dispeker. "I see Mr. Tucker has a sense of business," he said. She smiled, but did not respond.

"See what I mean, Mr. Bing?" Tucker went on. "I'm just trying to be reasonable. That's your word—reasonable."

"Very well, Mr. Tucker, I will pay you five hundred dollars per performance. *That* is reasonable."

"Well, I'm not gonna send for a dictionary and argue over a word, Mr. Bing, but *I* don't think five hundred is reasonable. I mean, here I am, a guy on the way up, working hard, always studying, trying to be better. . . . I get invited to Verona, I'm a *big* hit there—I mean, Tullio Serafin would tell you if he was here. . . . Well, what I'm saying is that for an artist of *my* caliber—"

"*All* Metropolitan artists are of the highest caliber," Bing interjected, cutting off not only the monologue but the logic behind it.

"Maybe so," Tucker retorted, "but I'll bet they didn't have to struggle like I did."

At this point, Thea braced herself for whatever appeals to sympathy Tucker was now about to try.

"You know, Mr. Bing—well, maybe you *don't* know—that I was a cantor in the service of God for a lot of years. I had to support my wife and my children—I had two boys then, but I've got three now—so I sold cloth down in the fur market, Mr. Bing. The cloth they use to line expensive fur coats. Fur coats that I could never buy my wife, Sara—not even imagine, let alone buy— because I had my children to take care of and I had all those voice lessons to pay for. I don't say this very often, Mr. Bing, but I've had to struggle. I'm not tryin' to sell you a sob story, you understand, these are just the plain facts."

"And no doubt your struggling has made your art all the greater," Bing said.

"Well, maybe so, but—I mean, I have children to think about!"

"Many people have children, Mr. Tucker."

"Yeah, but I've got *three* children!"

"Many people have *many* children, Mr. Tucker."

The telephone on Bing's desk rang. As he took the call, Richard looked at Thea and rolled his eyes. She acknowledged his distress with a look of concern—and secretly breathed a sigh of relief that he hadn't trotted out snapshots of the Tucker boys.

By eleven-thirty, the exchanges between the two men had become more vigorous, and the atmosphere more heated. To Tucker's chagrin, Bing had not upped his ante one dollar.

"Tell you what," Tucker said, "I'm gettin' pretty hungry. What do you say we grab a bite of lunch—just the three of us? There are lots of good places to eat around here. We can continue this later, maybe over a good dessert. How about it, Mr. Bing?"

"This is a business transaction, Mr. Tucker. I do not negotiate contracts at a lunch table, and I do not eat meals at my desk. We will do business in this office, and only in this office. Lunch will have to wait until some other day."

A few minutes past noon, as waves of office workers streamed along Broadway on their lunch hours, Bing issued his final offer.

"Seven hundred dollars per performance, Mr. Tucker—and not one penny more!"

"No!" Richard shot back. "Seven-fifty! Not one penny less!"

It was now Tucker's move—his *last* move. On principle, he would not back down; the Brooklyn boy deep within him could never accept that kind of defeat. But what if Bing said no? Would the $700 offer still stand? Or would the unrelenting Bing immediately withdraw it?

"We're haggling over fifty bucks," Tucker said. "Let's flip a coin for it."

"Let's do *what?*" Bing asked.

"You know, flip a coin," Tucker went on. "Let's say if it's heads, you win and I get seven hundred. If it's tails, you pay me seven-fifty. Fair enough?"

Before Bing could respond, Tucker produced a shiny new quarter. He handed it to Thea and told her to toss it into the air. Bing rose from his chair in time to see the coin land on the carpet in front of his desk.

In a moment, the three were huddled over it.

"Heads! *Damn!*" Tucker exclaimed.

Bing was still recovering his composure as Tucker eagerly shook his hand. He seemed the picture of a cheerful loser.

"As the saying goes, Mr. Bing, 'win some, lose some,' " he declared philosophically. "Today I had the luck of the Irish. The hell of it is, I'm Jewish. So, seven hundred it is!"

Three decades later, Sir Rudolf Bing and Thea Dispeker each reflected on the event. "Shall we say it was the most unorthodox negotiation I can recall," said Sir Rudolf. "I don't believe Richard ever asked me for another increase. If we differed, it was basically over repertoire, and even that was not very often. He was very easy to deal with—especially when compared to some of the other tenors, who were next to impossible at times—and he always gave his best when he performed."

Thea Dispeker saw the coin toss as especially revealing of the Tucker psyche. "Throughout the meeting, he was adamant about that fifty-dollar difference," she remembered. "The strategy of tossing a coin suddenly removed his ego from the negotiating. It was no longer pride, but sport. Though he lost, he was able to declare it a matter of chance, something over which neither he nor Mr. Bing had any control."

Tucker's own attitude, expressed in later years, was decidedly less philosophical. "I took a hell of a bath over that one," he said. "Considering how many times I sang that season, that twenty-five-cent piece ended up costing me about twenty-six hundred bucks!"

As of 1949, Richard Tucker's future could hardly have been brighter. With no noteworthy experience to his credit, he had parlayed an auspicious debut at the Metropolitan into a solid and expanding career. He had been at the Metropolitan only three seasons when, in his first venture in a foreign opera capital, he had been acclaimed in Verona, and his tutelage under Tullio Serafin there had prepared him for Toscanini's *Aida*. Even his recording career at Columbia was off to a promising start.

Through Thea Dispeker, Tucker had also begun to gather about him his "team," as he called them—a closely knit group including Thea as his personal representative, Al Gins as his attorney, Joe Garnett as his coach, Alan Chester as his cantorial conductor, and, as always, Paul Althouse as his teacher and confidant. Soon, Tucker would add four others to this "team": Elizabeth Winston, his first press representative, whom he found through Thea Dispeker; Alex Alexay, his accompanist, whom he met through Jan Peerce; Kitty Lederman, his and Sara's longtime secretary; and young John Gualiani, his European representative, who would introduce himself in a café in Milan.

In the midst of such excitement and promise, it never occurred to Tucker or to anyone involved with him that the very source of all his success—namely, his voice—would ever fail him. Yet it did—and with virtually no warning. In mid-May 1949, at the conclusion of the Metropolitan tour, he sang a performance of *La Bohème* in Minneapolis. Surrounded by a familiar cast—including Bidú Sayão and Mimi Benzell, who had sung Mimi and Musetta to his Rodolfo in the *Bohème* recording for Columbia—Tucker sang with his usual finesse, and was well received by the local critics. But in the last act, he told Sara afterward, he had difficulty keeping his tone in focus. "He complained that some of his tones sounded raspy," she remembered. "He felt as if more air than actual sound was coming from his throat."

Tucker attributed this odd sensation to being tired—or perhaps to an emerging case of the flu. Two days later, he felt fine—but could not sing at all. "His speaking voice was slightly hoarse, but otherwise he had no trouble talking," Sara recalled. "Yet every time he tried to vocalize, the tones would sound awful and finally crack—even in the middle of his range. Nothing like that had ever happened to Richard before, and he was absolutely beside himself."

Immediately, Tucker sought out Paul Althouse, who recommended a throat specialist in Philadelphia. Until he could be examined and treated, Althouse cautioned, Richard must say nothing to anyone about his condition. Otherwise, the press would seize upon his illness, make it a news item, and therefore compound his problems.

What the specialist found when he peered through his laryngoscope were severely inflamed vocal folds—the so-called vocal cords—which were no longer "approximating," or maintaining the proper closeness to focus the tone. Tucker, not unexpectedly, asked for medication to cure his condition. "There is no medicine I can give you," the physician told him. "You are on the verge of developing nodules on your vocal folds—and if you aren't careful, you'll soon need to have them surgically removed. Right now, Mr. Tucker, the best medicine for you is about two weeks' rest—in complete silence, away from your family, and away from New York."

What ensued were two weeks of mental agony—for Sara almost as much as for Richard.

"I made reservations for us in Miami," Sara remembered. "On the doctor's orders, I spoke for Richard wherever we went—and he communicated with me by writing on a pad. He tried as best he could to distract himself—he swam a lot, lay in the sun, took long walks, anything." As the days wore on, he grew despondent. "There were many times when he just started to cry, he was so frustrated and worried. Seeing him cry made me shudder—Richard had always been so confident, so unshakable, until now. He would write on his pad, the tears streaming down his face, 'What am I going to do if I can't sing? Is it really all over so soon?' "

At the end of the two-week period, he and Sara flew from Miami directly to Philadelphia, where he was again examined by the throat specialist. This time, the laryngoscope revealed pink, healthy vocal folds. The elated patient was told to resume his singing, but at a more prudent pace. "The first time Richard tried his warm-up routine after we got back home," Sara remembered, "he was so happy I thought he would turn cartwheels. His voice was every bit as perfect as before."

When Tucker asked what might have caused the inflammation of his larynx, the physician answered that there were several possibilities, among them, a tendency for the throat to become too dry during a performance. The doctor recommended that Tucker use any of the popular lozenges to keep his throat well lubricated when he was singing. After trying a few imported varieties, he finally settled on drugstore Vicks'. From then on, each of his Metropolitan costumes had tiny pockets sewn into sleeves and waistband—each a receptacle for a cough drop that could be discreetly retrieved in the middle of an act. "The cough drops became a standing joke with some of the other singers," Sara recalled. "But, say what they may, Richard never had another vocal problem."

Apart from the terror of momentarily losing his voice, Tucker had one other disappointment awaiting him—this one from Rudolf Bing. Tucker's name did not appear on the cast list for Bing's opening-night *Don Carlo;* the honor went instead to the more established Bjoerling. It was some comfort, at least, that Tucker's name appeared in the second cast for *Don Carlo*. This disappointment aside, however, Richard soon found himself the recipient of Bing's largess as well. Bing accorded him first-cast honors in Strauss's *Fledermaus* and Mascagni's *Cavalleria rusticana,* two of the five new productions Bing intended to mount during his first season as general manager. Soon, another plum came Tucker's way—Tamino in *The Magic Flute,* his first Mozart role—and, after it, an opportunity to sing his first Faust in the Metropolitan. Of the flurry of activity he engaged in during the first six weeks of the 1950/51 season—the *Flute* on November 25, his first *Don Carlo* on December 2, the *Fledermaus* premiere on December 20, *Faust* on January 14, and the new *Cavalleria* with Zinka Milanov as Santuzza on January 17—Tucker would say, in retrospect, "In two months, I moved into the front ranks faster than I had in all of my first two years at the Met."

Bing's opening-night *Don Carlo* was an unqualified success with the critics and the public. Under the stage direction of Shakespearean veteran Margaret Webster, and the baton of Fritz Stiedry, the first cast brought together an Olympian ensemble— Bjoerling as Carlo, Robert Merrill as Rodrigo, Cesare Siepi as King Philip II, Delia Rigal as Elisabetta, Jerome Hines as the Grand Inquisitor, and Fedora Barbieri as Princess Eboli. Their superb singing, coupled with the perfection of the sets, occasioned a rare moment of complete agreement among the major New York critics.

Well received though *Don Carlo* was, the most popular new production of the season was *Fledermaus*. It was heard nineteen times during the season, each performance a standing-room-only sellout. The production was not only the public's pet but Bing's as well; it justified his conviction that well-chosen operettas had a rightful (if occasional) place at the Metropolitan. He began by assembling a cast extraordinary by any standards—Tucker as Alfred, John Brownlee as Dr. Falke, pretty Patrice Munsel as Adele, the fiery Ljuba Welitch as Rosalinda, Risë Stevens as Orlofsky, and Set Svanholm as Eisenstein. Only Risë Stevens, to whom the "pants role" of Count Orlofsky had little appeal, required more than nominal persuasion to join the cast. As it was, she extracted a promise from the new general manager that she would only have to sing five of the nineteen performances.

For months, Bing vacillated over the nonsinging part of Frosch, the comic jailer. With varying degrees of seriousness, he considered such established comedians as Ed Wynn, Bert Lahr, Milton Berle, and even Groucho Marx. Through Robert Merrill, initially, he discussed the part seriously with Danny Kaye. Kaye's schedule, however, precluded a commitment for a run of nineteen performances. Ultimately, Bing awarded the role to former vaudevillian Jack Gilford, whose Frosch was one of several high points of the production.

In Garson Kanin, Bing found a stage director who, though he was a newcomer to the Metropolitan and to *Fledermaus,* pos-

sessed unquestioned Broadway credentials. The recruitment of
Kanin underscored the new emphasis on acting and stage direction in Bing's Metropolitan, and in the case of *Fledermaus* it occasioned a dramatic as well as musical triumph. With song lyrics
provided by Howard Dietz, Kanin wrote an English libretto that
brought the light comedy of the plot directly to the audience.
Conducting honors went to Fritz Reiner, whose operatic credentials—*primo maestro* at Dresden, at Covent Garden, then, as of 1949,
the Metropolitan—more than established his musical authority.

Kanin, the newcomer, was at first in awe of Reiner's authority on the podium, but the conductor's authoritarian ways soon
turned Kanin's reverence into discontent. By the time the major
rehearsals began in October 1950, their working relationship had
degenerated into a memo-writing campaign. As to the reasons,
Bing would later write that it was "because Kanin was an enthu-
siast and Reiner had not an ounce of that quality in his tightly
controlled personality." As is clear from some of their on-paper
exchanges, Kanin's lack of familiarity with opera led him to suggest some dramatic elements that Reiner thought incalculably naïve—as in the former's appeal to Reiner to conduct the overture
facing the audience instead of the orchestra.

Other suggestions were well within the director's traditional
province, but Reiner refused to discuss them. For instance, when
Kanin asked him to consider using the "Acceleration Waltz" for
the ballet in the ballroom scene, Reiner replied in a memorandum, "I will play 'Southern Roses' because I like it better." Exchanges of this sort led Bing to write Reiner and express his concern that this attitude did not indicate "a very happy attempt to
establish a friendly relationship with a guest stage director." Reiner
did not feel compelled to answer Bing.

Reiner had already put Bing into the middle of a dispute over
the rights to an "official" cast recording of *Fledermaus*—a dispute
between Columbia Records, with whom the Metropolitan had
signed an agreement for an "official" version, and RCA Victor,
which intended to market its own *Fledermaus* album with Reiner
as the conductor. Reiner's loyalties to RCA Victor put him on
thin ice with Bing, and the open tension that soon pervaded the
ensemble rehearsals in *Fledermaus* upset their already fragile relationship.

During one of the rehearsals for the second act, where hus-band-and-wife Eisenstein and Rosalinda flirt with each other in disguises in Count Orlofsky's ballroom, Kanin staged the scene so that the principals would drink their champagne while reclin-ing on oversize pillows, accenting the orgylike atmosphere of the all-night ball. In the middle of the rehearsal, Reiner halted the proceedings—none too tactfully, according to Kanin's recollec-tions—and ordered the principals to stand and face him while singing. Kanin politely countered that such static singing would ruin any semblance of realistic acting in a crucial scene. He asked Reiner at least to try the scene the way he had staged it—to which Reiner firmly replied, "No!"

At that point, Bing walked onto the stage and called for a ten-minute break. He asked both Reiner and Kanin to restate the basis of their disagreement. Kanin patiently tried to make a case for the importance of the dramatic credibility of the scene—and Reiner cut him off again.

"I am the conductor of this production," Reiner said flatly, "and *I* will tell the singers how they will stand, and where they will look when they sing. The music, not the comedy, is what matters here. Singers cannot sing lying down—I will not have it!"

Within the week, Bing decided the issue firmly: he replaced Reiner with one of his archrivals, Eugene Ormandy. Mindful of earlier tensions, Ormandy told the principals at his first rehearsal with them, "Let us all try to carry out the director's conception. If he wants you to sing standing on your heads, by all means let us try it."

Tucker, always remembering Paul Althouse's dictum not to get involved in opera-house politics, had given no opinion to anyone about the tension between Kanin and Reiner. When Bing commended him for his neutrality, he said simply that he was there to learn the music from the one, and the drama and com-edy from the other. Kanin, as the critics soon affirmed, had taught him well: he managed to tap into Tucker's natural instinct for comedy. For the first time, Tucker actually seemed comfortable on the stage; gone were most of the stiff movements and ges-tures, replaced by lively, natural-looking comic touches. Not only did he seem equal to the efforts of such experienced performers as Svanholm, Welitch, and Brownlee, but he added a discernible spark to the action and contributed to the outright enjoyment that became a hallmark of the popular *Fledermaus* run.

The fun reached a climax during the jail scene in a performance on New Year's Eve, in which Bing himself appeared with two of his assistants—all of them dressed as cleaning women, alternately mopping the jail and flailing their mops at the audience, finally revealing their identities by pulling off their charwomen's wigs. In the ballroom scene, the cast took liberties with the English lyrics of the familiar "Chacun à son goût" and made sporting fun of their new manager. It fell to the cast's mustachioed Orlofsky—Risë Stevens, brandishing an extra-long cigarette holder in one hand, and a glass of real champagne in the other—to deliver these couplets, to the audience's and Bing's amusement:

> The operas that must be your choice
> If you like plays that sing
> Are solely dependent on one voice—
> The voice of Rudolf Bing!

Midway through the nineteen-performance *Fledermaus* run, and well into the season, Tucker negotiated his new contract with Bing by way of Columbia Artists Management. When he saw what Bing was offering, he was elated. In the 1951/52 season, four new productions were to be mounted—*Aida, Rigoletto, Carmen,* and a revival of Mozart's *Così fan tutte,* which Metropolitan audiences had long awaited since it was heard last in 1927. In all but *Aida,* which he declined on the advice of Paul Althouse, Tucker was to be the first tenor on the playbills. He could not help but view this windfall of starring roles in new productions as a wholehearted act of faith on Bing's part, a willingness to invest heavily in his career.

Tucker strove to repay Bing's investment in him because it presented the kind of challenge he thrived on. But pure necessity lay beyond the challenge. For his future, like the plays that sing in Orlofsky's couplets, was also solely dependent on one voice— the voice of Rudolf Bing.

8

Q: *Some of your first recordings of full operas were made in Italy with Maria Callas. What was she like to record with?*

A: *In front of the microphones, when the tape was running, she was a great Leonora in* Forza, *and a hell of an* Aida. *When the tape wasn't running—well, I liked Maria, but she could be a pain in the ass.*

By the end of his first season as general manager, Rudolf Bing had firmly established himself, in the words of critic Howard Taubman, as "the Lord and Master of that Thirty-Ninth Street temple of temperament as well as art, the Metropolitan Opera House." Taubman might have added that the new Lord was distinctly biblical—he gave, and he also took away. In Bing's second season, 1951/52, Tucker was the benefactor of the giving, and Robert Merrill the object of the taking away.

Late in March 1951, when Bing was preparing for the Metropolitan's annual spring tour, Merrill received word from Paramount Pictures that he should plan to be in Hollywood from April through July, shooting his first motion picture. Unfortunately for Merrill, Rudolf Bing expected him to be on a train to Atlanta and points West for Met tour performances in April and May. As he watched a case of conflicting contracts develop before his eyes, Merrill regretted his hasty decision to sign a contract with Paramount. The whole affair had begun rather as a lark, with a screen test leading to a contract in 1950. Naïvely, Merrill had signed a lucrative contract without realizing that Paramount would demand his services so soon.

Bing's initially harsh reaction led Merrill's management to issue an ultimatum, essentially demanding to be released from most of the tour.

At a press conference on April 8, 1951, Bing publicly answered the ultimatum. Over a breach of contract, he said, he had just fired Robert Merrill.

Richard and Sara were at home in Great Neck, enjoying a cocktail with friends, when newsman John Cameron Swayze announced the dismissal on television. Merrill, according to Swayze, was "unavailable for comment." Later in the evening, when Tucker finally reached him by phone, Merrill was no less incredulous than Tucker.

"Never try to back that man into a corner," Merrill cautioned him. "I'm telling you, the bastard plays hardball!" Tucker advised him to avoid any further confrontations, especially in the press, by letting his management handle the situation for him.

The "hardball" was merely in its first inning. The game went on for a year, until contractual matters were finally resolved and Merrill was reinstated in March 1952. Bing maintained the loss was mainly Merrill's—and it did cost him most of a season, at the peak of his prowess—yet most felt it was also the Metropolitan's. Coupled with Leonard Warren's, Merrill's ravishing voice had made the Met's baritone ranks richer than at any point in the recent past. Even in the golden days of the early 1920s, when in the same season the programs boasted legendary sopranos like Ponselle, Galli-Curci, Jeritza, and Rethberg, augmented by tenors like Gigli, Martinelli, Lauri-Volpi, and Pertile, the Met had never been able to list more than one of the three major baritones of the day—Titta Ruffo, Pasquale Amato, and Riccardo Stracciari—on the same season's roster. The loss of Merrill—even on a matter of principle, as Bing kept reiterating to the press—threatened to have its effects on the 1951/52 season in general and the musical quality of the ensemble Bing had assembled for the much-talked-about *Così fan tutte* revival in particular.

A few days after the headline-making firing, Tucker was about to fly to San Francisco to sing a cantorial concert when he encountered Bing in the Met vestibule along 40th Street. Bing casually inquired how the *Così* rehearsals were progressing, and how Richard was faring in them.

"Fine, just great," Tucker said. "In fact, after I get back from California, I'm looking forward to the next round."

"I've heard of California," Bing said wryly. "That's where Hollywood is, isn't it?"

Bing, whose long, thin nose was keen to most of the goings-on among his artists, probably knew that Tucker had been talked about in the newspapers when Jesse Lasky and Louis B. Mayer were casting the M-G-M film *The Great Caruso*. The Metropolitan, naturally, was a logical place to begin scouting, and Lasky couldn't help but notice the uncanny physical resemblance Tucker bore to Caruso. As it was, Richard was never formally approached. The role quickly went to young Mario Lanza, who was a "hot property" by virtue of his success opposite Kathryn Grayson in *The Toast of New Orleans*. For Tucker, nevertheless, there was a small consolation: he had been heard (but not seen) singing Schubert's "Ständchen" in the film *Song of Surrender*, starring Wanda Hendrix, Macdonald Carey, and Claude Rains, released in 1949. This was Tucker's single encounter with filmmaking. Thereafter, he went to Hollywood only to appear in concert at the Hollywood Bowl.

Had Robert Merrill become another Mario Lanza at Paramount, his dismissal from the Metropolitan might have been easier to take. As it was, he wasted ten weeks in front of the cameras, costarring with Dinah Shore in a vehicle called *Aaron Slick from Punkin Crick*—a cornpone plot posing as a comedy, whose hillbilly title, Merrill remarked afterward, "made me want to go out and buy a spittoon." If the title made the public clear its throat, the film made them clear the theaters. In the parlance of filmdom, *Aaron Slick* was a "no-return property."

At the Metropolitan, however, Bing's hard line against Merrill appeared to have cost the Metropolitan relatively little—at least in the new Mozart production. The return on *Così fan tutte*, both at the box office and in the critics' columns, was nothing short of phenomenal.

This elegant comedy of manners had not been heard at the Met since the late 1920s. It had taken this Mozartean gem more than a century and a quarter to reach the Metropolitan (it had premiered in Vienna in 1790). Though its implicit theme of sexual infidelity had caused furrowed brows in the nineteenth century, the high comedy and lilting melodies of *Così fan tutte* made a lasting mark on New York audiences this time around.

Alfred Lunt, fresh from the play *I Know My Love,* costarring his wife, Lynn Fontanne, accepted Bing's invitation to direct *Così.* This was headline-making in itself. By 1951, Lunt's theatrical career was approaching its fortieth year, and his reputation rivaled Barrymore's.

Lunt had a remarkably good English libretto to work with, and a chiefly American cast to bring *Così* to life. Except for Australian-born John Brownlee, the production's Don Alfonso, the cast—Patrice Munsel (Despina), Blanche Thebom (Dorabella), Frank Guarrera (replacing Merrill as Guglielmo), Eleanor Steber (Fiordiligi), and Tucker (Ferrando)—was entirely native-born. The Steber-Tucker casting not only ensured the prominent representation of the Paul Althouse studio but also displayed two faultless technicians whose stamina became their separate trademarks. The striking-looking, ebullient, and down-to-earth Eleanor Steber not only attained an awesome record for annual appearances—in one year she sang 275 opera, concert, and radio performances—but also managed, on February 9, 1952, to follow a matinee Desdemona in *Otello* with an evening performance of Fiordiligi in *Così.*

One of the most memorable moments of the opening night of *Così* a few days after Christmas 1951 was Alfred Lunt's surprise appearance onstage, just after conductor Fritz Stiedry had mounted the podium. Dressed as a servant in a powdered wig, Lunt walked onstage with the busy gait of efficiency. In one hand, he carried an overly long lamplighter's wand, which he wielded like a sword at the row of authentic-looking footlights he had commissioned for the apron of the stage. As the rod made its way behind each footlight's ruby-colored shade, an electrician backstage made the footlight glow and then shine brightly. Lunt pantomimed his displeasure if one light would faintly glow and then go out—only to rekindle when threatened with a pointed finger. His finger would then point in mock disapproval of a latecomer, or to silence someone coughing loudly in a box near the stage. (One of Bing's assistants had been planted for this purpose.) When all the footlights were finally beaming, Lunt stepped back a few paces to admire his work, and then pointed his finger in the direction of Fritz Stiedry. The conductor's baton rose and fell in a downbeat, and the performance began. Because of Lunt's marvelously pantomimed lamplighting, the curtain rose with the comic tone already instilled in the waiting audience.

The curtain revealed a warmly colored, intimate set, at the back of which was an inner curtain bearing a monogram of Mozart's initials. This rear curtain brought the principals nearer to the footlights, and defined the perimeters of the large Metropolitan stage so that the action of the comedy would be closer to the audience. The costumes of the ladies were a spectacle in themselves and made the two women look, said Francis Robinson, "like Dresden figures."

Those in the audience who might have known the Italian text would have had to get used to English words for familiar melodies—Fiordiligi's "Per pietà" aria, for example, became "Grant me my peace"—but, like the critics, audiences generally found themselves charmed by the beauty of the Mozart "line," no matter what language it was expressed in. The roar of applause that followed Tucker's "Un'aura amorosa"—the first-act apostrophe to love, which he sang in English as "My love is like a flower"—amply proved the depth of this charm.

The critics failed to warm even half as much to the new production of *Aida* that opened the 1951/52 season, despite the expense and preparation that had gone into it. Many judged the sets not only awkward but a distinct departure from Verdi's own specifications—a complaint registered especially during the invocation to Ptah, "Nume, custode e vindice!" which Radames, Ramfis, and the immense chorus sang facing the audience, the opposite of Verdi's own directions. The stentorian tenor Mario del Monaco, who had been engaged by the Met while he was appearing with the San Francisco Opera, won the critics, as Radames, only in such moments as the climax of the Nile Scene, where he could thunder his "Sacerdote! Io resto a te!" at a volume level not heard since Caruso. But in the score's calmer moments, the critics generally reaffirmed *The New York Times* assessment of his Met debut the season before—namely, that he seemed to know how to sing only "at forte or louder." Whether the New York *Daily News* assessment of Del Monaco's debut was warranted—"We can forget him," wrote critic Douglas Watt—he failed to come into his own as Radames or Otello in this, Bing's second season. Irving Kolodin, for one, judged Del Monaco's first Otello "screamed rather than sung, ranted rather than acted."

Del Monaco was one of two much-publicized Italian tenors who joined the Metropolitan ranks at Bing's invitation. The other was Giacinto Prandelli, whose more lyric voice placed him in Tucker's repertoire—the Duke in *Rigoletto,* Pinkerton in *Butterfly,* Alfredo in *Traviata,* and Rodolfo in *Bohème.* Despite Prandelli's formidable reputation in Italy (Toscanini had chosen him for La Scala's first postwar season, and Prandelli had also created *Peter Grimes* there), he did not remain long at the Metropolitan. He returned to Italy in 1955, and continued to distinguish himself there. Prandelli's Metropolitan tenure was of no moment to Tucker, who rather liked him and, at any rate, never saw him as a threat.

In light of the *Aida* reviews, Tucker could not have been sorry that he had declined Radames in the new production. No doubt he was pleased by the critical reception accorded the new *Rigoletto* production, which *New York Times* critic Olin Downes judged "most interesting and exciting" when it was first seen and heard on November 15, 1951. Irving Kolodin assessed Leonard Warren's Rigoletto as having progressed from "manly to mature to magnificent"—a judgment that applied equally to Tucker's Duke of Mantua. Both Kolodin and Downes warmed to Tucker's refinement of technique, and to the different moods he brought to such diverse musical moments as "Parmi veder le lagrime," the "E il sol dell'anima" duet with Gilda, and "La donna è mobile." As the season took Tucker from Mozart to Verdi, his grasp of each composer's style won him continuous approval and demonstrated the deepening of his artistry. It remained for Bizet's *Carmen,* however, to display Tucker's much-improved acting and carry his name beyond the opera house to the general public.

If *Carmen* ever had a more prismatic interpreter in the title role than Risë Stevens—voluptuous, earthy, and white-hot in her alternating moods of passion and anger—it must have been in Bizet's own imagination. Had she sung nothing but *Carmen* (which, in one season alone, she performed thirty-seven times), Stevens would have ensured her fame. Though she was arguably less-equipped vocally than Bruna Castagna or Rosa Ponselle, who set differing standards for the role in the 1930s, Stevens somehow pleased the critics and the public more than almost all of her predecessors. Born in New York City and a Juilliard graduate, she decided early in her career to make her mark in a handful of roles. Though her self-abbreviated list would eventually include Octavian, Dalila, and Laura in *Gioconda,* it was her Carmen that made her highly individual mezzo-soprano voice and alluring, sensual beauty so memorable at the Metropolitan.

In Bing's new production, the previously dethroned Fritz Reiner was given another try with a new stage director, British-born Tyrone Guthrie. In this working relationship (unlike Reiner's with Kanin), there were minimal sparks, and Reiner's reading of the Bizet score was one of the most-acclaimed aspects of the new *Carmen.* The sets, designed by Rolf Gérard, helped Guthrie solve a "problem of Nature" between Stevens's Carmen and Tucker's Don José: Risë Stevens was several inches taller than Tucker, even when he wore built-up boots. Almost every scene utilized steps or else platforms of varying height, which enabled Guthrie to distract the audience's attention from differences in stature and at the same time keep the action from becoming visually static.

The staging of the final act would not have been static even if it had been performed in a cubicle. When Tucker, as the now-deranged José, took his revenge on Stevens's volatile Carmen, the acting was anything but old-school. Several critics reported that on opening night the audience actually gasped when José grasped Carmen's throat and plunged his dagger into her groin. "Whether it was mass hypnosis we will never know," Francis Robinson wrote later, "but there was the *sound* of a stabbing." Stevens played the final moments of her death scene framed by a window overlooking the bullring below; she grasped the window's torn red curtain, and as her life ebbed away, the curtain slowly ripped, ring by ring, from the window.

This last act had been meticulously rehearsed. "He was a real taskmaster," Miss Stevens recalled of Guthrie, "and he drove us to work a great deal at night on the rooftop stage of the Old Met, particularly on that final act." For all the principals, the results were telling—but especially so for Tucker. "As an actor, Tucker is all right if you give him something to clutch," Guthrie remarked after two weeks' work with him. Said his Carmen thirty years later, "It's true that Guthrie made Richard a better actor. He exposed him to a quality of direction he wouldn't have known otherwise." The results even showed on the television screen, when the pair performed the torrid death scene for Ed Sullivan on "The Toast of the Town."

Robert Merrill had returned to the Metropolitan and had joined the *Carmen* cast as Escamillo when, on December 11, 1953, Risë Stevens and Tucker sang a performance for the short-lived Theatre Network Television Corporation. The Stevens-Tucker-Merrill *Carmen* was beamed by closed-circuit telecast into movie theaters across the country, but with variable results technically. Though popular interest in *Carmen* drew sizable audiences, the poor quality of the television picture could not be overcome, and further telecasts were eventually canceled. Still, the publicity surrounding the *Carmen* telecast—if not the telecast itself—kept Tucker, Stevens, and Merrill much in the public eye.

The 1952/53 season, Bing's third, brought new productions of *La forza del destino* and *La Bohème*. Giuseppe di Stefano shared honors with Tucker in the latter, and Tucker garnered first-cast honors in *Forza*. Apart from Alberto Erede's conducting and the singing onstage, the best feature of the *Bohème* production was arguably its Rolf Gérard sets. The stage direction by Joseph L. Mankiewicz—the Hollywood filmmaker who would eventually direct Elizabeth Taylor's financially disastrous *Cleopatra*—was innovative in ways not wholly pleasing to Puccini aficionados. In the first act, for instance, where the text specifies that Mimi leaves the garret arm in arm with Rodolfo while they proclaim their love in the duet "O soave fanciulla," Mankiewicz had Rodolfo close the door while they remained in the garret—indicating none too subtly that their relationship was about to be consummated then and there. Critics and audiences generally preferred Puccini's way of handling the lovers' sex lives, and Mankiewicz's innovation was soon dropped.

So was the policy of giving half the *Bohème* performances in English, using a translation by Howard Dietz, the English lyricist of the *Fledermaus* production. The story of *La Bohème,* unlike *Fledermaus* or *Così fan tutte,* was familiar and not dependent on lyrics to make any of its dramatic points. Dietz had complicated matters by writing end-rhyming lines in all the major arias. Though Tucker did not find them troublesome (he had had far less to work with as Rodolfo on the "Chicago Theatre of the Air"), the critics and public concurred that the English couplets robbed

Bohème of much of its inherent "singability." When attendance figures for the English and Italian performances made clear that the English ones had no real appeal, Rodolfo's Narrative returned from "Your tiny hand is frozen" to "Che gelida manina," as it had always been.

La forza del destino has become so completely associated with Richard Tucker that it is hard to imagine a time when he did *not* sing it. In fact, it entered his repertoire on November 10, 1952, the opening night of the season. The new production afforded a marvelous blend of voices, ensured by the casting of Zinka Milanov as Leonora. Whether paired with the sonorous Cesare Siepi as Padre Guardiano in the moving prayer "La Vergine degli angeli," or in her solo moments, Milanov's singing refreshed memories of past golden ages; her soaring pianissimi in "Pace, pace, mio Dio!" evoked Ponselle's Leonora a generation before her. Tucker's Don Alvaro led the critics to the same conclusions they had drawn about his Duke in *Rigoletto:* he had the security of technique and command of dynamics to meet the challenges of the aria "O tu che in seno agl'angeli," and then, with Leonard Warren, to create unsurpassed lyrical pathos in the haunting "Solenne in quest'ora," and build the dramatic tension to a fiery climax in "Invano, Alvaro!" The same critics underscored the absence of these qualities in *Forza's* second cast, when Del Monaco sang Alvaro and, in the words of the *Times,* "transformed the final duet into a shouting match."

No one was more elated at Tucker's success as Alvaro than Paul Althouse, at whose constant urging Tucker had declined the role until the spinto quality of his voice had completely emerged. At sixty-four, Althouse had been in declining health, which had caused him to curtail his teaching. Though he took on no new pupils, Althouse remained close to Tucker; they were in contact by phone almost daily. Tucker continued to visit his mentor to vocalize for him before most of his performances.

On a snowy Friday evening in February 1954, Richard and Sara were having their Sabbath Eve meal when Mrs. Althouse— a vibrant young woman whose strawberry-blond hair led her husband and everyone else to call her "Red"—anxiously telephoned them and urged them to hurry into midtown Manhattan. "Red told us that Paul was failing rapidly," Sara recalled. "The doctors had done all they could for him. He was still conscious, and Red wanted Richard to be able to see Paul a last time." Althouse was alert when his wife took Richard to his bedside. Determined as he was to keep his composure, Richard soon broke down; he held his mentor's hand and poured out his feelings for the man who had fathered his career. "Without you, Papa," Richard said through his tears, "I'd have been just another tenor trying to make it and not knowing how. Tomorrow afternoon, I'm singing *Traviata* on the radio, and I would like more than anything else for you to hear me. Every word, every note, I'll be singing for you."

On Saturday, February 6, 1954, a few minutes before four o'clock, Paul Althouse died. The last music he heard was Tucker's voice on the radio, singing Alfredo's aria, "De' miei bollenti spiriti," a celebration of the unbridled hope of youth—a quality that Althouse had fostered in the young Richard Tucker a dozen years before.

The day after the funeral, Richard, still very distraught, once more paid his respects to Mrs. Althouse. The moment he saw her, he broke down again. "He was like my own father—you know that," he said. "Everything I did, it was always with Papa. What am I going to do now, Red?"

"Just remember what Paul taught you," she answered. Tucker took her advice to heart.

With one exception, after Althouse's death Tucker never took another voice lesson. That single exception merely proved the rule. "Once I thought maybe it would be good to learn some new things from a teacher," he admitted. "This fellow knew who I was, of course, and asked me to do some scales. When I finished, he looked at me kind of funny and said, "I don't know why you're here, Mr. Tucker, there's nothing you need from any teacher!' So, I just keep doing what I've been doing all along—what I learned from Paul."

Three weeks after Paul Althouse's funeral, Tucker received a telephone call from Dario Soria. With Walter Legge and Maria Callas's sponsor-husband, Giovanni Battista Meneghini, Soria owned a one-third interest in Angel Records. At the time he called Tucker, he was completing plans for a series of complete opera recordings, eventually known as the Angel/Soria Series, most of which were to be recorded at the Teatro alla Scala in Milan. To maximize their appeal, the recordings would feature the best of European and American casts. The first two operas the partners had chosen were *La forza del destino* and *Aida*. Maria Callas, not unexpectedly, was to star in each.

Soria asked Tucker whether he would be interested in recording both operas under his direction. Two separate sessions were to take place at La Scala in the summers of 1954 and 1955, with *Forza* being recorded first. Soria said that the cast was still tentative, except for Callas, though preliminary agreements had been reached with Tito Gobbi to sing Don Carlo, and with Herbert von Karajan to conduct the Scala Orchestra.

Though Tucker did not say so, the mention of Karajan led him to tell Soria that he needed time to think about the offer. The reason had nothing to do with musical matters; rather, it centered on Karajan's wartime association with the Nazis. From 1938 through 1945, Karajan had been maestro of the Berlin Opera, and was said to have been a favorite of Hitler. As had his fellow conductor Wilhelm Furtwängler's, Karajan's ties with Nazism had led Toscanini to refuse to conduct in Salzburg with either conductor even after the war was over. "I would not mingle," Toscanini had said angrily, "with Furtwängler, Karajan, and others who worked for Hitler and the Nazis."

After Richard and Sara had mulled over the offer, Tucker placed a call to Soria.

"I can't make a record with Karajan," he told Soria. "My Jewish people would never forgive me."

Tucker's refusal came as a complete surprise to Soria. "I know what you're saying, Richard, but we must remember that the war is over. I am an Italian, and my people suffered, too—at the hands of Mussolini, and indirectly at the hands of Hitler because of their alliance."

"I know the war is over," Tucker answered, "but for me as a Jew, that's not really the point. The fact is, this man was associated with a government that murdered six million of my people. The war could be over a hundred years and nothing is going to erase what the Nazis did."

Trying his best to understand and mollify Tucker, Soria reminded him that the essence of religion is forgiveness.

"That's the difference between us as Christians and Jews," Tucker answered. "I can forgive someone for what he does to me personally, but I'm not God—*I* don't have the power to forgive what is done to others. If this man was a friend of the Nazis—and he's never denied that he was one of them—then I'm not going to honor anything he does by having my name associated with his. It's that simple, Dario—it's a matter of principle."

When Tucker put down the phone, he weighed what he had said and assured himself that even if he had lost a great opportunity, he had done what was right. Nevertheless, the lost opportunity stuck with him and made him regret that he had to make certain decisions on a moral rather than an artistic basis. Subsequently, Tucker recounted the conversation at length to Rabbi Levinthal, who assured him that he had made the proper decision. The rabbi told him to pray that another opportunity would come his way in the future.

Some ten days later, Tucker was, in fact, saying his morning prayers when the telephone rang. His *tefillin* was still entwined in his fingers when he picked up the receiver. Dario Soria was on the other end of the line.

"Today is your day, Richard!" Soria said excitedly. "I just returned from Milan, and we all want you even more than we want Karajan. I'm happy to tell you that Tullio Serafin will conduct *Forza* and *Aida*."

Tucker was momentarily speechless. "Dario, this is just incredible!" he exclaimed. "Here I am, saying my morning prayers—why, right now I feel as if God were looking out for me!"

At the Caffè Marino, near La Scala, not long after the Tuckers had arrived in Milan for the *Forza* recording session, a young Italian-American approached Richard and Sara and introduced himself. "My name is John Gualiani," he said politely, telling Tucker eagerly that he had been introduced to him backstage at the Metropolitan after a *Gioconda* in 1946, and had also heard him as Alfredo in the *Traviata* radio broadcast. At the Tuckers' invitation, Gualiani joined them for a bite to eat.

Richard was pleased to learn that the young American spoke letter-perfect Italian. After the war, having served in the Pacific theater, Gualiani explained, he had relocated from New Jersey, where he was born, to Milan, where he had lived since 1948. He planned, he said, to continue his music studies in Milan. Tucker, much impressed by him, soon asked Gualiani to serve as his and Sara's interpreter. By the end of his stay, Tucker had invited Gualiani to act as his European representative, handling every detail of his appearances there. Gualiani eagerly accepted.

Tucker found the young man a virtual encyclopedia of operatic lore, and enjoyed the sightseeing sojourns that Gualiani began to plan for them. One of the first was a visit to the Casa Verdi, which Verdi planned, built, and endowed as a home for retired musicians. Completed in 1902, the spacious grounds of the home also contain the composer's burial place. Verdi is entombed next to his wife, soprano Giuseppina Strepponi, in a small chapel at the rear of the Casa's courtyard. Inside the Casa, on a large white wall in a foyer near the entrance to the building, Verdi's life work as a composer is enshrined; the titles of all his operas surround a carved relief of Verdi's face, crowned with laurel leaves.

Tucker read aloud the titles of the operas and said in wonderment to Sara, "How could one man accomplish all of this? It's unbelievable!"

Many of the Casa's residents were understandably eager to meet the "young American tenor from the Metropolitan," some having heard his imported recordings and others knowing his name from his Verona triumph. Several of them approached John Gualiani for an introduction. Giovanni Bambacioni, a dramatic tenor who had made an auspicious debut in the mid-1890s, held Richard enraptured as he told him how he had taken over several of Caruso's roles in those early days because Caruso's voice was too lyric for them. For all his promise, Bambacioni admitted, his gargantuan voice had been incapable of much subtlety. In Turin, when Toscanini heard Bambacioni after he had already been offered a performance of *Mefistofele,* the conductor had ordered the offer withdrawn.

Baritone Enrico Molinari, who had retired to the Casa several years before, was also introduced to Richard and Sara. A contemporary of Gigli, Molinari had been well received by the Italian critics in the Verdi repertoire—and, offstage, had been widely known for his womanizing. After a few minutes of talk about opera and singing, Molinari proceeded to introduce his wife—a small, impish woman whom Sara thought to be "about a hundred years old."

The wiry lady, perhaps wondering whether the Tuckers knew of her husband's past paramours, added proudly, *"I* am his *legitimate* wife!"

Although some time had been allotted the Tuckers for sightseeing, Dario Soria kept the *Forza* recording sessions on a tight schedule, owing to the limited availability of the Scala theater and orchestra. Gobbi could not come to Milan and had to be replaced by Carlo Tagliabue, but Maria Callas's singing was incandescent, and Tucker's was of his usual high standard. As Tucker was recording an alternate version of "O tu che in seno agl'angeli" one afternoon, a representative of the Scala management asked him to meet with Antonio Ghiringhelli, La Scala's general manager. Tucker had no advance word about what Ghiringhelli might want with him, but nevertheless he scheduled an appointment the next day. During the meeting, to Tucker's surprise, Ghiringhelli asked him to sing *Forza* at La Scala.

"He wants me to do six performances," Richard told Sara excitedly when he returned to their hotel. "I'm only supposed to be here for the month of May, which I'm pretty sure I can arrange with Mr. Bing. The rehearsals are scheduled for the week of May 1, and the last performance is supposed to be May 25." Though she found it odd (and said so) that one of the world's leading opera houses would make an offer to a foreign tenor with relatively little lead time—and, at that, purely on the strength of a recording session that Ghiringhelli himself had not heard—Sara agreed that the prestige of a Scala debut was worth any reasonable cost, so long as it could be worked out with Rudolf Bing.

After some initial reluctance, Bing readjusted the last weeks of Tucker's commitments for the spring of 1955 so that Tucker could arrive in Milan late in April, in time for the May 1 rehearsals. With La Scala much on his mind, he prepared only one role for the 1954/55 season at the Met—the title role in *Andrea Chénier,* which Bing revived chiefly for Zinka Milanov, who became the Met's first Maddalena in the twenty-two seasons since Ponselle had last sung it. Opening night of the new production went to Del Monaco, who had been thoroughly prepared by conductor Fausto Cleva and who finally won over the majority of New York critics in his manly portrayal of the poet-rebel. Yet when Tucker sang the role for the first time a few weeks later, the contrast in refinement and nuance was again apparent in the critics' columns.

During the first week of April, Tucker received a transatlantic call from La Scala. It was Ghiringhelli, informing him that he would be needed no later than April 17, not May 1 as originally arranged. Taken aback by such a request, especially in light of his contract, Tucker explained that there were no luxuries of time at Rudolf Bing's Metropolitan. He had already gotten several concessions from Bing to be able to arrive by May 1, and he feared no earlier date was even remotely possible.

Ghiringhelli was emphatic that, no matter who sang Alvaro, *Forza* would have to be moved ten days ahead in the spring schedule.

"But what about our contract?" Tucker asked incredulously. "The contract I signed with you says very plainly that I'm not to start rehearsing until May 1."

Ghiringhelli countered that the management always reserved the right to change the season's schedule, no matter what a contract said. In such cases, he went on, the management did its best to inform its artists as much in advance as circumstances permitted.

With no recourse but to say no, Tucker let the Scala opportunity pass. The role of Alvaro, he heard a few weeks later, went instead to Giuseppe di Stefano, who had never sung such a weighty part before. Alvaro marked Di Stefano's entry into the lirico-spinto repertoire—an entry that Tucker considered entirely premature, and one that gradually cost Di Stefano, in Tucker's judgment, the purity and ease of his lyric voice.

Some time later, Tucker mentioned the Scala debacle to basso Cesare Siepi, who merely shook his head. "That's the way they do things in Italy," Siepi said with a laugh. "Everything is last-minute, and nobody knows what anybody else is doing. Somehow, things get done and the curtain eventually goes up."

Siepi reminded Tucker, nonetheless, that he was legally owed the fee that Ghiringhelli had contracted to pay him. La Scala, after all, had broken the agreement, not Tucker. Siepi urged him to demand the money and, if nothing else, give it to a charity. When Jussi Bjoerling learned of the incident through Siepi, he suggested that Tucker donate the money to the Casa Verdi. Eventually, however, Tucker just grew disgusted with the whole situation and let the money issue drop. La Scala audiences would wait fourteen years before hearing his voice.

As the summer recording sessions for *Aida* approached, Tucker decided that a cruise would be a suitable balm for his disappointment with La Scala. He and Sara booked passage on the *Andrea Doria* for mid-July 1955, hoping to have a leisurely time aboard ship and arrive completely rested for the recording session. The cruise took eight days in all—seven to reach Naples and an additional day to go from Naples to Genoa. Though memories of seasickness on his honeymoon still haunted him, Tucker's stomach finally fared better than his patience. By the time Naples came into view, he was so restless and bored that he could hardly contain himself. Under the guise of paying homage to Caruso at his tomb in Naples, Richard left the ship. From Naples, he and Sara went on to Milan by train.

John Gualiani, who was now handling all the details of Richard's trips to Italy, had reserved a suite for the Tuckers at the Hotel Duomo, a magnificent structure dating from the 1890s and located within walking distance of La Scala. John arrived at the hotel on the appointed day, not realizing that Richard and Sara had arrived ahead of schedule. He then had trouble locating them; improbable as it seemed, the Hotel Duomo register listed not one but three Richard Tuckers, all from the United States. When the Metropolitan's Tucker had been found, Gualiani immediately steered him to the Via Manzone, where a new kosher restaurant had just opened.

After a night's rest, at Richard's request, John drove him to Verona, where he and Sara renewed their acquaintances from Tucker's *Gioconda* success eight years earlier. In the evening, they went to the Arena, where they took in a performance of *Carmen;* the cast included Mario del Monaco as Don José and Giulietta Simionato in the title role. This was unusual for Tucker, who as a rule did not go out of his way to hear other tenors—nor, for that matter, to hear performances other than those in which he was personally involved. But Tucker made exceptions for Del Monaco, whom he considered one of the greatest dramatic tenors of the postwar years.

After the *Carmen* performance, the Tuckers paid a call on Del Monaco in his dressing room; he and Tucker talked about the role of José, and the differences between the Verona and Metropolitan productions of *Carmen*. As they exchanged good-byes, each promised to treat the other to a lavish dinner, either in Milan or New York—a promise neither's schedule permitted him to keep.

Dario Soria and Walter Legge had a twenty-day contract with the Scala theater, orchestra, and chorus to record *Aida*. To make the most of the rather tight schedule, they arranged some sessions in the mornings and others in the afternoons, and allowed an hour's lunch break in between. The opera was recorded more or less in sequence, which called for Tucker to sing "Celeste Aida" during the morning of the second day. His first "take" of the aria went faultlessly onto the master tape, which pleased Tucker as much as it did Soria, as the producer, and conductor Tullio Serafin. Afterward, Serafin pointed out Giovanni Martinelli, who was sitting in one of the boxes to the right of the stage. Retired from the Metropolitan and living most of the year in New York City, Martinelli was spending the summer at Lago di Como and attended the recording session at Serafin's invitation. Tucker found the older man's presence more puzzling than flattering, because Martinelli had never exhibited any great fondness for Tucker's singing. Nevertheless, when Tucker finished "Celeste Aida," Martinelli signaled his approval, and, in return, Tucker called out a thank you.

At the Hotel Duomo, after the session, Richard and Sara received a call from industrialist Fredric R. Mann, the Philadelphian whose philanthropy and love of music sustained, among many other ventures, the Mann Auditorium in Tel Aviv. Mann, his wife, and daughters were vacationing in Milan and hoped to see the Tuckers during their stay. As the Manns were acquainted with Soria, Serafin, and other members of the cast including Fedora Barbieri and Tito Gobbi (available, happily, for this second recording), Tucker extended an invitation for them to attend one of the later recording sessions.

During the rehearsals as well as the first two days of actual recording, Maria Callas had been distant and restrained. As the first-act sessions progressed, she did not seem in full command of her voice, and her mood slowly turned from gray to black. When Tucker and Fedora Barbieri joined her in the trio following "Celeste Aida," where Aida makes her initial entrance, Callas put them through seven different takes. Afterward, she protested to Serafin that she was not happy with any of them, though she was willing to let the engineers splice the best segments of each rather than record it again. Privately, Serafin agreed with Soria that no important differences were discernible from one take to the next.

When the Fredric Manns visited La Scala on the ninth day of the sessions, Tucker had hoped they might hear most of the Nile Scene being recorded. Before they arrived, Callas had already sung several takes of "O patria mia," most of which pleased everyone but her. She was again in a black mood, and though Tito Gobbi escaped her harshness, she spoke curtly to Fedora Barbieri and even more harshly to Serafin, one of her most important mentors. From time to time, Tucker attempted to soothe her, but she rebuffed him. Privately, she complained to Meneghini and Soria that she disliked Tucker's habit of calling her "Mary."

While Tucker was recording "Pur ti riveggo," Callas began pacing behind him onstage, until the sound engineers finally had to stop the tape because of the noise her heels were making. She used the break to issue her salvo against the Manns—and, indirectly, against Tucker.

"I want everyone in this theater to realize," she said firmly, "that the music of *Aida* is *very* sacred to me."

The rest of the principals nodded their understanding.

"For me to make a record of this sacred music," she continued, "I must have complete cooperation in this theater. No one must distract me at any time!"

Innocently, Tucker—whom she had just distracted during his aria—asked her who or what might be interfering with her concentration.

"Those people in that box," she said loudly, pointing her finger at the Manns. "They must leave this theater *now!*"

Tucker was dumbstruck. He could hardly believe what he heard.

"But—but, Mary," he pleaded quietly, "that's Fred Mann and his family. They're my friends! Please don't make a scene over them, will you?"

"I just told you, Richard, this is *very* sacred music," she repeated. "Those people are distracting me, and either they will leave this theater or *I* will leave!"

Before Tucker could say anything else, the Mann family quietly left their box and were on their way out of the theater. As Tucker had told everyone that he had invited the family, Callas not only knew that they were Richard's and Sara's guests, but also knew full well who Fredric Mann was.

Humiliated as he felt, Tucker had the rest of the Nile Scene to record before he could seek out Mann and apologize to his family for Callas's rudeness. The rest of the afternoon session was tense but reasonably smooth—at least until the time came to record the final moments of the scene, in which Amonasro's plotting is disclosed and Amneris, set upon vengeance, confronts her rival, Aida. The climactic moment belongs to Radames, whose "Sacerdote, io resto a te" ("Priests, I surrender to you") must be sung powerfully and at a high tessitura.

Claiming dissatisfaction with the blend of voices, Callas made Tucker and the others record the scene's final moments twelve times in a row.

Later that evening at the Hotel Duomo, after he had made amends to Fredric Mann, Tucker spoke frankly with Tullio Serafin about Callas's inexcusable rudeness. He was angry and hurt, and said so to Serafin.

"Sometimes she has to make trouble in order to sing well," Serafin said. "Some singers are like that. Lauri-Volpi needed to argue, to fight. So did Maria Jeritza—and you should have heard them curse each other when they first sang *Turandot* at the Metropolitan! So it is with Callas. Sometimes she needs to fight—it is her nature."

Tucker found the maestro's explanation considerably wanting.

"You must also remember, Richard, that you have a perfect technique and she knows she does not," Serafin went on. "On the recording, you sound better than she does, and this makes her jealous. Why do you think she made you sing 'Sacerdote' so many times?"

Tucker said he didn't know.

"Because she thought that if you kept repeating it, your voice would get tired and your technique would deteriorate. Then the two of you might sound equal on the recording."

"Who the hell does this dame think she is? If that's the game she wants to play, somebody better tell her to pull this crap with another tenor," Tucker said angrily, forgetting that Serafin's comprehension of English did not extend to Brooklyn slang. "Just out of spite, I'll sing that goddam line till six o'clock in the morning—and the last time will be just as good as the first!"

Tucker could forgive Callas the personal slights she occasionally aimed at him—including her reference to him in print as "another singer, a tenor, who also made a debut at Verona when I made mine." He thought her childish more often than not, yet he could not bring himself to dislike her. Nevertheless, he found it impossible to understand, let alone forgive, her rudeness to the Manns. Though he remained cordial and generous when they were reunited at the Metropolitan—first in *Lucia* in 1956, the season of her celebrated debut as Norma, and again in 1965, when she returned to the Met in *Tosca*—he could never entirely warm to her again. With Callas, it was indeed a personal rather than an artistic reaction. Although he might have preferred Zinka Milanov and Renata Tebaldi in most of his repertoire (as she seems to have preferred Giuseppe di Stefano in hers), Tucker unfailingly acknowledged Callas's lack of peers as a singing actress.

As foreign to his nature as was the "get even" score-settling that often marked artistic relationships at the Metropolitan, after the *Aida* recording session Tucker found it hard to resist a little goading when Callas gave him the opportunity. When they were reunited in 1956, for example, Callas hardly troubled to inquire how he had been, and instead kept touting a young baritone she had been impressed by in Italy.

"The next time you are in Italy," she told Tucker emphatically, "you *must* hear this boy—and tell him that I told you about his voice."

"I think I'll wait," Tucker said indifferently. "If he's half as great as you say he is, he'll be singing with me before long anyway."

Fully aware that such displays of ego challenged her own, he took advantage of another opportunity—this one years later onstage, during the first act of *Tosca,* following the duet "O dolci mani." The two were holding their intimate pose as the tumultuous applause continued when Callas whispered, "Why is it, Richard, that whenever I sing with you, I feel good?"

"It's simple, Mary," he answered with a straight face. "When you're singing with me, you're in the big leagues."

9

Q: *Do you ever feel, as some singers do, that there is a price to pay because fans won't leave you alone?*

A: *I hear some of my colleagues talk like that and I just shake my head. Who do they think really pays the bills? Let's face it, we're not rock-and-roll stars, and our fans are almost always considerate. My fans love me, and I love them—and when I say it, they all know I mean it.*

The arrival of Maria Callas at the Metropolitan Opera was a watershed event in Rudolf Bing's management. Her debut as the tragic heroine of Bellini's *Norma* on the opening night of the 1956/57 season marked the arrival of perhaps the only first-magnitude star not already visible in the galaxy Bing had assembled. Her name, added to the existing roster of Metropolitan artists, ensured that on nearly every cast list excellence prevailed at the Met.

Between 1955 and 1960, Metropolitan audiences would not only hear Maria Callas but sopranos Renata Tebaldi, Zinka Milanov, Licia Albanese, Birgit Nilsson, Victoria de los Angeles, Eleanor Steber, Dorothy Kirsten, Leonie Rysanek, and, in 1961, Leontyne Price. The coloratura ranks boasted not only Roberta Peters but Lily Pons, then in the twilight of her career—and Joan Sutherland would arrive not long afterward. Bassos Cesare Siepi, Jerome Hines, George London, and Bonaldo Giaiotti complemented such stellar baritones as Leonard Warren, Tito Gobbi, Robert Merrill, Martial Singher, and Ettore Bastianini. The mezzo-soprano ranks glistened with Risë Stevens, Fedora Barbieri, Marian Anderson, Regina Resnik, and Rosalind Elias. The roster of tenors boasted Richard Tucker, Jussi Bjoerling, Giuseppe di Stefano, Mario del Monaco, Jon Vickers, Carlo Bergonzi, Nicolai Gedda, and, soon, Franco Corelli, who would make his debut in 1961, in the same performance in which Leontyne Price made hers.

The roster of conductors Bing had gathered was no less impressive—Bruno Walter, Pierre Monteux, Dimitri Mitropoulos, Max Rudolf, Fritz Stiedry, Karl Böhm, Rudolf Kempe, Erich Leinsdorf, and *Wunderkind* Thomas Schippers, among them.

In such heady company, Richard Tucker not only prospered but passed a turning point in his career. When Callas was beginning her tenure with the Metropolitan, Tucker was celebrating his thirteenth season with the company. He had more than twenty roles in his repertoire, and uniformly good reviews to his credit. Thirteen years into his career, he had clearly reached his earliest goals, and he had proven himself with Rudolf Bing and with his colleagues. In every part of his life, there were tangible signs of success. In material terms, he had long ago passed the point of having to worry about his finances; he was earning more than enough to keep his family in a grand style. And he had at last built a steady, if not vociferous, following among the operagoing public.

Still, every age has had its supply of fine singers whose names, when mentioned, occasion kind words from colleagues and nods of approval from opera savants. Tucker would have been one such singer had he done nothing more than sing the roles already in his repertoire and play out a pattern of stability. Every age has also had its legends—a Patti and a De Reszke, a Melba and a Caruso, a Ponselle and a Gigli. Given the choice between a fine career and a legendary one, Richard Tucker—a man with a sense of mission, and a persistent challenger of odds—could be happy only if aiming for the legendary. Tucker now made a conscious decision to strive for what Caruso had achieved—not merely because Caruso had achieved it, but rather because of the challenge it represented. To pursue any lesser goal, in the Tucker world view, would be distinctly second-rate.

Tucker was well aware what it took to rise to such a challenge: belief in himself, and a clear awareness of his strengths and his limitations. His voice remained his first and foremost asset; it was now a full-bodied spinto tenor, and showed signs of becoming still more dramatic. His tone had lost none of its silvery lyricism, yet it had taken on a clarion quality in its upper reaches. "You seldom heard the kind of overtones Richard had in his upper register," Risë Stevens recalled. "His high notes rang. They had strength, but they also had warmth." Though his voice was growing weightier, his solid technique permitted him the luxury of adding heavier roles to his repertoire without having to leave behind the lyric ones of earlier seasons. Over the years, this remained a Tucker trademark: even in his twenty-first season, he would follow Manrico in *Il trovatore* and Radames in *Aida* with letter-perfect Mozart singing in the lyric role of Ferrando in *Così fan tutte*.

If his voice was his greatest asset, his acting remained at least a question mark with many critics. The verdict of most reviewers was that he was still unable to create a wholly believable love interest. In general, his acting reflected little of the abandon that characterized his singing. Often, his movements seemed calculated rather than spontaneous, and externally ordered rather than inwardly motivated. Now and then, to be sure, there were glimpses of another Tucker in the final moments of *La Bohème,* in "Mamma! quel vino è generoso!" in *Cavalleria rusticana,* and in "Un dì all'azzurro spazio" in *Andrea Chénier.* But for the most part, as critic W. J. Henderson once wrote of Gigli, his acting seemed "merely a matter of form—and not very good form, at that."

As he charted his course, the realist in Tucker made him confront his liabilities. If his acting was not always well received, it had noticeably improved under the direction of Garson Kanin, Alfred Lunt, and Tyrone Guthrie—and, he reasoned, it would continue to improve under other stage directors, provided that he worked at it. But, long-term, he felt his acting would be a lesser hindrance than two other obstacles that had to be overcome: first, his lack of European experience and, second, his limited publicity value outside opera and the cantorial tradition.

Of his debits, his lack of European experience seemed the most tangible and the easiest to rectify. Though neither he nor Sara was especially fond of going abroad for weeks and sometimes months at a stretch, they were keenly aware of Richard's need to prove his acceptance in the capitals of Europe. Unlike others such as Bjoerling, Di Stefano, and Del Monaco, Tucker had had no European exposure except for the Verona *Giocondas* of 1947. His La Scala debut had fallen through and, with memories of Verona possibly fading, Tucker feared that unless he could again prove himself abroad, his career would be incomplete. He knew that without a European career he would never be regarded as an "international" artist. Hence, in 1956, with the encouragement of Michael Ries, his agent at Columbia Artists Management, Tucker began actively seeking foreign engagements.

Tucker's publicity value outside the necessarily limited fields of the world of opera and cantorial music presented a more formidable obstacle to be overcome. Though he had sung on tour across the country with the Metropolitan and had built a respectable following from his Chicago radio broadcasts, Tucker was still not well known outside New York City in 1956 and he had no "identity" as far as the general media were concerned. Tucker did not feel comfortable when being interviewed, and he often left even the operatic press with an impression foreign to those who knew him well. "[Tucker] gives off an aura," Met historian Quaintance Eaton once wrote, "of a rather humorless dignity, profound religious feeling, and a businesslike approach to his career." Needless to say, these were not qualities that excited the celebrity-hungry media. No journalist would have described Maria Callas as possessing "a rather humorless dignity"—even if it had been true.

In 1952, Thea Dispeker, hoping to help Tucker shape a new public image, urged him to retain Elizabeth Winston as his press representative. A native New Yorker and an associate of public-relations wizard Constance Hope, Elizabeth Winston had become an independent agent after leaving the Hope organization. When she took on Tucker, she already numbered Van Cliburn, Jascha Heifetz, and Helen Traubel among her clients. "I found Richard to be just as Thea had described him—very warm, considerate, a genuinely lovely man," Miss Winston recalled. "As with everybody who had anything beyond the most casual association with him, I was immediately taken to meet Sara and his three boys. He wanted everyone to know his family, and to feel a part of their lives."

One of Winston's immediate strategies as his press agent, therefore, was to bring his family-man image to the American public. First she persuaded comedian Sam Levenson to feature

Richard and the Tucker boys on his New York–based television show. The opening of the spot actually featured the boys making "complaints" about their singing father, after which Richard made a "surprise" appearance and asked the boys to harmonize as he sang "Goodbye, Good Luck, God Bless You" and "Tell Me (That You Love Me)"—two appropriately wholesome selections, the latter from one of his recent Columbia recordings. He enjoyed these appearances, not only because he was a proud father but also because Levenson's easy-going patter removed the tension he felt in most interview situations.

However, by far the greatest of Elizabeth Winston's early television coups for Tucker occurred when the staff of Edward R. Murrow's popular "Person to Person" series asked her to recommend a musical celebrity whose family life would be interesting to viewers. She had already arranged "Person to Person" appearances for Van Cliburn and Helen Traubel. This time she suggested Richard Tucker. Murrow informally interviewed Richard and Sara, and after the CBS camera crews and technicians checked their Great Neck home for the feasibility of a "live" telecast, they were approved as guests and a date was set for the program.

The format of "Person to Person" was novel in its day. Murrow's idea was to bring the television cameras into the homes of celebrities while he interviewed them by coaxial cable from the CBS studios in Manhattan. Commonplace as the format might seem today, this kind of living-room-to-living-room intimacy had never been done on television. Lacking today's hand-held video cameras, solid-state technology, and mobile broadcasting units, it was an enormous technical feat, especially when one considers that the smallest television camera weighed nearly as much as a Cadillac engine and that blinding studio lights were needed to capture and transmit a clear black-and-white image.

Two weeks before the telecast, CBS crews put in a row of telephone poles in the rear lot of the Tuckers' home. Inside, wooden tracks were carefully laid for the cameras, and nearly five miles of wire were routed through the downstairs rooms. In a day when every announcer and guest was tethered to the control room by wires, guests wore power packs as a short-distance alternative. Men were given the choice of a power pack, strapped above the hips and hidden by the suit coat, or a microphone cable that ran beneath the shirt. In the rehearsals, Tucker tried the trouser-leg rigging, but during the final run-through his eyes suddenly crossed when he tried to sit down. Fearing the prospect of an "electrical *bris,*" he opted instead for the power pack.

Just before air time, the boys told Sara that some of their neighborhood friends had asked if it might be "all right to ring the doorbell and walk in while the show is on." A consultation between the master of the house and the boys' disappointed friends took care of that crisis—and at last, at eight o'clock in the evening, the cameras went on and the familiar profile of Edward R. Murrow, crowned in a wreath of cigarette smoke, appeared on the monitors in the Tuckers' living room. On the air, Murrow conversed with Tucker in his paneled music study and in the dining room, where the table was set for a traditional Sabbath Eve meal. Eventually, Murrow interviewed the whole family, including Levi Perelmuth, then eighty-five.

The "Person to Person" telecast, to everyone's satisfaction, netted more than nine thousand letters and postcards, all clearly indicating that the wholesomeness of the Richard Tucker family had registered across the nation. Coupled with major stories that Elizabeth Winston arranged in the print media—a feature story by Winthrop Sargeant in *Life* proclaiming that the "World's Greatest Tenor is a Cantor from Brooklyn," and the *Time* feature on tenors in which Rudolf Bing predicted that Tucker would one day rival Caruso in the public memory—the "Person to Person" program did much to transform Richard Tucker into a public figure.

Had the "Person to Person" cameras peered unseen into the Tucker home almost any day during the Metropolitan season, the scenes they would have captured would not have been very different from the ones that had been telecast. Most weekday mornings would have found Richard and Sara seated at the round breakfast table in their kitchen. Tucker's early-morning routines had been established early in his marriage, and he rarely varied them. As soon as he awoke, he recited the ritual morning prayers, bathed, and joined Sara at the table by nine or nine-thirty.

About ten o'clock, he would be on his way by train or by car to downtown Manhattan. Nonsinging days in the city were carefully scheduled because of the many people and places he had to visit—Michael Ries at Columbia Artists Management to discuss bookings, Elizabeth Winston to review promotional materials, Wall Street brokerage houses to tend to his stock-market investments, perhaps a rehearsal with coach Joseph Garnett, and almost always a visit with old friends like Ben Herschaft from his fur-market days.

Tucker made it a point to return to Great Neck by six-thirty, in time for the evening meal. During warm stretches in the spring and autumn months, he occasionally played softball with his sons or joined them on the basketball court for a few foul shots. He and Sara often took a long walk after dinner, keeping a leisurely pace and saying hello to their neighbors as they walked.

At this point in his career, when he was singing, Tucker would be in his dressing room early, in ample time to put on his costume and makeup unhurriedly, and also to be able to pay an encouraging call on other cast members. "You can't imagine what a boost it was," basso James Morris recalled, "to have an artist of his accomplishments call on you in your dressing room and tell you that he was pulling for you, and that you were going to be 'just sensational.' " Another of his youthful protégés, Anna Moffo, added that the confidence-building often continued between acts. "Just before the curtain would go up on an act in which I might have especially taxing music to sing, Richard would be waiting for me outside my dressing room. 'Annie, you've already got 'em in the palm of your hand,' he would tell me. 'You're going to make this act come alive, and I'm going to be right there beside you!' Who wouldn't give their very best with encouragement like that?" Though veteran artists hardly needed—or sometimes entirely appreciated—such dressing-room coaching sessions, they accepted this ritual as part of Tucker's nature.

Life once reported that after a performance, whether at the Metropolitan or on tour, Richard and Sara would spend an average of two hours greeting his fans backstage. Whatever the average, Tucker was extremely generous toward his fans and was sincerely interested in them. He inquired about their families, and about their work; he signed their autograph books, record jackets, programs, and anything else they wanted him to inscribe. He always introduced Sara, who would jot down the names and addresses of fans who might have brought mementoes, or who might want autographed photos. Each gift or request was acknowledged no more than a week afterward, usually in a handwritten letter. It was no exaggeration, as his son David remarked, to say that Richard Tucker was as devoted to his fans as they were to him. "Invariably," David recalled, "he was the first one to arrive at the theater, and the last one to leave."

Tucker's generosity also extended to aspiring young singers who wanted an audition, hoping to gather from him an assessment of their chances for a career. In all such cases he was encouraging but unhesitantly candid. "My father wasn't about to encourage someone who had too little to work with," Barry Tucker recalled. "He knew that his opinions carried a lot of weight, not only with young singers but with their voice teachers and with their parents. It wasn't his style to deceive someone about their chances for a career."

Barry remembered one such audition, involving a young soprano whose mother brought her to audition for Tucker at the WEVD studios. "This poor girl was so nervous that she fluffed the first line of her aria, over and over. Dad went over to the piano, put his arm around her shoulder, and went through it with her note by note, tapping out the meter with his finger. Finally she settled into the music and finished the aria—and, naturally, the girl's mother immediately wanted to hear what he thought. He said what he had to say—that the girl didn't have the basic voice and musicianship to make it to the Metropolitan. But the way he said it was so gentle, yet so honest, that the young girl's feelings were never hurt."

When a *Herald Tribune* reporter asked whether he ever grew weary of this time-consuming devotion, Tucker responded, "When I was a cantor, I was on call twenty-four hours a day in case the rabbi was called to another responsibility. The congregation expected many things of me, and I was partially responsible for their well-being. If they had any problems that they brought to me, it was my responsibility to help solve them. I'm not talking about two or three people—I'm talking about a thousand-member congregation in the Bronx, and more than two thousand at the Brooklyn Jewish Center. So, how could I possibly object to something as simple as signing an autograph for a hardworking person who has paid good money to come and hear me sing?"

Whenever possible, Richard and Sara involved their sons in Tucker's career. To varying degrees, all three frequented the Metropolitan and were "regulars" in the goings-on backstage. As adolescents, all three had elements of their father's personality, although none was entirely like him. All three inherited Tucker's passion for the athletic field—all were exceptional baseball players, and both David and Henry were lettermen in football, basketball, and baseball in high school. Tucker was particularly proud of his sons' achievements in football and basketball because, like him, they were short in stature, yet muscular and well coordinated.

Of the three, Barry was the most extrovert: he was the plotter, the deal maker, the strategist. What he sometimes lacked in patience and self-discipline, he made up in the kind of bravado and "street savvy" that had always characterized his father. David was the brightest, scholastically, and was by far the most disciplined of the boys. He was the complete achiever, the one who inherited his father's intensely focused energy and relentless pursuit of long-term goals. Henry, the youngest, claimed the greatest share of Tucker's warmth, patience, generosity, and understanding. His pace was less aggressive than his brothers', though, perhaps more than they, Henry had his father's ability to intuit a person's basic needs and bolster his self-image.

Early on, each boy had learned to lead two lives: one when their parents were at home, and one when they were away. As Richard's career continued to build, demanding more and more traveling, he and Sara would put their housekeeper, Dorothy Mallory, in charge when they were away.

Being black, Catholic, and Southern, Dorothy was initially mystified by the Tuckers' Jewish ways—especially by Levi Perelmuth's Orthodox customs, which he could articulate only in Yiddish. He seemed equally mystified by her Catholicism, and the small statues of the Virgin Mary and the crucified Christ on every wall of her quarters. Overall, the elder Perelmuth—who the Tucker boys came to call "Zadie," from the Yiddish word for "grandfather"—viewed Dorothy rather amusedly, as he would someone from another civilization, a foreigner whose language and behavior seemed to operate by some different and puzzling logic of their own.

Mr. Perelmuth loved to recount Dorothy's idiosyncrasies to Sara and Richard in Yiddish—until, over the years, Dorothy picked up enough Yiddish to be able to eavesdrop.

"*Zie iz meshugge,*" he once told Sara with a laugh, recounting one of Dorothy's foibles while she stood nearby putting away the dishes. "What Papa was telling me," Sara remembered, "was that the way Dorothy did things was crazy—and on top of that he was also sure she cheated when he played cards with her."

"I am *not* crazy," Dorothy suddenly said in her defense. "And another thing, Mr. Zadie, I don't cheat at cards, either!"

Dorothy was frequently a victim of the boys' practical jokes—most of which Barry invented and orchestrated. One spring day, Barry talked Henry into ringing the doorbell and summoning Dorothy to talk to a nonexistent salesman who was supposedly waiting at the garage-door entrance to the house. Meantime, Barry and David, armed with a garden hose, had hidden in the garage—and when Dorothy innocently opened the door, they turned the hose on her. Not to be outdone, she armed herself with a watering can, systematically hunted them, and "baptized" each of the culprits.

But, more often than not, Dorothy covered for them—and occasionally had to go to extraordinary lengths to do so. As Sara recalled, "One Friday night, just after our Sabbath supper, Richard and I took a walk and visited one of our neighbors. When we came home, the boys were unusually quiet—the kind of quiet a mother soon learns to be suspicious about. I checked for damage, but couldn't find anything. The next day, when we returned from temple, the smell of fresh paint wafted down the staircase. I followed my nose and discovered that a whole section of a wall had been patched and painted in one of the bedrooms. The night before, while we were away, Barry and Henry had gotten into a wrestling match. Dorothy told me later that Henry won, but Barry and the wall had lost." Dorothy, the perennial protector, had helped the boys tack a freshly ironed bedsheet over the hole. The sheet disguised the damage until she summoned a plasterer the next day.

Tucker, perhaps remembering his own boyhood excesses, was often oblivious to his sons' pranks. When he learned of them, it was usually after the fact, and he was generally forgiving if not always tolerant of their behavior. If they damaged things, he meted out what he considered appropriate punishment—usually reducing their allowances, or giving them an earlier curfew. A temperate father, but nevertheless a firm disciplinarian, Tucker rarely lost his temper with his sons—but when he did, no one ever forgot the ensuing eruption.

What triggered his temper was any disrespect shown Sara—by anyone, anywhere, but especially by his sons in his own home. "Dad had a very high boiling point, and never lost his temper in public," Henry Tucker recalled. "For someone to get him mad, they would have to do something really thoughtless—that's about the only reason he would get angry. But not with us. All we had to do was say one cross word to Mother in his presence—then it was all over."

Barry Tucker remembered one such incident. "Once, as a teen-ager, I was in a rotten mood—complaining about everything, for no particular reason. I was sitting at the dining-room table in my underwear, with my sleeves rolled up, and was supposed to be doing my homework. This was in the middle of winter, so Mother told me to go put on something warm and then finish my homework. Dad had just gotten home, and was standing by the front door shaking the snow off his coat before hanging it up. Just then I mouthed off to Mother—and, knowing my mood, I must have said something way out of line.

"The next thing I knew, there was a big wooden hanger sticking in the dining-room wall, about a foot from my head. My father *exploded*. I heard him yell, 'The next time you talk back to your mother, I'll make you eat that hanger!' I took off through the garage, still in my underwear, and waited at a neighbor's house until Mother came looking for me."

Not even David, who was generally the best behaved of the three, escaped his father's wrath. A sometime practical joker like his brothers, David once offered his mother a "loaded cigarette." Sara, who occasionally smoked, innocently lit the cigarette while watching television with Richard. David stood by, waiting for the cap inside the cigarette to detonate. When the charge went off, David laughed, but unfortunately, something had gotten into Sara's eyes. Startled, she said loudly, "I can't see anything!" Richard imagined that the charge had blinded her—and immediately flew into a rage.

"I don't think I ever saw him get so mad," Sara remembered. "David took off running, and Richard went after him. Anything that got in his path—furniture, you name it—Richard

just threw it out of the way. David ran into the garage, and I
could hear Richard screaming at him. Thank God, the car was
between them." Sara was equally thankful that David's reflexes
were as keen as they were. In his fury, she discovered afterward,
Richard had hurled a shovel at David, narrowly missing him.

In the late 1950s, as his sons approached college age, Tucker felt
freer to pursue a European career. The responsibilities and joys
he felt as father, coupled with the security of his status at the
Metropolitan, had been the main reason that he waited until his
thirteenth season to try to build a career abroad. But with Barry
enrolled at the University of Cincinnati and David preparing to
enter Tufts University, Tucker seriously began to consider offers
to sing abroad. Meanwhile, he saw to it that they, too, broad-
ened their knowledge of the rest of the world—beginning with
their own country. "In my junior year in high school," Barry
recalled, "Dad arranged to sing only three concerts during a whole
summer, so that the whole family could go on an extended vacation from the East Coast to the West." Interspersed with concerts in Minneapolis, Denver, and Los Angeles, the vacation took
the Tuckers to most of the familiar tourist sites of the American
West—Pike's Peak, the Grand Canyon, Colorado's Estes Park,
Brice Canyon, and Central City.

"It was part of my father's basic philosophy," Barry Tucker
recalled, "to want us to see that there was much more to this
country than what he had already experienced in New York. After
that summer trip to the West, he told us, 'Boys, you're now ready
for Europe.' "

The feelers Tucker and Michael Ries had issued to opera houses
overseas began to yield responses almost immediately. Between
October 1956 and January 1957, Tucker received formal offers to
debut in London at Covent Garden, in Vienna at the Staatsoper,
and in Florence at the Maggio Musicale, or May Festival, in the
birthplace of Italian opera. As he was weighing the merits of each,
the American National Theater and Academy, in conjunction with
the State Department, approached him to make an extended concert tour in the Orient in mid-1957. Suddenly, Tucker found
himself in the pleasant circumstance of having to choose among
several lucrative offers.

The offer from Vienna was no small surprise. Considering the prominence of Herbert von Karajan at the Staatsoper, Tucker was astounded that Vienna seemed eager to have him; Karajan, after all, wielded enormous influence as an impresario, and was aware that Tucker had refused to record under him. Karajan had a chance to issue a refusal of his own, and did so in the offer that he conveyed to Tucker through John Gualiani, in which Karajan stipulated that he did not wish to conduct for Tucker in Vienna. This was more a relief than a rejection, as far as Tucker was concerned; had Karajan offered to conduct for him, Tucker would have asked for someone else—and would likely have jeopardized his Staatsoper debut.

In Vienna, he was to debut in January 1958 as Cavaradossi in *Tosca,* and would also sing Rodolfo in *La Bohème.* In *Tosca,* he would sing with Hilde Zadek as Floria Tosca, and Paul Schoeffler as Scarpia, with Rudolf Kempe conducting. In *Bohème,* Teresa Stich-Randall would portray Mimi, and Berislav Klobucar would conduct.

Luck favored Tucker when Covent Garden's impresario, Rafael Kubelik, agreed to schedule his London debut, also in *Tosca,* in January 1958—only a matter of weeks before he would appear in Vienna. Zinka Milanov was tentatively scheduled to sing Floria Tosca in London, and either Alberto Erede or Alexander Gibson would conduct.

For all of the appeal of London and Vienna, however, the prospect of singing in the Orient held the greatest appeal for Tucker, as he and Sara had never traveled to the Far East. He had been invited through the State Department, which lent additional prestige to the offer. He had heard stories of frenzied audiences, lavish receptions, and unparalleled scenery from Eleanor Steber, who had sung in the Orient the previous year. He had also noted the far-reaching publicity Steber had received during her tour. All of this made him decide to accept the Far East offer, even though it meant having to say no to Florence and its Maggio Musicale because the dates conflicted.

When Tucker received the itinerary for the Far East tour, he wondered how his voice would fare in a totally different climate, with so many performances to sing. Fortunately, he was blissfully unaware of the 110- to 120-degree temperatures he would face in the Orient. His schedule called for him to give concerts in

Bangkok, Singapore, Kuala Lumpur, Hong Kong, Taipei, Seoul, Pusan, and Manila, and he would spend almost three weeks touring most of the major cities in Japan. Scanning the dizzying schedule, he sensed that, except for the two-or-three-day layovers slotted for Singapore, Hong Kong, and Tokyo, he would be going from the concert platform to an ambassador's function to an airplane. If the tour had been any less exotic and challenging, he might have objected. As it was, he couldn't wait to leave San Francisco for Bangkok, his first stop on the tour.

The repertoire he planned to sing was basically the range of arias, oratorio selections, and songs he had incorporated into his regular concert appearances, many on the advice of Alex Alexay, his longtime accompanist. The Canadian-born Alexay, who had also accompanied Peerce, had first played for Tucker in Pittsburgh on January 23, 1949. At the time, Tucker had sung but one other concert, in Montreal in mid-October 1947—an appearance that had not been received by the critics as well as Tucker had hoped. Writing in the *Montreal Gazette,* the reviewer Thomas Archer had praised Tucker's "robust voice, ringing high notes, and completely authentic Italian diction," but had taken him to task for his "penchant for big effects," and for a repertoire that "became monotonous in the course of the program."

Alexay encouraged Tucker to abandon some of the more obscure *Lieder* selections he had sung in Montreal, and replace them with familiar Italian and French arias or songs. "The main thing I encouraged him to do," Alexay remembered, "was to start each segment of the program with something really big—'O tu che in seno' from *Forza,* 'Cielo e mar' from *Gioconda,* or maybe 'Parmi veder le lagrime' from *Rigoletto.* This was the reverse of the way recitalists usually began their programs. Most of them started with light and often obscure songs so that the voice would gradually warm up. To me, that was kid stuff and it used to bore me to death. Richard needed hardly any warm-up, so I got him to begin with a big aria. It allowed him to put himself in command immediately, which was very much the way he was on the opera stage."

Alexay, unfortunately, had to withdraw from the Far East tour when his wife became critically ill a few weeks before the Tuckers were scheduled to leave. In his place, Tucker retained

Erwin Jospe, who had accompanied him in some of his cantorial appearances in Chicago.

Jospe and the Tuckers arrived in Bangkok shortly before 2:00 P.M. on May 4, 1957. Tucker and Jospe spent the rest of the afternoon reviewing the four basic programs Tucker had prepared with Alex Alexay. The "A" program, the one chosen for Bangkok, was the one Richard sang most frequently on the tour. He began with a group of demanding arias—"If with all your hearts" from Mendelssohn's *Elijah,* followed by "Sound an alarm!" from Handel's *Judas Maccabaeus,* "Una furtiva lagrima" from Donizetti's *L'elisir d'amore,* and "Che gelida manina" from *La Bohème.*

After an intermission, as had Alexay in his concert appearances with Tucker, Jospe played two selections alone—usually a Chopin nocturne and perhaps a tarantella. Then, Tucker returned to the stage and sang a group of English and American songs; typically, he chose Nordoff's "Can Life Be a Blessing?" Weaver's "The Abbot of Derry," Taylor's "A Song for Lovers," and Edwards's "Awake, Beloved!" (He had planned to sing a few popular songs from *The King and I,* but was told, fortunately ahead of time, that the film had been banned in Thailand because of its supposed immorality.) He concluded the "A" program with the Flower Song from *Carmen,* and sang Neapolitan songs by Paolo Tosti for encores.

Programs "B," "C," and "D" involved variations mainly among the arias in the first part of the program. In Saigon and Singapore, for example, he followed "Sound an alarm!" with "Il mio tesoro" from Mozart's *Don Giovanni* and "E lucevan le stelle" from *Tosca.* Occasionally, he included a Neapolitan gem of the variety of Nutile's "Mamma mia, che vo' sapè?" which had come to the Orient a half-century earlier on an imported Victor Red Seal recording by Caruso.

To his pleasant surprise, Tucker also discovered that his own recordings had a considerable following in the Far East. This partially accounted for the intensity of the audiences' reception and enthusiasm in the many capitals in which he sang.

Wherever he appeared, the reviews he received—most of them written by qualified English or American reviewers living in the Far East—were of the highest order. In Seoul, where seven thousand Koreans packed a theater designed for four thousand, Tucker's oratorio singing was praised as having been executed "with a precision that can be best described as instrumental," and his Mozart singing led the reviewer to commend his "exemplary finesse, fine sense of line, and impeccable articulation." In Manila, the *Chronicle* maintained that he "seemed to fall in love with his audience," to the point that he not only "contained his annoyance when some people over-enthusiastically clapped *on*, not after, his prolonged, climactic note in 'E lucevan le stelle,' " but also "sang for them with all the verve and gusto he was capable of" in a string of encores that included "Vesti la giubba" from *Pagliacci*, "La donna è mobile" from *Rigoletto*, and Leoncavallo's ballad "Mattinata."

In Hong Kong he sang twice—and he pulled out all the stops in his first appearance. At the expansive Empire Theatre on May 21, 1957, the audience in the auditorium rose en masse and cheered him for nearly five minutes when he walked onstage. As shouts of opera titles rang out from the crowd, he knew instantly that he was facing a knowledgeable and opera-starved audience. As he bowed repeatedly to their cheers, he cupped his hand to his ear, as if to tell them that he was ready to sing their requests. The gesture yielded even louder cries for the familiar arias of Verdi, Mascagni, and Puccini. Amid them could be heard an occasional shout of "Mozart! Mozart!"

Turning to Erwin Jospe—who had given up any thought of beginning the concert until the crowd grew less vociferous—Tucker said over the cheering, "If they want me *this* bad, I'm gonna give 'em something they'll never forget!" For the next two hours, according to the Hong Kong newspapers, he did just that. With no time away from the stage except during Jospe's two solos, he picked arias from all four of his programs—and, when the mood struck him, he simply called out titles to Jospe, building the audience to a feverish pitch. By evening's end, he had sung not only the Mendelssohn and Handel oratorio pieces, but had added, "Champs paternels" from Méhul's sacred opera *Joseph,* "M'appari" from Flotow's *Martha,* "Mamma! quel vino è generoso!" from *Cavalleria,* "O tu che in seno agl'angeli" from *Forza del destino,* "Una furtiva lagrima" from *Elisir d'amore,* and "E lucevan le stelle" from *Tosca*—an incredibly taxing sequence that he *capped* with "Il mio tesoro" from *Don Giovanni,* before Jospe played his solo pieces. Jospe, too, had to make additions, even playing excerpts from Gershwin's "Rhapsody in Blue" for the cheering audience.

The reviewer Ernst Gottschalk, writing in the *South China Morning Post* the next day, praised the "magnificently commanding voice of Richard Tucker" and the "technique and art with which he used it." The oratorio gems, though not well known to the audience, "made it clear at once," said Gottschalk, "that one was listening to a singer of operatic pre-eminence, a singer who does not rely solely on the immediacy of the appeal of a splendid voice but who has the ability to use such a beautiful voice for expressive and dramatic purposes." Commented the reviewer for the *China Mail,* "the large and friendly audience had the opportunity to hear one of the finest voices and greatest singers in the world." Added the Hong Kong *Standard,* "the artistry and musicianship which has made [Tucker] so renowned only made us wish that he could stay among us."

Only once did he encounter any form of hostility during the Far East tour. In Taipei, anti-American rioting broke out shortly before Richard and Sara landed. Although no attaché met their plane, they thought nothing of it because U.S. Ambassador Carl Rankin, who had made the flight with them, had given them no advance warning of any trouble. When the Tuckers and Jospe reached the Grand Hotel in Taipei, they were told the concerts had been canceled—and a harrowing series of events ensued.

"Richard was supposed to inaugurate Taipei's new auditorium, but the government had declared martial law and had imposed a strict curfew," Sara remembered. "No one was allowed on the streets after dark, which meant that Richard couldn't perform. I sensed something was wrong at the airport, because there were Formosan soldiers in battle gear all over the place. From what we could gather, an American GI had killed a Formosan who was reputed to be a voyeur, spying on the American soldiers' wives. Apparently, the Formosans wanted to try the GI, but the Army had whisked him out of the country for his own safety. In retaliation, the Formosans launched a series of demonstrations, which led the government to impose martial law."

At the Grand Hotel, the Tuckers heard intermittent gunfire from their first-floor suite. "Our room had large French windows that opened onto the street," Sara recalled. "I was petrified because in the midst of all the chaos, anyone could have walked into our room and shot us in our sleep."

The manager of the Grand Hotel did his best to entertain the Tuckers, and gave them a dinner party in the hotel's lavishly decorated dining room. During the meal, as the stewards served wine, Tucker lightened the tension by singing a chorus of the "Libiamo" from *La traviata*. But at the end of the meal, he and the other guests found themselves staring at a detachment of Formosan soldiers.

"We were still in the dining room when the curfew siren sounded," Sara remembered. "Before we knew what was happening, an armored car came to a halt in front of the hotel. Formosan soldiers poured into the lobby, their rifles in their hands, and came into the dining room. We didn't move for fear we would be shot. The soldiers just stood there, looking around the room, and then staring at us. Finally, one of them said something, and they all turned on their heels and left the hotel."

In the streets, the gunfire continued sporadically through the night. The next morning, the manager of the hotel admitted to the Tuckers that he could no longer hope to guarantee their safety.

"We were told we had one last chance to get out of Taipei that day," Sara said. "There was one flight that would take us out of Formosa, if we could get to the airport safely. We had to have a special stamp for our passports in order to board the plane—but the local library, which issued the stamps, had been burned to the ground in a demonstration. Finally, the hotel manager got the stamps for us, and got us to the airport in one piece. For a moment, we thought the Formosans were going to detain us. But after the manager from the hotel told them that we were part of a State Department tour, and that we had had nothing to do with the problems in Taipei, they put us on a plane and let us go."

Later, Tucker learned that one of his predecessors had had a similar experience in Taipei. Thirty-two years earlier—to the very day, May 24—a Canadian tenor, one Edward Johnson, had sung in Taipei in the middle of Chinese Communist–supported riots in Formosa in 1925.

In Korea, President and Madame Syngman Rhee offset this single instance of anti-Americanism by giving the Tuckers a warm diplomatic reception. At the invitation of the president, Tucker sang for the guests at the presidential palace. After a luncheon-

and-tea afternoon reception, the Austrian-born Madame Rhee presented Sara with a *kakemono,* an ornately embroidered scroll that had been crafted by Korean war widows.

Several Korean cities held warm memories for the Tuckers—especially Richard's concert in Seoul, the diplomatic reception of President and Madame Rhee, and, in Pusan, a moment of comedy that occurred just before Richard's concert there. "We stayed at a U.S. Army compound in Pusan," Sara remembered, "and the accommodations were not what you would call luxurious. Late in the afternoon on the day Richard was to sing, I decided to take my shower and begin to get ready while he rested for the performance.

"The shower was kind of primitive and the water none too warm, but at least it worked—for a while, anyway. Just as I was about to rinse the shampoo from my hair, the water suddenly stopped running. I turned the faucets on and off, and nothing happened. I called to Richard to come and help me, and he couldn't get a drop of water out of the plumbing, either.

"By this time, I was shivering, frustrated, and covered with soapsuds. I kept shouting to Richard, 'Do something! If you don't, I'm never going to make it to the concert!' He said he'd call the commander of the base.

"All of a sudden, I heard a very loud siren. At first I thought it was an air raid or some kind of military alert, and I panicked. I thought, what am I going to do now? Wrap myself in a towel and run to a shelter?

"Soon I realized that the siren was from a fire engine. That was some consolation—until it pulled up in front of our door. 'God help us!' I yelled to Richard, 'this place is on fire!' I started reaching for towels and robes. Richard was in the next room, and seemed to be paying more attention to what was going on outside than to my anxiety. I couldn't figure out how he could be so calm!

"The next thing, I heard footsteps on the roof of the place. I grabbed a towel, feeling sure that any second the firemen might have to chop a hole in the roof or something. I kept yelling for Richard, but he was already outside and couldn't hear me. That made me mad, because I expected him to worry about my safety before his own.

"Just as I got a towel around me and was ready to run out

of the shower, the water suddenly came back on. I heard some more footsteps on the roof, and in a few moments the fire engine pulled away.

"Richard sauntered into the bathroom, as if nothing had happened, and said, 'Are you done in there yet?' I was still scared. I wanted him to assure me that the men put out the fire. 'Are you absolutely sure they got it all?' I asked.

"He looked at me like I was crazy. 'Fire? What the hell are you talking about,' he said with a laugh. 'The cistern on the roof was empty, so the men filled it with a fire hose.' "

Overwhelming as his reception in the Orient was, Tucker treasured two private memories that endured far longer than all the dinner parties, testimonials, and cultural-exchange affairs. One involved an incident in Kuala Lumpur. There, Tucker was greeting a long line of well-wishers backstage after his concert, and as the line gradually thinned, he and Sara took notice of an impoverished-looking teen-age boy who they thought must be awaiting parents or relatives.

After a while, they began to wonder if the youth was lost. Eventually, Tucker asked one of the interpreters to question the boy about his parents' whereabouts. Haltingly, the boy said he was alone. He reached inside his shirt and pulled out a frayed news clipping. The interpreter recognized it as an announcement of Tucker's concert, clipped from a newspaper in the city of Seremban—nearly a hundred miles away. Under further questioning, the boy said that he had walked and hitchhiked all the way to Kuala Lumpur "just to touch the American who made music come from his throat." When Tucker had the interpreter ask the youth why he walked such an enormous distance, he answered that if Tucker had come to Malaysia all the way from America, it was only fitting that he should make the journey to Kuala Lumpur to see him and touch him. Tucker listened incredulously as the interpreter explained that the boy intended to hike through the night back to Seremban. Tucker gave one of the attachés money to feed and clothe the boy and see to his safe return home.

A second memorable moment took place on the streets of Yokohama, Japan, after Tucker and Erwin Jospe had finished a rehearsal and were waiting for someone from the embassy to take them back to Tokyo. Sara was waiting with them as a wispy young girl, no more then ten years old, approached Tucker and shyly asked one of the interpreters in their party whether she could present a gift she had made in her provincial school. When the interpreter relayed her request to Tucker, he smiled and said he would gladly accept her gift—but he was scarcely prepared for what she gave him.

The girl took his hand and, with a proud smile, slipped onto his finger a delicately carved bronze ring. On the face of the ring, she had painstakingly etched his initials. She had worked on it for months, she said, because her teacher had told her that Richard Tucker, a great American, would be coming to her country to sing for her people. The touching simplicity of her gesture deeply affected Tucker, and he fought back tears as he accepted her gift.

Franco Corelli had been the talk of London opera circles in the 1956/57 season, when he sang Cavaradossi to Zinka Milanov's Tosca in one of the best-received productions of the Covent Garden year. The next season, 1957/58, Corelli's prominence as an Italian tenor was rivaled by two American-born tenors who happened to be appearing in London at the same time. One of them, Richard Tucker, was to follow Corelli as Cavaradossi at Covent Garden. The other, Mario Lanza, was to appear in concert at the Royal Albert Hall.

Had Rafael Kubelik, the newly installed musical director of Covent Garden, been able to adhere to his original policies, the British public might not have heard Richard Tucker at all. For, according to Kubelik, Tucker represented what the new management did not want: he was a visitor rather than a native, he was essentially an Italian tenor, and, worst of all, he was an opera *star*. Kubelik, like Rudolf Bing, disliked so-called stars—and especially the "visiting artist" kind. "They come and go and have no idea of real artistic cooperation," he had said of them in his first press conference as musical director. He might have added that most of them would not have agreed to come to Covent Garden with the additional stipulation Kubelik had in mind—namely, that they should sing all their performances in English. The cornerstone of his management planning, he announced early on, would be "productions sung in English by English artists."

Kubelik's plans as musical director, however, soon went awry:

the British wanted internationally acclaimed artists (or, to use the forbidden word, *stars*), and the artists wanted to sing in the languages to which they were accustomed. Had Kubelik refused to bend his posture, Covent Garden would not have attracted (as it did in the 1956/57 season) Zinka Milanov in *Tosca* and *Il trovatore,* Victoria de los Angeles in *Madama Butterfly,* and Maria Callas in *Norma.* Whether Tucker might have agreed to sing *Tosca* in English, as he had *La Bohème* at the Metropolitan, was immaterial by the time he signed his contract: when Kubelik had approached Franco Corelli the season before, Corelli's management had firmly declared that he would sing Cavaradossi in Italian or not at all.

The January night when Tucker made his Covent Garden debut, Mario Lanza asked to attend the performance. Tucker saw to it that Lanza and his wife, Betty, would sit with Sara and their London agent in the Tucker box. As the Covent Garden boxes were small compared to the Metropolitan's, prime seating space was a bit limited. Lanza, not wanting to call attention away from Tucker and the stage, insisted that he sit in the rear of the box, out of the public's view. Sara understood and appreciated the gesture, knowing well of Lanza's celebrity—a fact underscored by the eight thousand screaming fans who packed the Royal Albert Hall for each of his concerts.

Between acts, fearing photographers and autograph seekers, Lanza stayed in the box with Betty and Sara. He talked about Richard, Sara remembered, as if he were discussing Gigli, Martinelli, or one of the other tenor idols of his youth. He wanted to know how Tucker had got his start in opera, how much he practiced vocalizing each day, how long he spent preparing various roles—the full gamut of in-the-business questions, which Sara answered as best she could.

After the final curtain calls, Lanza asked Sara how Tucker liked to wind down after performing. She answered that usually he liked to go to a good restaurant, eat a late-night meal of eggs, lox, fresh bread, orange juice, and a piece of pie or other pastry, and enjoy a highball or two with his guests.

"Tonight, I've got just the right restaurant for the two of you," Lanza said. "We'll call it the Café Lanza, our suite at the Dorchester Hotel. We don't want to let you and Richard get away from us without some more time together. So you come to our suite as soon as you get done backstage, and I'm going to have everything that Richard likes to eat."

When Richard and Sara were ushered into the foyer of the Lanzas' enormous suite at the Dorchester, a butler escorted them to the long dining table that dominated one of the rooms. True to Lanza's word, every item that Sara had mentioned was awaiting Tucker at the head of the table; there were even two tall glasses of fresh orange juice, and the exact brands of bourbon and mix that Tucker preferred.

"You'll forgive me, Richard, but the only thing I forgot to ask Sara was how you like your eggs," Lanza said apologetically. "I'll have the cook fix them right now, so they'll be nice and hot for you."

As the two men sat at the table and talked, Tucker ate leisurely while Lanza drank large quantities of mineral water and German beer. Lanza ate nothing all evening, and explained that he was on a strict diet. He was suffering from periodic attacks of gout and high blood pressure, and was doing his best to rid himself of the fifty-or-so pounds he had gained in Italy, in exile from troubles that had plagued him in Hollywood.

"Richard, you wouldn't believe what they put me through to get thin," Lanza said, telling of sanitarium confinements, diet pills, and intravenous feeding, all for the sake of the cameras.

For the rest of the evening, the two men talked like long-lost friends, about their childhoods, years of vocal training, first breaks, their religious backgrounds, ethnic roots, family lives— topics normally reserved for classmates at a reunion, and unusual for two men who had nothing more in common, ostensibly, than their American birthplaces and tenor voices. In retrospect, Sara reflected, "It was as if Mario wanted to figure out why Richard's life had gone one direction, and his own life another. He was very subdued that night and seemed to hang on to every word Richard spoke. He seemed to want and need a friendly ear, and in Richard he found one." Lanza was happiest, Sara observed, when he was talking about his boyhood in Philadelphia, his mother and father, and his children. His career, in contrast, seemed far less fulfilling. "Richard and I both got the impression," Sara said, "that, for all his wealth and great success, Mario wasn't really happy. Something important, something very basic, seemed missing from his life."

As for Lanza's gossip-column reputation for boorish behavior, the Tuckers saw nothing resembling it. "First of all, Richard paid no attention to anybody's so-called reputation, particularly as it was reported in a secondhand way," Sara pointed out. "He felt there were always two sides to every story, and that the celebrity's side often wasn't heard. As for Mario, he was the essence of a gentleman—as Richard liked to say of him, he was 'a regular guy.' He was extremely polite, warm, friendly, and very well-spoken. We knew him only briefly, but we felt he was really our friend."

When the Lanzas and the Tuckers said good-bye at three-thirty in the morning, they vowed that they would spend more time together—maybe even plan a trip when the Lanzas returned to the States. But Mario Lanza never returned home. Eighteen months later, while undergoing an intravenous treatment for weight-loss, he died in a sanitarium in Rome. He was thirty-eight years old.

Tucker arrived in Vienna on a bitter-cold January afternoon, armed with a folio of London reviews that in the main were as favorable as those he had received in the States. Ernest Newman, the veteran critic of the London *Sunday Times,* wrote that his Cavaradossi "had all the verve of his great predecessors in the role," and was sung with "extraordinary command of technique" and "genuine finesse in phrasing and line." Tucker hoped for the same reception from the Vienna critics, and was confident after his first rehearsal for *Tosca,* despite the differences between the Covent Garden and Staatsoper productions. Chief among these differences was one of language: while Tucker was accorded the privilege of singing the role in Italian, the rest of the cast would sing their parts in German. The only exceptions would be the better-known duets, which his Tosca, soprano Hilde Zadek, would also sing in Italian.

John Gualiani met Richard and Sara at the famed Sacher Hotel, where they were booked for a ten-day stay. Natalie Eisenstadt, a friend and former neighbor from Brooklyn days, joined them at the Sacher on the day of the final *Tosca* rehearsal. With little time between his opening and closing performances of *Tosca* and the *Bohème* sandwiched between them, extensive sightseeing was out of the question. So, they stayed mainly in the area of the

Sacher, where Tucker's chief contact with Vienna's delights was his daily ration of *Sachertorten*.

We have Tucker's own word, attested to by John Gualiani, that Vienna was the site of the greatest single performance of his entire career. The performance took place not on the stage of the Staatsoper—though, to be sure, the acclaim he received there was phenomenal—but instead in the pulpit of the venerable old synagogue in Vienna's Jewish quarter.

Over dinner on a Sabbath Eve, Dr. Akiba Eisenberg, chief rabbi of the historic Seitenstettengasse synagogue, had extended an invitation to Tucker to conduct *Shabbos* services the next morning. The rabbi tendered the invitation rather apologetically, as the congregation had no money to pay Tucker. No doubt, he would have declined their stipend anyway, just for the privilege of singing a service in the same synagogue in which the first of the long line of modern cantors—Salomon Sulzer, whose liturgical works Tucker had first studied under Cantor Weisser—had sung *Shabbos* services a hundred years earlier.

Tucker immediately accepted the rabbi's invitation—and in a matter of hours, word had spread through the Jewish quarter that *Hazzan* Tucker, whose cantorial recordings had long ago established his reputation in much of Europe, would sing the morning services.

Sara Tucker would never forget the emotion that *Shabbos* morning:

"The synagogue was already full by the time we arrived, and there was a large crowd awaiting us outside. As we made our way to the steps, we saw a warm and familiar face in the crowd. Emanuel List, the great bass, was living in Vienna and had come to share this moment with us. He and Richard embraced, and they entered the synagogue together.

"As is the custom in an Orthodox congregation, the women sat in the gallery upstairs, so Natalie Eisenstadt and I took our seats with Rebbitsin Eisenberg, the rabbi's wife. There were people everywhere—upstairs in the gallery, downstairs in the sanctuary, and in the hallways, anywhere a person could find room enough to stand.

"What was so haunting was the congregation itself. Many of the people were older—over fifty or sixty years old, maybe—and then there were youngsters in their teens. It was as if a middle generation was missing—the parents of the children, the sons and daughters of the elders, victims of the Nazi death camps of the Holocaust.

"I will never forget the emotion and the power of Richard's prayers that morning as he stood beneath the immense, sky-blue dome of the synagogue. There was no choir, and he sang alone. But I like to think that there *was* a choir singing with him—an unseen choir of the Viennese Jews murdered by the Nazis. Their souls were Richard's choir."

John Gualiani, who was present, heard an outpouring of vocal power and drama that he had never heard before. "I knew Richard's voice intimately," Gualiani said, "and that day he sang more powerfully than at any other time in my memory. As a Gentile, I couldn't follow what he was singing the way the congregation could. So I just listened to the beauty of his voice. Believe me, this was a once-in-a-lifetime moment.

"Later, I asked him whether he was aware himself how incredibly he had sung that morning. He told me that he realized it, and that he felt he had never sung better in his life."

Natalie Eisenstadt remembered the emotion of the congregation even after the service had concluded:

"The elderly people, especially, sat in their seats and cried. For nearly twenty years, they had not heard the prayers of a *hazzan* like Richard Tucker. They were so moved by his singing that they surrounded him like a king, hoping to embrace him and thank him personally. As Sara and I and the rebbitsin left the upstairs gallery, we saw elderly women actually kneel down and kiss Richard's feet, they were so moved."

In tribute and in gratitude, many in the congregation formed a procession, walking fifteen blocks with the Tuckers, from the synagogue on the Judenstrasse to the Sacher Hotel.

On the night of his debut, Tucker was his unshakable self as he sat at his dressing table putting the final touches on his makeup. There was a knock at the door, which he first took to be a signal to take his place backstage. When Sara opened the door, Herbert von Karajan walked briskly into the dressing room.

"Mr. Tucker," the maestro said with a click of the heels, "I welcome you to the Staatsoper. I wish you good luck in your performances."

Protocol thus carried out, Karajan bowed politely to Sara and made his exit. Tucker admired him for the gesture. "He was a gentleman," he said of the event in retrospect. "He had his obligations and I had mine."

As it had in London, "Recondita armonia" worked its charm in Vienna. The ease and fluidity with which the climactic phrase— "Tosca! sei tu!"—rang out in the two-thousand-seat auditorium primed the audience for a *Tosca* the Viennese would long remember. With Paul Schoeffler as Scarpia, Hilde Zadek sang and acted the title role memorably, and delivered a commendable "Vissi d'arte." The critics recorded, nevertheless, that the evening belonged to Richard Tucker. His "E lucevan le stelle" merited one of the most prolonged ovations anyone could remember, and the suaveness of his "O dolci mani" led one critic to write that "surely his throat is lined with the purest of silver." The audience showed its enthusiasm at the end of the performance, when he was accorded some twenty curtain calls.

Happy and hungry—his usual state after a well-received performance—Tucker changed into street clothes, gathered Sara, Natalie, and John, and made his way through the backstage crowd, returning handshakes and stopping to sign programs on his way to the stage door. Preparing himself for the freezing weather outside, he gave an extra tug to his wool muffler and swung open the large metal door to the street.

A wave of cheers greeted him as the door made its arc. Newspaper accounts the next day estimated that between seven and eight hundred people stood waiting for him in the bitter cold.

As the mob surged forward, many of them waving programs and envelopes, he shouted to John Gualiani, "For God's sake, take care of Sara and Natalie! I'm not moving!" With the help of interpreters, the crowd soon grew quiet and orderly. One official of the Staatsoper told Tucker that almost all the people wanted an autograph or, preferably, a signed photograph; as was apparently the practice among many Vienna opera lovers, most had prepared postpaid envelopes, hoping that Tucker's management would send them a photo. John helped gather the envelopes and stuffed them into shopping bags, empty boxes, anything he could find in the backstage area. Meanwhile, Tucker shook as many hands as he could, and signed more than a hundred programs before he asked the interpreter to tell the crowd that he would somehow answer their written requests.

Sara and Natalie had arrived safely at the Sacher well before Tucker and John made their way to the hotel. Sara had looked forward to a quiet dinner as a foursome in the hotel dining room, but Tucker suddenly altered their plans.

"Have them send up some food," he said. "We've all got work to do."

From midnight until four-thirty in the morning, sustained by sandwiches, orange juice, and tea, Tucker signed his name to nearly five hundred publicity photos—almost the entire stock he had brought to Europe from Columbia Artists Management. Many were of recent roles, but as the stock dwindled, there were several photographs from the late 1940s. When he ran out of those, he signed hotel stationery. Sara, Natalie, and John, like three workers on an assembly line, stuffed and sealed the mailing envelopes.

At fifteen minutes till five, the exhausted foursome deposited their bundles in the mail slots in the Sacher's lobby. Vienna's Mario Cavaradossi, to borrow a phrase from Longfellow, had "earned a night's repose."

10

Q: It's always been very clear that you have a strong sense of self, and, as you say, a very strong will. Some might say that you have a very big ego—maybe too big?

A: Oh, now and then some people at the Met might say, "Tucker's the Number One Tenor in the World—just ask him." I'm not that egotistical. There's room enough for everybody, I've always said. I believe in myself, sure. But as long as the people and the critics list me as one of the greats, that's good enough.

After his successes in London and Vienna, Tucker's return to New York was to a degree anticlimactic. The bulk of his appearances at the Metropolitan were as Lenski in the new production of Tchaikovsky's seldom-heard *Eugene Onegin,* in which he had opened the 1957/58 season. *Onegin* had not been staged at the Metropolitan since 1921, when Giovanni Martinelli had sung Lenski to Claudia Muzio's Tatiana and Giuseppe de Luca's Onegin. In the new Rolf Gérard–designed revival, Tucker was in the presence of a strong cast—George London as Onegin, Rosalind Elias as Olga, and Lucine Amara as Tatiana. Yet he disliked the role of Lenski and soon grew weary of it.

Not even the best-known moment in the opera—Lenski's aria, which Tucker sang in English as "What is the coming day preparing?"—was sufficient inducement for him to keep the role in his repertoire. He eventually dropped it because, he told the *New York Times,* "My public doesn't like me in a role where I die in the second act."

Nevertheless, *Eugene Onegin* did afford Tucker the opportunity to sing under the baton of Dimitri Mitropoulos, for whom he had the highest esteem—as did Mitropoulos for him. "Of the spinto and dramatic tenors I have worked with at the Metropolitan," Mitropoulos once told the New York Philharmonic's Bruno Zirato, "Tucker is not only the one whose [vocal] production is the best, but also is the one I can always count on. He is the one whose standards are to me the highest, and it is rare when he fails to meet them."

Mitropoulos's reference to Tucker as one of the Metropolitan's "spinto and dramatic tenors" is especially significant—not only in regard to the new roles Tucker had now begun to study but also because Bing had assigned several newly arrived lyric tenors to roles with which Tucker had long been associated. Between 1955 and 1958 a number of lyric tenors had made respectable debuts at the Metropolitan—among them Giuseppe Campora, Carlo Bergonzi, Eugenio Fernandi, Nicolai Gedda, and Flaviano Labò. To varying degrees, each fell heir to lyric roles Tucker had sung during his first decade with the Metropolitan. Fernandi made his debut as Pinkerton, Gedda distinguished himself as Faust, Labò as Edgardo in *Lucia,* and Bergonzi made a strong impression in *Tosca, Bohème,* and *Lucia* as well.

Except for Faust, whose range did not entirely suit him as his voice grew heavier, Tucker kept these roles in his own repertoire and returned to them from time to time—especially Cavaradossi in *Tosca* and Rodolfo in *La Bohème,* which remained among his favorites. More frequently, however, he concentrated on his "specialties"—the Duke in *Rigoletto* (which, interestingly, he shared with Peerce, although it did not bring the two of them into personal contact), Don José in *Carmen,* Enzo in *Gioconda,* and Alvaro in *Forza del destino*—roles that his maturing dramatic voice fit handsomely. There were further challenges in the offing as well. Between these roles and Otello, the weightiest dramatic role in the Italian repertoire, there lay such enticements as Radames in *Aida,* Manrico in *Il trovatore,* Calaf in *Turandot,* and Dick Johnson in *La fanciulla del West*—all of which would eventually enter Tucker's Metropolitan repertoire.

In the decade that had elapsed since Tucker had signed his long-term contract with Columbia Records, the recording industry had followed an unpredictable course. The "renaissance at a new speed" which *High Fidelity*'s Roland Gelatt had envisioned with the advent of the Columbia LP had indeed occurred—but not in the form

Zinka Milanov, as Maddalena in <u>Andrea Chénier</u>, acknowledges the applause of (left to right) Rudolf Bing, Tucker, and Robert Merrill in the final performance of her career, April 13, 1966. (Louis Melancon/Metropolitan Opera Archives)

The Mario Lanzas greet Tucker after his Covent Garden debut in Puccini's <u>Tosca</u>, January 1958. Like Frank Sinatra, whom Tucker greatly admired, Lanza's highly charged singing made him a Tucker favorite. Left to right are conductor Alexander Gibson, Richard and Sara Tucker, John Coast (of Columbia Artists Management), and Betty and Mario Lanza. (Elizabeth Winston)

With Leontyne Price during a break in the recording sessions for RCA's <u>Madama Butterfly</u>, Rome, 1962. (John Ross/Courtesy of Hubert Dilworth)

After a concert in Tokyo during his 1957 tour of the Far East, Tucker demonstrates a phrase while signing autographs. (Elizabeth Winston)

Paying a mid-afternoon visit to Arturo Toscanini at Lago Maggiore, Italy. (Mrs. Richard Tucker)

Onstage in Saigon, 1957, with Erwin Jospe at the piano. (Elizabeth Winston)

David Tucker (extreme left) receives an informal voice lesson from tenor Giacomo Lauri-Volpi (seated), while John Gualiani, Sara, and Richard listen. "Leave the boy with me for a year, and I'll give him a technique," Lauri-Volpi said—to which Tucker politely answered no. (Dr. David N. Tucker)

Tucker with his "first ladies" on the evening of the gala performance marking the silver anniversary of his Metropolitan debut, April 1970. Left to right are Renata Tebaldi, Leontyne Price, and Joan Sutherland. (Henry Grossman/Time-Life, Inc.)

As Radames in Aida in his first performance of the role at the Metropolitan, January 1965. Though Tucker had sung Radames in concert under Toscanini, he waited sixteen years and twenty-six roles later until he felt ready for Aida's demands. (Frank Dunand/Metropolitan Opera Archives)

With Francis Robinson, then Assistant General Manager of the Metropolitan, at the celebration following Tucker's silver anniversary gala, April 1970. (Henry Grossman/Time-Life, Inc.)

After his silver anniversary gala, Tucker receives an embrace from Franco Corelli. Tucker considered Corelli a peerless Calaf, Romeo, and Werther and envied his enormous popularity. Corelli genuinely admired Tucker and envied his immunity to nervousness. Though initially rivals, the two became warm friends. (Henry Grossman/Time-Life, Inc.)

Terence Cardinal Cooke presents special cufflinks to Tucker on the occasion of his and Sara's thirty-fifth wedding anniversary, February 1971. The Tuckers celebrated the event in grand style at the Plaza Hotel in New York City. (Bill Mark)

With Sara, receiving from New York Mayor John V. Lindsay the coveted Handel Medallion, the city's highest cultural award. Tucker was given the award in 1970 for "distinguished achievement in the arts and dedicated service to humanity." (Whitestone Photo/Courtesy of Alix B. Williamson)

(ABOVE) As Canio in the Franco Zeffirelli production of Leoncavallo's *I pagliacci, with Teresa Stratas as Nedda, 1970. "Not even Olivier could have equaled Tucker's acting as Canio," Schuyler Chapin declared. (Henry Grossman)*

(ABOVE LEFT) As Rodolfo in Verdi's Luisa Miller, with Montserrat Caballé in the title role, 1967. As they did not have a language in common, Tucker and Caballé had to improvise offstage—she addressed him in German and he answered her in Yiddish. (Louis Melancon/Metropolitan Opera Archives)*

(LEFT) With Robert Merrill in concert at Carnegie Hall, 1973. "He was an original, my friend Ruby," Merrill said years after Tucker's death. "I still think about him—and I always end up asking him, wherever he is now, 'Why did you leave us so soon?'" © (Beth Bergman)*

In concert with Sherrill Milnes, at the Ravinia Festival in Chicago, 1969. Tucker judged Milnes's promise immense from the first time they were paired in La forza del destino. During one of the rehearsals, Milnes remembered, Tucker grew impatient with what he considered awkward stage directions. "Listen, kid, forget this stuff," Tucker told Milnes. "When this rehearsal is over, I'll show you how Lennie Warren and I used to do it." (Courtesy of Sherrill Milnes)

With conductor James Levine after a concert performance of Verdi's Simon Boccanegra in Cleveland, Ohio. "One of my most touching memories of Richard," Levine has said, "happened on the day of my debut. Just as I was about to leave my dressing room for the podium, Richard called me and said, 'Don't be nervous, Jim—remember, you're the greatest, and they're gonna love you.'" (Hastings-Willinger & Associates)

La Juive was much on Tucker's mind when he visited soprano Rosa Ponselle, then living in retirement in a villa near Baltimore. Ponselle, who had sung Rachel to Caruso's Eléazar a half-century earlier, heard Tucker sing several sections of the score during his visit. "By all rights," she said later, "Richard's Eléazar would have been definitive." (Baltimore News American)

For years Tucker lobbied for a fully staged Juive in America. The New Orleans Opera gave him his wish. Here, as Eléazar, Tucker intones a prayer in the Passover Scene. (Courtesy of Gerald Fitzgerald)

Receiving an honorary doctorate from the Reverend Theodore M. Hesburgh, president of the University of Notre Dame, 1965. Two other distinguished recipients were Bernard Jan Cardinal Alfrink (left), Archbishop of Utrecht, and National Security Adviser McGeorge Bundy. (Bruce Harlan/University of Notre Dame)

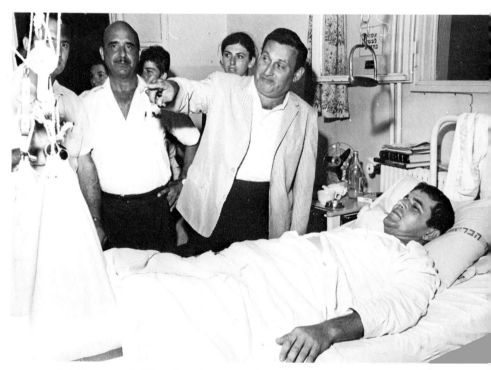

Visiting wounded Israeli soldiers in a military hospital near Tel Aviv, in the aftermath of the Six-Day War, 1967. (Arie Kanfer)

Conductor Dimitri Mitropoulos greets the Tuckers at the Lydda Airport, on their arrival in Israel. (Isaac Berez)

Entertaining American troops on a makeshift stage at the Tan Son Nhut Airport in Saigon, Vietnam, 1967. (JUSPAO/Saigon)

(LEFT) With sculptor Milton Hebald during a sitting at Hebald's studio in Rome. (Mrs. Richard Tucker)

(BELOW) On the dais with conductor Zubin Mehta, greeting Israeli prime minister Golda Meir, Tel Aviv, July 1973. (Ilan Brunner)

(BELOW LEFT) After Richard's death, Sara Tucker became "the keeper of the flame" of her husband's memory. She is shown here with their family on the occasion of Lee Tucker's bar mitzvah. Left to right are Barry Tucker; his wife, Joan; Larry and Jackie Tucker; Dr. David Tucker; his wife, Lynda; Lee Tucker; Henry Tucker; Sara Tucker; Amy, Andrew, and Robert Tucker. (Dr. David N. Tucker)

Luciano Pavarotti and Placido Domingo greet Sara Tucker at the Third Annual Richard Tucker Music Foundation Gala, Carnegie Hall, January 1979. (By permission of Placido Domingo and Luciano Pavarotti)

that Gelatt might have hoped. Neither at Columbia nor RCA Victor had there been a groundswell from the record-buying public for more classical music; instead, the threefold technical advances of a long-playing format, full-frequency reproduction, and stereophonic sound (introduced late in 1957) were being used to their fullest commercial advantage in the popular-music market. For Tucker and other classical artists, whether opera singers or instrumentalists, the major companies' preference for "mood music" à la Mantovani, the Cascading Voices, or the One Hundred and One Strings had signaled steadily diminishing royalty payments in spite of the strong initial market for classical LPs in the late 1940s.

By the summer of 1956, Tucker's royalties from his series of Columbia "official cast" recordings of the late 1940s and early 1950s—*La Bohème, Fledermaus, Cavalleria rusticana, Pagliacci, Così fan tutte, Madama Butterfly,* and *Lucia*—had so declined that the company gave him nothing new to record. Despite his newfound success at home and in the highly acclaimed Soria Series on the Angel label abroad, Tucker considered himself a Columbia artist and was offended by what he considered the company's increasingly indifferent attitude toward him—or, more to the point, toward the contract he had signed with them in 1946.

This contract, his attorney, Al Gins, reminded Columbia, called for Tucker to record at least one opera per year, or else an album of arias and songs on which he and Columbia's Artists and Repertoire staff would agree. Columbia was to pay him $10,000 a year in two equal semiannual installments, all finally adding up to those "six figures" he had been so proud of in 1946. The wording of the contract guaranteed payment whether or not any recordings were made or released—though quite naturally the good-faith assumption of both parties was that new titles would be recorded and issued regularly.

Yet when Tucker was given nothing to record in the last half of 1956, Columbia balked at paying him the next $5,000 his contract called for. Instead, the company wanted him to agree to a new arrangement—namely, for him to allow Columbia to place the contractual amounts in escrow accounts, and pay him only when the royalties from the recordings had actually been earned.

Tucker was quick to point out—as had Bing when Columbia had made the suggestion to the Metropolitan—that this was not the agreement Columbia Records had negotiated. According to Tucker, Columbia continued to press the issue—until, through Al Gins, he threatened to file suit against Columbia for breach of contract. This threat was eventually withdrawn when Goddard Lieberson, now president of CBS/Columbia, helped resolve the payment issue out of court.

Whether because of diminishing returns in the opera market or, as Tucker privately held, because of his threatened lawsuit, Columbia Records offered him no more complete operas to record in the States, and Tucker's ten-year contract expired in 1956. After a year of minimal appearances in the Columbia studios in 1957, however, the company did arrange a complete *Rigoletto,* to be recorded under the aegis of the Electrical Musical Industries/Philips interests in Europe, and to be released in the States on the Columbia "Masterworks" label. The cast was to include Gianna d'Angelo as Gilda and Renato Capecchi in the title role; Francesco Molinari-Pradelli would conduct. The sessions were to take place at the San Carlo Opera in Naples. At the end of the Metropolitan season, before going on tour, Tucker therefore finalized arrangements with John Gualiani for another stay abroad.

On this occasion, the Tucker sons accompanied their parents to Europe. The Tuckers arrived in Italy in May, stopping first in Rome. John Gualiani, as usual, had arranged their itinerary; they were to stay at the Grand Hotel for four days and then journey to Capri and Naples. They had no more than checked in when Gualiani chanced to meet tenor Giacomo Lauri-Volpi and his wife in the lobby of the hotel. When Lauri-Volpi learned that Tucker would be staying briefly in Rome, he extended an invitation through Gualiani for Sara and Richard to visit his villa. The Tuckers accepted and asked if David might come too. They agreed to a midday visit—only to find that "midday" to the Lauri-Volpis, who arose at 6:00 A.M., meant ten in the morning.

Mrs. Lauri-Volpi, the former soprano Maria Ros, had furnished the palatial villa according to her husband's classical tastes; even the perfectly manicured garden, Richard thought, somehow symbolized Lauri-Volpi's personality and art. One large room of the villa was dedicated entirely to Verdi, whose life-size marble likeness stood at the center; programs from Lauri-Volpi's four decades as a Verdi tenor adorned each of the walls. "All that I have in life," the sixty-six-year-old Lauri-Volpi told Tucker, "in some way can be credited to the works of Giuseppe Verdi."

During the course of the midmorning visit, Lauri-Volpi went to the piano and struck up the chords to "Recondita armonia" from *Tosca*. He asked Tucker to sing the aria—to which Richard replied, only half-jokingly, "At this hour?" He sang it, nevertheless, and earned Lauri-Volpi's highest praises. "Yours is a 'Carusiano' approach to Cavaradossi," he said. "Like Caruso's, it is a strong approach—very verismo, dramatic, a *forte* approach. It is quite different from the approach of a bel canto tenor like Alessandro Bonci."

Tucker replied that he had heard much about Bonci; he knew Bonci was considered Caruso's peer in many quarters, yet he knew nothing about Bonci's approach to singing or how it might have differed from Caruso's. This was all the prompting Lauri-Volpi needed to sing "Recondita armonia" himself—smoothly, securely, and with all the fire and drama of a tenor in his prime. The style he illustrated traced to the bygone era of Bonci, Giuseppe Anselmi, and Fernando de Lucia—a nineteenth-century approach permitting a liberal use of alternate loud and soft attacks, with considerable altering of the time values of the written notes.

Lauri-Volpi concluded the aria with a stentorian high note that gave no hint of his age. At John Gualiani's request, he followed this with "A te, o cara" from *I puritani,* with which he had graced the first Maggio Musicale in Florence in 1933. Lauri-Volpi struck the aria's climactic D-flat squarely on center—to Tucker's amazement—and held it several beats longer than the score specified, just as he had done in long-ago performances.

"That," Lauri-Volpi said with a modicum of modesty, "is the style of Bonci."

On leaving the Lauri-Volpi villa after a warm and pleasant two-hour visit, Tucker said to his son, "By God, if he ever decides to come back to the Met, a lot of tenors will be washed up!" Not unexpectedly, he did not include himself among them.

The recording sessions for *Rigoletto* at the San Carlo opera afforded Tucker his first extended stay in Naples. The sessions were as tightly scheduled as the ones Dario Soria had produced in Milan for Angel Records. Still, there was nominal time between "takes" for Tucker to visit the local tourist sites and enjoy

the summer sun. "Whenever Richard had a day off," said John
Gualiani, "he immediately asked directions to the nearest body of
water—he didn't care if it was a lake or an ocean, as long as he
could swim in it. Sara would pack a picnic basket of his favorite
snack foods—sliced peaches, cheese, melon, maybe some yo-
gurt—and we'd all head for the beach."

On one such day off, Capri proved an ideal site for a day of
swimming and relaxing. As the beauty of Capri came into view,
Tucker was so buoyed by the scene that when the ferryboat
docked, he serenaded the waiting cabbies. "At the dock, there were
seven cabs lined up waiting for passengers," Gualiani remembered. "To them, Richard looked like any other American tourist, so each one started bargaining with him to ride in a particular
cab. Richard stretched out his hands as if to say that he couldn't
make up his mind. Then he burst into 'Questa o quella' from *Rigoletto,* singing, 'Which cab—this one or that one?' " The im-
promptu aria earned Tucker an enthusiastic round of applause from
the cabdrivers—and also netted him free rides to and from his
hotel.

In Naples, the Tuckers stayed at the Excelsior Hotel, where,
to their pleasant surprise, they learned that former President Harry
Truman was also vacationing there. Tucker had first met Truman in 1948, when he had defeated Thomas E. Dewey against
formidable odds for the Presidency. Tucker had helped the Truman campaign and had subsequently sung at the annual Jeffer-
son-Jackson Democratic fund raisers in Manhattan. Truman had
reciprocated by inviting Tucker to entertain at the White House—
the first of many invitations Tucker would receive, not only from
Truman but from Presidents Eisenhower, Kennedy, Johnson, and
Nixon as well. Of all of them, however, it was Truman whom
Tucker held in the highest regard, primarily because of the key
role he had played in the independent statehood of Israel.

When the former President learned that the Tuckers were at
the Excelsior, he invited them to lunch in the hotel. During the
informal affair, Tucker steered the conversation to the rebirth of
Israel a decade earlier. He listened eagerly to Truman's recollections of the events leading to the United Nations vote, and to his
candid descriptions of Abba Hillel Silver, Chaim Weizmann, David
Ben-Gurion, and other Israeli leaders. Tucker then broached the
subject of a visit by Truman to the land he had helped father.

"Over there, you're a national hero, Mr. President," Tucker told him. "You'll be given a hero's welcome by the Israeli people. Will you go?"

"I'd love to go—but I can't," Truman answered. "Once you've been President, everything you do, and anyplace you go, you're not doing on your own but as a statesman. If I were to go to Israel, the other side would make something out of it. There's already been too much trouble in the Mideast, and I'm not one to add to it."

After the luncheon, Truman invited the Tuckers and John Gualiani to join him for a long walk. The group had no more than left the lobby when a crowd of Neapolitan urchins gathered about them and begged money from the former President. He reached into his pocket and extracted a roll of *lire* and, forgetting the exchange rate, was ready to distribute the roll among the crowd. He hesitated, and then asked Tucker's help. "Richard, you probably understand this money, so figure out what to do for these kids," Truman said. Tucker took the money—two hundred *lire* in all—and led the children to a nearby *dolceria,* where he bought each one a pretzellike delicacy.

"You're pretty damned good with money, Richard," Truman said laughingly. "I could've used you in the White House."

The revival of Verdi's *Simon Boccanegra* was a high point of the Metropolitan's 1959/60 season, and a personal triumph for Leonard Warren. *Boccanegra* was the first opera he had learned; Wilfred Pelletier had coached him in the lyric-baritone role of Paolo Albiani, in which Warren made his debut in 1939 in a cast that included Elisabeth Rethberg as Amelia and Giovanni Martinelli as the young patrician Gabriele.

The star of that *Boccanegra* production, however, was not Warren but the veteran baritone Lawrence Tibbett. By the time Warren got his first chance at the part of Simon, in the 1949/50 season, Tibbett had announced his retirement from the Metropolitan. Supporting Warren's Simon were Astrid Varnay as Amelia, and Tucker as the young Gabriele. Though Warren's dramatic ability was still in a chrysalid stage, he made a deep impression on the critics in *Boccanegra*—so much so that Rudolf Bing revived it expressly for him ten years later, in the 1959/60 season, by which time he had matured into a consummate actor-singer.

When the curtain rang down on the first performance of that new production on March 1, 1960, the critics judged Warren's Simon Boccanegra a perfect character study and elevated his performance to the lofty plane of Feodor Chaliapin's Boris Godunov, Antonio Scotti's Baron Scarpia, and Ezio Pinza's Don Giovanni. The dramatic power of Warren's characterization, coupled with the ravishing beauty of his voice and the perfection of his technique, even helped to offset the fact that the Amelia of the production, Renata Tebaldi, had been unable to leave Italy for New York in time for the first performance and had to be replaced by Mary Curtis-Verna.

As he had ten seasons before, Tucker again sang Gabriele to Warren's Simon in the new production. By now, Tucker had become accustomed to the laborious process by which Warren created a character—a process marked by an unrelenting perfectionism, and an equally unrelenting capacity for self-doubt. This latter ingredient in Warren's psychology was one that Tucker accepted and easily tolerated, but that nonetheless remained incomprehensible to him. Others were equally mystified by Warren's insecurities, especially during the preparation of a role. "Leonard would worry so much over a new part that it sometimes spilled over to the rest of the cast," Roberta Peters remembered. "This was almost counterproductive, because the others had their own roles to be concerned about. I don't think he was ever aware of how childish all this worrying and fussing made him seem."

On the evening of March 4, 1960, three days after his triumph in *Simon Boccanegra,* Leonard Warren was feeling insecure and unappreciated. Tucker sensed it immediately from the tone of their conversation as they waited in the wings to sing a performance of *La forza del destino.* At first, Tucker charged off Warren's obvious depression to the inclement Manhattan weather—there was snow everywhere, nearly fifteen inches of it, the worst snowfall in more than a decade. It had almost detained Renata Tebaldi again, though she had been able to fly into Manhattan in time to rehearse for the *Forza* performance.

Warren made his entrance in the second act. The audience

showered him with a familiar kind of applause, but later, after he and Tucker joined voices in "Solenne in quest'ora," the shouts of *"Bravi!"* were almost deafening. The two had sung the duet so many times that the music was second nature to them. Still, this night they outdid themselves. As critic Howard Taubman would write the next day in *The New York Times,* "A listener would have had to go back many years to recall a performance of comparable beauty."

The audience was now primed for Carlo's majestic solo aria, "Urna fatale del mio destino." Howard Taubman's account of the ensuing scene conveys clearly the reception Warren was given: "He sang it with a perfection he had taught his admirers to expect. As he ended it, he spread out his arms in a habitual gesture with an air of triumph, and he was greeted by an outburst of applause from the packed house."

All eyes were still on him as the Surgeon (a minor character, sung that night by Roald Reitan) entered the scene, announcing that Alvaro had escaped death. The way they had rehearsed the scene, Warren was to sing the words "O gioia! o gioia!," then clutch a small portrait of Leonora in his hands and launch into the cabaletta, "Ah! egli e salvo!"

The two words rang out. "O gioia!"—the phrase punctuated by that dark, sonorous voice—and then again, "O gioia!" even more dramatically. A tier above the stage, Wilfred Pelletier sat in his box and silently approved the beauty of Warren's delivery. Twenty years earlier, he had taught him how to sing the same phrase over and over, letting the colorations of the voice make each repetition seem different.

A few boxes away, Agathe Warren proudly applauded her husband and waited for the brief bit of stage business with the Surgeon to conclude before Leonard sang the cabaletta. He stood there, the portrait in hand, just as he had rehearsed the scene. But he didn't move. He seemed frozen in a peculiar pose. A moment later, the portrait slipped through his fingers. Its tiny frame shattered as it struck the stage floor. The audience was puzzled. Was this part of the action? Or had he dropped it accidentally?

An instant later, his towering figure pitched forward. His massive chest, then his head, struck the floor with unrestrained momentum. The audience gasped. The fall was too real.

Backstage, it seemed an eternity before the curtain was rung down. In the wings, Tucker shouted, "Lennie! Lennie!" His voice broke the eerie silence in the theater.

Tucker and Osie Hawkins, the stage manager, were the first to reach Warren's side. It was clear to both of them that something was radically wrong. Blood trickled from Warren's nose, broken in the fall. Under the heavy and ornate costume, his enormous chest seemed motionless; they could not tell whether he was breathing. In desperation, Tucker cradled Warren's head in his arms and alternated with Hawkins giving him mouth-to-mouth resuscitation. Soon Dr. Adrian Zorgniotti, the Metropolitan's house physician, was on the scene; he had called an ambulance on his way backstage.

A stagehand brought a small oxygen tank from a first-aid cabinet backstage. When Dr. Zorgniotti opened the valve to feed oxygen into the rubber mask, he heard a steady rush of air; the oxygen was escaping through the sides of the mask. Leonard Warren was dead.

Backstage, Monsignor Edwin Broderick, one of Agathe Warren's guests that evening, intoned the Latin phrases of the last rites of the Roman Catholic Church. At ten-twenty, Dr. Zorgniotti pronounced Leonard Warren dead. On the death certificate, he wrote the words "massive cerebral vascular hemorrhage."

At ten-thirty, Bing stepped before the curtain.

"This is one of the saddest nights in the history of this great theater," he said somberly. There were gasps of "No!" from the audience.

"May I ask you all to rise," Bing said mournfully. In an instant, everyone in the packed theater was standing.

"I ask you to honor the memory of one of our greatest artists, who died in the midst of one of his very greatest performances. I am sure you will agree that it would not be possible to continue."

Slowly, sorrowfully, the audience filed out. The programs they left behind now had an unsettling significance—*La forza del destino,* the force of destiny. For Warren's colleagues in the remaining *Forza* performances—especially Mario Sereni, who now assumed the role of Carlo—the "Urna fatale del mio destino" was impossible to hear without reliving the tragic moment.

The death of Leonard Warren haunted Tucker well after the Metropolitan season drew to a close. In time, he came to grips with the suddenness of it, chiefly because Warren's physician disclosed that he had been under treatment for chronic hypertension. In a curious way, this partly relieved Tucker: it accounted for the sudden death of a man who had had no real vices, who had seemed the personification of self-control. But the suddenness of Warren's passing did little to relieve the sense of loss Tucker felt—a loss that made itself acutely felt, among other places, in Buenos Aires, where Alvaro served as Tucker's debut role at the Teatro Colon later that summer on August 16, 1960. Though he would sing a number of roles during his six seasons at the historic theater—the Duke in *Rigoletto,* Mario in *Tosca,* Enzo in *Gioconda,* Andrea Chénier, and Des Grieux in *Manon Lescaut*—his first *Forza del destino* in Buenos Aires haunted him because Warren was to have sung with him. On the night of the performance, under the baton of Fernando Previtali, baritone Aldo Protti took his place.

Leonard Warren's death had hardly become a reality to many when, in the autumn of 1960, the Metropolitan lost two more artists from its star ranks. On September 9, word came from Stockholm that Jussi Bjoerling had died of a massive coronary. He had been plagued by a weakened heart for some time, but had disregarded his physicians' advice to curtail his drinking. Then, on November 2, conductor Dimitri Mitropoulos died in Milan, after suffering a heart attack during a rehearsal of Mahler's Third Symphony at the Teatro alla Scala. He had been hospitalized several times after suffering a serious coronary in 1959, yet had refused to alter his work schedule. A few minutes before he went to the podium on that same November afternoon, the sixty-four-year-old maestro described himself to one of the players as "an old automobile that still works."

Minutes later, he toppled from the podium and was rushed to the hospital in an ambulance. He died en route.

One of the most immediate, most tangible effects of the death of Mitropoulos was the uncertainty that now faced the new Cecil Beaton production of Puccini's *Turandot,* last heard at the Metropolitan in 1929 with Lauri-Volpi as Calaf and Maria Jeritza in the title role. Mitropoulos was to have conducted the new production, which was scheduled to premiere on February 24, 1961.

Eventually, Bing persuaded Leopold Stokowski, then nearly eighty, to conduct in Mitropoulos's place. This was a premiere that Tucker had anticipated eagerly because he had negotiated for the role of Calaf for the 1960/61 season, and felt reasonably certain that he would sing in the first performance.

Given its heavy demands, Tucker opted to sing his first Calaf outside New York when the Houston Grand Opera Company mounted a *Turandot* production in the autumn of 1960. A Houston tryout not only enabled him to test how well he could pace himself in *Turandot* but also brought him in closer contact with the Houston Endowment Corporation, which was then in the process of planning a new performing-arts complex. The planning group tentatively approached Tucker about opening the new complex, to be named in honor of Houston philanthropist Jesse H. Jones.

Tucker's first appearance as Calaf in Houston on November 17, 1960, was an artistic triumph. "His singing was tender, as is needed in 'Non piangere, Liu,' " said the Houston *Post*, "yet defiantly self-assured, as is demanded if the final act is to have any dramatic credibility." He had no difficulty with the weight of the role and was therefore primed for the premiere of the new Metropolitan production. But, to his chagrin, Bing assigned the premiere to another Calaf: a young, stunning-looking Italian tenor who strode into the Metropolitan from La Scala and in short order established himself as the favorite of the public, of many of the critics—and of Rudolf Bing.

Onstage, Franco Corelli, to reiterate *Time* magazine's years-earlier description of his leonine predecessor Martinelli, seemed "the six-foot incarnation of all Latin gallantry." His assets for the opera stage were possibly the greatest of any dramatic tenor in recent memory. Physically, he was not merely handsome but, to quote Bing, "he looked like a god"—an aquiline profile, a perfectly sculpted physique, thick auburn hair, and deep, dark eyes. Even his legs—"as long and shapely as Cesare Siepi's and a little more youthfully fleshed," judged Quaintance Eaton in her appraisal in *The Miracle of the Met*—netted Corelli widespread press coverage when his costumes allowed him to display them.

For all the perfection of his features, however, Franco Corelli's voice remained his most singular asset. It was wholly distinctive, yet at the same time reminiscent of the best attributes of

some of his predecessors. The timbre, or tone color, of his powerful voice had a baritonal tint similar to Caruso's (though dis-
similar in overall sound). The compass of Corelli's voice well exceeded most others, including Caruso's: only Giacomo Lauri-Volpi
(with whom Corelli coached) could so easily negotiate interpolated high Cs, D-flats, and Ds. And though many other tenors
boasted a more pristine technique (Corelli's, it was said, was largely
self-taught), the Corelli voice had an animal vitality that took hold
of listeners and virtually conquered them.

Corelli's Metropolitan debut—as Manrico in *Il trovatore* on
January 27, 1961—may have earned him mixed reviews from the
critics (compared to what was written of the stunning debut performance of Leontyne Price, the evening's Leonora), but the reaction of the public—and even of some of his tenor colleagues—
was unequivocal. His nearest competitor in the dramatic repertoire, Mario del Monaco, had returned to Europe in 1959, just
before Corelli was engaged. Del Monaco is said to have refused
Bing's contractual offers to return to the Met as long as Corelli's
name was on the roster.

Tucker's reaction to this new arrival was less forceful than
Del Monaco's—but perhaps only publicly so. As far as Tucker's
career was concerned, Franco Corelli could not have arrived at
the Metropolitan at a worse time. With Del Monaco back in Italy, Tucker now had an unrestricted vista of dramatic roles ahead
of him. For a time, Carlo Bergonzi attempted two of these roles—
Manrico in *Trovatore* and Radames in *Aida*—but his voice was
plainly too lyric for them at that stage in his career. Canadian-
born Jon Vickers, who made his debut in 1959/60, had a far more
dramatic voice than Bergonzi, but not the proper timbre for most
Italian parts. Tucker, whose timbre and technique suited these roles
thoroughly, was therefore in a position to inherit them—until
Franco Corelli arrived.

Though Tucker deliberately remained oblivious to the public reaction to new tenors, he was too much a realist to ignore
the reaction Corelli garnered. In a rare moment of envy, he
quipped to Sara, after hearing of the electricity Corelli generated
at his debut, "If I was Italian instead of Jewish, and if I had legs
like his, my audiences wouldn't just yell *bravo,* they'd carry me
around on their shoulders!" From then on, this became Tucker's
pet explanation for the different responses he and Corelli engen-

dered from Metropolitan audiences: he was Jewish and, unlike Italians, Jews were "foreigners" in the opera world.

It is likely that Corelli was Tucker's implicit reference point when he elaborated on this explanation in his long interview for the Wiener Oral History Project. "I admit there were moments," he told Janet Bookspan, "when I used to say to Sara, not in a sense of jealousy, of course—well, I *will* say jealousy, yes—that if I were not Jewish or if I changed my name, how much higher could I have gone?"

Though he would have been loath to admit it, he regarded Corelli as his one and only rival—both for the acclaim of the Metropolitan audiences and for the favor of Rudolf Bing. Almost from the evening of Corelli's debut, Tucker must have felt himself losing his preferential status with Bing. Over a period of time, Bing's favoritism showed clearly in the numerous concessions he granted Corelli—concessions Tucker would never have thought to ask for, because he predicated his relationship with Bing on his eagerness to do more, not less, than the general manager would have expected of him.

This headline-making news item from February 1956 attests literally as well as figuratively to the lengths to which Tucker had gone to earn Bing's favor:

> Richard Tucker made it to the Metropolitan Opera just in time to sing the role of the Duke in *Rigoletto* when tenor Eugene Conley became ill. Rudolf Bing wanted Mr. Tucker to replace him, but Mr. Tucker was in Bloomington, Illinois, for a concert.
>
> The Texaco Company, sponsor of the Saturday matinee broadcasts, arranged for a private airplane to pick up the tenor at Springfield after his concert, but the weather had closed in. The airfield at Indianapolis was open, however, and Mr. Tucker was driven there. It took six hours.
>
> Mr. Tucker took off from Indianapolis and arrived in New Jersey about 11:30 Saturday morning. A limousine whisked him to a barber shop on West Fortieth Street. At about 1:00 P.M. the singer entered the Metropolitan. He had no time for lunch before getting into costume, and was onstage at 2:00 P.M. when the curtain went up.
>
> Mr. Bing told the story to the radio audience prior to the broadcast of the opera. Mr. Tucker was in superb voice and received an ovation from the audience. If he was sleepy, he did not show it.

This account contrasts pointedly with Bing's own account of a later incident involving chartered planes, hired limousines, and a leading tenor—but this time Franco Corelli:

> . . . Corelli has a dog that must go with him everywhere. The dog can ride with us in the chartered plane, but on a scheduled flight it must go in a container and the container must go in the luggage compartment. Even with my connections with the president of Eastern Airlines, . . . there is nothing I can do. So Corelli had to stay with the company and fly our chartered plane, which he didn't want to do. After a performance in Cleveland, without telling anybody, he hired a car, and drove off at midnight. He found to his great surprise that it took him nine hours to drive to New York. Then he couldn't fly to Atlanta, because he couldn't take the dog, so we arranged for him to take the train. I had him picked up by limousine, because otherwise he couldn't have found the station, the track, the train, or the compartment. They [Corelli and the dog] arrived with two minutes to spare.

"If I hadn't put up with this sort of thing," Bing concluded, "somebody at another opera house would have, and would have paid Corelli a higher fee, too." Tucker could not fathom this reasoning from the same general manager who had summarily dismissed Lauritz Melchior because he considered him "unprofessional."

As Corelli's popularity mounted, Tucker's sense of having been displaced began to show in his negotiations with Bing. Uncharacteristically—and, at times, rather petulantly—he asked to be excused from previously negotiated performances, as if to underscore that Richard Tucker could progressively but quietly withdraw from the Metropolitan and, if unappreciated there, would do his singing elsewhere. By the end of the 1960/61 season, Tucker's requests for releases from his contract began to trouble Bing. Sensing Tucker's state of mind (with help, no doubt, from Tucker's managers at Columbia Artists), Bing expressed his concern in writing, all the while trying to reassure Tucker of his importance to the Metropolitan:

> As you well know by now, I can never quite resist you, even though this time I am making a great effort. I have told you very clearly how I felt about your suggestion to cut your appearances either wholly or partly. I think it would be unwise in your own

interests and it would certainly be of severe damage to the Metropolitan, which is a responsibility I cannot assume.

You have achieved the position of one of the world's leading tenors and I would gravely offend against my duties if I voluntarily agreed to release you from an agreement that has been mutually and happily reached. I am sure you must understand this position and I trust that you may have many more years at the Metropolitan and I certainly look forward to having you back next season.

Despite other similar letters of reassurance, Bing's favoritism toward Franco Corelli showed itself more openly as the years went on—though not necessarily at Tucker's expense. After he left the Metropolitan, Bing plainly acknowledged his favoritism toward Corelli—even admitting in his memoirs that he and his assistant, Robert Herman, had once gone to Corelli and had dropped to their knees to beg him to cover for an indisposed Carlo Bergonzi. Tucker, had he witnessed this, would have questioned who indeed was running the Metropolitan.

However deeply Tucker felt about any rivalry with Franco Corelli in the early 1960s, Corelli himself caused it to dissipate and, finally, to disappear. Just at the time Corelli had taken a patent on the role of Calaf opposite Birgit Nilsson in *Turandot*, Corelli sought out Tucker after a rehearsal for *Tosca*. To Tucker's surprise, Corelli seemed somewhat nervous.

"Richard, would you do me a favor?" Corelli asked. His question seemed serious but somehow tentative, revealing a boyish shyness.

Tucker was puzzled at what he could possibly do for his rival.

"Would you let me watch you sing 'O dolci mani'?" Corelli asked. "I would like to see how you sing it."

Tucker was so touched by this gesture that he hardly knew what to say. His initial reaction was to make a joke of it. "To sing it right, Franco," he said, "you have to be Jewish." Corelli laughed—and soon Tucker sang for him. From that moment on, their "rivalry" ended. The two great tenors became friends, and at last shared a mutual admiration.

11

Q: You keep up such a hectic schedule, even for a tenor just starting a career. You've been doing it for almost thirty years. What's your secret?

A: Well, I have Paul Althouse to thank for my technique, which keeps me going. But Sara and I have said to each other, "Look, it can't go on forever." I'd hate to hang around till people say, "You should have heard him when he was good!" I hope I can retire gracefully, still be a cantor, and maybe sing six months and then teach someplace for six months. But that's later on, not now.

In his first decade as general manager, Rudolf Bing had led Metropolitan audiences to expect at least three new productions each season. In the 1960/61 season, his eleventh, Bing commissioned a total of five new productions—one of them, Verdi's *Nabucco,* a Metropolitan premiere. Four of the five were major revivals. One of them—Gluck's *Alceste,* last heard with Flagstad in 1951—proved an ideal vehicle for the long-awaited Metropolitan debut of Eileen Farrell, whose superb voice had been compared often with Flagstad's and who was already hailed as one of the greatest voices America had yet produced.

Another revival—of Puccini's *Turandot,* not heard since 1929—gave Franco Corelli one of his greatest roles, and would also earn Tucker his share of accolades in later seasons.

Flotow's *Martha,* which Caruso had popularized in the 1910s, was also revived after an absence of thirty-three seasons. Now, Tucker, Victoria de los Angeles, Giorgio Tozzi, and Rosalind Elias brought it to the Metropolitan in an English translation. Though the musical direction and the staging (by Carl Ebert) of *Martha* were well received, the English translation of the libretto fared poorly with the critics, the public, and even many of the cast members. ("The crassest chore . . . ," Irving Kolodin later wrote, "was the substitution of new words for 'The Last Rose of Summer' in place of Tom Moore's.") In the performance of April 13, 1961, Tucker supplied his own remedy for his best-known moment in *Martha,* and sang "M'appari" in Italian. The audience responded with a prolonged ovation.

Later, when asked backstage why he had done so, Tucker replied, tongue in cheek, "I wanted to let my fans know how Caruso sounded."

In Bing's 1961 end-of-the-season radio address, he confirmed that a new production of Puccini's *La fanciulla del West* would open the 1961/62 season. The anticipation only increased when Bing announced the principals in the cast of the revival— Tucker as Dick Johnson, and Leontyne Price as Minnie. The confirmation that Price had been granted opening-night honors had an impact that went well beyond the *Fanciulla* revival. As Irving Kolodin would later write, "For a Negro to appear in a leading role on a Metropolitan opening night marked a social change as significant as any in years." But as the much-anticipated date approached, deepening labor problems at the Metropolitan threatened not only the opening-night *Fanciulla* but the entire season as well.

The focal point of the labor problems was the inability of Bing's administration to agree to the terms demanded by the Metropolitan Opera orchestra, as negotiated by its union. The problems were long-standing. Throughout Bing's first decade as general manager, the orchestra players had been given an average wage increase of a mere 1 percent per year. Bing himself had once labeled this "a pittance," but he allowed it to continue. Publicly, he justified his actions on the basis of the Metropolitan's mounting annual deficits. But, privately, he acknowledged a basic philosophical opposition to organized labor in the arts.

Bred as he was in a land of uncompromising standards, Bing could not fathom why a labor union representing an orchestra should be allowed to dictate to the management which players would perform in the pit—let alone at what price. Whenever his conductors complained of incompetent playing in the orchestra, Bing longed for the days in which a Toscanini could order any musician dismissed instantaneously—without any paperwork, peer evaluations, grievance procedures, or other trappings of organized labor. Similarly, he longed for a simpler time when musicians' salaries had been negotiated by the management and orchestra in a calm and amicable way.

Indeed, neither calm nor anything resembling amicability had characterized negotiating sessions between Bing's administration and the American Federation of Musicians, which represented the orchestra members. Early on, the AFM called for a base-salary increase of almost $100 a week. Bing and the Metropolitan's board of directors labeled the sum exorbitant, and countered with an offer of a mere $8-a-week increase. This disparity in the offers and counteroffers continued throughout the summer of 1961 until, in the opinion of Bing and Anthony A. Bliss, then president of the Metropolitan Opera Association, the situation had reached a point of no return.

Bliss, in a brief statement to the media during the first week of August, acknowledged that the upcoming season was "no longer a possibility." Bing, who had interrupted a vacation in the Dolomites to be present at Bliss's press conference, nodded his agreement. But the press—and, certainly, most of the affected musicians—speculated that the Bliss-Bing posture was a strong-arm tactic intended to force a settlement.

At this point, the ranks of Metropolitan artists began to divide perceptibly (if not necessarily publicly) over the lingering strike and the deadlocked negotiations. Risë Stevens, who had recently concluded her singing career, appealed directly to President Kennedy to intervene and settle the strike. Leontyne Price—who, like Tucker, had an opening night in an important revival at stake—made a similar appeal to the White House and asked that Arthur Goldberg, then Secretary of Labor, be given a presidential mandate to resolve the dispute. Kennedy did so—despite Bing's response (to *The New York Times*) that "it will not help a bit."

Arthur Goldberg worked ceaselessly to effect a compromise and salvage the season. His very presence gave Tucker, among others, a renewed sense of optimism about the outcome of the negotiations. Goldberg had made Tucker's acquaintance at the Concord Hotel in the Catskills, where each year Tucker officiated as cantor for the High Holydays services. Though as a singer Tucker had no official role in any of the negotiations, he spoke freely and frequently with Goldberg during the often intense sessions, and after the strike had been settled, Goldberg even invited him to officiate at a special seder for United Nations delegates. Goldberg respected Tucker's staunch support of the striking musicians throughout the negotiations—a stance probably traceable to Tucker's own garment-district roots. But out of deference to both Bing and Goldberg, Tucker shied away from taking sides in statements to the media. Still, Tucker did sing at a special benefit concert for the orchestra players, an event held in cooperation with the New York City Opera during the negotiations.

Ultimately, Goldberg succeeded in having both sides agree to accept voluntary but binding arbitration. The season was therefore restored—and Bing privately claimed Goldberg's achievement as a victory for management. It was difficult to characterize the results in any other way. The orchestra members received no raise until 1964, when the Goldberg arbitration agreement expired—and even then the musicians received only a portion of what they had originally demanded. Yet for the moment, at least, tensions were eased. Under the baton of Fausto Cleva, Metropolitan audiences could finally be transported to the Gold Rush setting of Puccini's long-absent *La fanciulla del West*.

The irony of the mammoth gold curtain of the Metropolitan Opera House slowly revealing the interior of the Polka Barroom in the Gold Rush settlement of Cloudy Mountain, California, was just as apparent to the 1961 opening-night audience as it had been in 1910, when the opera had premiered at the Met under Toscanini's baton. On that memorable occasion, Caruso had created the role of Dick Johnson, and Emmy Destinn the role of the barmaid Minnie. A half-century later, Richard Tucker donned the same brown leather jacket his predecessor had worn—courtesy of Gloria Caruso, the tenor's daughter—and sang Dick Johnson to Leontyne Price's Minnie.

At its premiere, Puccini's score had been mildly received, while the plot of *Fanciulla* (based on the stage play by David Belasco) seemed too much like an old-fashioned melodrama—even by 1910 standards. Subsequent revivals, both here and abroad, had generally borne the same pattern of criticism: reviewers usually praised the advanced score, with its similarities to Debussy and Ravel, but tended to lament the libretto to which it had been wed. But the 1961/62 Metropolitan revival—a production lent by the Chicago Lyric Opera as part of a consortium arrangement—was an exception to the rule. To reiterate Irving Kolodin's appraisal, Belasco's West now seemed "as much a dream world of romance and fantasy as the Nagasaki of *Butterfly* or the China of *Turandot*."

The principals of the *Fanciulla* revival virtually ensured its musical success. Tucker's voice had now blossomed into the penultimate stage of dramatic tenor (the final stage would become evident only at the end of his life, in *La Juive*), and his burnished middle voice and clarion top notes were tailor-made for the role Puccini had written for Caruso. Baritone Anselmo Colzani, a recent arrival at the Metropolitan, was equally well suited to the role of Sheriff Jack Rance. And vocally, Leontyne Price could not have been a finer Minnie.

Price's success not only caused a sensation on opening night, but also a sold-out house for the second performance on October 31, 1961—a night that promised to be as auspicious as the first. Once again, Tucker's rich tones and Price's dark, luscious voice vitalized Puccini's score throughout Act I. The momentum continued into the second act, where Price's vocal and dramatic power had made the tension of the Card Scene with Rance unforgettable on opening night.

As the scene progressed, this same chemistry was again in evidence—until, in the middle of one of Colzani's moments as Rance, most of the audience saw Price momentarily turn away. Tucker saw her cover her mouth and heard her try to clear her throat. He assumed that she was experiencing a sudden dryness of the throat—the problem he overcame with his ever-present cough drops.

After clearing her throat, Price again faced Colzani and the Card Scene continued. But as the drama unfolded, it became clear that Price was having problems. Again she cleared her throat and continued to sing—but soon the tones in her middle voice lost their focus. Since much of the Card Scene lies in that range, her worsening hoarseness could not be disguised. Her voice was leaving her—and she was powerless to do anything about it. Tucker, attempting to help, tried to pass a cough drop to her. But nothing worked; by the end of the Card Scene, all that was left of her magnificent voice was a husky whisper.

Tucker watched her begin to panic and tried to reassure her. He whispered that she must now focus all her attention on her acting. "Just *think* Minnie—you're in a play, that's all!" he told her. "Speak the words! Let the orchestra carry you!"

Great artist that she is, Price acted the remainder of the scene impeccably, leading an already aware audience to accord her a standing ovation for finishing the scene. In the final act, Dorothy Kirsten took her place, and did so in all but one of the remaining *Fanciulla* performances of the season. Price's sudden loss of voice (with which Tucker could readily sympathize, given his own trouble in 1949) was eventually traced to an acute virus infection. After a lengthy rest in Rome, she returned to New York in splendid voice—and, like Tucker, was never beset by vocal problems again.

Of Tucker's concern for her, Price would later say, "I had a very helpful colleague that night. Richard was the experienced artist, and I learned from him—especially about courage under duress."

When he undertook the role of Johnson in the revival of *La fanciulla del West,* Tucker was forty-eight years old and, many thought, at the peak of his powers as a singer. Though as self-assured as always, he himself wondered how long his good fortune could last. When *Opera News'* Florence Stevenson broached the subject with him a few weeks after his first *Fanciulla,* he admitted that his future had become a discussion topic at home. "My wife and I can't stand sympathy," he said candidly. "We know that after fifty, there's only one way a tenor's voice can go. Nobody wants to pay ten dollars to hear an old man. After I'm fifty, I mean to retire gracefully into teaching."

However sincerely Tucker may have believed that his career was nearing its end, it had been (to borrow a phrase once applied to Caruso's) "one long crescendo," and had already assured him a prominent place in musical history. He took pride as well as comfort in the fact that his personal life had been equally fulfilling and had been spared any real tragedy. By his own description, he had always been "as healthy and strong as a team of horses," and he offered his energy and endurance as proof of his claim. If his doctors occasionally disagreed, pointing to his rounded girth (he weighed 190 pounds, at five feet seven) and the high-cholesterol diet he favored, he paid them little heed. He had no conception of his own mortality.

Yet, Tucker was no stranger to death. "A cantor, like a rabbi," he once said, "comes to see death as an unhappy but real part of life, because he's around it so much." Tucker had first confronted the reality of death as a teen-ager, when his mother died virtually in his arms. For twenty years, he was spared the grief of another loss—until his brother, Louie, died suddenly of a heart attack, leaving a wife and children whom Richard and Sara helped to sustain afterward.

The death of his only brother, sudden as it was, deeply affected Tucker—not only because of the sadness it brought Louie's wife, Celia, but also because of the grief his father was to experience. Sam Ticker had outlived his elder son, to whom he had remained devoted even amid the many downward turns of Louie's adult life. A few years later, perhaps hoping to put aside an unhappy memory and begin a new life away from Brooklyn, Sam relocated in Miami, and never returned to New York even for a family visit. In his mid-seventies, his health rapidly declined; he died in Miami in 1958.

In the spring of 1962, four years after his father's death, Richard again faced what to him was almost a parental loss: Sara's father, Levi Perelmuth, who had lived with them sixteen years, began to fail. He had been under treatment for various maladies, but had remained in stable condition until a few months before his ninetieth birthday. As his health worsened, his doctors concluded that he would have to undergo surgery—a sizable risk for someone his age, and one that neither Sara nor Richard felt they had the right to decide on alone.

Dutifully, they contacted Sara's brothers for advice—including Jan, from whom they had been estranged for nearly ten years. After a lengthy discussion with the Peerces—a discussion that never strayed from the subject at hand (thus bringing the couples no closer together than they had been)—Sara and Richard concurred that the doctors should do anything within reason to prolong her father's life.

On the morning of May 19, 1962, Richard awoke late. He had slept uneasily during the night, as he was preoccupied with the condition of his father-in-law. A few days earlier, as he and Sara had weighed the decision to operate, he had called on Rabbi Levinthal for guidance. The essence of prayer, the rabbi reminded him, was not merely resignation but hope. As Richard recited his morning prayers, he thought about Levi Perelmuth and remembered Rabbi Levinthal's advice—and yet, inwardly, he had forced himself to accept the prospect that his father-in-law might die.

A few minutes before ten o'clock, the phone rang in Richard's and Sara's bedroom. He was in the bathroom and had just begun to shave when he heard the telephone. He answered it quickly, anticipating word from the hospital; it was only Barry on the other end of the line, calling from his Wall Street office on a business matter. In a few minutes, Richard hung up and went back into the bathroom to finish shaving.

As he shaved he felt a sharp pain when he moved his arms. Soon he had a burning, aching sensation in his chest. At first he dismissed it as indigestion, and imagined that he was merely paying the price for having eaten too late the night before. But then he began to feel nauseated. His hands trembled and he began to perspire profusely. He must be coming down with a virus, he told himself. Then came a viselike tightening in his chest—an almost unbearable pressure, as if heavy blocks had been laid across his breastbone. He began to feel dizzy, and started for the kitchen to tell Sara he was ill.

He never reached the kitchen door. He collapsed in the hallway, and almost immediately lapsed into unconsciousness.

Dorothy Mallory rushed to him as Sara frantically called Dr. Sam Doskow, their personal physician. When his answering service could not immediately contact him, Sara called another physician, Dr. Irving Wecksell, who had supervised her father's hospital care. In a matter of minutes, Wecksell was on his way to Melville Lane, and had called for an ambulance as he left his office.

When Wecksell arrived, Tucker was ashen-colored and was breathing irregularly, although he was now conscious. Enormous beads of perspiration rolled from his forehead and cheeks, and his robe was virtually soaked. Later, at the Long Island Jewish Hospital, Dr. Wecksell was able to verify his initial diagnosis: Tucker had suffered a heart attack. Wecksell put him into the intensive-care unit, where his heart rate could be continuously monitored.

By eleven o'clock that night, Tucker was conscious and his condition had begun to stabilize. Sara sat at his bedside, wiping his forehead with a moist towel and urging him to rest and not to worry. As his sons gathered around him, their sense of helplessness showed plainly on their faces. Their father lay in front of them, oxygen tubes protruding from his nostrils and intravenous needles penetrating his forearms.

In a low whisper, he called Barry close to him. "Get ahold of Michael Ries at Columbia Artists," Tucker said anxiously. "Nobody must know about this, do you understand? Make up anything—but don't tell *anybody* that there's something wrong with my heart."

Dr. Wecksell, a cardiologist, had cautioned Sara that Richard might deny the reality of his heart attack—a common problem among strong-willed men. Almost immediately, Wecksell's caution proved prescient: Richard refused to grant that there was anything wrong with him other than a bad case of indigestion. He had merely eaten something that hadn't agreed with his system. Even when Wecksell showed him the tracings of the electrocardiogram series, explaining what the tests verified, Tucker barely paid any attention. It was a stomach problem, he argued, and nothing else.

Tucker had been in a private room for nearly a week when Levi Perelmuth died in the Mount Sinai Hospital in Manhattan. Amid Sara's grief, she chose not to tell Richard that her father had died. "I knew very well that Richard would forget about his own illness and want to be with me," she said. "But, as it was, he found out anyway." The morning of the funeral, she learned, Richard had read the obituary in the previous day's *New York Times*.

Sara was already on her way to the funeral home on the Lower East Side when Richard telephoned their Great Neck home. David was still home and answered the phone. "Dad was absolutely livid that no one had told him," David remembered. "He ordered me to get in the car and come and get him. He said he was checking himself out of the hospital."

Tucker was fully dressed and standing in the lobby of the hospital, still arguing with Dr. Wecksell over leaving, when he caught sight of David's car. Wecksell insisted on going with him when Tucker ordered David to drive him to the East Side, so that he could pay his respects to Sara's father.

At the funeral home, the Peerce and Tucker families were

shocked when Richard walked into the room. Jan and Alice Peerce, who knew of his heart attack, were among the first to express their concern for his health, and were touched by his presence. Yet they and their families could hardly mask their shock at his appearance. "Richard was shaky and his skin had a grayish color," Sender Peerce remembered. "I didn't think he was going to make it through the day without going back to the hospital."

At Tucker's request, the simple pine coffin in which, following Orthodox tradition, Levi Perelmuth would be buried, was opened so that Richard could see his face one last time.

After the burial, Tucker, having reassured himself that he still had the strength of an oak, then sat *shivah* for the person who, perhaps even more than his own father, had shared his family life and had shaped him as a man.

With Michael Ries's cooperation, Columbia Artists Management helped keep the news of Richard's heart attack from the press. Obviously, they could not prevent his hospitalization from becoming public knowledge. It made the news wires almost as soon as he was admitted to the emergency room. Officially, "physical exhaustion" was given as the reason for his hospitalization. According to *The New York Times* account, he was put "under observation" because he had been keeping too hectic a schedule.

Privately, Tucker put more stock in the *Times* account than in the counsel of his doctors—who, not unexpectedly, insisted that he would have to alter both his diet and his pace. They warned him that his "delicatessen diet" of eggs, cheeses, and other cholesterol-rich foods would only complicate his condition. So would the self-imposed demands of his performing schedule. He dismissed both warnings. There was nothing wrong with him to begin with, he insisted.

Except to Sara, Tucker refused to acknowledge that he ever had any heart ailment. "Deep inside him, Richard probably accepted it," Sara felt. "But not on the outside. He kept up a good front." At least once, however, he dropped the mask. In the autumn of 1962, several months after the heart attack, he paid a routine call to Alix B. Williamson, his new press agent. Earlier, he had reluctantly left Elizabeth Winston when she told him that she felt she had taken his career as far as she could. Williamson, an aggressive and imaginative publicist, was soon recommended to him. Tucker later would credit her with much of his success in the media.

Alix Williamson's offices, like Elizabeth Winston's, were located at 119 West 57th Street—on the same floor, at that. Miss Winston happened to be leaving her office just as Tucker was opening the door to Alix Williamson's suite. She had not seen Tucker for more than a year, but had been distressed when she heard of his hospitalization. "I can't explain what came over me," she recalled, "but when I called out to him, I burst into tears. Even though he and I were no longer working together, I still thought he was one of the most wonderful men I had ever known. I think that's what made me cry—I was afraid *for* him."

Elizabeth Winston's sincere reaction made Tucker momentarily abandon the façade. He took her in his arms and comforted her, and was deeply touched by her obvious fear for his health. "Don't you worry about me," he said softly, his words slowed by his own emotion. "I'm gonna be all right—that's what I keep telling myself. I'll beat this damned thing somehow."

After the *shivah* for Sara's father, Richard heeded his doctors' suggestion—to Sara's surprise and relief—that a week or two of rest, away from the pressures of New York City, would do him good. Rudolf Bing offered to release him from his tour performances so that he could recuperate fully. Other than the Metropolitan tour, Tucker's only major upcoming commitment was a July recording date at the newly built RCA facilities in Rome, where he was scheduled to record *Madama Butterfly* with Leontyne Price, under Erich Leinsdorf's direction. This was the third in the series of five complete operas he would make in Rome for RCA, all part of the company's renewed commitment to recording operas.

Preceding *Butterfly* were complete recordings of *Il trovatore* with Leontyne Price, Rosalind Elias, Leonard Warren, and Giorgio Tozzi, and *La traviata* with Anna Moffo and Robert Merrill. RCA planned to follow them with recordings of *La Bohème,* with Tucker singing Rodolfo to Anna Moffo's Mimi and Merrill's Marcello, and *La forza del destino,* which he would record with Price, Merrill, Tozzi, mezzo-soprano Shirley Verrett, and basso Ezio Flagello. These recordings not only did much to revivify RCA's much-touted "Red Seal standard" of an earlier age but also established Tucker as one of the most listened-to tenors in the recording industry. Of *Madama Butterfly,* which would occupy his attention in the summer of 1962, *High Fidelity* was to write later, "The manliness and yet ease of line which Tucker creates as Pinkerton in 'O quant'occhi fisi' with Leontyne Price is reminiscent of the dynamic performance recorded five decades earlier by another pair, Enrico Caruso and Geraldine Farrar."

Agreeing that a restful vacation before the *Butterfly* sessions might be good for him, Tucker booked a flight to Jamaica and rented a suite facing the beach at the Round Hill resort hotel.

On arriving, Tucker was delighted to learn that Prince Rainier and his Princess, the former Grace Kelly, were also staying at Round Hill. Naturally, the royal couple was the object of endless attention from the media, and the *paparazzi* were in abundance in the dining room, on the dance floor, on the beach—everywhere the Rainiers surfaced during their stay.

Tucker himself saw to it that his and Sara's table was near the Rainiers' in the hotel dining room. This, Sara remembered, was but the first sign that Richard was seriously star-struck. Before going to dinner, he fussed with his tuxedo, sprayed himself with liberal quantities of Mark II, his favorite cologne, and spent an extremely long time preening himself. At dinner, he was almost too preoccupied to eat. Throughout the several-course meal, he couldn't keep his eyes off Princess Grace.

"We've just got to meet her—I mean, them," he declared.

"For God's sake, leave them alone," Sara said. "They've got enough to contend with here."

But Tucker kept staring, hoping the Princess would recognize him. "She probably knows who I am," he assured Sara. He played with his food a few more minutes, all the while gazing none too discreetly at Princess Grace. Sara found it embarrassing—and said so.

"Do us all a favor and eat your dinner," she told him. "You're making a fool of yourself."

He ate a few more bites, but was soon staring again. Finally, his obsession got the better of him. "This is it, I'm going over to their table," he informed Sara. "You coming with me?" Before she had time to protest, he was leading her by the hand to the Rainiers' crowded table.

Princess Grace looked at him and smiled slightly. He was sure she recognized him. Sara was equally sure the Princess hadn't the faintest idea who he was.

"Your Highness, I am Richard Tucker from the Metropolitan Opera," he announced himself with all the flair of Alfredo encountering Violetta in *La traviata*. He was at his courtly best, taking the Princess' hand in his, bowing as properly as a nineteenth-century Parisian *chevalier*. Princess Grace nodded politely. "You see, my wife and I—this is my wife, Sara—we're vacationing here, too, so we thought we should say hello. We hope you and the Prince have a wonderful stay here."

Dutifully, Princess Grace introduced the Tuckers to Prince Rainier and to their dinner guests. After pleasantries were exchanged and the Prince told them they "must see Monaco someday," Richard and Sara made their way to the dance floor.

"So, are you satisfied now?" Sara chided him. "You've met Presidents—and now you can tell your grandchildren that you met a real-life Princess."

"What are you getting at?" Tucker asked innocently. "I was just trying to be neighborly. I mean, we're both Americans, she used to be in the business and I'm in the business, and it's real proper that I should go and—"

"You're full of it, just dance!" Sara cut him off playfully.

Dessert had arrived when they returned to their table. For about five minutes, Tucker spoke in sentences that did not include some reference, direct or indirect, to the flaxen-haired goddess at the next table. But soon he was staring again, mindlessly twirling his spoon in his Cherries Jubilee.

"Are you going to eat that or make jam out of it?" Sara said.

"You know," he said, "I think it would be wonderful for us to dance with the royal couple. I mean, it would be real memorable—you could dance with the prince, and I'll dance with the princess. Wouldn't that be great?"

"Do yourself a favor, and do them an even bigger one," she answered. "Eat your dessert, and for God's sake stop gawking at her."

"Who the hell is gawking? I'm just trying to be friendly, that's all. It would be friendly of us to dance with them."

"Use your eyes. They're eating, not dancing."

"Well, they may be eating now, but they'll probably dance afterward."

"Forget about dancing. Your dessert is melting."

He gave Sara a look of defiance.

"This is it, Sara—I'm gonna do it. I'm gonna walk over to that table, and I'm asking her to dance. That's that!"

"Go ahead and try it!" she said in an equally defiant voice. Under the table, he felt her feet lock around his ankle. "If you so much as try to get out of your chair," she said under her breath, "I'll hang on to your leg with my feet—and you'll either fall flat on your face, or else you'll have to drag me across the floor with you. So take your choice."

He finished his Cherries Jubilee.

Thanks to his father, David Tucker made news in 1962. *Opera News* was the first magazine to report (straight from the proud father) that "David Tucker has been accepted by Cornell Medical School." For several months, Tucker spent much of his time talking about David when he gave interviews. To make certain no one thought that the university had been influenced in any way, he always quickly added—as he had to *Opera News*—that "Cornell accepted David immediately on the strength of his grades." In fact, this was no small accomplishment, as David was only in his junior year at Tufts when Cornell accepted him.

But while medicine proved to be David's enduring calling, it was not his first. In his late teens, Tucker's middle son had been drawn to singing. While at Tufts, David studied voice with Frederick Jagel, who was teaching at the New England Conservatory in Boston.

All three of the Tucker sons had tenor voices of varying quality. Barry, who had a performer's psyche and genuinely loved to sing, was gifted with a highly discriminating ear but an undistinguished voice. Both David and Henry had more refined voices— and most listeners agreed that of the two, Henry's held the greater promise. Although he, too, studied voice for a time, Henry did not seriously consider a singing career. But David was quite serious about singing—especially after receiving encouragement not only from Jagel but also Giacomo Lauri-Volpi, for whom David had sung briefly in Rome. Lauri-Volpi had even gone so far as to offer to teach him—an offer that Tucker, speaking for David, quickly but politely dismissed.

As David's interest in singing deepened, he asked his father to give him lessons—a request that Tucker repeatedly rejected until, during a stay at the Eden Rock Hotel in Miami, David persisted until he broke down his father's opposition. The "lesson," however, proved more humiliating than Tucker's initial refusal to help. "He put me off for about two days before he actually agreed to listen to me sing," David remembered. "He and Mother were still in bed one morning when I went into their room and all but insisted that I get the lesson he'd promised me.

"Dad told me to sing scales—which I did, though it was obvious he wasn't paying any attention to me. About two minutes into this 'lesson,' he got out of bed, went into the bathroom, and started shaving. I stopped singing and he yelled from the bathroom, 'Keep going, I can hear you all right.'

"The next thing I heard was the water running in the shower. He kept insisting he could hear me, but it was obvious the lesson was over before it ever began."

David, his brother Henry recalled, "wanted to find the nearest rock and crawl under it, he was so humiliated."

Later that summer, David cajoled his father into attending a voice lesson with a Broadway voice teacher who purported to have "the" method by which David's lyric voice could be refined. The "method" involved singing the nonsense-word *woo* in place of actual scales. After some ten minutes of enduring not only the oppressive heat but also the eerie howling that the method called for, Tucker none too politely walked out of the studio. At home that evening he told Sara, "What I heard this afternoon puts voice teachers another notch lower in my book. This guy runs a studio for werewolves."

Out of necessity, David accepted his father's complete lack of encouragement, and tried as best he could to discern Tucker's technique while watching him in performances. But on one notable occasion, a Tucker concert at the Brooklyn Academy, David's self-study plan thoroughly backfired. "Richard was in perfect voice, and sang marvelously in the first part of the program," Sara remembered. "David was sitting only two or three rows from the stage, to be able to watch his father up close. The other boys were sitting with me, along the side of the auditorium. As the program went on, I could see that Richard was getting edgy—something was making him nervous, and he was losing his concentration. Finally, I leaned over to Barry and Henry and said I was sure something was wrong with their father. I could hardly wait for the intermission so I could go backstage and talk to him."

When Sara reached the dressing room, Tucker was pacing the floor. She asked him what was wrong.

"Get that goddamned kid away from the stage and out of my sight!" he bellowed. "It's bad enough that he sits there and stares down my throat, like I'm some kind of freak on display. What's worse, he mouths the words to every aria! He's got me so fouled up I can't think!"

Near the end of the intermission, David was hastily ushered to a distant row, where he remained for the rest of the concert.

Apart from his interest in singing, how much promise there was in David's voice remained the basic issue for Sara and Richard. They concurred that David did not have a voice distinctive or refined enough to attempt a career with. So, after a series of blunt and no doubt painful discussions with his father, David turned all his energies to medicine.

It would be tempting to read into Tucker's blunt counsel and refusal to encourage David more than the facts warrant—perhaps a father-son rivalry of classical proportions, or even a replay of the Peerce-Tucker conflict within the same household. What militates against either view is Sara Tucker's place in the scenario. Her relationship with David was a close and special one—more so, however she might deny it, than with Barry or Henry. Of the three, Barry was the closest to his father. Henry was less so, but mainly because he relocated in California not long after he graduated from law school. David became close to his father only late in Tucker's life—but even then he remained even closer to his mother.

Had Sara heard the promise of a voice in her son—as she had in young Rubin Tucker three decades earlier—she would have encouraged David at all costs. She knew he had both the ambition and the drive to become a serious singer. David was as fiercely competitive as his father had always been—which made Sara blanch at the prospect of his attempting to compete with the growing legend of his father. Yet her basic concern for David was one of inherent ability. As it was, she felt his strengths lay elsewhere.

David was in his first year at Cornell when he met Lynda Schwartz, a student nurse at the Cornell Medical Center. They had been dating only a few weeks when he invited her to a Saturday-evening dinner in Great Neck so that she could meet his family. By the winter of 1963, Lynda was a frequent guest in Great Neck, and it became clear that David took more than a passing interest in her. But Sara was caught entirely off guard when David told her that he wanted to marry Lynda—not later, but in the very near future.

Sara was awaiting Richard's return from an out-of-town concert when David made his announcement—and, to say the least, the news did not set well. Sara had no reservations about Lynda. But she was afraid that marriage at such a young age would complicate David's life and ultimately prevent him from graduating from medical school.

Sara was running short of arguments when she saw Richard getting out of a cab at the bottom of the driveway. She couldn't restrain her anxiety long enough for him to reach the front door. She flung it open, stood on the porch, and called out to him.

Tucker raced up the driveway, imagining something dire.

"Do something!" Sara pleaded with him, pointing into the house. "Your son wants to get married!"

Richard thought she meant Barry, who was engaged at the time. He couldn't fathom why Sara seemed so anxious—until he learned that David, not Barry, wanted to get married. Then he, too, objected.

"I can't let you go through with it," he told David in his sternest fatherly tone. "You haven't had enough experience with women."

All three sons looked at one another and tried not to laugh—they knew one another's pasts only too well. When that argument made no impression, Tucker changed strategies and claimed that Orthodox custom mandated that the eldest son must marry first. All eyes were now on Barry, who shrugged his shoulders and said that he was in no hurry to get married.

David held his ground, bolstered by his brothers. Finally, Richard and Sara yielded, but only after David swore that his

progress in medical school would not suffer because of his marriage. David and Lynda were married in August 1963, after a ten-
month courtship. When his second year in medical school went
along just as smoothly as his first, his parents breathed a sigh of
relief. And in his third year, when David was named one of three
recipients of cash awards for his research into viruses, Richard
Tucker, according to Sara, was "the proudest father in New York
City."

One year after his heart attack, Tucker was still denying that he
had had one. Repeatedly emphasizing his invulnerability to
everything except the common cold and momentary indigestion,
he primed himself meanwhile for the demands of the role of
Manrico in *Il trovatore*—a dramatic role on which Corelli had put
his stamp since his arrival at the Metropolitan. Tucker had considered Manrico as early as 1955, but had waited until he had the
endurance for the part's well-known demands. Now, despite a
fully diagnosed heart ailment, he declared himself ready to sing
Trovatore.

Manrico had long been regarded as a "specialty role" for
tenors because of its unusual requirements—especially in the third
act, where the voice must negotiate the lyric demands of the brief
duet with Leonora, "Quale d'armi fragore," then proceed to the
intricate legato of "Ah sì, ben mio" and its rarely heard trills—
and conclude the act with two interpolated high Cs in the climactic "Di quella pira."

Not even Caruso had been at his best in *Trovatore*. Although
his Victor Red Seal recordings of arias from the opera had given
him a permanent association with *Trovatore*, Caruso had actually
dropped the role early in his Metropolitan career. In the next
generation, only Martinelli and Lauri-Volpi had sung Manrico with
distinction. In Tucker's time, prior to Corelli's Manrico, perhaps
only Bjoerling had consistently negotiated its demands to the
critics' satisfaction—usually fortified, according to his colleagues,
by a tankard of German beer between the second and third acts.

Both in his first performance of *Trovatore* on December 11,
1963, and in subsequent ones in New York or on tour, Tucker
proved himself, said critic Miles Kastendieck, "a natural for this
role vocally." Though he sang "Di quella pira" a half-tone
downward (as had Bjoerling and almost every other tenor except

Corelli and, earlier, Kurt Baum), Tucker managed, as critic Louis Biancolli observed, "to sing an impeccable 'Ah sì, ben mio,' adding the forgotten trills as only a cantor could negotiate them, and then trumpeting out the big climax—all with the eager, throbbing voice of a newcomer."

The other principals—Leontyne Price as Leonora, Robert Merrill as the Count di Luna, and Irene Dalis as Azucena, with Thomas Schippers conducting his first *Trovatore*—led the *Herald Tribune*'s Alan Rich to label it "a dream cast," although "the big news of the evening was Richard Tucker's first Manrico." Echoing the sentiments of the rest of the New York critical fraternity, Rich judged Tucker to have been "in superlatively good voice, investing the flow of the Verdian legato with all the power and the glory that he commands at his best. You had to pinch yourself to remember how long Tucker has been singing at the Met, because he has the vocal stride of a man of half his years."

After his triumph in *Il trovatore,* Richard's relief over David's unbroken progress in medical school turned to elation when David proudly announced that Lynda was expecting. From then on, Tucker became the doting grandfather-to-be, hovering over Lynda and chiding David for not being what he considered properly protective of her.

Where the line was drawn between "proper" protection and outright overprotection was never clear. As far as Tucker was concerned, any time Lynda ventured outside their apartment, or lifted a finger to do even the lightest of housework, the well-being of his future grandchild was somehow in jeopardy. Medically, David and Lynda knew better, but they good-naturedly welcomed Tucker's constant attention. He began visiting them several times a week, and if David wasn't home, he immediately took over whatever Lynda was doing. It was not uncommon to see the Metropolitan's *primo tenore* vacuuming the carpet.

The "expectant grandfather" had but one regret—and one he could do nothing about. He was committed to record *Forza del destino* in Rome as part of his RCA contract. The sessions were scheduled from mid-July to early August—precisely when the baby was due. Tucker wanted more than anything to be in the waiting room and to be among the very first to see his newborn grandchild. If the child was a boy, he especially wanted to participate in the *bris,* or circumcision ritual. He had participated in the rite many times as a cantor, but this would be singularly meaningful: it would mark the entrance of his first grandson into the Jewish faith.

Inevitably, while Tucker and Robert Merrill were in the midst of a "take" of the "Invano, Alvaro!" duet in Rome that July, the baby—a boy, Larry—was born in Manhattan. At the Grand Hotel in Rome, after the recording session, the cast of *Forza*—Leontyne Price, Giorgio Tozzi, Shirley Verrett, Merrill, and conductor Thomas Schippers—joined Richard and Sara in a toast to the first member of the newest generation of the Tucker family. The next morning, after checking the recording schedule and finding that he had no singing to do on the day of the *bris* (the eighth day of the child's life, according to Jewish law), Tucker went to the producer of the sessions, Richard Mohr, and asked if he could fly to New York for the ceremony and return the next day.

Mohr denied his request.

Tucker appealed to him repeatedly, and each time Mohr patiently reiterated his objection: he reminded Tucker that he had signed a contract saying that he would be available throughout the sessions so that RCA could schedule him as necessary. When Tucker pointed out that on the day of the *bris* he was not scheduled to record anything, Mohr countered that the schedule was subject to change for any number of reasons—many beyond his control, necessitating that Tucker be available at all times, as he had agreed in his contract.

The dispute cast a pall over the recording sessions, and some of the cast members found themselves with divided loyalties. Some felt that Mohr was being insensitive, at the very least—and Mohr no doubt resented some of their attempts to intercede on Tucker's behalf. Ultimately, Tucker informed Mohr that he was leaving for New York; he was not about to be away from his family on such an important occasion.

Mohr did what he felt Tucker had forced him to do. Acting on orders from RCA, he informed Tucker that the company would file suit for breach of contract if he left Rome during the recording sessions.

Nonetheless, on Monday, August 1, 1964, Tucker stood at David's side at the Schwartz family home in New York as his newborn grandson entered the Jewish faith. As David recited the ancient benediction—"Blessed art Thou, O Lord, our God, King of the Universe, Who consecrated us with Thy commandments, and has commanded us to bring this child into the covenant of our ancestor, Abraham"—Tucker led the traditional response, "May he also enter into the study of the Law, into marriage, and into good deeds."

As soon as the ceremony concluded, Richard and Sara were on a plane to Rome. They were away only two days, and hoped that their prompt return would give Richard Mohr a reason to drop any further talk of lawsuits and contract violations. Mohr had not softened, however, and now claimed that the recording schedule had been disrupted. As a result, the remaining sessions were tense.

In the end, Mohr, according to Tucker, "sounded my death knell in the recording business." He elaborated in his lengthy Oral History interview of 1973: "People wouldn't believe that a company like RCA could drop me because they didn't want me to attend the circumcision of my grandson." Whatever Mohr's version of the sequence of events, the incident ended Tucker's lucrative association with RCA. Nevertheless, he considered it worth any cost, any penalty, to be able to hold David's firstborn at his *bris*. Ten years would pass before RCA invited him back into the fold. In the intervening years, by his own choice, he made no commercial recordings at all.

On November 25, 1963, a week before his first *Trovatore*, Tucker received the following letter at his Long Island home:

Dear Mr. Tucker:
I want to take this opportunity to advise you that, with the imminence of our opening a new opera house, planning has to be done even further ahead than usual.
Both the last season in this house and, of course, the first season in the new opera house will, as a whole, be seasons of major importance, and we can assume that both these seasons will find worldwide attention and publicity.
It is my hope that within the next three or four weeks we will be able to organize tentative first plans for these two seasons. Needless to say, it would be my hope that you should be involved in both seasons and, on the assumption that you, too, would care to participate prominently, this letter is to ask you to be good enough

as far as possible not to commit yourself otherwise for these two seasons until we have been able to make our suggestions to you.

It would be terribly unfortunate if any previous commitments you might have made would then make it impossible for you to participate in our two festive seasons, and I hope, certainly, that you will be able to keep yourself available for the time being.

Yours sincerely,
Rudolf Bing

A new Metropolitan Opera House had been the subject of on-and-off discussion since early in the century. From the day he arrived in 1908, Giulio Gatti-Casazza, general manager in Caruso's day, had bemoaned the house's major limitations—an impossibly shallow backstage area, no storage space for scenery, and no large-scale rehearsal quarters. Benefactor Otto H. Kahn, sensing Gatti-Casazza's distress, assured him that a new Metropolitan Opera House would be built "in two or three years." As Francis Robinson wrote, it took "fifty-eight years, four months, one week, and five days for this to come to pass."

By November 1963, when Bing wrote Tucker, the new and partially completed Lincoln Center for the Performing Arts had marked its first season. Of the four theaters in the Lincoln Center complex, Philharmonic Hall, the site of the opening-week concerts, was the first to be completed. Among the musical riches of the opening week in September 1962—a week of concerts by the New York Philharmonic, the Boston Symphony, the Cleveland Symphony, the Philadelphia Orchestra, and the Juilliard String Quartet—Tucker sang twice in the inaugural concert with Leonard Bernstein and the New York Philharmonic. He was heard in Vaughan Williams's *Serenade to Music,* and also in the "Veni Creator Spiritus" from Mahler's Eighth Symphony.

By late 1963, when Bing apprised Tucker of "the imminence of our opening a new opera house," the construction of the New Met (as it had been dubbed by the press) was proceeding on schedule, and a new opera had been commissioned for opening night: *Antony and Cleopatra,* by American composer Samuel Barber. Justino Díaz would create the role of Antony and Leontyne Price, Cleopatra, at the world premiere.

Bing's request that Tucker avoid commitments that might conflict with the high points of the last season in the Old Met and the first in the New was a request that, as Columbia Artists'

Michael Ries subsequently wrote to Bing, might not be possible for Tucker to honor. Early in December 1963, Ries replied:

> . . . I have before me an agreement which Mr. Tucker must act upon, in which he has been asked to sing for the opening of the Jesse H. Jones Hall for the Performing Arts in Houston. Just this week, the building contracts [for Jones Hall] have been let, and the hall is to open probably in September or October 1966. If what we understand is true, this is very near the time the new Metropolitan is to be ready. . . .
>
> A conflict may be inevitable if construction proceeds at the same pace for Jones Hall and the Metropolitan. Perhaps if you can suggest something firm to us in the number of roles and performances you envision for Mr. Tucker, we can give you a firm answer. We see no difficulties, however, with Mr. Tucker appearing (if the roles and sequence are to his satisfaction) in the final season in the current theater.

In response, Bing replied that he could not as yet offer "something firm," as Ries had requested. Tucker, not wanting to lose the Houston opportunity, accepted the invitation to open the Jones Hall for the Performing Arts, in either *Trovatore* or *Aida*. As luck would have it, precisely as Michael Ries had speculated, Jones Hall was completed just as the Metropolitan was receiving its final touches. Under the baton of the Houston Grand Opera's Walter Herbert, Tucker would open that new hall as Radames in *Aida*.

Meanwhile, *Aida* had formally entered Tucker's Metropolitan repertoire on New Year's Day 1965, when he sang his long-awaited first Met Radames to Leontyne Price's soon-to-be-legendary Aida. Radames became his twenty-seventh role, and earned him reviews on a par with those he had received as Manrico. After his first performance, Harold C. Schonberg wrote of Tucker's "manly, ringing voice," and especially the power he exhibited in the closing moments of the second act, where, wrote Schonberg, "his voice could be heard over the orchestra, full chorus, and the other principals." Critic Howard Klein, reviewing a subsequent Price-Tucker *Aida,* ventured a comparison with two prominent colleagues. "Franco Corelli may be more robust in the role [of Radames], and Carlo Bergonzi more suave," Klein thought, "but Mr. Tucker blended the qualities of each in a movingly dramatic performance."

Throughout the Old Met's last season, 1965/66, Tucker

maintained a dizzying pace, shuttling from the opera stage to the concert platform and defying Sara's growing concern for his health. In a nine-week period between January and mid-March 1966, he sang nearly twenty performances, several with regional companies. Typical of his self-imposed schedule were closely spaced performances of *Manon Lescaut, Tosca, Aida, Fanciulla, Trovatore,* and *Bohème* at the Metropolitan, *Carmen* in New Orleans, *Rigoletto* in Philadelphia, and *Andrea Chénier* in Pittsburgh, separated by demanding concerts of opera, oratorio, and cantorial music in Ohio, Minnesota, and California.

In the summer of 1965, Tucker allotted time during his Metropolitan tour appearances to accept an honorary doctorate from the University of Notre Dame. Among the many honorary degrees he subsequently received (from Adelphi University, St. John's University, Combs College, and the University of Miami), Tucker's Notre Dame doctorate held a singular significance for him. To Illinois industrialist Alfred C. Stepan, his longtime friend who had recommended his doctorate, Tucker brimmed, "Imagine, me being honored by one of the greatest universities in the world—a Jewish cantor who never got to finish high school! *Big* leagues, Al!"

It had taken Stepan a mere four sentences to nominate Tucker to the Reverend Theodore M. Hesburgh, president of Notre Dame: "Richard Tucker is the best husband I know. Richard Tucker is the best father I know. Richard Tucker is the best tenor I know. We would do well to consider conferring an honorary degree upon him." The board of trustees and Father Hesburgh concurred. With presidential adviser McGeorge Bundy and NAACP director Roy Wilkins, they honored Tucker "for the humility with which he has accepted and treasured the gift of his voice from God, and the reverence with which he has turned to Him." Tucker reciprocated by volunteering his services as a fund raiser for the university's multimillion-dollar "Summa" Campaign of the mid-1960s.

When he planned the final season for the Old Met, Bing accorded Tucker the honor of singing Rodolfo in *La Bohème* in the last full opera performance from the venerable old house. On the day of the performance—the matinee of Saturday, April 16, 1966—Tucker was recuperating from a head cold and was still somewhat congested when he went onstage. For a few moments in "Che gelida manina," he had difficulty with the tempo because his hearing was slightly impaired; he recovered his timing as the much-anticipated high note approached and sang it with his usual abandon and precise intonation. He was in fine form throughout the rest of the broadcast.

That evening, when the Old Met's gold curtains parted for the last time for a Gala Farewell, Tucker again stood at center stage—this time with Zinka Milanov. They were to sing the fiery duet from the second act of *Andrea Chénier*—a reprise of the final performance of Milanov's legendary career, which had taken place earlier that same week. Then as well, Tucker had been her Chénier—he had personally asked Bing for the honor.

Twenty-eight years had passed since Milanov's Metropolitan debut. During her long reign, she had sung more than 450 performances in New York or on tour with the company. Her final performance on Wednesday, April 13, 1966, was electrifying and memorable. "A good deal of the ravishing Milanov voice still remains," judged the *Daily News'* Douglas Watt, "and she performed with sweep and authority. Tucker too was in magnificent voice, and their big second-act duet brought down the house."

Watt and other New York critics wondered aloud why Milanov had elected to retire while her voice was still reasonably near its prime. Neither she nor the Metropolitan disclosed that Bing had thought otherwise. Bing, not she, drew her career to a close. "I had wanted to sing in the new theater," she said in a recent interview, "but Mr. Bing said that he could not allow it."

At that Gala Farewell, a week after her final *Chénier,* generations of stellar singers came and were seated onstage to pay their respects to the Old Met—Lotte Lehmann, Marian Anderson, Lily Pons, Elisabeth Rethberg, Bidú Sayão, Marjorie Lawrence, Stella Roman, Rose Bampton, Richard Crooks, Frederick Jagel, Raoul Jobin, Alexander Kipnis, and Giovanni Martinelli, then in his eighties—but it was Zinka Milanov's entrance that touched off the most thunderous applause. For all of the musical splendor of the evening's riches—among them scenes from *Der Rosenkavalier* with Montserrat Caballé, Judith Raskin, and Rosalind Elias, *Manon Lescaut* with Franco Corelli and Renata Tebaldi, a magically spun "D'amor sull'ali rosee" from *Trovatore* by

Leontyne Price, and an entire Immolation Scene from *Götterdämmerung* with Birgit Nilsson—it was the Milanov-Tucker *Chénier* duet that garnered the most frenetic applause of the night. Afterward, the assembled artists joined voices in a chorus of "Auld Lang Syne" that marked the end of one epoch and the beginning of another.

12

Q: You're singing now almost more than at any earlier time in your career. Don't you ever want to slow down and take it easy?

A: No, not until I have to. Why slow down if you're still on top? Right now, I'm "hot," as they say—you know, more offers than I could accept if I wanted to. Taxes take a pretty big bite out of the gross, so, like any other business, I make it up in volume. I sing a lot— but money's not the big thing. I owe it to my public to keep singing as long as the voice is still there.

In the winter of 1966, not long before the Old Met received its last illustrious audience, Richard and Sara Tucker celebrated their thirtieth wedding anniversary. Appropriately, the Old Met had a place in the scenario. The afternoon he celebrated his anniversary—Saturday, February 12, 1966—Tucker appeared as Radames in a broadcast performance of *Aida*. Leontyne Price, once again, was his Aida; Zubin Mehta conducted. Tucker, said *New York Times* critic Howard Klein, was fully "in his stride," exhibiting "his familiar declamatory style, clarion top, clear diction, and plenty of breath"—even interpolating a finely focused high B near the end of the second act.

After the performance, he and Sara were taken by limousine to the banquet room of the New Yorker Hotel, where they received three hundred guests—a Who's Who of art, politics, religion, and society in Manhattan, observed the *Times*. But the nostalgic moments for the Tuckers were with their longtime friends who attended the celebration—couples whose married lives had begun when theirs had, friends from their early years in Manhattan, the Bronx, and Brooklyn during Richard's years as a young cantor. These were the people to whom he remained closest—

people who, like Ben Herschaft, he could pull aside whenever they called him "Richard" and say, "What's with this 'Richard' stuff, Bennie? Have you gone high-hat on me? I'm Ruby to you."

As Tucker stood with Sara in the receiving line, the magnitude of the celebration must have made him keenly aware of the breadth of his success—regardless how one would choose to define or measure it. In material terms alone, he had progressed from a $5-a-day job in the fur market to an annual income of nearly $300,000. He had once netted $25 a week as a cantor. Now, at the Park Synagogue in Chicago—which Rabbi Alvin Kleinerman and a dedicated group of trustees had built up chiefly around Tucker's cantorial reputation—he commanded an average of $70,000 for the Rosh Hashanah and Yom Kippur services alone.

His success as a parent was similarly unquestionable. Barry had entered Wall Street before graduating from New York University and had married Joan Kramer in June 1965. Henry would soon graduate from Tufts and would graduate from Brooklyn Law School, later joining a large Wall Street law firm and eventually relocating for a time in Los Angeles. Later, Henry would represent a number of his father's colleagues in his Madison Avenue entertainment and commercial law practice in New York. David would graduate from the Cornell Medical School in 1967, and would intern under renowned eye surgeons in the United States, Europe, and South America, eventually entering private practice in Cincinnati, Ohio.

Tucker would always unabashedly trace each success to the day he married Sara. Many of the sites and scenes of their early life were now only memories—the Grand Mansion, the Rumanian cafés along Delancey Street, the Jolson Theatre, Ye Eats Shoppe, the Hippodrome, Temple Adath Israel, and soon even the Old Met. But on his anniversary, in the presence of political figures, celebrities, and longtime friends, Tucker could renew his vows with the woman whose foresight, strength, and complete confidence had been the cornerstone of his emergence as one of the greatest singers of his time.

In the presence of their friends, Richard gave Sara a diamond to commemorate their anniversary. As photographers captured the moment, their flashbulbs reflecting in the facets of the immense stone, Tucker whispered to her, "This is the one your mamma would have wanted to see." When he awoke the next morning in the comfort of their Long Island home, he found a handwritten note on the adjacent pillow. "No diamond, whatever its size, can ever compare to you," Sara wrote. "Throughout these many years, you have kept the promise you made me. Like a rosebush, you have blossomed every year, and in more ways than you will ever know, you have indeed made me proud of you."

At age fifty-two, thirty years into his marriage and twenty-one into his career, Richard Tucker felt blessed. In some of the interviews he gave, he reflected on this. "The good Lord blessed me with a voice, a calling, and of course He puts a lot of responsibility on my shoulders," he told a New York interviewer in 1966. Still, privately, as he told his friend Ben Herschaft, he could not help but see his career in realistic terms—especially given his age. "It's scary, Bennie, because nobody can go on forever," he admitted. "It's got to start slipping away sometime—what the hell, I'm no kid anymore. But until it does, I'm stayin' in high gear."

Overdrive would have been the better metaphor, when one looks back on the accomplishments of the last decade of his life. Gambler that he was, he was ready for higher stakes. As Tucker felt himself nearing some vague deadline, a sense of restlessness led him to raise those stakes even higher.

Little else would explain why, between 1966 and 1975, he advanced his career into nothing but high-risk territory. As if driving himself to prove the literal truth of the "American Caruso" label—nothing more than a public-relations slogan, originally—Tucker undertook increasingly dramatic roles long associated with his predecessor's memory: Canio in *Pagliacci,* Samson, and finally Eléazar in *La Juive.*

Were this not enough, between 1969 and 1972 Tucker chose to concentrate a great part of his career in Italy, opting for debuts before the extremely demanding critics and audiences of Milan and Parma, and returning to other capitals—Rome, Florence, and Verona—in roles that were anything but safe ventures. As Giuseppe di Stefano would eventually say of this period of Tucker's career, "Any man who could sing *Manon Lescaut* in Rome, *Ballo in maschera* in Florence, *Il trovatore* in Parma, *Aida* in Verona, and choose *Luisa Miller* for his debut at La Scala—now, *this* was a tenor!"

Some of these European performances impinged on Tucker's Metropolitan schedule during the premiere season of the new opera house. As it was, the High Holydays, coupled with the opening of the new Jones Hall in Houston, kept Tucker from the new Met until November 1966, when he sang three performances of *Aida* between November 7 and 26. In Houston, a month earlier, he had sung three other *Aida*s (with Tucci, Colzani, and Tozzi) at Jones Hall. Soon afterward he left for Europe, where he was heard for the first time in Barcelona, as Riccardo in *Ballo,* and in Budapest, as Cavaradossi in *Tosca.*

The response he received in each capital, however, more than compensated Tucker for his absence from the excitement of the new Lincoln Center. In Barcelona, where the popularity of his operatic recordings led the press to dub him *"el tenor mas grande del America"*—"America's greatest tenor"—he was lauded by *El correo Catalan* for his "exemplary technique, clarion yet lyric voice, and 'native' Italian diction." (A youthful spectator at this first Tucker *Ballo* was, interestingly, tenor José Carreras.) In Florence, the respected critic Leonardo Pinzauti echoed these same sentiments, declaring that Tucker "fully justified his great reputation . . . not merely in the solo moments, where he shone as expected, but equally so in [the] demanding ensembles."

Tucker's appearance as Cavaradossi in *Tosca* at the Erkel Theatre in Budapest proved to be the only performance of his career in a Communist country—by his own choice. "The Communists, especially the Russians, want artists on their [that is, the Communists'] own terms," he told Janet Bookspan in his Oral History interview. "I have always given the Communists a standing offer. I will sing anywhere, in any opera house they have, if three conditions are met. First, they have to pay me fifty thousand dollars for one month of singing. Second, they have to let *me* distribute the money in the Jewish communities wherever I sing. And, third, I have to be allowed to sing at services in every synagogue along the way. But you can't dictate to Communists, and they won't accept any of my terms."

Due to the swiftness and ruthlessness with which the Soviets crushed the Hungarians during their ill-fated revolt of 1956, Tucker personally considered the people of Hungary to be involuntary participants in the Communist bloc. For this reason, and perhaps to attempt to establish a reputation (and possibly leverage) in a Communist-controlled country, he did not insist that all his terms be met—especially the $50,000 fee—when he negotiated his contract with the Hungarian National Theatre. Politically, however, no minds were changed.

But, musically, the Budapest *Tosca* performance was an unequivocal success. At the close of the opera, Tucker was ushered to the front of the stage by way of an iron door near the curtain—a symbolic gesture reserved for the artist who has clearly been the star of the performance.

In the spring of 1967, after these first European triumphs, Tucker opted for more distant ports: he agreed to sing for nothing in the battle zones of Vietnam. The impetus for his decision to entertain the troops was a conversation he had with Robert McNamara, then Secretary of Defense under President Lyndon Johnson, at a White House state dinner honoring Ethiopian Emperor Haile Selassie in February 1967. After Tucker had sung for the distinguished group, McNamara asked whether he might consider a USO engagement, perhaps in the relative safety of Bangkok.

Unknowingly, McNamara had touched on not only Tucker's patriotism but also his lingering feeling of having owed his country a debt since his deferment during World War II. Tucker saw a chance to repay that in Vietnam. After nominal discussion with his family, he worked out an agreement to sing a Passover seder in any battle zone the Defense Department would choose. He added a proviso that Sara be allowed to travel with him—and he volunteered to pay their expenses.

Initially, the Defense Department balked at permitting Sara to accompany him, but eventually Tucker prevailed by pointing out her familiarity with the area, owing to their own Far East tour of ten years before. Sara, in turn, persuaded the Jewish Welfare Board to purchase *mezuzahs*—small scrolls of prayers traditionally placed at the entrance of a home—to be given to each of the Jewish soldiers at the seders.

In mid-April, the Defense Department coordinated the shipment of some eighteen tons of kosher delicacies to sites in Saigon, Nha Trang, and Da Nang, where seder services were to be held simultaneously on April 24. Not only were the requisite sacramental wine, *gefilte* fish, matzoh, and lamb sent to the three sites, but also hundreds of new kitchen utensils for their kosher preparation.

Tucker officiated at the main site, in an enormous field tent erected on a base in Saigon. He shared the dais with Rabbi William Rosenblum, a distinguished military chaplain and for many years rabbi of the Temple Israel congregation in New York City. Two others, Rabbi Samuel Sobel and Reverend Benjamin Fairchild, an Episcopalian chaplain, participated in the seder as well. An estimated sixteen hundred servicemen, varying in rank from privates to colonels, attended the seder. In a letter written to Rabbi Israel Levinthal on April 28, Tucker described the event himself:

> I don't believe I will ever see anything like it again. They came in fatigues and full battle dress, their rifles still on their backs, but with *yarmulkes* instead of their helmets, and many of them with prayer shawls draped over grenades that hung from their belts. So young and so innocent-looking, all of them!
>
> There were Gentiles who came with their Jewish buddies, and we welcomed them. Even some *shvarzes* [blacks] joined us! They told Sara that they had never heard a cantor, and besides, their friends told them that the food was going to be great.
>
> Sara was named "Mother of the Seder" and the boys presented her with a beautiful corsage, and it made her very happy. In turn, she presented over five hundred *mezuzahs* to the troops. We want them to remember that they have a home waiting for them when this nightmare is over. I am going to try to sing as much as I can. I hope to continue to Da Nang, Camrahn Bay, and somewhere near an airbase outside Saigon, giving a concert each day for all the branches of our Armed Forces.

Tucker dispatched the letter from an aircraft carrier (coincidentally, the *Bonhomme Richard*) in the Gulf of Tonkin. There, amid the distant sounds of artillery along the coast of North Vietnam, he gave a concert for 3,500 men on the deck of that carrier—at eight o'clock in the morning. The choice of the hour, he said later, was by no means his own. "When the Captain told me eight o'clock, I said, 'Sir, I don't even spit before nine.' But the Captain said it was the best time for the boys, so I went ahead and sang. There was an accordion player accompanying me, and I started out with 'You'll Never Walk Alone.' Pretty soon, I saw faces peeking out of gun turrets, and fellows laying down their tools—and then they really started coming."

The Associated Press later reported that Tucker sang arias from *Aida, Gioconda,* and *Forza del destino,* capping them with

Neapolitan songs and a medley of Broadway show tunes. To Sara, who was not permitted to travel past Saigon, he remarked later on the irony of "singing 'Cielo e mar' on an aircraft carrier, looking at the real sea and sky, but seeing shells bursting in front of the clouds."

While touring the battle zones, Richard and Sara took down an estimated 700 telephone numbers and messages—greetings from soldiers to their families in the States, all of which Tucker promised to relay. When he returned to New York, Tucker found his plan thwarted by New York Telephone, to whom he appealed for help in making and paying for the long-distance calls. From one echelon of its administration to the next, New York Telephone said no to him on grounds of setting a precedent.

When the final "I'm-sorry-but-policies-won't-permit-this" came from the executive offices, Tucker lost his restraint and railed (over the phone, quite appropriately) at the "cheap bastards who run that goddamned monopoly," accusing them of some involvement, overt or covert, in every social ill he could list on the spur of the moment. For a time, he was tempted to relate to the newspapers what he considered the company's insensitivity; in the end, he restrained himself, and he and Sara placed the calls, one by one, at their own expense. "For many of the families we called," Sara remembered, "our messages were the only assurance they had that their husbands or sons were still alive."

The joy and relief these calls brought to the families they contacted slightly offset Tucker's anger at New York Telephone, but only slightly. After the last calls had been made some two months later, he was still seething at the company. As his own private protest, he made a point of going to the company's executive headquarters in Manhattan and hand-delivering his payment for the final bill.

With shellbursts of Vietnam still fresh in his memory, Tucker flew with Sara to Israel to appear in a series of concerts at the Mann Auditorium in Tel Aviv in the summer of 1967. He had first sung in his ancestral homeland nine years earlier, at the invitation of the Israel Philharmonic Orchestra. Since then, he had appeared eight times. He was justifiably proud of having been invited back so frequently. "The Israeli people are a critical audience," Tucker remarked to Janet Bookspan. "The agent who brought me to Je-

rusalem, Henry Haftel, warned me that my reputation in America would do me no good in Israel. If the Israelis don't like an
artist, they give him very lukewarm applause and send him
home—and he isn't invited back. Thank God, they took me into
their hearts."

In his Tel Aviv engagements of 1967, Tucker shared honors
with Roberta Peters. Erich Leinsdorf conducted. The last of the
concerts took place on Saturday evening, June 3—the eve of the
Six-Day War. Tucker recalled that concert movingly:

"Earlier in the week, before the June 5 concert, Israel began
mobilizing her troops, getting ready for an attack. When the mo-
bilization started, the American Embassy was on the phone to Sara
and me, pleading with us to go back to the States. I said, 'I'm
not leaving, I'm staying right here and I'm going to sing.' Roberta told them the same thing. She's a very courageous girl, and
she felt we had a commitment to keep to our people. But the
embassy kept insisting. 'We know how you feel,' they said, 'but
you can do more for us in America than you can do here.' Still,
we held to our word, and we stayed.

"By Saturday, we were without a conductor. Leinsdorf had
left the country without even notifying the orchestra! Fortunately, a very talented Israeli boy, Sergiu Comissiona, who went
on to become conductor of the Baltimore Symphony, took
Leinsdorf's place at the last minute.

"I went on, and I sang my heart out. Every word I sang, I
kept looking at their faces—knowing that the attack was coming,
wondering if I would ever see them again.

"At the Metropolitan they'll tell you that I know how to keep
my emotions under control, how to walk that fine line between
keeping a tear in the voice without getting tears in the eyes. That
night in Tel Aviv, I was in trouble and I knew it. In a way, I
made it worse for myself by singing *Shabbos* songs and some
cantorial pieces for encores. It was *so* hard to sing those Yiddish
and Hebrew words, with all the suffering that they contain, when
Israel herself was at knife-point!

"I kept myself in one piece only because I had to concentrate
on *staying* in one piece—that's all that kept me going through my
encores. The last one I remember singing was 'Shir Hacheirut'—
a tribute to the *Halutsom,* the Jewish pioneers. I didn't want to
go, and the audience kept applauding, so I sang 'Hatikvah,' the

Israeli national anthem. I knew I shouldn't sing anything more after that—but somehow I just couldn't leave the stage.

"After the applause finally died down, I just stood there and didn't move. I decided I would speak to them and tell them that the embassy told me to go back to the States. Then I thought I would ask the people if there was some word, some message, they wanted me to take back.

"The applause kept on, so finally I raised my hands to try to quiet things down. A lot of people were crying—I could see them very plainly because I always insisted the lights had to be up. They grew quiet, and I started to speak. I said one word—just one word, believe me—and I broke up. I couldn't face them. I bit my lips and kept trying to talk, but every time I started I couldn't get past saying 'I-don't-want-to-leave-you-but—' and then I would break up.

"Finally, I just opened my hands as if to say, 'I can't go on, I can't even talk.' I walked off the stage, fell into Sara's arms, and cried like a baby.

"We left Tel Aviv on Sunday morning. The next day, the Six-Day War started. Sara and I were in New York only briefly, because we had to leave for Italy right away. I was scheduled to sing *Andrea Chénier* in Florence early in July, and the way the rehearsal schedule was set, I had to be there early.

"As soon as I sang my last performance in Florence, I worked out a deal with El Al [the Israeli airline] to get me into Tel Aviv. Every night I had watched the news, I'd read the papers and the magazines—and I kept seeing the faces of these brave people. I thought to myself, 'If you can sing for your American troops in Vietnam, the least you can do is sing for your Jewish people when they need you.'

"I had to work the El Al deal under the table because of the restriction on civilian travel. I didn't even tell Sara until I had worked it all out. She said to me, 'You don't think you're going alone, do you? I'm going where you go!'

"The morning after we arrived in Tel Aviv, we were taken to a small airport and were flown to a desert commando base in a one-engine Cessna plane. They warned us ahead of time that because the plane flew so slow, it would be an easy mark for enemy fighter planes, or for their desert raiders.

"The Israeli writer Itzhak Nimsovitch and a young accompanist who played the accordion flew with us. When we landed, the airmen and the soldiers—they were so young, girls as well as boys—were all waiting for us. The welcome we got is too un-believable to express in words—they made me feel like a mes-siah. Some of them shouted that I was like David, ready to take my life into my hands to sing for them. They began shouting, 'Hazzanuth! Hazzanuth!'—the Hebrew word for cantorial music. They didn't want popular music, or even patriotic songs. They wanted sacred music, the music of David.

"The very next morning, we flew back to Tel Aviv, and then went to visit the wounded soldiers at the Tel Hashomer Hospi-tal. One of the head surgeons took us through the different units. He showed us how some of the soldiers even made artificial limbs for the others, because they couldn't get them from the outside world.

"In the wards, I saw scenes that will haunt me for the rest of my life. I stood at the bed of a young boy who had lost one leg; I sang softly to him while the doctors tried to save the other leg. I sang for a boy who had once played the violin, but had lost his arm in battle. It was all so very, very sad—and there was so little to say, so little I could do but sing to them.

"The most haunting moment of all came later that day, in another ward. I saw this gaunt-looking man, maybe in his forties but looking much older, hobbling toward me on a crutch. He had one leg—the other was gone practically up to the hip. I found out later that he had been in charge of burying the dead, and had stepped on a land mine. When I saw him hobbling toward me, I said to him, 'Slow down! Let me come to you!' I went over to him and asked what I could do for him. He said, 'I just wanted to see with my own eyes that you came!'

"Then I said to him, trying to be reassuring, that I was sorry about his tragedy. I can still see the look on his face when he said to me, 'What is there to be sorry about? What's a leg? I still have two arms. I still have two eyes. I'll make it all right!'

"He was a fighter, a survivor. In that one man, that hollow-looking soldier, I saw the whole story of Israel."

In the fall of 1967, Tucker began negotiations with the South Af-rican Symphony to sing ten opera and concert performances in four cities—Johannesburg, Cape Town, Pretoria, and Durban. He was to make his debut in *La traviata* at the Civic Theatre in Johannesburg on August 28, 1968, and would subsequently appear in a cantorial recital as a benefit for Johannesburg's Yeshiva College. Alex Alexay would accompany Tucker in his concert performances.

During the negotiations, overseen by Johannesburg agents Percy Tucker (no relation) and H. Sol Liebgott, Tucker insisted on a provision in his contract that did not entirely endear him to the South African government. The provision was prominently titled "concerts for non-white audiences" in the draft Tucker forwarded to Liebgott in May 1968. The provision prompted this reply from Liebgott, which Tucker received on June 8, 1968:

> It is very difficult to arrange at this stage, as you requested, concerts for non-white audiences. . . . The major problem is the audience. At the last concert arranged for non-whites, only thirty people turned up—and admission is usually free. But please rest assured that we will do our best to adhere to your request.

Ultimately, Tucker continued to insist, and a concert for blacks was arranged, though attendance would indeed be limited because it was planned only *after* Tucker arrived in Johannesburg. Still, the concert gave him a great sense of satisfaction in having persisted and won a small victory.

But before that trip, on the morning of June 9, 1968, Tucker arose early, intending to go into Manhattan to, among other business matters, prepare a response to Liebgott. However, the morning news brought a devastating report: during the night, Robert Kennedy had become the victim of an assassin's bullet.

Tucker postponed his plans in order to follow the tragedy on television. That same morning, he received a telephone call from the late Terence Cardinal Cooke, of the Archdiocese of New York. The cardinal told Tucker that the Kennedy family wanted him to sing at the senator's funeral Mass in St. Patrick's Cathedral. Tucker had known the Kennedys only in the casual way that most artists knew them—through occasional invitations to entertain at the White House, or at fund raisers like the annual Alfred E. Smith dinners in New York. He was by no means a close friend of Robert Kennedy, and was therefore all the more touched by being asked to sing at the funeral.

Popular singer Andy Williams, who was a Kennedy family

friend, also sang during the service. Williams's softly sung, slowly paced rendition of "The Battle Hymn of the Republic" captured the greater public attention, but Tucker, deeply affected himself, sang a moving performance of the "Panis Angelicus" that rang memorably through the cavernous cathedral.

The virtual conquest of the opera capitals of Italy that marked Richard Tucker's last years continued apace with his debut at the Teatro dell'Opera in Rome, in February 1969, as Des Grieux in Puccini's *Manon Lescaut*. Though twenty years had passed since he had first sung Des Grieux to Licia Albanese's delicately spun Manon Lescaut, the role remained Tucker's favorite, apart from Eléazar in *La Juive*.

His only comment to the Roman daily *Il popolo di Roma*, when he arrived for his first rehearsal on January 29, was simply, "The weather in New York could have been a lot better." This was indeed an understatement. For several days, he and Sara had been sequestered in Great Neck, anxious to leave but prevented by the deepening snow mounds surrounding their house. Tucker paced the floor and tried to distract himself any way he could—reading back issues of the *Wall Street Journal,* watching game shows on television, anything to pass the time. As their original departure was to have been before Sara's birthday on January 28, he had planned to give her a party in Rome. But as the weather grew worse, he began to wonder whether they would go to Rome at all.

Sub-zero temperatures, coupled with the snow and high winds, kept both the La Guardia and Kennedy airports closed. Even the telephone was out of order for a time, preventing Tucker from staying in contact with John Gualiani, to keep Gualiani apprised of the weather situation and the subsequent changes in their arrival time. Fortunately, La Guardia reopened on the afternoon of the 28th, and TWA gave the Tuckers priority status. At long last, they were on their way to Rome.

"We were in the air about an hour," Sara recalled, "and we weren't saying much to each other—you know, just sitting there, not exactly mad at the weather, but very disappointed that we had to start such an important trip with all this confusion. I was staring out the window, dejected, when Richard told me the stewardess had a message for me. I looked up and saw her hold-

ing this big birthday cake—it even had my name on it. It took a
second or two for it to register with me. Before I could make up
my mind to laugh or cry, the whole crew was singing 'Happy
Birthday' to me, and Richard was helping them pass around glasses
of champagne to all the passengers. Even with all that he had on
his mind—from the weather to his Rome debut—he gave me one
of the best birthday parties of my life."

By the time the Tuckers arrived in Rome and checked into
the Grand Hotel, it was after 1:00 A.M.—and it was nearly 4:30
A.M., Rome time, when they fell asleep. Nevertheless, Richard
was up and about early the next morning, and even managed to
arrive at the theater fifteen minutes before the ten o'clock rehearsal call. Once the rehearsals were under way, Tucker began
to relax and to enjoy Rome. He took in the historical sites with
Sara, conductor Thomas Schippers, John Gualiani, and anyone else
who wanted to join them. He sampled the *cuccina alla Judea* to
which his friend, sculptor Milton Hebald, introduced him in the
Jewish districts of Rome, and also consumed large quantities of
fresh fruit, *cappuccino,* and *bel paese* cheese.

Tucker especially looked forward to sojourns with Hebald,
who often flew to meet him wherever he was singing in Italy—
Rome, Milan, Parma, Verona—and, in favorable weather, would
take Tucker on long, annotated walks. Hebald enjoyed pointing
out the intricacies of classical art and architecture, the significance
of various monuments, and otherwise educating Tucker in Italian
culture. For Hebald himself, these sessions had a second purpose
as well: he was already making preliminary sketches for a bronze
bust of Tucker. Neither man would have imagined that only a
few years later, copies of that bust would be placed in the Mann
Auditorium in Tel Aviv, and in the Richard Tucker Memorial
Park on Broadway in Manhattan.

One of the most memorable of the evenings Tucker spent in
Rome prior to his *Manon Lescaut* debut came at the invitation of
the family of his tenor-idol, Beniamino Gigli. Soprano Rina Gigli,
Gigli's daughter, was living in a custom-built home on the grounds
of her parents' immense villa on the Via Storchio. Her mother,
then nearly eighty, lived in the villa itself amid a retinue of servants.

When the Tuckers accepted her invitation, Mrs. Gigli had her
servants prepare a five-course meal for the Tuckers. She saw to

it that Richard ate more than his share of the main course, a special lasagna dish that Gigli himself had favored after his performances. Though Tucker pleaded with her to come to the Teatro dell'Opera for his debut—even promising to have her chauffeur-driven—it was clear that she was no longer well enough to venture much outside the grounds of her villa.

When she told Richard how much she regretted not being able to hear the tenor voice most frequently compared to her husband's, he rose from the table and sang "Donna non vidi mai" to her. In return for this spontaneous and, for him, very emotional musical moment, the tenor's widow presented Tucker with one of the many medals Gigli had been awarded during his illustrious career.

The debut performance of *Manon Lescaut* was scheduled for March 3, 1969. On the day of the performance, Tucker agreed, in a moment of impetuousness, to be photographed by RCA's Rome publicity bureau. The session called for still photographs to be taken of him in front of the statue of Mario Cavaradossi at the famed Castel Sant'Angelo, the setting of Act III of Puccini's *Tosca*. Though the weather was agreeable, Tucker had to climb and then reclimb so many stairs that he became short of breath. Sara, always aware of his heart condition, began to worry—only to have Richard dismiss her concerns and, in a calculated show of bravado, tell her that he could "take these steps two at a time and never break my stride."

Despite Sara's fears, the photo session in no way weakened him for what lay ahead that evening in *Manon Lescaut*. The crowds had begun queuing up in mid-afternoon—and, to be fair, many of them entered the theater skeptically. Probably few doubted the quality of Tucker's voice, having heard the recordings he had made in Rome for RCA in the early 1960s. But many doubted whether, at fifty-six years old, Tucker could portray a credible Cavaliere des Grieux.

The critics' columns the next day give a clear indication of the majority opinion. At the outset of the period in which he was to reach the pinnacle of his career, Tucker had indeed passed a severe test.

As regards his acting in the part of the youthful Des Grieux, the consensus was that he could scarcely have been bettered. The critic for *Il giornale d'Italia,* directly addressing the matter of

Tucker's age, wrote, "It is generally agreed that Des Grieux, when sung by an artist no longer young, has been much less effective. Yet Richard Tucker was able to render Des Grieux's love for Manon with so much impetuosity, so much fervor and desperation, that he *became* the young Cavalier before our eyes." Guido Pannain, writing in *Il tempo,* added that by singing such a youthful part Tucker "risked more, but in the long run obtained a great success with equally great dignity in the high quality of his characterization."

The greatest accolades, however, were reserved for his voice. Among four of the major critics then writing in the Rome newspapers, not one of them had anything but the highest praise for his technique. Renzo Rossellini, critic for *Il messagero,* labeled him "a tenor of the authentic Italian school, following the footsteps of predecessors in a lineage now all but lost. In his voice, there is tradition—the evanescence of memories of the unsurpassable Caruso, but preserved with it the power and the flavor of the art of Beniamino Gigli and the young Giuseppe di Stefano."

"Twenty years have passed since Toscanini gave us Tucker in those priceless NBC broadcasts of *Aida,"* wrote Pannain in *Il tempo.* "Yet his voice, to our astonishment, seems to have escaped the insidiousness of time." Capping such accolades, the critic for *L'Unità* stated flatly, "We do not have anyone in Italy today who can sing as Tucker does."

By March 1969, John Gualiani was satisfied that Tucker's long-awaited La Scala debut would finally occur. In Milan, arrangements for the revival of *Luisa Miller* and a hopeful replay of Tucker's 1968 Met triumph in that opera were progressing on schedule.

Then Gualiani received a message from Luigi Oldani, of the Scala management, that took him back fifteen years. Would Tucker, Oldani asked, please make himself available three weeks earlier than his end-of-April contract had specified? Gualiani was almost too incredulous to answer.

Oldani went on to explain that the management now wanted Tucker to open the much-publicized International Fair, in which 112 nations participated. "Imagine, Oldani wanted Richard to sing four performances of *Ballo in maschera* only fifteen days before he was to make his debut in *Luisa Miller,"* Gualiani recalled. "There was Richard, preparing for the debut he had waited so long to make, and the management wanted him to change his plans again. It was déjà vu!"

And then, almost as a footnote to his request, Oldani asked Gualiani whether Tucker knew *Ballo in maschera.*

"He's only been singing it for twenty years," Gualiani replied. "But that doesn't mean he's going to want to sing it when he's trying to be ready for *Luisa Miller."*

When Gualiani telephoned, Tucker was dumbfounded. "Richard said to me, 'What the hell—?' He actually considered it, though—probably because he was afraid that if he didn't sing the *Ballo* performances, they might cancel his debut. But in the end we got around it by using his Metropolitan contract as an excuse. We said he couldn't leave New York a day earlier than the contract called for." This time, Tucker got his way.

Even before his income matched his life-style, Barry Tucker had become accustomed to jetting in and out of Europe, sometimes arriving on the day of his father's performance and leaving for the States the next morning. When Barry arrived shortly before the *Luisa Miller* debut, he found his father engrossed in a letter from Giacomo Lauri-Volpi. John Gualiani had translated it for him from Italian.

When Barry asked what the letter said, Richard handed him the translation:

> I write not to add to your thoughts, which naturally, I understand, are considerable as you finalize your preparations. Rather, I write merely to ask you to bear in mind a few matters concerning La Scala audiences, and this mystifying opera of our beloved Verdi, *Luisa Miller.*

Lauri-Volpi went on to remind Tucker that *Luisa* was easily one of the most controversial of Verdi's operas, viewed from the perspective of more than a century of critical reaction.

> I sang *Luisa Miller* in Florence more than thirty years ago, and the reaction was much the same there as it had been in New York several years before, when I sang it with Rosa Ponselle at the Metropolitan. Some thought the opera weak, commonplace, and monotonous, especially compared to its immediate successors, *Rigoletto* and *Trovatore,* whereas others thought it one of Verdi's absolute masterpieces. It is a role which, though very difficult, I sang well

because of my technique; in fact it was I, you may be aware, whom the management of the [Florence] Maggio Musicale called when Gigli had to decline the role because he did not have the technique for it.

I succeeded because I knew how to pace my voice. As your elder, my friend, I want to remind you of the importance for you to do the same. I cannot say this enough, especially in the final act. There you must pace your voice and keep your reserves, for otherwise this opera is unendurable even for the best of tenors.

Lauri-Volpi ended his letter by underscoring that the Milan public would be strangers to *Luisa Miller*. The opera had last been given under Toscanini near the turn of the century—and even then it had not been uniformly well received. "This strangeness on the audience's part, their not being familiar with more than one or two arias," Lauri-Volpi wrote, "may make them less demonstrative. Mentally, you must not let their reaction deter you from giving your best."

Just how prophetic Lauri-Volpi's words were became clear at Tucker's debut the following evening. As the event had been abundantly promoted, there were no vacant seats in the venerable La Scala theater on May 20, 1969. Barry found his father predictably self-assured and eager for the opening curtain. He and his mother stayed backstage until the last minute, then were shown to their seats in the orchestra section.

The applause that greeted Tucker was vociferous. The first act—quaintly titled "Love" by the composer, to set it apart from the remaining two acts, "Intrigue" and "Poison"—progressed fluidly from beginning to end, with Tucker in exquisite voice. The applause, however, was anything but enthusiastic as the act went on.

At the first intermission, Tucker sat in his dressing room, alternately puzzled and concerned about the audience's indifferent response—all the while trying to keep in mind Lauri-Volpi's admonitions. Barry, meanwhile, pushed through the intermission crowds, looking for John Gualiani. When he found him, Barry asked bluntly, "What's wrong with these people? Why the hell are they so cold?"

"Go back to your seat and don't worry about it," John told him. "Like Lauri-Volpi said, they don't know the music well enough to react. But wait till the next act."

In Act II, during the melodious but unfamiliar music to which the love triangle of Luisa, Rodolfo, and Wurm is set, a burst of applause greeted the minor-key strains of the woodwinds and strings introducing Rodolfo's lament, the familiar aria "Quando le sere al placido."

We have the word of the critic from *Il giorno* that as soon as Tucker finished the last dramatic phrase in the aria, "The theater erupted in a demonstration that went on for approximately five minutes. Rarely in the history of this theater have such ringing top tones, surging musicality, and vivid personality been wedded in the performance of a single Verdi aria."

Mindful of Lauri-Volpi's advice that he pace himself, Tucker had more than his customary reserves in the opera's concluding act. "All of the facets of his performing that have long been reported—the flawless diction, the unerring intonation, the power, the refined legato—were there in abundance in the final act," said *Il giorno*. "And much else was there, too: a polished actor, a man of genuine emotion, an artist who turned the clock back to the time of Pertile and Gigli.

"Whether or not the music is deserving of the mature reputation of Verdi is one matter, and remains arguable. That Richard Tucker—an American Jew—is among the greatest tenors who have sung at the Teatro alla Scala is now beyond any dispute."

The audience seemed in clear agreement: more than two hundred people awaited him backstage, hoping for an autograph. True to form, he left the theater only after the last program had been signed.

Florence, the scene of two earlier triumphs—his debut as Riccardo in *Ballo in maschera* in 1966, and his return (just after the Israeli Six-Day War) in *Andrea Chénier*—welcomed him repeatedly between 1969 and 1972. At the Maggio Musicale in 1969, he sang his first European performance of *Il trovatore*. His Leonora, Montserrat Caballé, remembered the thunderous ovations he received, especially after the taxing third act. "As they did in Rome and Milan," Caballé said, "the people of Florence regarded him as one of their own, a true Italian tenor. They came backstage—crowds of people—and said over and over, 'Where have you been? Why aren't you here all the time?' They loved his singing because his was the most virile tenor voice of its time—certainly the most virile I have ever heard."

Tucker returned to Florence some six months later, to repeat his triumph in *Ballo in maschera*. Subsequently, Florentine audiences would hear his Duke in *Rigoletto*, Canio in *Pagliacci*, and a third series of *Ballo in maschera* performances. Florence was the site of some of Tucker's greatest triumphs in Italy and a city of warm personal memories as well—as when he and Sara and their close friend Natalie Eisenstadt once found themselves stranded in Florence's Excelsior Hotel in the midst of December ice storms. Unable to celebrate Hanukkah in a more traditional way, the three of them bought candelabrum-size candles at a nearby shop; they celebrated each night by lighting another candle and exchanging whatever small gifts they could find to buy. Wanting at least a hint of communal ceremony during this all-important time in the Jewish calendar, Richard led Sara and Natalie to the nearby Church of All Saints, where they observed the pageantry of Midnight Mass on Christmas Eve.

Tucker returned to New York from Florence at the end of December. He had originally been scheduled to sing in *Aida* on the September opening-night performance of the Met's 1969/70 season, with Price, Merrill, and Irene Dalis. But owing to labor disputes (once again finally settled at the eleventh hour), that opening did not take place until December 29, making it the latest opening of any Met season in its history. It was a triumphant performance nonetheless, and because of its lateness it made headlines across the country.

The 1969/70 season as a whole was to become one of the most memorable in Tucker's career. This was the season that marked the twenty-fifth anniversary of his Metropolitan debut and the full flowering of his artistry in the role most associated with Caruso, Canio in Leoncavallo's *I pagliacci*.

Through the greater part of 1968, often at his summer home near Rome, director Franco Zeffirelli designed the sets and costumes for a new production of the double bill of *Cavalleria rusticana* and *Pagliacci*. As an actor-turned-director, Zeffirelli had always envied the great tenors. "I would give my right arm to be a tenor," he said, "just to be able to produce that sound—those notes—in front of thousands and thousands of people."

As Zeffirelli would both design and stage the new *Cav* and *Pag* double bill, he had a great deal of say in casting the principals. For the first performance of the new productions—originally scheduled for September but, because of the labor disputes, rescheduled for early January 1970 as a benefit for the Metropol-

itan's Production Fund—Zeffirelli, Bing, and the two conductors, Thomas Schippers for *Cavalleria* (later to be replaced by
Leonard Bernstein) and Fausto Cleva for *Pagliacci,* concurred on
the following casting:

In *Cavalleria rusticana,* Franco Corelli would sing Turiddu,
Grace Bumbry would portray Santuzza, Nedda Casei would sing
the role of Lola, and Frank Guarrera would be heard as Alfio. In
Pagliacci, Tucker would portray Canio, Sherrill Milnes would sing
Tonio, and William Walker would appear as Silvio. Teresa Stratas was to sing the role of Nedda, though she would be replaced
at the first performance by Lucine Amara.

Tucker came to Franco Zeffirelli with the reputation of a great
singer who had developed into an effective but decidedly limited
actor. After the first two or three rehearsals, Zeffirelli's formula
for characterizations ("The key," said Zeffirelli, "is to mold the
basic nature of the actor to that of the character he is to portray")
began to work a special kind of magic. Whatever he had heard
of Tucker's marginal acting, Zeffirelli disregarded as he watched
Richard transform himself into a tragic character of near-classical
proportions.

"At last," Zeffirelli told Bing at the general rehearsal, "I have
a tenor I can *really* work with."

At the premiere of the production on the evening of January
8, 1970, from Canio's invitation to the villagers to "Come one,
come all!" to his final cry, "The comedy is ended!" Richard Tucker
created a character that no one who saw it is likely to forget. "It
was like a flame at the beginning, when Canio's jealousy slowly
begins to overtake him," said Francis Robinson. "As the story
unfolded, Richard made the flame become a fire. When he began
'No, Pagliaccio non son!' and he stripped away the trappings of
the clown, the fire became white-hot."

Marilyn Horne—then about to make her Metropolitan debut
as the co-star, with Joan Sutherland, of another of the season's
new productions, a revival of Bellini's *Norma*—thought Tucker's
characterization of Canio "shattering—just incredible." Luciano
Pavarotti considered it "one of the truly *great* performances I have
ever seen—not merely of Canio in *Pagliacci,* but any performance, anywhere."

"Not even Olivier," said Schuyler Chapin, "could have
touched Richard Tucker in *Pagliacci.*"

Precisely how Franco Zeffirelli effected this transformation lies perhaps more in his insights into Richard Tucker the man than in his actual direction of Richard Tucker the artist. Zeffirelli's philosophical departure point for a successful characterization was the "fit" between the inner nature of the actor and that of the character portrayed. Zeffirelli saw a far more complex person than Quaintance Eaton's man of "rather humorless dignity, profound religious feeling, and a businesslike approach to his career." Though Tucker impressed many people as being no more than this at base, that "sensible" man was largely an extension of the public image that he had carefully shaped over the years—the *hazzan,* the paterfamilias, the holy man/family man/businessman who happened to make his living in opera.

Zeffirelli's penetrating insights led him to see a private man, the "real" Richard Tucker, a man whose basic nature contained within it Canio's essential attribute—a volatile energy that could be contained only by hard-learned self-control, a self-control that, when it suddenly evaporates, does so with cataclysmic results. However free Tucker was of other essentials of Canio's makeup— jealousy and a basic insecurity as a man—he understood the sensual, the passionate—and his rare losses of self-control were almost always based on a breach of trust by someone he genuinely cared for. In this basic similarity, Zeffirelli found and shaped his Canio.

The ultimate test of *Pagliacci,* for director and tenor alike, was the reception it received abroad when Zeffirelli was invited to stage *Cavalleria* and *Pagliacci* in Florence. There, as in Manhattan, the usually reserved critics found themselves groping for superlatives when the production premiered on January 2, 1971.

"Tucker's Canio," wrote Alfredo Mandelli in the weekly magazine *Oggi illustrato,* "was nothing short of phenomenal. One hardly knows where to begin in praising it. His voice was fresh, powerful, romantic—and, in the final scene, scaldingly hot. At fifty-seven years old, he seemed no more than twenty on the stage. He demonstrated once and for all how Canio can be sung with absolute drive, in the true *verismo* tradition, without sacrificing a shimmering, limpid, finely focused tone quality. Tucker's technique is so perfect that it is certainly arguable whether there is another tenor anywhere who can measure up to it."

Writing in *La nazione* on January 3, the day after the first performance in Florence under Riccardo Muti, critic Leonardo Pinzauti underscored that "without any doubt the focal point of the performance was the incredible Richard Tucker, who left us in such awe that we wonder which we should admire more: his technical bravura, his musicality, his perfect control, or the intensity of his acting. Not only is his voice a marvel that seems to know no age limits, but his portrayal of Canio, from beginning to end, is a lesson in melodrama."

Tucker's first Canio was but two weeks behind him when, on January 25, 1970, he marked his twenty-fifth year at the Metropolitan Opera. For the previous two years, Rudolf Bing had sent him semiannual reminders that Tucker and the administration should work together to plan a gala performance befitting his many years of first-rank singing. Each of these "gentle reminders" carried a caveat that the planning would have to be done much in advance, owing to other singers' schedules.

As Bing would relate after the gala, Tucker bet him that he could personally plan and cast the event in less than a week. And, Bing readily conceded, Tucker had won the bet. After a meeting of minds with Columbia Artists' Michael Ries and Ronald Wilford—and with the usual input from Sara and his sons—Tucker decided to appear in four of his best-known roles: Alfredo in Act I of *La traviata,* Mario in Act III of *Tosca,* Radames in Act III of *Aida,* and, naturally, Enzo in Act II of *La Gioconda.* His choices (notable for the absence of *Pagliacci* and other recent successes) were based on the availability of a production (*Traviata, Tosca, Gioconda, and Aida* were all essentially new productions, no one of them being more than five seasons old) and the availability of a particular *prima diva* for each.

Rather to Bing's surprise, with no real advance notice Tucker landed three of the four "leading ladies" he had decided on: Joan Sutherland, Renata Tebaldi, Birgit Nilsson, and Leontyne Price. Dispensing with the formality of "engraved invitations," he telephoned each of them and asked them to make room in their schedules for a gala on April 11, 1970. Based on his notes and recollections of the telephone calls, not one of these First Ladies of the Metropolitan asked who the others were. He volunteered the information to Leontyne Price, who kidded him, saying, "I'll bet you've got this written down in front of you, Richard, and there's a blank space for you to fill in 'Joan,' 'Birgit,' 'Renata,' or 'Lee' when you dial the number!"

Only Birgit Nilsson was not available; Tucker had wanted her to sing Floria Tosca to his Mario Cavaradossi. Though she could not join him, Nilsson asked if she might appear with him at another benefit gala of his choice. Tentatively, they agreed to discuss later a joint concert, perhaps in Stockholm, in memory of Jussi Bjoerling. Out of deference to Nilsson, Tucker deleted *Tosca* from the gala, rather than ask another soprano to appear in her place.

The other principals he chose for each of the operas—Rosalind Elias, Cornell MacNeil, and Robert Merrill—were veterans like himself, with whom he had sung and recorded many times over the years. In smaller parts he chose among relative newcomers like Joann Grillo, Jean Kraft, and Leo Goeke, who had either sung with him or in whose careers he had a personal interest. The overall casting made for exquisite moments, in all of which Tucker was seen and heard not just as the "star" but rather as a vital member of an ensemble and the foremost member of a stellar cast. Formidable as was his ego, this was how he had viewed himself through all his twenty-five seasons and he considered it important that this be reinforced at the gala.

Only once did he have the entire stage to himself—in Act II of *La Gioconda,* appropriately, when he turned back the clock a quarter-century and sang "Cielo e mar," re-creating the moment that had launched his career. In the audience, applauding wildly just as they had twenty-five years before, were many of the friends who had known him from his boyhood in Williamsburg and Boro Park, his years in the fur market, or his tenure as cantor of Temple Adath Israel or the Brooklyn Jewish Center.

Apart from the journalistic spreads the Richard Tucker Gala was accorded in the pages of *Life, Newsweek,* and other periodicals, critic Irving Kolodin—never one to mete out unearned accolades—afforded this assessment of the subject of the gala in the pages of the *Saturday Review:*

> It would be stretching the truth to say that Tucker never has sung better, for leading tenors—which he has been from the very first—must live on their capital, however carefully they try to harbor their assets. Tucker has long been celebrated as one of the most abstemious of recent decades where vocal vices are concerned. Thus, if

the natural attrition of more than four hundred performances at the Metropolitan alone has taken its toll of pristine tonal purity and vocal shimmer, he sang quite well enough for any sometime listener to discover just why he still ranks among the day's top tenors. For that matter, it is hard to think of one among them who could have taken this series of stints in sequence and done them all as well.

To be sure, there were other top tenors—most notably Franco Corelli, then in his tenth Metropolitan season and the beneficiary of a new production of Massenet's *Werther,* and other veterans on the order of Carlo Bergonzi, Jon Vickers, and Sandor Konya. Others, newcomers to these shores, were emerging from chrysalid stages—Alfredo Kraus, James McCracken, Placido Domingo, and Luciano Pavarotti, the latter two making debuts in the same season. Yet, for all of them, Richard Tucker was a standard-bearer—"the master of us all," Pavarotti told him admiringly. Though one of the last of the great tenors of the immediate postwar rosters—Bjoerling, Tagliavini, Di Stefano, Del Monaco—Tucker remained a *primo tenore* who was still at the peak of his powers.

Someone else in such an enviable position might have taken a rational pause, assayed a quarter-century's triumphs, and decided that the time had come to coast to a gradual stop. Tucker, now in a race of his own making, chose instead to accelerate.

As Irving Kolodin was to write in another *Saturday Review* essay only a few years hence, "Curious that a man who devoted so much thought and effort to the care of his voice did not guard as carefully something even more precious—himself."

13

Q: *Your repertoire is so extensive that it's hard to think of one of the great tenor roles that you don't sing. Are you thinking of new ones?*

A: *You always have to think ahead. I could do some Wagner—Walther in* Meistersinger *and* Lohengrin. *But I'm not going to be satisfied till I get the Metropolitan to give me La* Juive. *That's the one I've wanted for years.*

Well before Tucker had planned his twenty-fifth anniversary gala, Rudolf Bing, in a sense, had begun planning his own. Late in 1968, he addressed a long memorandum to the Metropolitan's board indicating that he intended to step down as general manager in June 1972, and that unless his successor were to be chosen from within, the new manager would have to be available by August or September 1971. Elsewhere in the memorandum, Bing reaffirmed his belief in the necessity of a single locus of power within the Met—"It is impossible to departmentalize and it is imperative that final decisions on all matters rest in one hand"—thus arguing against dividing responsibilities among several top-echelon administrators, one of several variants of management plans then under discussion.

After marking his silver anniversary in peak form, Tucker had no fear for his tenure under a new general manager. Apart from repertoire, there was little for him to negotiate with a new management. With Franco Corelli, he was the highest-paid tenor on the roster, thus eliminating even the possibility of salary disputes; when other Metropolitan superstars got an increase, Tucker got the same (and sometimes more) as a matter of form. Even the

negotiations for roles gave him only periodic concern; his repertoire was enviably broad, from Rodolfo in *La Bohème* to the
weightiest Verdi parts, and most of his roles were in popular operas. But Tucker viewed his ample security only as so many chips
in a poker game. He would use it with the new management to
garner the one role Bing had never granted him: Eléazar in Halévy's *La Juive*.

Tucker's correspondence reveals that he had made his interest in Eléazar known to Bing as early as 1961, and that by the
autumn of 1962 he was actively lobbying for a new production
of *La Juive*. That Bing thwarted his lobbying is, in retrospect,
obvious—and the arguments and counterarguments each man used
against the other are interesting to unravel. At base, Bing was
unable to grasp fully why Tucker should have wanted to sing
Eléazar in *La Juive* at all.

The conventional answer, even among some of Tucker's
colleagues, was that he was "chasing the shadow of Caruso."
Eléazar proved to be Caruso's final role and, in the opinion of
most critics, was also his greatest triumph as an actor. Tucker,
who had marched one by one through nearly all the roles Caruso
had sung at the Metropolitan, was now, so the reasoning went,
aiming toward Caruso's crowning achievement. Others saw a
more immediate explanation: he was Jewish, and by title *La Juive*
is a "Jewish opera."

Neither, however, is a satisfactory explanation. While Tucker
was always conscious of his "American Caruso" image, it was
never a major consideration in the order and manner in which he
selected his roles. If anything, Paul Althouse's commandment that
all of his tenor pupils disregard Caruso's career as a model of how
to build a repertoire haunted Tucker every time he considered a
new role.

When Tucker decided that he wanted to portray Eléazar in
La Juive, he was interested only secondarily in the fact that Caruso had sung it. True, he was curious enough about Caruso's
approach to the music that when he visited Rosa Ponselle, then
in retirement in an expansive villa near Baltimore, he reviewed
parts of the score with her. But, in the end, Tucker's curiosity
had its own well-defined goal: he was not out to equal Caruso's
Eléazar, he was out to become *the* Eléazar for all time.

Nor was the fact that Tucker was Jewish a principal reason

for his attraction to the role. Caruso, after all, was not Jewish, and yet found the role similarly attractive; the same applied to Giovanni Martinelli, who succeeded Caruso in the part, and to Adolphe Nourrit, the tenor who created the role of Eléazar in the mid-nineteenth century. Tucker was attracted to the role primarily because, as Nourrit once observed, Eléazar is a genuine dramatic character requiring a genuine dramatic-tenor voice: he is a self-righteous old man, a considerable departure from the flashy, sword-bearing, stereotyped tenor heroes. But, unlike Nourrit, Caruso, Martinelli, or any other Gentile playing the part, Tucker would bring to the role his own unique set of advantages.

To account for his attraction to the role, however, is not quite to account for Tucker's attraction to the opera itself—and it was the story, as much as the role, that gripped him. The libretto of *La Juive*—which warrants a synopsis, because of its importance to Tucker and its unfamiliarity even to most opera enthusiasts— is not, contrary to what one might think, a story of Jewish triumph over persecution. Rather, it is a story of a persecuted Jew's revenge against a Roman Catholic cardinal, a story of the mindlessness of religious prejudice, told in a fifteenth-century context.

Jacques Fromental Halévy, composer of the opera, was attracted to the text (by playwright Eugène Scribe) because of his own Orthodox Jewish background. The Scribe libretto was based on the conflict between Cardinal Brogny and a wealthy goldsmith, Eléazar, whose daughter, Rachel, falls in love with a Catholic prince. To win her, the prince pretends to be Jewish, but during a secret Passover service held out of the sight of Catholic persecutors, the prince's ignorance of the Jewish rituals betrays his Christian identity.

The Christian-Jewish conflict inherent in the love story of Rachel and the prince is but a subplot, however. Early in the action, it is made clear that Brogny, before he had entered the seminary, had launched a pogrom in Rome against the Jews—and as a result of the pogrom, Eléazar's two sons had been murdered by the vengeful Catholic mobs. Brogny, married and a father at the time, soon lost his wife and only daughter in a mysterious fire that destroyed his home. They were presumed dead, although the daughter's body was never found. After this personal tragedy, Brogny entered the priesthood.

When the cardinal and the goldsmith again confront each

other, in another city at another time, hatred—not only hatred of each other but the hatred of each for everything the other represents, Christian oppression and militant Jewish resistance—engulfs them and leads them on a path of self-destruction. Brogny, hating all Jews with a virulence matched only by Eléazar's toward Brogny, learns of the relationship between Rachel and the prince and, as a form of grotesque punishment, launches another pogrom. He orders both Rachel and Eléazar publicly boiled in oil.

Minutes before Rachel is to be executed, Brogny offers to spare her life if she will renounce her Judaism and convert to Christianity. When she refuses, Brogny orders her thrown into the caldron of oil. Moments later, after her anguished screams have ceased, her lifeless body becomes visible in the seething caldron.

Eléazar is taken to the caldron next. The goldsmith maintains a stoical posture—yet Brogny intuits that Eléazar holds the answer to the fate of Brogny's own daughter and wife. Eléazar stands above the caldron, maintaining his defiant silence. Brogny breaks the silence: if Eléazar will reveal the whereabouts of Brogny's daughter, his life will be spared.

"Behold your child!" Eléazar bitterly declaims, pointing to Rachel's body. His vengeance complete, Eléazar then hurls himself into the caldron.

This story had two levels of attraction for Tucker. On one level, he was attracted to the dramatic potential of the role of Eléazar. On another, he saw the drama as a vivid moment in the long and tragic history of life in the Jewish ghettos of Eastern Europe.

A heritage of fear and uneasiness with the powerful and dominant Christian world—the legacy of a life spent in the Eastern European Jewish ghettos—was as much a part of the Ticker or the Perelmuth lineage as it was of any other European Jews whose ancestors had been the victims of oppression. In the Old World and then in the New, from one generation to the next, accounts of the pogroms, polemics, and forced conversions were passed on as part of the oral history of the Jewish people.

Richard Tucker learned this history from many sources—his father, his father-in-law, and the rabbis with whom he served as a *hazzan*. The moment he read the sketch of the libretto of *La Juive*—in an old edition of the *Victor Book of the Opera*, published not long after Caruso's Eléazar had rekindled interest in the opera—Tucker read much more than a grand-opera plot: he felt he was reading history itself. From then on, to be able to sing Eléazar for his generation—not merely to sing a great dramatic-tenor role, but rather to bring the story itself to the public in spectacular form—became, for Tucker, not just a hope but an obsession.

There were those among his Gentile colleagues and friends—capital among them, Rudolf Bing—who never understood this obsession. Tucker did not fault them; he merely felt that they could not grasp his heritage as an Eastern European Jew. There were also those among his Jewish friends—ones who disapproved of his friendship with Catholic prelates like Francis Cardinal Spellman, Terence Cardinal Cooke, or Father Ted Hesburgh, and also disapproved of his occasional fund raising for Catholic charities—who wondered why he devoted himself to the cause of singing an opera in which a Jew is as much a villain as a hero. Perhaps they did not fully understand Tucker—a tolerant man, a man who believed he had a part to play in unifying people, perhaps by showing, through Eléazar, that history's darkest ages need not repeat themselves.

Much earlier, in 1962, Tucker began his long quest by approaching Bing about a revival of *La Juive*. He lobbied in the manner he knew best—"Show them they need the product, and then show them that yours is the best." He pointed out to Bing that *Juive* had been performed approximately every other season at the Metropolitan from 1919 through 1935, when Caruso or Martinelli had sung Eléazar, but the Metropolitan had not given *Juive* since 1935. Tucker went on to argue that he personally could sing Eléazar more definitively than any of his predecessors, since he was already well schooled in the French tradition, his voice was now weighty enough—and, of course, he was a *hazzan*.

In arguing his singular credentials for the role, Tucker inadvertently gave Bing his best counterargument. Suppose, Bing retorted, that the Metropolitan mounted a new *Juive* and built it around Tucker as Eléazar. No doubt Tucker would be brilliant in the role. But what other tenor could step in if Tucker was indisposed? Rather than argue the merits of the opera itself—although Bing did note for Tucker's benefit that *Juive* was a poor box-office draw, and had been given only two or three times a season in the 1920s and 1930s—he invariably pointed to Tucker's indispensability to every performance.

Patiently, deliberately, Tucker attempted to circumvent Bing's logic by attempting to demonstrate the drawing power of *La Juive*. Through Ruth M. O'Neill, then vice-president of Columbia Artists Management, he worked closely with the Friends of French Opera—a New York society than headed by Frank Forest, once a prominent radio tenor—to mount a concert performance of *La Juive,* to be conducted by Robert Lawrence. Tucker personally raised a great deal of the money and planned for two performances—one in Carnegie Hall and the other at the Brooklyn Academy of Music, both set for mid-March 1964.

Most of the cast members in the performances were young singers, and thus spotlighted Tucker's Eléazar all the more prominently—the single strength, as the reviews soon showed, of the performances. Every other aspect, including the opera itself, was poorly received by most New York critics. A few lodged complaints about extensive cuts in the score—made for the sake of trimming *Juive*'s five-hour length to something more reasonable. Others found much else to lament—as Harold C. Schonberg bluntly wrote in *The New York Times* the next day:

> Those who have been wondering if *La Juive* contains other material so good as the one popular aria can now set their curiosity to rest. . . . The plain fact is that the opera is a monument of banality and boredom.
>
> A stronger performance might have helped the cause. The orchestral playing was sloppy, the direction without spirit, and some of the singers were not up to the demands of their roles. Making allowances for all that, it is still difficult to see what our forebears saw in *La Juive*. Could it be that they were content to sit in bovine indifference until THE aria came along?
>
> The star of the evening was Richard Tucker. At least he had THE aria. As presented last night [i.e., with numerous cuts], Eléazar has relatively little to do, and the role does not go above a B-flat. Mr. Tucker found the music entirely comfortable. And when he came to "Rachel, quand du Seigneur," he sang it with fervor, fullness of tone and a professional sheen to his work.

Schonberg concluded his assessment of Tucker's Eléazar with a frank comment. "Mr. Tucker has wanted to sing in *La Juive* for many years," he wrote. "Now he can rest content. The chances would appear very remote for a staged revival. The world is in enough of a mess as it is." Sickened but undaunted by such reviews, Tucker was left with little in his defense except—as he pointed out to Bing—that the Carnegie Hall performance had sold out five weeks in advance. Bing countered, as usual, with the question, "And what would have happened if you had gotten sick?"

Tucker had continued lobbying for a *Juive* production throughout the 1960s—through Columbia Artists Management, through more appeals to Bing directly, and, when he felt it safe, through appeals to influential board members as well. In April 1965, the New York *Daily News* reported Tucker had said that "he has been promised the necessary funds for the production and knows he could sell out at least nine benefit performances. So far, Bing has turned the project down partly because if the tenor were not around there would not be a replacement in the role, and partly because Bing considers the opera outdated." Undaunted, Tucker began organizing another concert performance of *Juive,* this one to be sung under the auspices of impresario Denny Dayviss in London, at the Festival Hall. Through Dayviss, Tucker planned the performance for the spring of 1973—when Bing would have retired and a new general manager would be firmly in place at the Metropolitan.

In the interim, Italy beckoned Tucker once again—this time to make his debut in Parma at the celebrated Teatro Regio. The site of numerous Verdi productions and revivals, the Teatro Regio long ago earned a reputation for having the most critical audiences in all of Italy. (The Parmese were fond of repeating a story involving a tenor who wanted to leave town after a merciless booing at the Teatro Regio the night before. The next morning, even the porters at the train station rebuked him and refused to carry his baggage.) Sara had heard enough of the rudeness of the Parmese audiences to make her urge Richard not to sing at the Regio. He brushed off her worries, and not only accepted the invitation but agreed to debut as Manrico in *Il trovatore.*

Baritone Renato Bruson and soprano Katia Ricciarelli, then at the very beginning of her career, partnered Tucker in what proved to be the only disappointment of his Italian career. In a letter he wrote to Francis Robinson on January 21, 1971, the day after the *Trovatore* performance, Tucker said:

. . . I am happy to report that I sang very well indeed, and won the admiration of not only the public but also the orchestra and chorus, and, of course, our dear old friend Alberto Erede, who conducted. But the evening did not go off as expected. First, the baritone, Bruson, got ill between the second and third acts, and because he was not applauded well after "Il balen," he swore never to return.

Then, after I sang the beautiful "Ah sì, ben mio" and the "Di quella pira," I received a tremendous ovation. But in the last act duet with Azucena, "Ai nostri monti," some idiot whistled upstairs in the balcony, where they allow food and wine—but he was immediately shushed. Some people think this was planned by my colleagues (tenors). Of course, the critics here played up the whole thing—why, I don't know. Is one whistle from an idiot or a drunk more important than the whole opera? I guess they can't understand how an American can sing so beautifully and with such an Italian pronunciation. It is hard for them to accept.

Di Stefano came up from Milan to hear me, and came backstage with his family, which made me feel good.

After my tremendous successes in Florence, this has certainly been a letdown. But I am strong, and my sincerity for Art will help me carry on for many years, I hope.

Fortunately, Tucker's subsequent London appearance, in the concert performance of *La Juive,* proved a counterbalance to his disappointment over the Parma *Trovatore.* The reviews, although not uniformly laudatory for the opera as a whole, repeatedly singled out Tucker for artistic honors. Critic Philip Hope-Wallace, writing in the *Arts Guardian,* judged Tucker "in splendid shape, giving the 'Rachel' aria with immense passion and that moulding of which we hear glimpses yet in Caruso's wonderful recording."

Desmond Shawe-Taylor, the highly respected critic of the London *Times,* decried the quality of editing the score had seen, and afterward rendered a balanced judgment both of *La Juive* and Tucker as Eléazar:

> Halévy has decided merits; but with the exception of Eléazar's "Rachel, quand du Seigneur," he seems curiously unable to write an aria. How then did we manage to have such a good time? Partly because this Scribe libretto about Jewish persecution gave the composer scope for some splendid trios (even though we lost one or two of these) and duets, especially that for Rachel and her royal rival, Eudoxie; and partly because the opera was so finely cast.
> London has heard little of Richard Tucker, a leading Metro-

politan tenor since the war, now in his late fifties. When I first heard him, at Verona in 1947 in *La Gioconda,* singing with Maria Callas, he produced some of the most luscious and finely controlled tenor tone I had ever encountered; today, although he has lost that sweetness (which is not really required for Eléazar), he still combines a smooth line with a dramatic intensity that can sweep the house off its feet, as it did in his big aria.

Swedish impresario Goeran Gentele, of the Stockholm Opera, had officially become the Metropolitan Opera's new general manager when, on April 22, 1972, the company honored the recently knighted Sir Rudolf Bing at a gala unmatched since the closing of the Old Met. Of the forty-two artists who sang in his honor— among them tenors Luciano Pavarotti, Placido Domingo, James McCracken, Sandor Konya, Jon Vickers, and Franco Corelli— Tucker was the senior artist, matched in tenure only by Robert Merrill. Appropriately, the two were to sing "Invano, Alvaro!"—the high-tension duet from the fourth act of *La forza del destino.*

Tucker, on the night of the Bing gala, strode into the Metropolitan a would-be conqueror prepared to do battle. He was well aware that the best in the world had been assembled for this gala. He had come to prove to the operatic public and the millions who would watch the gala by television satellite, on tape, that even among long-term tenor rivals like Corelli and Vickers, or popular newcomers like Pavarotti and Domingo, Richard Tucker alone would predominate.

Robert Merrill shared a dressing room with him that night. "Richard and I," Merrill said, "were always known for our lack of nerves before going onstage. But that night, I admit, *I* was nervous—and so was everybody else. It was absolutely crazy backstage. Forty-some artists, the cream of the crop—imagine Caballé, Sutherland, Price, and Nilsson, all on the same stage— the 'big leagues,' to use a Tuckerism. Richard and I were scheduled to open the second half of the program, which meant that we had to spend a lot of time waiting in the dressing room. There were television monitors in the dressing rooms, and the tension mounted as the program went on. I mean, these people were singing their hearts out—even if they were shaking in their shoes.

"I was getting so nervous I thought I'd need diapers. And do you know what Tucker was doing? He was pacing the dressing room like a caged animal—believe me, he couldn't *wait* to go on! He was strutting around like a general. Every now and then, he'd stop pacing and glance at the television when one of the other tenors came on. Once, he looked at the monitor, then looked at me and barked, 'Tell him he better sing his ass off! When you and I hit that stage, I'm gonna make his own mother forget him!'

"It seemed hours before we were told to take our place by the curtain and get ready for our signal to go on. When the time came and we got our cue, Tucker actually turned around to me after the applause mounted and said, 'All right, Merrill, no goddam bunting in this game! Home runs!'

"He strutted out there ahead of me—I swear, his feet were six inches off the ground. The applause was so loud that I could hardly hear the first bars of the music. I was still shaking until we got to 'Le minaccie, i fieri accenti,' the second part of the duet. Tucker was so far in his stride—I mean, *banging* out the notes like a cannon, he was so hot—that I wasn't sure I was keeping up with him. But when we got into the second part, I realized we were 'on,' and I started to calm down. By the end of that duet, we were so into each other's pace that even the vibratos in our voices were one-to-one! When we let go of those final high notes, the audience split the roof. The applause went on so long it had to be cut down when the video tape was shown.

"As soon as we got offstage, Tucker looked at me and said, 'We showed 'em! Let's see any of 'em follow *that!*'"

Part of the explanation for the perfection of Tucker and Merrill's *Forza* duet lay in a finely honed sense of each other's performing style—a consequence not so much of their singing together at the Metropolitan as of their much-publicized recitals. These concerts were the brainchild of Michael Ries, who managed both Tucker and Merrill at Columbia Artists. By January 1973, when they sold out Carnegie Hall and made headlines, the Tucker-Merrill concerts had earned them a broader public following than either man would have guessed.

These joint recitals were unique in several respects. Apart from Jean and Édouard de Reszke late in the nineteenth century, the American concert stage was rarely a platform for two male vocalists. Usually, joint recitals involved a man and a woman, or perhaps a male vocalist and a male instrumentalist. Though two men might appear in concert, almost never would they appear in a long run of engagements such as Michael Ries persuaded Tucker and Merrill to agree to do. Once the two agreed, they tapped in one another a reserve of energy that awed their colleagues: from their Carnegie Hall debut in January 1973 onward, they were booked for seventeen joint appearances through April 1974, with options for a dozen more through 1975.

Tucker's operatic calendar for this same period was nothing short of staggering—especially for a man of sixty. For the 1973/74 season alone, he was scheduled to sing thirty-three performances throughout the country, in *Il trovatore, Tosca, Rigoletto, Simon Boccanegra, Aida,* and *Pagliacci.* He had also taken a giant step in his quest for a Metropolitan production of *La Juive:* he had negotiated two fully staged performances with the New Orleans Opera, which he was to sing on October 18 and 20, 1973. There were also inquiries from Barcelona, where the Teatro Liceo was considering a *Juive* production for the 1974/75 season.

Both New Orleans and Barcelona, Tucker reasoned, would give him increased leverage with Goeran Gentele. Then, on July 18, 1972, Gentele was killed in an auto accident while on vacation in Sardinia. In the aftermath of the tragedy, Gentele's assistant—affable Schuyler Chapin, whom Tucker had known at Columbia Records early in Chapin's administrative career—was named acting general manager. Soon, Chapin's acting appointment would be made permanent by the Metropolitan board of directors.

Richard Tucker was never busier—and never happier, most of his colleagues thought—than in the 1972/73 opera season. By his own admission, he was "singing everywhere, and packin' in the crowds." His description to an interviewer of a "typical" three months' performing in the spring and summer of 1973 seems almost dizzying. "I've sung about fifteen concerts recently and, let's see, around ten performances with the Met. To give you an idea of what I would call my typical month, I sang in Cleveland, left there for San Francisco to sing two concerts—one in Frisco itself and the other at a nearby college—then I sang in Los Angeles, spent some time with my son Henry while I was there, and from Los Angeles I backtracked to catch the Metropolitan tour in Atlanta. I ran down to Miami to visit my son David, backtracked to Atlanta to meet Sara, went with her to our home in Great Neck, and then I took off for San Antonio for another *Pagliacci.* I went on to Dallas, where I caught up with the Met tour, sang an *Aida*, went to Minneapolis and did a *Trovatore* there, and flew back to Chicago to sing a joint recital with Bob Merrill. I caught a plane to Miami, spent two days with the grandchildren, and then flew north to catch up with the Met tour in Detroit."

As the names of cities cascaded on, the interview seeming more like a geography lesson than a description of a tour, Tucker capped his monologue with a predictable show of self-assurance. "I just got home last week, I spent a couple of days at my favorite spa in New Jersey, I'm in perfect voice, fresh as a daisy, and I've even got a suntan!"

With Merrill, he was becoming more visible to the public than at any point in his career—especially after the release of the "live" recording of their Carnegie Hall debut, and their appearance on national television with Arthur Fiedler and the Boston Pops Orchestra. *Variety* dubbed them "the hottest act in town," and *TV Guide* described their Boston Pops appearance as "a musical tour-de-force by two of opera's greatest artists, . . . two Brooklyn-born showmen who clearly love what they are being paid to do."

There was no mistaking their enjoyment—or the "tour de force" their program involved. They opened with the duet from *La Gioconda*, "Enzo Grimaldo, Principe di Santa Fior," and progressed through "Invano, Alvaro" and "Solenne in quest'ora" from *La forza del destino*, "Au fond du temple saint" from *Le Pêcheurs de perles*, and "Sì, pel ciel" from *Otello*.

Interspersed among the duets were Merrill's singing of "Adamastor, re dell'onde profonde" from *L' Africana*, "Deh vieni alla finestra" from *Don Giovanni*, "Non più andrai" from *Le nozze di Figaro*, "Nemico della patria" from *Andrea Chénier*, the Credo from *Otello*, "Di provenza il mar" from *Traviata*, and "Zazà, piccola zingara," from Leoncavallo's *Zazà*.

Tucker matched this with Mozart's "Misero! o sogno!" (K. 431), "Una furtiva lagrima" from *L'elisir d'amore*, "Giorno di pianto" from *I vespri Siciliani*, "Mamma! quel vino è generoso!" from *Cavalleria rusticana*, Goldfadden's Yiddish lullaby "Rozshinkes mit Mandlin," and Leoncavallo's "Mattinata."

As they refined and expanded their basic program, tailoring it to various audiences and locales, they added songs from *Fiddler on the Roof*—Merrill rendering "If I Were a Rich Man," Tucker

singing "Sunrise, Sunset," and, as a finale, the two of them singing "L'Chaim! To Life!" In the finale, they incorporated a bit of
stage business of Merrill's invention: between choruses of
"L'Chaim!" they choreographed a folk dance, some of the steps
inspired by Yiddish dances they had seen as boys in the Brooklyn
Jewish community.

On tour with their "act," Merrill and Tucker became predictably close, much more so than at any previous point in their
careers. Merrill adjusted to the idiosyncrasies of Tucker's highly
structured life: his love of Chinese food ("It's as kosher as you
get in small towns"), his penchant for arriving at a theater far
ahead of time, his constant telephone calls to Sara, his sons, his
bookies, and his railing at quarterbacks during televised games
("Look what the hell he did, Bob! I just lost fifteen hundred bucks
because he can't figure out which end of the goddamned ball to
throw!").

When they weren't traveling or rehearsing, Tucker and Merrill
were busy promoting themselves. The joint recitals proved an
unexpected bonanza income-wise, and they were eager to promote the concerts at nearly any cost. London Records, which
produced their Carnegie Hall recording, found them indefatiga-
ble. Mitchell Krieger of London's Classical Division said of them
in a 1973 memo to retailers, "There is *nothing* that these two guys
won't do to help promote sales of their records. In one twenty-
four-hour period in Chicago, they gave a fantastic joint recital at
the Auditorium Theater, taped *two* TV programs, appeared on a
major FM station, held an autographing session at one record store,
and stopped in at another store. At the first store they signed almost three hundred record albums! They were scheduled so tightly
they barely had ten minutes to breathe. Merrill asked, 'Couldn't
we do something else?' Tucker added, 'Only four appearances—
that's not a day's work.' "

Near the end of the 1973/74 season, Tucker's preoccupation
with work began to concern his family, colleagues, and even the
Metropolitan management. Zinka Milanov, then in retirement,
watched Tucker's schedule escalate in the early 1970s. When Milanov encountered Sara after a performance one evening, she asked
her pointedly, "Why is Richard singing so much?" Sara had no
answer, having repeatedly asked her husband the same question.
"Whatever his reasons," Milanov said, "he is singing *too* much.

He may not think so, but he is inviting trouble." When Sara relayed Milanov's comment, Tucker dismissed it. "I'm like a kid, I've got so much energy," he retorted.

Yet *Pagliacci,* for all his bravado, had begun to betray him. Schuyler Chapin has recorded in his memoirs a vivid description of the aftermath of one such performance. "As part of an experimental program," Chapin wrote, "we had taped [for television] *Cavalleria rusticana* and *Pagliacci.* Tucker sang Canio in the latter, a role that he loved, and it was an especially brilliant performance. I remember thinking at the time that [he] was almost like a lightbulb about to burn out. At the end he was totally exhausted and stood backstage before bowing, bent over, trying to catch his breath."

Somewhat earlier, critic Irving Kolodin broke precedent and wrote Tucker a personal letter of concern after witnessing what he would later describe as a *Pagliacci* of "urgent, fiercely personal, almost ominously intense" proportions. Kolodin's letter:

> I was present at your performance of *Pagliacci* a few nights ago and was much impressed by the all-out effort you bring . . . and how the audience responds to it.
>
> At the same time, I could not but feel that such an expenditure of physical energy bears with it a stress that may not be altogether wise. Having been acquainted with you these many years, I take the liberty of suggesting that you consider this aspect. . . .
>
> I know that you are not the kind of performer who can deliberately ease off, or hold back, but I think your sincerity as an artist would carry to the audience at less physical force than you are now exerting.

Some ten days later, Kolodin received this handwritten reply:

> Words cannot express my gratitude for your sincere thoughts on my behalf. I certainly appreciate your comments but knowing me through the years, I have always given of myself to the utmost, whatever the music and its interpretation demanded. I can only say I will try to withhold a bit more than the night your heard me in *Pagliacci,* and am happy that you enjoyed it.

His promise to "withhold a bit more" was momentary and fleeting. Anna Moffo, who sang Nedda to Tucker's Canio in one of his last *Pagliacci* performances, remembered a scene similar to the ones Chapin and Kolodin described. "I was especially attuned to

Richard, both as an artist and as a man, because he had been such a mentor to me at the beginning of my career. I idolized him, and therefore noticed and scrutinized everything he did onstage. In his last *Pagliacci*s, he finished his performances so tired, so spent, that he hardly seemed the same person. That performance still haunts me. When we were getting ready for our curtain calls, I said to him, 'Are you sure you're all right?' He tried to pep himself up, and said to me, 'Don't worry about me, Annie, I'm fine!' "

Chapin recalled that at this same performance, when Tucker's curtain calls came, "I saw him take hold of a fold in the curtain and actually pull himself upright in order to go onstage. Yet he insisted he was 'just a little tired.' "

Schuyler Chapin was among the first to learn of Tucker's twin triumphs in his quest for *La Juive:* RCA Records offered Tucker a contract to record excerpts from *Juive,* and from the Teatro Liceo in Barcelona he received final word that his Eléazar would indeed be the focal point of an elaborate production of the Halévy work. The RCA recording was to be made in the summer of 1974 at Covent Garden in London; the cast would include Anna Moffo, Martina Arroyo, and Bonaldo Giaiotti, with Antonio de Almeida conducting. The Barcelona performances of *La Juive* were to take place near Christmas 1974; Tucker had also agreed to sing a performance of *Carmen,* scheduled for Christmas Day.

Additionally, he finalized plans to sing *Ballo in maschera* in Florence in January 1974—an engagement that, as matters proved, nearly put an end to his Metropolitan career.

The trouble over the Florence engagement began when Chapin checked the Metropolitan schedule for January 1974. He saw immediately that Tucker would have to miss several performances of *Simon Boccanegra* in order to be in Florence (not Barcelona, as Chapin later recalled in his memoirs) for the *Ballo* rehearsals and performances. Chapin suddenly found himself in a predicament, because Tucker was vital to ticket sales for *Boccanegra* and could not be replaced easily.

Both in person and then by letter, Chapin reminded Tucker that the Metropolitan could not release him from his contract for the Florence performances. To Chapin's surprise, Tucker ignored the "reminder," but for reasons that he shared only with his family and with his managers. To Sara and his sons, he freely admitted that he had tired long ago of being the "drawing card" for *Simon Boccanegra*. He considered it a "baritone's opera" and, though he had retained it in his repertoire, he had lost his zest for *Boccanegra* after Leonard Warren's death.

His other reasons centered on the Metropolitan's management—though not exclusively on Schuyler Chapin, whom he liked. Tucker felt that after Bing's departure and Gentele's tragic death, the "management philosophy" at the Metropolitan had become loose and arbitrary. Tucker privately maintained that other singers were being exempted from contractual responsibilities, often for arguable reasons. If others were allowed exemptions, *he* would be allowed them—and this time he did not intend to yield any ground.

Chapin, Tucker felt, in this instance was attempting to "show his muscles," Bing fashion, to prove himself somehow to a number of board members who were dubious about his leadership. Chapin, as one might expect, saw the issue differently. Tucker would have to abide by the terms of his contract—or else, Chapin advised Columbia Artists' Michael Ries, "I'll be forced to dismiss him."

"The matter seemed settled," Chapin would later write, "until the afternoon of [a] *Boccanegra* broadcast when quite by accident I learned that he was leaving that night for [Florence] regardless of what we had discussed." Again, Chapin confronted him—to which Tucker said simply, "Don't worry, kid, everything will be fine." After the broadcast, over dinner with Barry and, later, in long-distance calls to David and Henry, Richard reviewed what Chapin had said. Finally, Henry asked him bluntly, "What the hell do you need with the Metropolitan at this point in your career?" Tucker had no answer.

The next day, a Sunday, after the Tuckers were airborne, Chapin sent a telegram, firing Tucker for breach of contract, but promising not to inform the news media in the hope that the disagreement could be settled.

At that point, Chapin recalled, "All hell broke loose. Mrs. August Belmont telephoned and later wrote me that I was 'impetuous.' Members of the board with whom I'd had almost no personal contact began calling and asking what I'd done. Subscribers, finding out somehow through the operatic underground, began assailing me for assassination of character, imperialistic tendencies, and even lack of sympathy to singers. At home the phone began ringing at 3:00 and 4:00 A.M. with threatening voices saying: 'Chapin, get out. You've ruined the Met.' "

The "firing" of Richard Tucker was short-lived. Through Michael Ries, a formal apology was arranged and, as Chapin wrote in his memoirs, "the incident was shelved."

In Barcelona, at the Teatro Liceo, the management gave Tucker a royal welcome and moved him deeply by the care they had taken in preparing the *Juive* production. During the negotiations, he had asked that actual kosher food be used, if possible, in the opera's Passover Scene. On the day of the first performance, December 14, he learned that the management had even sent to Paris for the proper matzoh, completing a Passover table of the highest-quality kosher foods. This attention to detail—"Things he asked about but never would have insisted on," Sara remarked—contributed to a *Juive* that may have been the finest single performance of his entire career.

Barcelona critic Juan Lluch, writing in *El Noticia Universal,* devoted a half-page to a review headlined "The Apotheosis of Singing: Richard Tucker's Triumph in 'La Juive' ":

> Tucker arrived in Barcelona a "name" singer, someone whose singing has long been admired the world over, especially on his phonograph recordings. Many will recall his prior appearances here in "Andrea Chénier" and "Ballo in maschera" several years ago. Those of us who heard him then, heard a voice in its full bloom, although the tenor himself was at least fifty years old. None of us, I venture, would have been prepared to hear this same artist again—at age sixty—and hear an authentic dramatic tenor still very much at his peak. Venerated as he is, his triumph as Eléazar in "La Juive" took him to new heights—and ones which no amount of words will adequately convey.
>
> This prodigious Tucker, this phenomenal Tucker, is impossible to compare to any other tenor singing today: Tucker is Tucker, from the first note to the last note, and his vocal production is so natural, so free, yet so enviably powerful that it is difficult to locate any peer. Certainly he has none as Eléazar. No one—and, again, words fail here—could possibly sing with more fervor the second-act cavatina, "Dieu que ma voix tremblante," or with more majesty the great aria, "Rachel! quand du Seigneur." Nor could anyone have created a character so complex, so torn with conflicting

emotion, as his Eléazar. Richard Tucker in "La Juive" will always be, for those fortunate enough to have heard it, the apotheosis of opera singing.

The performance left Sara Tucker with a curious memory. "During the Passover Scene, his singing was so superb, so moving, and the mood so deeply religious that a glow seemed to surround him. It was almost like a halo—and many people commented about it to me afterward. I kept telling myself that it was the stage lighting, but deep inside I felt it was something of an omen."

After the performance, backstage in his dressing room, Sara told Richard of this eerie experience. "Aw, get off it," he huffed. "I can think of at least a half-dozen places where I could've done better. Don't be putting a halo around my head until I get it perfect."

The Christmas Day performance of *Carmen* netted him another set of laudatory reviews, although for Tucker and for the Barcelona public, *La Juive* was his triumph. He returned to New York a victor, and returned to the Metropolitan fold in good graces. He was now ready to use his success in Spain to move toward a Metropolitan *La Juive*.

Just after New Year's Day, 1975, Schuyler Chapin telephoned with the news that Tucker had awaited for more than a decade: the funding for a production of *La Juive* was all but guaranteed. Beverly Sills was to sing Rachel, and Nicolai Gedda would sing the role of Leopold, the second tenor in the opera; Paul Plishka was to sing Cardinal Brogny, and Leonard Bernstein would conduct the revival. Only a few preliminary meetings in which both Chapin and Tucker would be involved now had to be scheduled. Eagerly, Tucker checked his calendar when Chapin asked him to set a date for the initial meeting. They agreed to meet at the Metropolitan on Thursday, January 9.

That day, Tucker told Chapin, he was scheduled to return from a joint concert with Robert Merrill in Kalamazoo, Michigan.

14

Q: *Years from now, what do you wish to be remembered for?*

A: *I think for pleasing my fans, my admirers, and for being a good and kind parent, and for what Jewish people call* shem tov—*leaving behind a good name.*

Except for a bumpy descent, the flight to Kalamazoo was pleasant but routine. Merrill napped part of the way; Tucker had a highball, and leafed through an issue of *Fortune*. Kalamazoo was simply another booking. There would be interviews to give, record albums to sign, and, if time permitted, a radio or television appearance. But once they landed and were on their way to the Holiday Inn West, where their lodging and rehearsals had been arranged, they gave up any thought of leaving the hotel. The inclement weather—a souplike fog, near-freezing temperatures, and a driving rainstorm—precluded doing much else. They would have dinner in the hotel dining room and afterward watch television in their adjoining suites.

On Wednesday, January 8, the day of their performance, both men were up and about by 9:00 A.M. Though Merrill was still a bit tired, both men had slept well and were ready for a quiet day—brunch in the hotel, an hour's rehearsal with David Benedict, their accompanist, in one of the hotel's conference rooms, a rest period of two or three hours in mid-afternoon, a light supper at six, then on to the auditorium in full dress at seven o'clock.

"Have you looked outside?" Merrill asked sardonically when

he rang Tucker's suite at ten o'clock. "Such a gorgeous day! Let's go play golf."

"How do we get to the auditorium?" Tucker grimly cracked. "Are we going by car or by boat?"

When Merrill hung up a few minutes later, Tucker made one of his regular calls to Barry at his downtown Manhattan office. As he often did when his father was on tour, Barry arranged a conference call, linking Sara and Richard so that for part of the conversation the three of them could talk. After Barry hung up, Sara asked Richard what he would be doing for the rest of the afternoon, so that they could arrange a later phone call.

"Bob's tired, so he'll probably take a nap," he answered. "I'll either stay here and get some rest, or may spend a few minutes at an audition. You remember the girl whose teacher wrote and asked me to listen to her if I came to Kalamazoo? Apparently she's near this hotel, so I might do that."

"Do yourself a favor," Sara said sternly. "If the weather is so bad there, don't go out in it. Ask the girl to send you a tape or something."

"We'll see, we'll see," he said indifferently. "Anyway, how about you? What are you up to today? Tell me so I can call you after Bob and I get done rehearsing."

Sara answered that she and Tillie Sussman, a friend from their early years on Thayer Street, would meet her in town for lunch and the two of them would go shopping. Sara said that afterward she might take in a movie. Richard agreed to call her late in the afternoon, at five o'clock sharp.

Downtown Manhattan had been spared the oppressive weather that had engulfed Kalamazoo. The weather was favorable enough, Sara thought, to walk rather than ride to Wolf's, a favorite delicatessen a few blocks from the Tuckers' apartment on Central Park South. After lunch, while walking along West Fifty-seventh Street, Sara saw Marilyn Horne; Ronald Wilford, of Columbia Artists Management, was with her. They all chatted briefly, and afterward Sara and Tillie completed a few errands.

Sara said good-bye to her friend at the Central Park South apartment. Remembering Richard's call, she looked at her watch. It was now four-thirty.

At twenty-five before five, the phone on Barry's desk rang.

"I have a call for you," his secretary said over the intercom. "It's Mrs. Merrill."

"Marion! How are you doing?" he greeted her, surprised that she would be calling at his office. "I was just sitting here waiting for Dad to call from Michigan."

"Barry," she said haltingly, "I want you to take down this number in Kalamazoo. You're to wait five minutes before you call. A doctor will be on the line as soon as the operator puts you through. Bob just called me and said your father has been taken to the hospital. I wish I could tell you more, but Bob was rushed, so that's all I know."

It could be anything, Barry told himself. A slip in the shower, maybe a fall on an icy sidewalk. The more Barry thought, the more limitless the possibilities seemed. Surely it was nothing serious.

At twenty minutes before five, he placed the call to Kalamazoo. At the other end of the line, a physician introduced himself.

"What's wrong with my father?" Barry asked abruptly.

"Now, just to be sure whom I am speaking with," the physician said, "this is Barry Tucker, am I correct?"

"That's right."

"And you are Richard Tucker's oldest son. Is that correct?"

"Yes, yes," Barry answered impatiently. "So, what's wrong with my father?"

"I don't know how else to tell you this, Barry, but your father suffered a massive coronary in his hotel room."

The doctor paused for a moment.

"And?" Barry asked, ignoring the pause.

"He was brought here to the hospital in an ambulance, but by the time it got here, there were no vital signs at all. I regret having to say this to you over a telephone, Barry, but I have just pronounced your father dead."

"Doctor, how do you know it's him?" Barry asked in disbelief.

The question momentarily threw the doctor—but it fit the pattern of denial that typically emerges in such a situation.

"Barry, I had tickets to your father's concert tonight," the doctor said sympathetically. "I've seen your father on television, and I've heard him in person over the years. Besides, Mr. Merrill has already made positive identification here at the hospital. I wish it were otherwise, but I'm afraid it's beyond question at this point."

Stunned, Barry thanked the doctor and hung up.

"Get my brother David in Cincinnati," he said to his secretary. In a moment, she was back on the intercom. "Your brother is in his office," she said, "but his receptionist says he can't come to the telephone."

Barry got on the line. "This is an emergency," he told the receptionist. "Tell David I have to talk to him."

"I'm sorry, Mr. Tucker," she said firmly. "Dr. Tucker is doing a surgical procedure, and I can't call him to the phone."

"I just told you, *this* is an emergency," Barry reiterated, his patience quickly draining.

"You will have to call back, Mr. Tucker, because—"

"Get him out!" Barry snapped. The nurse complied.

The moment he was called away from his patient, David knew intuitively what had happened. Later, he would tell his mother of the eerie feeling that gripped him, a feeling that precluded having to be told anything.

"It's Dad, isn't it?" he said quietly to Barry. "He's dead, isn't he?"

Immediately, David asked Barry where Sara was. "Be sure someone is with her. She mustn't be alone."

"That's the hell of it," Barry said anxiously. "I'm not sure where she is. I tried her at the apartment a while ago, but she was still out. She was supposed to go shopping, then she said something about a movie—she could be anywhere right now."

The same scenario suddenly occurred to both of them. In a matter of minutes, there would be news bulletins on television and radio. What if Sara were to hear them on the car radio? Or, worse, what if someone stopped her on the street and told her?

"Joan and I will find her," Barry assured David. "Get here as fast as you can, okay?"

Henry Tucker was in his Melrose Avenue office in Los Angeles when Barry called him. It was five minutes past two, Los Angeles time. Barry had become increasingly anxious over his mother's whereabouts, and had had no time to come to grips with the tragedy himself. Now he spoke hurriedly and bluntly to Henry.

"Your father just died of a heart attack, so get the first plane you can," he said. "Right now, Joan is on her way to the apartment to try to find Mother. I'm leaving to meet her, so I can't talk. I'll give you the details when I see you." And he hung up.

Two hours later, Henry was on his way to New York City. The five hours he spent in the air were the most wrenching five hours of his life.

If he doesn't call pretty soon, Sara thought to herself, *I'm not going to make it to the movie.*

Richard's calls were always prompt. If he said five o'clock, he meant five o'clock. It was now twenty past five. Finally, wondering whether Barry or Joan had heard from him, she called their Park Avenue home. Robert, their preschool-age son, answered the phone. Joan was now on her way to the Central Park South apartment, and had carefully instructed the children not to give their grandmother any hint of what had happened.

"Robert, this is Nannie," Sara said. "Who's home? Is your dad there?"

Robert's evasiveness quickly evaporated into tears. His sister, Amy, not yet ten, took the receiver from him. Amy, too, fought back tears.

"What's wrong with Robert?" Sara asked Amy. "Is your dad there or not?"

"No, he's not here right now, Nannie."

"Is your mother there?"

"No, Nannie. She's coming to see you."

Sara knew that Barry and Joan were expected at a dinner party. Her driver was to have taken them.

"Amy, is there something wrong with Poppie?" she asked pointedly.

"I—I can't talk to you right now," Amy said nervously.

"Amy, just tell me whether Poppie is all right."

"I think Poppie is sick, Nannie, but he's going to be okay. I can't talk now, Nannie. I have to hang up."

Jack Nash, president of Oppenheimer and Company, learned of the tragic news and dispatched a car and driver for Barry's use. As the driver sped up the West Side Highway, a bulletin came over the car radio. "Richard Tucker, the legendary American tenor who was to celebrate his thirtieth anniversary with the Metropolitan Opera this month, has just died of a massive heart attack in Kalamazoo, Michigan."

As Joan Tucker entered the circular driveway at 200 Central Park South, she heard a similar bulletin on her car radio.

Barry arrived a few minutes later. When he embraced Joan in the lobby, she found him remarkably clear-headed and in control. He *had* to be, he reminded her: the hardest part of the ordeal now lay before him.

From one of the doormen, Joan had learned that Sara had returned to the apartment in mid-afternoon. In all probability, she was alone. Barry and Joan quickly realized that there was no strategy, no plan to decide on: they would have to go to her apartment and tell her what had happened.

For all they knew, she might be watching television. She often did when she was alone in the apartment. If so, she would already know.

Stepping off the elevator on the building's tenth floor, Barry took out his key to the apartment. As he paused in front of its emerald-green door, he took a deep breath and put the key in the latch. The door swung open.

Inside, Sara was pacing like a caged animal.

"Just what is wrong?" she asked Barry sternly. "I know something is wrong, but everybody is keeping it from me!"

Barry eased her into a lounge chair.

"It's all over," he told her softly. "He's gone."

In Kalamazoo, Robert Merrill's ordeal was far from over. At four-fifteen, the telephone in his hotel suite had jarred him from an afternoon nap. The manager of the hotel had informed him that his friend had been rushed to the hospital. Merrill dressed quickly and, with David Benedict, made his way by cab up the fog-covered winding road to the hospital.

Once there, he was besieged by reporters. The hospital's security guards helped him avoid them temporarily, and escorted him to the emergency room. A doctor took him aside and told him that Tucker had been dead on arrival. The cause of death, he was told, was in all likelihood a massive coronary occlusion, though an autopsy would be necessary to confirm the exact cause.

Amid all the confusion, the mention of an autopsy made Merrill bridle. Though not an observant Jew in the sense his friend had been, Merrill was familiar with Orthodox funeral customs, and he knew that they expressly forbade autopsies. Jewish teachings prohibited any tampering with the body of the deceased; according to rabbinical tradition, the body was to be washed and dressed in linen shrouds, and burial was to take place as soon after death as possible. As best he could, Merrill explained this tradition to the attending physicians and, later, to the coroner. For legal reasons, they were unyielding.

When it appeared that an autopsy would have to be done before the body could be transported to New York, Merrill called Barry and explained the dilemma. Immediately, Barry placed two long-distance calls—one to Sanders Goodstein, a prominent family friend in Flint, Michigan, and the other to Father Hesburgh at Notre Dame. In their separate ways, both men would be sensitive to the dilemma and would know how to go about resolving it.

Sanders Goodstein contacted an Orthodox rabbi in the Kalamazoo area and secured his help in establishing with the hospital and county personnel that Tucker's religious beliefs prohibited an autopsy. Meanwhile, Father Hesburgh also used his considerable contacts to ensure that the family's wishes would be honored. Tucker's right to a traditional Jewish burial was at last guaranteed, and his body was prepared for transport to New York City the next morning.

Funeral arrangements were already on Barry's mind when, at half past seven, Schuyler Chapin called on Sara to offer his condolences. Earlier in the evening, Barry had arranged for his father's body to lie in state at the Riverside Chapel in Manhattan. Family, friends, and the public would be able to view the body and pay their respects the next evening, Thursday. The funeral would be scheduled for Friday morning.

But where would the funeral service be held?

The synagogue in which he worshiped would be the customary site, though the family's congregation in Great Neck would be too distant for the public, and the temple too small to accommodate the anticipated crowds. As Jewish law did not limit the service to a single location, what concerned Barry was what he felt would have mattered to his father—that he be accessible to the public that had supported his career.

"I have something I'd like to talk over with you about Dad's

funeral," Barry told Chapin after he had paid his respects to Sara.
"Would it be too much to ask to have the funeral service at the
Met?"

"I don't know that there is any precedent for it," Chapin replied, "but I will be happy to poll the board on your family's
behalf. You can count on my personal support, that I assure you."

By late evening, the Metropolitan board had approved the
Tuckers' request. Chapin had been authorized to plan the funeral
service with the family. An irony befell the planning when Chapin
looked at the rehearsal schedule for Friday morning, January 10.
The sets for *La forza del destino*—the very ones in use fifteen seasons earlier, when Leonard Warren had collapsed onstage and died
in Richard Tucker's arms—would have to be struck to accommodate the funeral service.

In Great Neck, messages of condolence began to arrive at the
Tucker home as soon as the dinner-hour news broadcasts had relayed the tragedy. During the next twelve hours, 135 messages
would be logged on legal pads by friends of the family. The one
hundredth message appearing in the logs had been cabled from
Rome; it was signed simply *La famiglia Gigli*.

Colleagues were among the first to send cables and telegrams. The words they chose were the ones that pervaded all the
messages the family would eventually receive. Mario del Monaco
wrote of the "pain and sadness" that had overcome him when he
heard the news in Rome. Sandor Konya, echoing the sentiments
of Carlo Bergonzi, Giuseppe di Stefano, and Ferruccio Tagliavini
in their separate messages, wrote of "the great loss of a dear friend
and wonderful colleague."

Placido Domingo, whose Metropolitan career Tucker had
helped advance, expressed the disbelief that everyone felt. "We
are shocked about the news of Richard's sudden and untimely
passing," he and his wife, Marta, wired. "We just saw him in
Barcelona and we cannot believe that he is not with us anymore."

The telegrams continued to pour into New York—some sent
directly to Great Neck, and others wired in care of the Metropolitan Opera House. "The loss of the great and irreplaceable artist
Richard Tucker," wrote Vladimir and Wanda Horowitz, was more
than the loss of a great tenor. Renata Tebaldi in her message to
Sara added that his death meant "the loss of such a treasured col-

league and wonderful man." Leonard Bernstein wrote simply, "We are all in mourning together."

Among the hundreds of letters the family would receive, many were from fans who had once stood in the long lines backstage, awaiting nothing more than a hasty autograph—but often finding themselves the object of Tucker's attention.

Scores of letters were intensely personal and reached far into Sara's and Richard's past. Many mentioned Cantor Rubin Tucker, not the Metropolitan Opera star.

The day before the funeral, the Tucker family received the written condolences of Rabbi Levinthal. "He was not only the world's greatest tenor," Levinthal wrote, "but, like King David, he was also the Sweet Singer of Israel—a great musical interpreter of the sacred prayers of our people, inspiring hope and faith in their hearts and souls." Recalling his tireless work for the Jewish homeland and the courage he showed by entertaining Israeli troops after the Six-Day War, the rabbi spoke of Tucker's "great love for Israel and the courage and confidence he helped to instill in the hearts of the battlers in Israel's defense."

"His name," Rabbi Levinthal concluded, "will be immortally enshrined in the hearts of all our people."

On Friday morning, January 10, 1975, as the funeral of Richard Tucker was about to begin, Robert and Marion Merrill sat with Franco and Loretta Corelli and other colleagues in the orchestra section of the Metropolitan Opera House. Merrill, by his own later admission, was still in a state of shock. When he had left Kalamazoo, a hospital administrator had unceremoniously handed him a sealed plastic bag. In it were the contents of his friend's trouser pockets. Merrill had still had the plastic bag in his hands when he arrived at La Guardia Airport.

As the hushed crowd awaited the arrival of the Tucker family, Franco Corelli gazed mournfully at the catafalque and casket at center stage. The night before, he had stood patiently in the long line at the Riverside Chapel, where the body of his friend and colleague lay in state. When the moment came for him to view the body, Corelli looked at the lifeless form and sobbed loudly. When he approached Sara to pay his respects, he said in a voice choked by tears, "This is so cruel, so unfair! Richard *loved* life."

Now, Franco Corelli and scores of Tucker's colleagues had come to mourn him. Risë Stevens, Eleanor Steber, Leontyne Price, Eileen Farrell, Roberta Peters, Rosalind Elias, and Victoria de los Angeles were among those present. Even Maria Jeritza, who had created Turandot at the Metropolitan when Tucker was merely a boy, came to the funeral to honor him.

A hush came over the immense audience as Sara Tucker was escorted into the auditorium by her sons. Dressed in black, with a black veil covering her head, she wept profusely as the funeral ceremony began.

Rabbi Mordecai Waxman, spiritual leader of the synagogue where the Tuckers worshiped, intoned the poignant words of the prophet Isaiah: "Thy sun shall no more go down; neither shall thy moon withdraw itself: for the Lord shall be thine everlasting light, and the days of thy mourning shall be ended."

Schuyler Chapin spoke not only for the Metropolitan Opera but for the music world as a whole. "Richard Tucker was an honest man in everything he did. His life as a human being and an artist were intertwined, each nourishing the other. To every performance, he brought one hundred and seventy-five percent of himself. He believed that the public was entitled to the best, every time he put his foot on the stage. He never failed them—just as he never failed his family or his friends."

During the ceremony, among the eulogies of Chapin, Cardinal Cooke, philanthropist Charles Silver, Rabbi Waxman, and Rabbi Alvin Kleinerman, Cantor Benjamin Siegel intoned the sacred music of the Psalms. At the close of the service, Cantor Herman Malamood, a young protégé of Tucker in the cantorate and in opera, chanted the wailing phrases of the memorial prayer "El Mole Rachamim."

As the last tones of the prayer resounded through the Metropolitan, a stillness enveloped the audience. Those who had given their eulogies and offered their prayers now made their exit, leaving the immense stage bare except for the catafalque and casket. Then slowly, hauntingly, the great gold curtain closed a final time for Richard Tucker.

Postlude

"Weeping may tarry for the night," says the psalmist, "but joy comes in the morning." For the family of Richard Tucker, the sun of the psalmist's morning was long in rising. What sustained them through the long night of their grief—and what has since sustained Tucker's innumerable admirers the world over—are his legacy as an artist and the memories of his warmth and generosity as a man.

To his admirers he left unforgettable musical moments—the lyric splendor of his youthful Rodolfo, and the abandon with which he sang "Che gelida manina"; the fire of his "Guardate, pazzo io son" as Des Grieux in *Manon Lescaut;* the broad phrases of "Un di all'azzurro spazio" in *Andrea Chénier;* the white heat of "No, Pagliaccio non son!"; and the absolute majesty of "Rachel, quand du Seigneur" in *La Juive.* Fortunately, all were recorded—not only commercially, but also on private recordings made of complete performances throughout his career. These recordings will ensure the permanence of Tucker's voice and artistry.

Almost thirty years have passed since Rudolf Bing told the media, "Caruso, Caruso—that's all you hear. I have an idea we're going to be proud someday to be able to tell people we have heard

Richard Tucker." A decade after his death, the breadth of Tucker's accomplishments are already proving Bing's prescience. Comparisons between Caruso and Tucker no longer belong in the realm of a publicist's creative writing, for no other tenor has yet come as close as Richard Tucker to the achievements that Enrico Caruso claimed.

The parallels between the two tenors are often striking—well beyond the fact that after singing the very same role, Eléazar, each died suddenly, and at the height of his acclaim.

Tucker's generosity, like Caruso's, vastly outstripped the few occasions on which he exhibited any uncharitable reactions. In particular, his generosity toward charitable causes was extraordinary. Conservative estimates suggest that in thirty years Tucker contributed his services to raising more than $200 million for a broad range of causes. In return, he received a wealth of honors—among them the First Annual B'nai B'rith Award, the Handel Medallion, the National Interfaith Council Award, the Louis B. Brandeis Medal for Service to Humanity, a gold medal from the City of Vienna for his cultural contributions, the State of Israel's first Artistic and Cultural Award, a gold plaque for distinguished service to Israel during its formative years, and the coveted Order of the Commendatore, Italy's highest civilian honor.

Shortly after his death, the Richard Tucker Music Foundation was chartered by his family "to perpetuate the memory of America's greatest tenor through projects in aid of gifted young singers." Conceived by Herman E. Krawitz, the foundation was formed and shaped by Barry Tucker with a nucleus of executive officers that included (with Sara as foundation president) John V. Lindsay, John McGrath, Howard M. Squadron, and Karen Kriendler Nelson, all of whom led the planning and fund-raising efforts of a board of directors encompassing many of Richard Tucker's artistic colleagues.

On October 31, 1976, at Carnegie Hall, Luciano Pavarotti, Mario Sereni, Renata Scotto, Anna Moffo, Gilda Cruz-Romo, Bonaldo Giaiotti, Elena Obraztsova, Giuseppe di Stefano, Jascha Silberstein, Richard Woitach, James Morris, Eve Queler, and Martina Arroyo launched the first Richard Tucker Music Foundation Annual Gala; on that memorable occasion, highlighted by videotaped excerpts of Tucker singing "Vesti la giubba" and "No, Pagliaccio non son!" James Levine, whom Tucker profoundly admired and regarded almost as family, served as accompanist. Another longtime friend, Alan King, was master of ceremonies. Then, as in each subsequent gala, all the performers donated their fees, to honor the memory of Richard Tucker and to further the cause of the Tucker Foundation.

Since 1976, the rosters of the annual galas have boasted the names of the greatest singers in opera throughout the world—all for the purpose, as Sara Tucker said in her address to the audience at the first gala, "of supporting and guiding American singers who are on the critical threshold of international recognition." In its first decade, the Richard Tucker Music Foundation has raised nearly a half-million dollars for this purpose, and has funded not only the continued studies of competitively selected young American artists but has also given sizable awards to opera training programs throughout the United States. In raising the funds to support these programs, the Tucker Foundation Annual Galas have also provided the public with some of the most memorable and highly praised musical events in the cultural life of New York City.

Richard Tucker's death in 1975 occurred, in retrospect, at the close of one operatic Golden Age and the beginning of another— the end of the postwar era of now-legendary singing that brought the Metropolitan Opera under Rudolf Bing to a level of prominence it had enjoyed under Giulio Gatti-Casazza in Caruso's era. Having achieved the longest tenure of any tenor in the history of the Metropolitan Opera other than Giovanni Martinelli—and inarguably attaining the greatest acclaim of any tenor America has yet produced—Tucker's legacy is secure. One may say of him, as critic W. J. Henderson wrote in his obituary of Caruso, that Richard Tucker, "in sincerity, in fervor, in devotion to his art, was the peer of any opera singer in history."

Man and artist, Tucker left his mark on the history of his time, and in so doing ensured for himself an immortality reserved for a very few. Poetically and nobly, the words of the great rabbis speak to its source:

> When Death comes whispering to me:
> "Thy days are ended."
> Let me say to him:
> "I have lived in love and not in mere time."

He will ask:
  "Will your songs remain?"
I shall reply:
  "I know not, but this I do know,
  That often when I sang my songs,
  I found my own eternity."

Afterword

Richard Tucker: An Artistic Appreciation

We remember Richard Tucker today as the greatest American tenor of worldwide fame whose career followed an unbroken line that ended with a tragic suddenness at its peak. In retrospect, Tucker's entire Metropolitan Opera career suggests a landscape of all peaks, no valleys. Already in 1945, when he made his debut, he was a remarkably well-trained artist of mature judgment—short on repertoire but exceptionally long on confidence. His first recordings of opera arias testify to the gleaming quality of his sound, to his excellent intonation, and to his firm grasp of the Italianate style. Perhaps even more convincing is his 1947 recording of the complete *La Bohème,* which already presents him in total command of a role that was to bring him much acclaim later on. For a Rodolfo of such a high international level, a meteoric rise to stardom was inevitable.

But Richard Tucker was an exceptionally long-lasting meteor. Outstanding tenors came and went during the next quarter century, but Richard Tucker was still there in 1974, still one of the company's pillars, still enlarging his already ample repertoire. An astonishing record of achievement, this, not only in terms of longevity, versatility (thirty roles at the Metropolitan alone), and popularity but also in terms of dependability: a year-in, year-out adherence to the vocal gold standard.

If Richard Tucker had any "off nights," I certainly never witnessed one, or even heard of it. He was, vocally speaking, a firm commodity who always fulfilled the highest expectations his name came to signify. Like Caruso, Gigli, and Bjoerling before him, he was not a naturally gifted actor, but he played his roles with total commitment and often with a fierce intensity. In any case, theatrical considerations mattered little once he began to sing. The voice itself was pure, evenly produced with rarely any audible effort. It was quite powerful, vibrantly alive, but free from the excessive vibrations that can invade sustained notes and threaten true pitch. As a matter of fact, Tucker's firm intonation was one of the most enviable weapons in his artistic arsenal.

From his early beginnings, Tucker displayed an intelligence in choosing roles that is rare in singers. Whenever he undertook a new assignment, he was ready for it. Basically a lyric tenor, he was blessed with a richer body and darker coloration of tone than most lyric tenors, whose resources cannot permit dramatic expansions as they mature. Tucker learned the parts of Radames in *Aida* and Canio in *Pagliacci* early in his career and, in fact, made excellent recordings of these operas in 1949 and 1951, respectively. Yet he did not appear onstage in these roles until 1965 (Radames) and 1970 (Canio), at ages 51 and 56, respectively.

Tucker's development into a "dramatic" tenor thus proceeded with great deliberation. His voice retained its basically lyric quality as the tone darkened: as Calaf, Manrico, Radames, and Canio he continued singing with a legato line that was rarely broken up to create enhanced dramatic effects. Perhaps eventually he, too, would have sung Otello, the coveted goal of many Italian tenors, as Caruso had planned to do had he lived beyond 1921. In any case, more for emotional than artistic reasons, it was the role of Eléazar in Halévy's *La Juive* that Richard Tucker regarded as his crowning achievement. He fulfilled a long-cherished dream when he brought that Hebrew patriarch to the stage in New Orleans and Barcelona.

The road to *La Juive* also represented a logical progression in French opera that led through the principal roles in *Faust, Carmen, Les Contes d'Hoffmann,* and *Samson et Dalila.* In an era singularly lacking in native French tenors who might have supplied the ideal combination of the right tone quality with innate stylistic expression, Tucker's accomplishments in French opera (which are only suggested on records) may also be viewed as a substantial contribution. His characteristically vital and ringing tones created an effect far beyond the reach of lighter-voiced French "specialists."

The clarity of Tucker's enunciation also served him exceedingly well in his native tongue. An early broadcast souvenir of the Metropolitan Opera's 1950 English-language production of Mozart's *Magic Flute* reveals him as a very effective Tamino. Later, he recalled with particular delight his role in the memorable 1951 production of *Così fan tutte* under Fritz Stiedry, who imparted valuable lessons to him in the Mozart style. He continued to enjoy singing in English (there are excellent recordings of operetta and musical comedy favorites to prove it) and even turned to the oratorio role of Handel's Samson toward the end of his career.

But the true focus of his career lay elsewhere. Richard Tucker was—by style, temperament, and a strong linguistic empathy— an "Italian" tenor: twenty-one of his thirty Metropolitan roles came from the Italian repertoire. Only the lack of that certain caressing of phrases that an Italian native acquires at birth betrayed the fact that Tucker's idiomatic command of the *sung* Italian was, in fact, the result of hard work, sound schooling, and thorough preparation.

He was a passionate singer. From the world of cantorial singing, which relies on strong emotion for its successful communication, he carried over into opera a style that rang with the ardor of personal commitment. His Riccardo, Enzo, Cavaradossi, Des Grieux, Alvaro, and Andrea Chénier (perhaps the best of his many roles, although such a choice is not easy to make) were all strongly etched and passionately delivered. Although he sang Alfredo in *La traviata* extremely well, I found it hard to reconcile that character's impulsive and immature nature with Tucker's sober and thoughtful stage personality, especially in the later years of his career.

There was a distinct manliness to his singing style. Even such a role as Edgardo in *Lucia di Lammermoor,* which is often undertaken by light-voiced tenors, would take on an unsuspected assertiveness in Tucker's interpretation. Conversely, while he certainly knew how to sing softly and *mezza voce, piano* was not

Tucker's favorite dynamic marking. He maintained a certain forcefulness in his singing and avoided at all times sounding precious and overly sensitive.

At times, more frequently onstage than in the recording studio, he allowed his "Italian" temperament to run away from him, though I, for one, always suspected that he remained at all times in full control. There was a characteristic "catch" in his voice—whether a residue of his long cantorial experience or a device adapted from such an earlier practitioner as Beniamino Gigli—which he would frequently employ to create a sense of heightened emotional involvement. In his 1954 recording of Verdi's *Forza del destino,* I felt that he actually allowed excessive emotion to compromise an otherwise outstanding vocal effort. (Fortunately, his second *Forza* recording, made in 1964, presents him in an equally fine vocal form and in far steadier emotional control.) In the theater, too, Tucker was not averse to a certain amount of gallery pleasing. Although the excellence of his singing alone would have assured him the applause singers thrive on, he made sure of it—by a slight sharpening of the pitch on a final note or some calculated gesture.

In the theater Tucker always created the impression that he gave his maximum effort without holding anything back. With the passing of time, the intensity with which he threw himself into his roles actually increased, causing concern that his health might be affected by his physical exertions. It was indeed a rather curious phenomenon that an artist who was able to pace his career with so much wisdom and foresight would then use his resources so unsparingly.

At the same time, when it came to his voice, Tucker knew how to conserve it from undue stress. Like Caruso and Gigli before him, he was not particularly anxious to flaunt his high C, for instance. Those who wish to be convinced that he could sing the note may check the conclusion of the *Ballo in maschera* duet with Eileen Farrell (Odyssey 35935) or his second recording of *La Bohème* (RCA), where he sings "Che gelida manina" in the original key. As far as I know, in the theater he usually sang that aria a half-step lower, more comfortably and more effectively. In any case, his high B-natural was a note he could unfailingly produce with triumphant ease.

High notes are essential to a tenor, and they are deprecated only by those who cannot sing them. But high notes serve little

artistic purpose if they exist without any organic connection to
the rest of the scale. Tucker's range was remarkably even: the basic quality of his tone remained unchanged as he went from low
to high register across the *break,* the crucial area where the "chest"
and "head" registers meet. There are instances of downright
treacherous passages (in *La Bohème* and *La forza del destino,* to
mention but two operas) that Tucker could negotiate as though
these difficulties did not exist.

Effortlessness, the art of concealing art, is the result of sound
technique, which, in Tucker's case, had many manifestations. His
command of florid music probably grew out of his cantorial expertise. Few of his operatic roles called attention to this aspect of
his art, but the easy flow and accurate articulation of the Duke of
Mantua's arias in *Rigoletto* and his rare early recording of "Una
furtiva lagrima" readily attest to it, as do the trills in Manrico's
"Ah sì, ben mio" from *Il trovatore.* By his own statement, he was
attracted to Handel's *Samson* at least partially because of the role's
florid requirements.

From his earliest recordings to the very end, there is an element of utter self-confidence that radiates from Tucker's singing.
He was an artist with a firm belief in the beauty of his tone, the
soundness of his technique, his readiness to function always at the
peak of his ability. This kind of self-confidence was part of the
man's makeup. Richard Tucker knew his worth: there was no false
modesty about him. He not only knew he was good, he simply
did not know anyone who was better.

Recording in the studio, discussing his work, he projected
no artistic aura, no glamour whatever. He was all business, down
to earth, to the point. I recall, in particular, an off-the-air conversation I had with him at radio station WQXR in New York
City. It was in 1969, following his debut at La Scala in Verdi's
Luisa Miller. As he recalled the enthusiastic reception the Milan
audience had given him, Richard said, "I showed them!" He did
not complete the thought, nor did he have to. He showed them
that this Brooklyn-born American had the voice and the heart to
sing Verdi not only beautifully but also idiomatically. He also had
the guts to prove it in Verdi's own Milan to a very demanding
audience. But there was no reason for Richard Tucker to feel in-
timidated. He *knew!*

GEORGE JELLINEK

Discography

compiled by Patricia Ann Kiser

OPERAS

Donizetti, Gaetano.
Lucia di Lammermoor.
Columbia SL 127 (1954).
CAST: Pons; Tucker, Guarrera, Scott; Metropolitan Opera Orchestra and Chorus; Fausto Cleva, conductor.
REISSUE: Odyssey Y2-32361 (1973).

Giordano, Umberto.
Andrea Chénier—Abridged.
Metropolitan Opera Record Club MO 826 (1958).
CAST: Curtis-Verna; Tucker, Sereni; Metropolitan Opera Orchestra and Chorus; Fausto Cleva, conductor.

Halévy, Jacques.
La Juive—Selections.
RCA ARL1 0447 (1974).
CAST: Arroyo, Moffo; Tucker, Giaiotti; New Philharmonia Orchestra; Ambrosian Opera Chorus; Antonio de Almeida, conductor.

LEONCAVALLO, RUGGIERO.
I pagliacci.
Columbia SL 113 (1951).
CAST: Amara; Tucker, Valdengo, Harvuot; Metropolitan Opera Orchestra and Chorus; Fausto Cleva, conductor.
REISSUE: Columbia SL 124 (with *Cavalleria rusticana*), Odyssey YS 33122 (1974).

MASCAGNI, PIETRO.
Cavalleria rusticana.
Columbia SL 123 (1953).
CAST: Harshaw; Tucker, Guarrera; Metropolitan Opera Orchestra and Chorus; Fausto Cleva, conductor.
REISSUE: Columbia SL 124 (with *I pagliacci*), Odyssey YS 33122 (1974).

MOZART, WOLFGANG AMADEUS.
Così fan tutte.
(Sung in English)
Columbia SL 122 (1952).
CAST: Steber, Peters, Thebom; Tucker, Guarrera, Alvary; Metropolitan Opera Orchestra and Chorus; Fritz Stiedry, conductor.
REISSUE: Odyssey Y3 32670 (1973).

PUCCINI, GIACOMO.
La Bohème.
Columbia SL 101 (1947).
CAST: Sayão, Benzell; Tucker, Valentino, Cehanovsky, Moscona, Baccaloni; Metropolitan Opera Orchestra and Chorus; Giuseppe Antonicelli, conductor.
REISSUE: Odyssey Y2 32364 (1973).

La Bohème.
RCA Victor LM 6095 (mono), LSC 6095 (stereo) (1961).
CAST: Moffo, Costa; Tucker, Merrill, Maero, Tozzi, Corena; Rome Opera House Orchestra and Chorus; Erich Leinsdorf, conductor.
HIGHLIGHTS: RCA Victor FTC 2156 (1961?).

Madama Butterfly.
Columbia SL 104 (1949).
CAST: Steber, Madeira; Tucker, Valdengo; Metropolitan Opera Orchestra and Chorus; Max Rudolf, conductor.
REISSUE: Odyssey Y3 32107 (1973).

Madama Butterfly.
RCA Victor LM 6160 (mono), LSC 6160 (stereo) (1962).

CAST: Price, Elias; Tucker, Maero; RCA Italiana Opera Orchestra and Chorus; Erich Leinsdorf, conductor.
HIGHLIGHTS: RCA Victor LM 2840 (1965).

STRAUSS, JOHANN.
Fledermaus.
(Sung in English)
Columbia SL 108 (1950).
CAST: Pons, Welitch, Lipton; Tucker, Kullman, Brownlee; Metropolitan Opera Orchestra and Chorus; Eugene Ormandy, conductor.
REISSUE: Odyssey Y2 32666 (1973).

TCHAIKOVSKY, PETER ILYICH.
Eugene Onegin—Abridged.
(Sung in English)
Metropolitan Opera Record Club MO 824 (1958).
CAST: Amara, Elias; Tucker, Guarrera, Tozzi; Metropolitan Opera Orchestra and Chorus; Dimitri Metropoulos, conductor.

VERDI, GIUSEPPE.
Aida.
Angel 3525 C/L (1955).
CAST: Callas, Barbieri; Tucker, Gobbi, Zaccaria, Modesti; La Scala Orchestra and Chorus, Milan; Tullio Serafin, conductor.
HIGHLIGHTS: Angel 35938 (1961).

Aida.
(From a broadcast performance of March 26 and April 2, 1949)
RCA Victor LM 6132 (1957).
CAST: Nelli, Gustavson; Tucker, Valdengo, Scott, Harbour; NBC Symphony Orchestra; chorus under the direction of Robert Shaw; Arturo Toscanini, conductor.

La forza del destino.
Angel 3531 C/L (1954).
CAST: Callas, Nicolai; Tucker, Tagliabue, Rossi-Lemeni, Capecchi; La Scala Orchestra and Chorus, Milan; Tullio Serafin, conductor.
HIGHLIGHTS: Angel 3531/L (1958).
REISSUE: Seraphim IC-6088 (1974).

La forza del destino.
RCA Victor LM 6413 (mono), LSC 2838 (stereo) (1964).

CAST: Price, Verrett; Tucker, Merrill, Tozzi, Flagello; RCA Italiana Opera Orchestra and Chorus; Thomas Schippers, conductor.
HIGHLIGHTS: RCA LM 2838 (1964).

Rigoletto.
Columbia ML 404 (mono), MS 901 (stereo) (1959).
CAST: D'Angelo, Pirazzini; Tucker, Capecchi, Sardi; San Carlo Orchestra and Chorus, Naples; Francesco Molinari-Pradelli, conductor.
REISSUE: Philips 7699 063.

La traviata.
RCA Victor LSC 6154 (1960).
CAST: Moffo; Tucker, Merrill; Rome Opera Orchestra and Chorus; Fernando Previtali, conductor.
HIGHLIGHTS: RCA Victor LM 2561 (1961).

Il trovatore.
RCA Victor LM 6150 (mono), LSC 6150 (stereo) (1959).
CAST: Price, Elias; Tucker, Warren, Tozzi; Rome Opera Orchestra and Chorus; Arturo Basile, conductor.
HIGHLIGHTS: RCA Victor FTC 2122 (1959?).

PRIVATE LABELS

Chicago Lyric Opera Gala. HRE 245.
CONTENTS: *Un ballo in maschera:* Ma se m'è forza perderti.—*Cavalleria rusticana:* Mamma . . . mamma.—*Tosca:* E lucevan le stelle, sung by Richard Tucker.—*Andrea Chénier:* Act IV duet, sung by Renata Tebaldi and Richard Tucker; Georg Solti, conductor (1956).—*Manon Lescaut:* Act IV, sung by Renata Tebaldi and Richard Tucker; Fausto Cleva, conductor.

GIORDANO, UMBERTO.
Andrea Chénier.
(From a 1958 South American performance).
HRE 350.
CAST: Tebaldi; Tucker, Bastianini; Oliviero De Fabritiis, conductor.

HALÉVY, JACQUES.
La Juive.
(From a performance on October 18 or 20, 1973).
HRE 212.
CAST: Galvany, Shane; Tucker, Plishka, Bullard; New Orleans Opera Orchestra and Chorus; Knud Andersson, conductor.

Great Tenor and Baritone Duets.
HRE 217-1.
INCLUDES: *The Pearl Fishers:* "Within the temple there," sung by Tucker and Weede (1946).

PONCHIELLI, AMILCARE.
La Gioconda.
(From a Buenos Aires performance of June 26, 1966).
TD 505.
CAST: Suliotis, Elias, Dominguez; Tucker, MacNeil, Washington; Bruno Bartoletti, conductor.

PUCCINI, GIACOMO.
Manon Lescaut.
(From a Caracas performance of June 2, 1972).
HRE 354 [possibly ERR 130-2].
CAST: Olivero; Tucker, Sardinero; Michelangelo Veltri, conductor.

"Recondita armonia": The Aria from Puccini's *Tosca* Sung by 22 Tenors.
HRE 377-1.
INCLUDES Tucker.

Richard Tucker at the Hollywood Bowl:
Live Performances 1951.
HRE 383-1.
INCLUDES: Arias from *Judas Maccabaeus, Andrea Chénier, Forza del destino, L'Africaine, Carmen, Cavalleria rusticana,* and songs by Leoncavallo and DeCurtis.

VERDI, GIUSEPPE.
Rigoletto.
(From a South American performance in 1967).
HRE 269.
CAST: Scotto; Tucker, MacNeil, Wilderman; Fernando Previtale, conductor.

MISCELLANEOUS

**A Dudele.*—Mimaamakim (Yiddish).
Columbia 57070-F.

The Art of Bel Canto.
Columbia ML 6067 (mono), MS 6667 (stereo) (1965).

**45 rpm record

WITH: Columbia Chamber Ensemble; John Wustman, piano or harpsichord.
CONTENTS: Giuseppe Giordani: Caro mio ben.—A. Scarlatti: Già il sole dal gange
(L'Honesta negli amori).—Rossini: Pieta, Signore.—Giuseppe Sarti: Lungi dal caro
bene *(Armida e Rinaldo).*—Gluck: O del mio dolce ardor *(Paride ed Elena).*—
Francesco Durante: Danza, danza, fanciulla; Vergin, tutto amor.—Antonio Cal-
dara: Sebben, crudele *(La costanza in amor).*—Giuseppe Torelli: Tu lo sai.—
Giovanni Legrenzi: Che fiero costume *(Eteocle e Polinice).*—Pergolesi: Nina.—
Francesco Veracini: Meco verrai (Roselinda).

★★ *The Art of Richard Tucker.*
WITH: Metropolitan Opera Orchestra; Emil Cooper and Fausto Cleva, conduc-
tors.
CONTENTS: *L'Africana:* O Paradiso.—*La Gioconda:* Cielo e mar.—*Carmen:* Flower
Song.—*Un ballo in maschera:* Di'tu se fedele.

Best of the Great Songs of Christmas, Album 10.
CSS 1478 (196–?).
INCLUDES TUCKER SINGING: The Lord's Prayer.

Cantorial Jewels.
Columbia ML 4805 (1949).
WITH: Chorus and Orchestra; Sholom Secunda, conductor.
CONTENTS: Kiddush.—Havdoloh.—Tzadik Adoshem.—Ki K'shimcho.—Yehi
Rotzon.—Yir'u eineiu.
ALSO ISSUED AS: Columbia FL 9502, CBS 72285, and Columbia Special Products
AML 4805.

★CAPUA, EDUARDO DI.
O sole mio.
Columbia 3-359.
WITH: Instrumental ensemble.

Celebrated Tenor Arias.
Columbia ML 4750 (1954).
WITH: Metropolitan Opera Orchestra; Fausto Cleva, Emil Cooper, conductors.
CONTENTS: *La traviata:* De' miei bollenti spiriti.—*Andrea Chénier:* Come un bel
dì di maggio.—*L'Africana:* O paradiso.—*Faust:* Salut! demeure.—*L'elisir d'amore:*
Una furtiva lagrima.—*La Bohème:* Che gelida manina.—*Carmen:* Air de fleur.—

★★45 rpm record
★7-inch 33⅓ rpm record

La Gioconda: Cielo e mar.—*Un ballo in maschera:* Forse la soglia attinse; Ma se m'è forza perderti.

Celeste Aida.
Columbia ML 6357 (mono), MS 6957 (stereo) (1967).
WITH: Orchestra; various conductors.
CONTENTS: *Aida:* Celeste Aida.—*Il trovatore:* Di quella pira.—*Faust:* Salut! demeure.—*La Bohème:* Che gelida manina.—*Rigoletto:* Questa o quella; La donna è mobile.—*Tosca:* Recondita armonia.—*Turandot:* Nessun dorma.—*Carmen:* Air de fleur.—*Tosca:* E lucevan le stelle.—*Cavalleria rusticana:* Mamma, quel vino è generoso.—*Manon:* Ah, fuyez, douce image.—*Il trovatore:* Ah, sì, ben mio.— *L'Arlesiana:* Il lamento di Federico.

The Fabulous Voice of Richard Tucker: Great Songs of Love and Inspiration.
Columbia ML 5797 (mono), MS 6397 (stereo) (1962).
WITH: Orchestra; Skitch Henderson, arranger and conductor.
CONTENTS: The exodus song.—I believe.—Tonight.—Climb ev'ry mountain.— Love letters.—Softly, as in a morning sunrise.—The sweetest sounds.—Shalom.— Love is a many-splendored thing.—Anniversary waltz.—You'll never walk alone.—With these hands.
REISSUE: *The Exodus Song,* Columbia ML 6167 (mono), MS 6767 (stereo) (1965).

★★*Faith alone—Someone is watching.*
Columbia 4-40487.

★★*Faithfully yours—Tell me.*
Columbia 2-G.
WITH: Orchestra; Percy Faith, conductor.

First Performance, Lincoln Center.
Columbia L2L 1007 (mono), LS2 1008 (stereo) (1962).
Recorded at opening concert in Philharmonic Hall, September 23, 1962.
INCLUDES TUCKER IN: Vaughan Williams: *Serenade to Music* (also available on Columbia MS 7177).—Mahler: "Veni Creator Spiritus," from Eighth Symphony.
WITH: Addison, Amara, Chookasian, Farrell, Tourel, Verrett-Carter; Bell, Bressler, Flagello, London, Vickers; New York Philharmonic; Schola Cantorum; Juilliard Chorus; Columbus Boychoir; Leonard Bernstein, conductor.

★★45 rpm record

★Flotow, Friedrich von and Verdi, Giuseppe.
Martha: M'appari tutt'amor;
Rigoletto: Questa o quella.
Columbia 3-259.
with: Orchestra; Emil Cooper, conductor.

Goldfaden, Abraham.
[Goldfaden Songs]. Columbia FL 9506 (1950).
with: Orchestra; Sholom Secunda, conductor.
contents: Faryomert, Farklogt (from *Doktor Almasada*).—Once there was a
shepherd (from biblical opera *Bar Kochba*) (sung in Yiddish).—*Shulamis* selections: Rozshinkes mit mandlin (lullaby); Shabes, Yomtov un rosch chodesh
(ballad); Oh, der Brunen, oh der . . . ! *(Die Schvue) (The well);* Flaker feieril
(Flicker, oh, flame).

Great Duets from Verdi Operas.
Columbia ML 5696 (mono), MS 6296 (stereo) (1962).
with: Eileen Farrell; Columbia Symphony Orchestra; Fausto Cleva, conductor.
contents: *Don Carlo:* Io vengo a domandar.—*Aida:* Pur ti riveggo.—*Simon
Boccanegra:* Vieni a mirar.—*Un ballo in maschera:* Teco io sto; non sai tu.—*Otello:*
Già nella notte.
reissue: Odyssey Y 35935 (197-?).

Great Love Duets.
Columbia ML 4981 (1955).
with: Dorothy Kirsten; Metropolitan Opera Orchestra; Fausto Cleva, conductor.
contents: *La Bohème:* Che gelida manina; Mi chiamano Mimi; O soave fanciulla; Quando me'n vo; Donde lieta.—*Manon:* Toi! Vous! . . . *Manon Lescaut:*
L'ora, o Tirsi; Tu, tu amore? Tu?; Sola, perduta, abbandonata.

The Great Songs of Christmas, Album 5.
Columbia CSP 238M (mono), CSP 238S (stereo) (196-?).
includes tucker singing: The Lord's Prayer.—O Little Town of Bethlehem.

Great Tenor Arias.
Columbia ML 4248 (1950).
with: Metropolitan Opera Orchestra; Fausto Cleva, Emil Cooper, conductors;
Columbia Symphony Orchestra; Wilfred Pelletier, conductor.

★7-inch 33⅓ rpm record

CONTENTS: *Aida:* Celeste Aida.—*La forza del destino:* La vita è inferno all'infelice (recit.) . . . Tu che in seno.—*Rigoletto:* Ella mi fu rapita (recit.) . . . Parmi veder le lagrime.—*I pagliacci:* Vesti la giubba.—*Cavalleria rusticana:* Mama, quel vino è generoso.—*Rigoletto:* La donna è mobile; Questa o quella.—*Martha:* M'appari tut'amour.—*La Juive:* Rachel, quand du Seigneur.—*The Pearl Fishers:* A cette voix quel trouble (recit.) . . . Je crois entendre encore.

★★*Hatikvah.*—*Ani maamim* (Jewish).
Columbia 8248-F.

★★*Hatikvah.*—*Jerusalem, Jerusalem* (Yerushala'im Shel Zahav).
Columbia 4-44284.

Hatikvah! Richard Tucker Sings Great Jewish Favorites . . .
Columbia MS 7217 (1969).
(Sung in Hebrew or English)
WITH: Chorus and orchestra; various conductors.
CONTENTS: Hatikvah.—Hava Nagila.—Kinereth.—Jerusalem of gold.—Tzena, tzena, tzena, tzena.—Sunrise, sunset.—The Exodus song.—Shalom.—Anniversary waltz.—The rover.

Israel Sings.
Columbia F1 9512 (1950).
(Sung in Hebrew)
WITH: Orchestra; Sholom Secunda, conductor.
CONTENTS: Tzena tzena tzena (hora).—Shir hacheirut (song of liberation).—Shir hapalmach (march) (song of the commandos).—Haemek hu chalom (hora) (The Emek is our dream).—Katsir baemek.—Sair eres.
REISSUE: Columbia ML 4806 (with selections from *Shulamis*)

Joyous Christmas, Vol. 5.
Columbia C10396 (196-?).
INCLUDES TUCKER SINGING: The Lord's Prayer.

★★Just for you.—Because.—Thine alone.—The song of songs.—For you alone.
Columbia 4-1619.
WITH: Columbia Symphony Orchestra; Alfredo Antonini, conductor.

★★45 rpm record

Kol Nidre Service.
Columbia MS 6085 (1959).
Music composed and conducted by Sholom Secunda.
WITH: Ben Irving, narrator.

Man of La Mancha.
Columbia S 31237 (1972).
CAST: Horne; Nabors, Tucker, Gilford; chorus and orchestra; Paul Weston, conductor.
INCLUDES TUCKER SINGING: I'm only thinking of him (with Madeline Kahn, Irene Clark).—Impossible dream (with Marilyn Horne and chorus).—To each his Dulcinea.—The Psalm.

Metropolitan Opera Gala Honoring Sir Rudolf Bing
(From the broadcast of April 22, 1972).
Deutsche Grammophon DGG 2530 260 (1972).
INCLUDES: Invano, Alvaro from *La forza del destino* with Robert Merrill; Metropolitan Opera Orchestra; Francesco Molinari-Pradelli, conductor.

Opera Favorites.
Columbia ML 2139.
INCLUDES: Act I Love Duet from *Tosca,* with Ljuba Welitch; Metropolitan Opera Orchestra; Max Rudolf, conductor.
REISSUE: Odyssey 32 16 0077 (1967).

Passover Seder Festival.
Columbia ML 5736 (mono), MS 6336 (stereo) (1962).
(Musical setting of the Hagadah and Passover prayers, sung in Hebrew).
WITH: Chorus; Alexander D. Richardson, organ; Ben Irving, narrator; Sholom Secunda, conductor.
CONTENTS: The Kiddush.—Ma nishtano.—Dayeiny.—Bochol dor vodor.—B'tsels Yisroel mimits royim.—Vayhi bachatsi haloyloh.—Ki lo noeh.—Adir hu.—Echod mi yodea.—Chad gad'you.—Hodu ladoshem.—Pis'chu li Shaarei tsedek.—Ribono Shel olom.—Tal tein.—Tal bo.—Ein kelcheinu.—Adon Olom.
ALSO ISSUED AS: CBS-Israel 72293.

Puccini and Verdi Favorites.
Columbia ML 6004 (mono), MS 6604 (stereo) (1964).
INCLUDES: La Bohème: Che gelida manina.—*Turandot:* Nessun dorma.—*Tosca:* E lucevan le stelle.—*Rigoletto:* La donna è mobile.—*Aida:* Pur ti riveggo.

Richard Tucker and Robert Merrill at Carnegie Hall
(From a recital of January 7, 1973).
London BP 26351-2 or Decca SXLA 7517/8 (1973).
CONTENTS: *La Gioconda:* Enzo Grimaldo, Principe di Santa Fior.—*L'Africana:* Adamastor, re dell'onde profonde.—*Don Giovanni:* Deh vieni alla finestra.—*Le nozze di Figaro:* Non più andrai.—Mozart: Misero! o sogno, o son desto (K.

431).—*I vespri siciliani:* Giorno di pianto.—*Andrea Chénier:* Nemico della patria.—*La forza del destino:* Invano, Alvaro.—*L'elisir d'amore:* Una furtiva lagrima.—*Zazà:* Zazà, piccola zingara.—*Cavalleria rusticana:* Mamma, quel vino è generoso.—*Otello:* Credo.—*Les Pêcheurs de perles:* Au fond du temple saint.—*Otello:* Sì, pel ciel.—Leoncavallo: Mattinata.—Goldfaden (Secunda): Rozshinkes mit mandlin.—*La traviata:* Di Provenza.—*Fiddler on the Roof:* If I were a rich man.—*La forza del destino:* Solenne in quest'ora.

Richard Tucker: In Memoriam.
Columbia D3M 33448 (1975).
CONTENTS: Verdi *Requiem:* Ingemisco tamquam reus.—*Rigoletto:* Parmi veder le lagrime.—*Aida:* Celeste Aida.—*Luisa Miller:* Quando le sere al placido.—*Manon Lescaut:* Donna non vidi mai; Guardate, pazzo son.—*Tosca:* E lucevan le stelle.—*Turandot:* Non piangere, Liu; Nessun dorma.—*La Bohème:* Che gelida manina.—*La fanciulla del West:* Ch'ella mi creda libero.—*Andrea Chénier:* Un dì all'azzurro spazio.—*La Gioconda:* Cielo e mar.—*I pagliacci:* Vesti la giubba.—*Les Pêcheurs de perles:* Je crois entendre.—*Carmen:* Air de fleur.—*L'Africaine:* O Paradis.—*Le Cid:* O souverain, o juge, o père.—*Joseph:* Champs paternels.—*La Juive:* Rachel, quand du Seigneur.—Giordani: Caro mio ben.—Torelli: Tu lo sai.—*Paride ed Elena:* O del mio dolce ardor.—Pepoli/Rossini: La danza.—Fusco/Falvo: Dicitencello vuie.—Anonymous: Tiritomba.—Gannon/Sieczynski: Vienna, my city of dreams.—Smith/Lehar: Yours is my heart alone.—Puffer/Cavalieri/Heuberger: In our secluded rendezvous.—*Carousel:* You'll never walk alone.—Boone/Gold: The Exodus song.—*Fiddler on the Roof:* Sunrise, sunset.—Goldfaden: Rozshinkes mit mandlin.—Yehi rotzon.—Yir'u eineinu.—Kiddush.—Kol nidre.

Richard Tucker Sings Arias from Ten Verdi Operas.
Columbia ML 6068 (mono), MS 6668 (stereo) (1965).
WITH: Vienna State Opera Orchestra; Nello Santi, conductor.
CONTENTS: *Aida:* Se quel guerrier io fossi! Celeste Aida.—*Un ballo in maschera:* Forse la soglia attinse; Ma se m'è forza perderti; Ah! Dessa è là.—*I Lombardi:* La mia Letizia infondere; Come poteva un angelo.—*I due Foscari:* Notte! perpetua notte; Non maledirmi, O prode.—*Simon Boccanegra:* O inferno! Sento avvampar nell'anima.—*Il trovatore:* Il presagio funesto; Ah sì, ben mio.—*Luisa Miller:* Oh! fede negar potessi; Quando le sere al placido.—*Rigoletto:* Ella mi fu rapita; Parmi veder le lagrime.—*I vespri siciliani:* E' di Monforte il cenno! Giorno di pianto.—*La forza del destino:* La vita è inferno; O tu che in seno agl'angeli.

Richard Tucker Sings Puccini.
Columbia ML 5416 (mono), MS 6094 (stereo) (1959).
WITH: Columbia Symphony Orchestra; Fausto Cleva, conductor.
CONTENTS: *Tosca:* Recondita armonia; E lucevan le stelle.—*Gianni Schicchi:* Firenze è come un albero fiorito.—*Turandot:* Non piangere, Liu; Nessun dorma.—*La Bohème:* Che gelida manina.—*La fanciulla del West:* Ch'ella mi creda libero.—*Madama Butterfly:* Addio, fiorito asil.—*Manon Lescaut:* Ah, Manon, mi tradisce; Guardate, pazzo son.

Robert Francis Kennedy—A Memorial.
Columbia D2S 792 (1968?).
INCLUDES TUCKER SINGING: Panis Angelicus (Franck) at the funeral service.

Rozshinkes mit Mandlin (Raisins with Almonds).
Living Archives Ltd. LAL-1977 (197-?).
CONTENTS: Goldfaden: Rozshinkes mit mandlin (*Rozshinkes mit mandlin,* CBS 81421).—Comments made in a 1962 WFMT/Studs Terkel interview, followed by the narrator's reading of excerpts from "In Memoriam: Richard Tucker" by Professor Jacob Cohen, commentary, June 1975, over the final scene of *La Bohème* by Puccini (Sayão, Tucker; Metropolitan Opera Orchestra and Chorus; Giuseppe Antonicelli, conductor, Odyssey Y 232364), fading into Mr. Tucker singing and commenting on Riboni Shel Olom from *Passover Seder Festival* (Ben Irving, narrator; Sholom Secunda, conductor, CBS LP 72293).

A Salute to Richard Tucker on His Silver Anniversary at the Metropolitan Opera.
Columbia M 30118 (1970).
WITH: Orchestras; various conductors.
CONTENTS: *Carmen:* Air de fleur.—*Aida:* Celeste Aida.—*Così fan tutte:* Un'aura amorosa (sung in English).—*La forza del destino:* O tu che in seno agl'angeli.—*Manon Lescaut:* Guardate, pazzo son.—*I pagliacci:* Vesti la giubba.—*La Gioconda:* Cielo e mar.—*Tosca:* E lucevan le stelle.—*La Bohème:* Che gelida manina.—*Luisa Miller:* Quando le sere al placido.

SANDER.
Eli, Eli.
Columbia 72198-D.

Songs from Sunny Italy.
Columbia ML 2155 (1951).
WITH: Columbia Concert Orchestra; Alfredo Antonini, conductor.
CONTENTS: Torna a Surriento.—Non ti scordar di me.—Mamma mia, che vo' sapè?—Dicitencello vuie.—Torna, piccina!—O sole mio!—La danza.—Tarantella napoletana.—Lolita.

Sorrento.
Columbia ML 5258 (1958).
WITH: Columbia Concert Orchestra; Alfredo Antonini, conductor.
CONTENTS: Core'ngrato.—Canta pe'me.—Torna a Surriento.—Non ti scordar di me.—Mamma mia, che vo sapè?—Lolita.—Tiritomba.—Rondine al nido.—Torna, piccina!—O sole mio.—La danza.

The Soul of Italy.
Columbia ML 6164 (mono), ML 6764 (stereo) (1965).
WITH: Columbia Symphony Orchestra; Nicolas Flagello, conductor.
CONTENTS: O paese d' O sole.—Reginella la campagnola.—I' te vurria vasa!—Tu, ca nun chiagne!—La bella aurora.—Senza nisciuno.—Signora fortuna.—Fenesta che lucive!—Occhi turchini.—L'alba separa dalla luce l'ombra.—Ohie meneche!—Mamma.

The Sound of Genius.
Columbia SGS 1 (1963).
INCLUDES TUCKER SINGING: Tonight from *West Side Story*.

Starring Richard Tucker.
Columbia ML 5062 (1955).
WITH: Columbia Symphony Orchestra; Fausto Cleva, conductor.
CONTENTS: *Un ballo in maschera:* Di'tu se fedele.—*Manon Lescaut:* Donna non vidi mai.—*Verdi Requiem:* Ingemisco tamquam reus.—*Andrea Chénier:* Un dì all'azzurro spazio.—*Iris:* Apri la tua finestra.—*Manon:* Ah fuyez, douce image.—*Luisa Miller:* Quando le sere al placido—*Il trovatore:* Ah! Sì ben mio; Di quella pira.

Stars for a Summer Night.
Columbia PM 1 (mono), PMS 1 (stereo).
INCLUDES TUCKER SINGING: *Tosca:* E lucevan le stelle.

A Treasury of French Opera Arias.
Columbia ML 6231 (mono), MS 6831 (stereo) (1966).
WITH: Vienna State Opera Orchestra; Pierre Dervaux, conductor.
CONTENTS: *Carmen:* Air de fleur.—*Werther:* Un autre est son époux.—*Joseph:* Champs paternels.—*L'Africaine:* O paradis.—*La Juive:* Rachel! Quand du Seigneur.—*Les Pêcheurs de perles:* Je crois entendre.—*Manon:* Ah fuyez, douce image.—*Werther:* Pourquoi me réveiller.—*Hérodiade:* Ne pouvant réprimer.—*Le Cid:* O souverain, O juge, O père.

★★ *Tzadik Adoshem.*—*Ki K-shimcho* (Hebrew).
Columbia D-206-3.

VERDI, GIUSEPPE.
Requiem.
Columbia M2L 307 (1964).
CAST: Amara, Forrester; Tucker, London; Philadelphia Orchestra; Westminster Choir; Eugene Ormandy, conductor.

★★*Rigoletto.*
La donna è mobile.—Questa o quella.
Columbia 4-41587.

Verdi Duets.
Columbia MM 798.
WITH: Daniza Ilitsch; Metropolitan Opera Orchestra; Max Rudolf, conductor.
CONTENTS: *Otello:* Già nella notte.—*Un ballo in maschera:* Teco io sto.

Vienna, City of My Dreams; Richard Tucker sings romantic favorites.
Columbia ML 5937 (mono), MS 6537 (stereo) (1963).
WITH: Columbia Symphony Orchestra; Franz Allers, conductor.

★★45 rpm record

CONTENTS: Vienna, city of my dreams.—I have been in love before.—Medley from *Boccaccio*.—Roses from Tyrol.—Darling, trust in me.—Lovesong of May.—Yours is my heart alone.—Medley from *The Count of Luxembourg*.—In our secluded rendezvous.—Love, you invaded my senses.—Wonderful world.—Frasquita's serenade.—I long for Vienna.

★★ *Vienna, city of my dreams.—I long for Vienna.*
Columbia ML 5937 (mono), MS 6537 (stereo).

Welcoming the Sabbath: A Friday Evening Service.
Columbia ML 5119 (1956).
(Sung in Hebrew)
WITH: Choir under the direction of Sholom Secunda.
CONTENTS: Lechu Neranenoh-L'cho Dodi.—Borchu.—Ahvas olom.—Mi chomocho.—Haskiveinu.—V'Shomru.—Eloheinu Velohei Avoseinu.—Kiddush l'Shabos.—Yigdal.—Shabat Shalom.
ALSO AVAILABLE AS: CBS 72286.

What Now My Love: Richard Tucker Sings Today's Popular Favorites.
Columbia ML 6295 (mono), MS 6895 (stereo) (1966).
WITH: Orchestra; Franz Allers, conductor.
CONTENTS: What kind of fool am I?—Sunrise, sunset.—What now my love.—Somewhere.—And this is my beloved.—More.—The rover.—When you're young.—Who can I turn to?—Melinda.—Never will I marry.—Why did I choose you?

★★ *What now my love.—The rover.*
Columbia 4-43893.

★★ *Yehi, Rotzon.—Uir'u Eineinu* (Hebrew).
Columbia D-206-5.

Yizkor: In Memory of the Six Million.
Ethnic Music Pub. Co. (1967).
Text by Samuel Rosenbaum; music by Sholom Secunda.
CAST: Sauler; Tucker, Da Silva, Schwartzman; Ithaca College Concert Choir and Orchestra; Thomas Michalak, conductor.

★★ 45 rpm record

Acknowledgments

This book would not have been possible without the assistance—whether offered directly to me, or to my associates in this project—of a long list of Richard Tucker's family members, friends, colleagues, and representatives. I should like to acknowledge my inestimable thanks to:

His colleagues in music, including (in alphabetical order) Licia Albanese, Alex Alexay, Richard Bonynge, Montserrat Caballé, Alan Chester, Franco Corelli, Gilda Cruz-Romo, Annamary Dickey, George Jellinek, Robert Merrill, Nan Merriman, Zinka Milanov, Sherrill Milnes, Anna Moffo, James Morris, Luciano Pavarotti, Rose Bampton Pelletier, Roberta Peters, Claudia Pinza, Stella Roman, Alfredo (Sadel) Sanchez-Luna, Bidú Sayão, Eleanor Steber, Dame Joan Sutherland, and Nina Morgana Zirato. Regrettably, I must thank five distinguished artists posthumously: Alexander Kipnis, Mario del Monaco, Wilfred Pelletier, Giacomo Lauri-Volpi, and last Rosa Ponselle, who in the course of my work as her biographer gave me many insights into the repertoire Richard Tucker sang, especially Halévy's *La Juive,* in which she starred with Caruso in the opera's 1919 Metropolitan revival.

My thanks also extend to the general managers, artists' representatives, public relations executives, legal representatives, and other administrators who played a role in this book. They include Sir Rudolf Bing, Herbert H. Breslin, Schuyler G. Chapin, Hattie Clark, Thea Dispeker, Laurence Wasserman, and Elizabeth Winston. Here too, regrettably, I must extend my gratitude posthumously to Dario Soria, Michael Ries, Gustave Haenschen, and Francis Robinson for recollections they shared or materials they provided.

I am thoroughly indebted to Irene Heskes for her continual assistance, limitless patience, and invaluable insights into Jewish liturgical music, the cantorial tradition, and immigrant Jewish life in general; to Dr. Stephen M. Schneeweiss for additional insights into Jewish-American life in New York City; and to Walter E. Afield, M.D., for his insights into Richard Tucker's personality makeup from the vantage point of a psychiatrist. Special thanks also go to Edwin F. Wilde for his understanding, interest, and support during the writing of this manuscript.

For technical information and recollections of Tucker's career, given to me recently or in the past, I am grateful to Carl E. Gutekunst, Myron Ehrlich, Bill Park, Peyton M. Hibbit, Carmen S. Savoca, William Seward, Hugh M. Johns, Joseph Tague, Edward E. Swenson, Maria Scajola Swenson, Charles Jahant, Howard Buck, Don Martin Jager, Eugene H. Cropsey, Edward S. Clute, Martin W. Laforse, Charles Snyder, Jr., and Joseph F. Tempesta.

I should like to extend special gratitude, on behalf of Irene Heskes as well as myself, to Cantor Joseph Mirsky, and to the family of the late Rabbi Israel H. Levinthal. For an understanding of the Tucker family lineage, I am especially indebted to Claire Nacman Witkowsky, daughter of Minnie Tucker Nacman, and also to Celia (Mrs. Louis) Tucker.

There are two notable exclusions from this list of acknowledgments, each of which needs an explanation. The story of Richard Tucker's career, especially the intricate and highly creative ways through which it was promoted at its zenith, is to a degree incomplete without the recollections of Alix B. Williamson, his public relations representative; regrettably, Ms. Williamson declined my request for an interview.

Similarly, Jan Peerce was unavailable (but did not decline an interview). I was fortunate, nevertheless, to have interviewed him at length in 1973, through Gustave Haenschen; I want to be clear, however, that none of the questions in that interview concerned Richard Tucker. The strained relationship between Peerce and Tucker was an open secret in the operatic world, although it rarely appeared in the news media. Peerce, in his memoirs, devoted less than a page to Tucker—and then only because his narrative required him to mention that Tucker had married his sister Sara. For her part, Sara Tucker would have been pleased had I avoided the Peerce-Tucker subject entirely, or else had opted (like Peerce) to include a nominal paragraph indicating that the two men were related by marriage but were not at all close. I have chosen instead to focus to a limited extent on this strained relationship, chiefly because Peerce played an important though minor part in Tucker's years of struggle, well before his Metropolitan Opera debut.

Lacking Jan Peerce's own viewpoint, however, I have tried to avoid a narrow interpretation of the nature of the strained relations between the two men, hoping instead to let the events I have recorded speak for themselves.

My academic disposition compels me to list briefly the primary sources I have utilized in refining my thoughts on Jewish tradition. I have relied principally on books, articles, or scholarly papers by Israel Chipkin, Simon Greenburg, and Zevi Scharfstein on Jewish-American education; Donald Jay Grout, Abraham Z. Idelsohn, and Eric Werner on Jewish music; Joseph Bram, Uriah Z. Engelman, Melville J. Herskovitz, Samuel Joseph, Anita Libman Lebeson, Jacob Lestschinsky, Cecil Roth, and joint works by Arieh Tartakower and Kurt Grossman, on Jewish sociology and emigration; and, last, in the specific areas of religion and theology, works by Alexander Altmann, Louis Finkelstein, Mordecai M. Kaplan, Israel H. Levinthal, Frederick J. Copleston, Harold H. Kushner, David Philipson, and Abba Hillel Silver.

My research was greatly helped by the cooperation of The New York Public Library, the Museum of Broadcasting in New York City, and the libraries of St. John's University, the University of Miami (Florida), the University of Notre Dame, and the Merl Kelce Library of the University of Tampa. I am indebted to our discographer, Patricia A. Kiser, music librarian at Trinity College; jointly, Ms. Kiser and I thank Robert A. Tuggle, archivist of the Metropolitan Opera company.

We all thank Gerald Fitzgerald of *Opera News* for making available to the publisher many important photographs.

The brief quotes with which these chapters open are from published as well as unpublished interviews with Richard Tucker. Many stem from interviews conducted by Janet Bookspan in the spring of 1973, under the auspices of the William E. Wiener Oral History Project. Accordingly, I wish to thank the American Jewish Committee and the directors of the Wiener Library, especially Irma H. Krentz, for their cooperation in this regard.

In quoting from these and various other printed or recorded interviews, I have often compressed an extended response (or, less frequently, have conjoined similar responses from different interviews on the same subject) so as to maintain both a logical and a literary "flow" in the narrative. Sources that are quoted verbatim, however, appear as indented extracts in these chapters. A single exception is a 1969 letter from Giacomo Lauri-Volpi to Tucker, the original of which has apparently been lost; what is quoted is reconstructed from the memories of John Gualiani and Barry Tucker, but parallels Lauri-Volpi's own recollections, which he summarized for me during our correspondence in 1978 and 1979.

It would be impossible to begin to repay the kindnesses of the many

personal friends of Richard and Sara Tucker, who not only endured innumerable rounds of questions but who treated me regally on every occasion. I thank especially Ben Herschaft, Emanuel (Manny) and Ruth
Schwartz, Julius Kushner, Dr. Danny Jacobson, Harold and Natalie Eisenstadt, William and Ide Levine, Sam and Selma Mintz, Kitty Lederman, Philip and Florence Robbins, and Harold and Tillie Sussman for
their intimate recollections of Richard and Sara Tucker and their family.
I also thank Alfred C. Stepan, Jr., and Giovanni Camajani, for permission to quote from their letters.

Special thanks go to Karen Kriendler Nelson, administrative director of the Richard Tucker Music Foundation, for her assistance in providing a range of documents and recorded interviews; to Gerhard Ot-
tinger, of Vienna, and Juame Tribo, of Barcelona, for furnishing complete
cast lists and reviews of Tucker's appearances in those cities; and especially to John Gualiani, who served for many years as European representative for Richard Tucker, and whose precise recollections of Tucker's career in the operatic capitals of Europe expedited my research to
an extent impossible to acknowledge fully.

To have been associated with Richard Tucker's immediate family
has been the high point of this project, and I shall always be indebted
to Barry and Joan Tucker and their children, Amy and Robert; to Henry
Tucker; and to Dr. David Tucker, his wife, Lynda, and their children,
Larry, Jackie, Andrew, and Lee. Most of all I am indebted to Sara Tucker,
who made me a guest in her home, introduced me to longtime friends
and associates, interceded when someone might not have been available
to me otherwise, unflaggingly tolerated my personal and often intrusive
questions, and, above all, opened her husband's and her life to me. I
hope these chapters repay the confidence she invested in me.

For my part, I am especially grateful to Michelle Morley, both for
her moral support and, on several occasions, her editorial suggestions.
In this same vein I owe particular thanks to Jerret Engle and Michael
Willis of E.P. Dutton, Inc., not only for their editing refinements but
also—as may be said equally of my literary agent, Howard Buck—for
their understanding and encouragement as this project evolved.

Most of all, I am grateful to my family, in more ways than I can
articulate. With my mother, Ruth R. Drake, and my sister, Julia Drake
Alfred, I share the deep regret that my father, James W. Drake, never
saw these pages in print. He died on June 13, 1982.

In spirit, this book is his.

JAMES A. DRAKE

Tampa, Florida

Index